CA Proficiency

Taxation 1 (NI)

2016–2017

Published by
Chartered Accountants Ireland
Chartered Accountants House
47–49 Pearse Street
Dublin 2
www.charteredaccountants.ie

ISBN: 978-1-910374-54-2

Typeset by Deanta Global Publishing Services
Printed by eprint, Dublin

Contents

3.6 Double Taxation Relief 39
3.6.1 Double Taxation Treaties 39
3.6.2 Unilateral Relief 39
3.6.3 Deduction Relief 40
3.7 Coming to or Leaving the UK – Tax Registration 40
3.7.1 Coming to the UK 40
3.7.2 Leaving the UK 40
Questions 40

Chapter 4 Trading Income **43**
4.1 Introduction 43
4.1.1 Definition of "Trade", "Profession" and "Vocation" 44
4.1.2 "Badges of Trade" 45
4.2 Basis of Assessment of Trading Income 46
4.2.1 Overlap Profits 47
4.2.2 Commencement of a Trade 47
4.2.3 Change in Accounting Date 50
4.2.4 Cessation of a Trade 52
4.2.5 Relief for Overlap Profits 53
4.3 Computation of Taxable Trading Income 54
4.3.1 Overview 54
4.3.2 The Adjustment of Profits – Allowable and Disallowable Items 55
4.3.3 Capital versus Revenue Receipts 55
4.3.4 Capital versus Revenue Expenditure 56
4.3.5 Tax Treatment of Common Expenses 58
4.3.6 Special Rules for Small Businesses:Cash Basis of Accounting and Simplified Expenses 68
4.3.7 Partnerships 72
4.3.8 Overseas Trades 77
Questions 77

Chartered Accountants Regulatory Board *Code of Ethics*

The Chartered Accountants Regulatory Board *Code of Ethics* applies to all aspects of a Chartered Accountant's professional life, including dealing with income tax issues, corporation tax issues, capital gains tax issues, inheritance tax issues and stamp duty issues. The *Code of Ethics* outlines the principles that should guide a Chartered Accountant, namely:

- Integrity
- Objectivity
- Professional Competence and Due Care
- Confidentiality
- Professional Behaviour

As a Chartered Accountant, you will have to ensure that your dealings with the tax aspects of your professional life are in compliance with these fundamental principles. Set out in **Appendix 2** is further information regarding these principles and their importance in guiding you on how to deal with issues which may arise throughout your professional life, including giving tax advice and preparing tax computations.

Overview of the UK Tax System

Learning Objectives

After studying this chapter you will understand:

- The principal legislation governing income tax and VAT.
- Who is assessable for income tax.
- The classification of income.
- The structure and operation of HM Revenue & Customs (HMRC).
- The administration procedures for tax assessment and collection.
- The hierarchy of the appeals system in the UK, including the First-tier Tribunal and the Upper Tribunal.
- The Chartered Accountants Regulatory Board *Code of Ethics*.
- The difference between tax evasion and tax avoidance.

1.1 Introduction

The main taxes levied in the United Kingdom (UK) can be classified as **taxes on income** and **taxes on transactions**. The main taxes on **income** are income tax and corporation tax. Individuals (including partners in a partnership) pay income tax on their income whereas corporation tax is charged on the profits of a company. Taxes on **transactions** include value-added tax (VAT), customs and excise duties, stamp duty (SD), stamp duty land tax (SDLT), capital gains tax (CGT) and inheritance tax (IHT).

The main taxes are sometimes categorised as 'revenue' or 'capital' taxes. Revenue taxes are charged on income and include income tax and corporation tax (on income profits of a company). Capital taxes include CGT (for individuals and companies) and IHT.

In addition, the main taxes may be referred to as 'direct' and 'indirect' taxes. Direct taxes are collected directly from the taxpayer and are taxes on income and profits. Direct taxes include income tax, corporation tax, CGT and IHT. VAT and customs and excise duties are examples of an indirect tax as they are levied on goods and services rather than on income or profits. Indirect taxes are not collected directly from the taxpayer.

This textbook for the Chartered Accountants Proficiency 1 syllabus concentrates on the main aspects of income tax and VAT. The objective of the Taxation 1 syllabus is to "understand and apply the legislation, procedure and practice" for income tax and VAT. From an income tax perspective, the aim of this book is to enable the student to calculate and advise on the income tax liability associated with different types of income (such as employment, self-employment, interest and dividends), as well as how to differentiate whether an individual is operating in an employed or a self-employed capacity. Calculating income tax is a step-by-step process, which can be broadly outlined as:

1. determining an individual's exposure to UK income tax, especially their domicile and residence;
2. recognising the classification of the income in question;
3. computing the amount of taxable income;
4. applying the various reliefs, allowances and deductions that are available from the Government; and
5. computing the income tax payable.

VAT is a tax on consumer spending and, as such, is often referred to as a tax on turnover opposed to profits. This book outlines the scope of VAT and explains how VAT liabilities are calculated in connection with supplies in the UK, within the European Union (EU) and, indeed, where a UK business is involved in transactions with suppliers and customers located outside the EU.

1.2   Legislation and Guidance

Income tax law is based on legislation contained mainly in the following Acts:

- Income and Corporation Taxes Act 1988 (ICTA 1988)
- Income Tax (Earnings and Pensions) Act 2003 (ITEPA 2003)
- Income Tax (Trading and Other Income) Act 2005 (ITTOIA 2005)
- Income Tax Act 2007 (ITA 2007)
- Capital Allowances Act 2001 (CAA 2001).

The legislation dealing with VAT is contained in the Value Added Tax Act 1994 (VATA 1994).

In addition, the annual **Finance Acts** (FAs), which are enacted after the Budget each year, amend the relevant legislation or create new legislative provisions. This textbook includes the provisions of Finance Act 2016, which is assessable for examinations undertaken in the summer and autumn of 2017.

Certain detailed tax rules relating to the legislation are set out in regulations that are issued by HM Revenue & Customs (HMRC) under powers conferred by the relevant tax legislation. Relevant tax case law, tax practice and HMRC guidance also play an important role in putting tax legislation into effect.

Decisions from the Court of Justice of the European Union (CJEU) and EU Directives are also influential and binding if enacted into UK legislation. EU consent is also required where tax measures support an industry sector or region under the State aid rules.

For tax purposes the United Kingdom includes Great Britain and Northern Ireland, including its territorial sea; it does not include the Isle of Man, the Channel Islands or the Republic of Ireland.

1.3   Classes of Taxpayer

Income tax is assessed on the following:

1. individuals, on their personal employment and/or self-employment income;
2. individuals in partnerships, i.e. each partner, on their share of the income from the partnership;
3. trustees, on the income from the trust; and
4. personal representatives of a deceased individual, on the income arising from the estate of the deceased person.

Married couples (including same-sex married couples since March 2014 in the UK, except in Northern Ireland) and civil partners are taxed as **individuals**, each entitled to their own personal allowances. (There is one exception to this rule: in certain circumstances the marriage allowance lets one spouse/civil partner transfer some of their own personal allowance to their spouse/civil partner.)

Where married couples/civil partners hold money in a joint bank account, the interest earned on that account will be split between each spouse/partner and will be taxed individually in their respective income tax computations/returns. Similarly, where a property is held jointly and rental income is earned from that property, each spouse/civil partner will be taxed on their share of the rental profits.

If a parent gives income, or assets that generate income, to their child, then the income is still treated as the parent's if the child is less than 18 years of age and is unmarried. However, this rule does not apply if the income is £100 (gross) a year or less. Income derived from parental contributions to a child trust fund does not count towards the £100 limit.

Income tax may be assessed by **self-assessment** (e.g. profits of a sole trader or a partner in a partnership) or by **deduction at source**, directly from an individual's income (i.e. employees under the PAYE system).

1.4   Classification of Income

The rules around the computation of income tax depend on the **source** of the income; different rules apply to different sources. Therefore the Income Tax (Trading and Other Income) Act 2005 classifies income as:

- trading income;
- employment income;
- savings and investment income;
- property income; and
- miscellaneous income.

A broad distinction is also made between non-savings, savings and dividend income. This distinction is important as it determines the order in which income tax is charged – income tax is charged first on non-savings income, then on savings income and finally on dividend income. The table below shows the classifications of income.

Classification of Income	Type of Income
Trading income – profits of trades, professions and vocations (**Chapter 4**)	Non-savings
Employment income – income from employment, pensions and some social security benefits (**Chapter 6**)	Non-savings
Savings income – income from savings, including interest (**Chapter 7**)	Savings
Investment income – income from investments, including dividends (**Chapter 7**)	Dividend
Property income – profits of property businesses, e.g. rental income (**Chapter 8**)	Non-savings
Miscellaneous income – e.g. post cost cessation receipts, income for royalties	Non-savings

1.4.1 Exempt Income

Specific types of income are exempt from income tax, they include:

- scholarships;
- betting and gaming winnings;
- many social security benefits (but note, the State retirement pension and Jobseeker's Allowance are taxable);
- certain tax-free investments, e.g. proceeds from National Savings Certificates and interest on Individual Savings Accounts (ISAs);
- gifts of assets including money (although these may be subject to inheritance tax, which is outside the scope of the CAP 1 syllabus);
- damages for personal injury; and
- payments received from insurance policies.

1.4.2 Foreign Income

An individual, who is subject to income tax in the UK, may derive some of their income from overseas sources. For example, the individual may own a property overseas which is let out, they may carry out their employment duties in another country or they may hold money in a foreign bank or shares in an overseas company. Depending on an individual's residence and domicile status (see **Chapter 3**), they may have to pay UK tax on overseas income.

In addition to the UK tax exposure on overseas income, the country where the income is generated/earned may seek to tax the income generated within its territory. For example, a rental property in the Republic of Ireland will generate rental income there, and may be liable to tax by the Irish Revenue. Generally speaking, relief will be available in the UK for any overseas tax suffered (subject to certain limits). The UK income tax implications of overseas employment income, property rental income and investment income (i.e. interest and dividends) will be dealt with in the relevant chapters.

1.5 HM Revenue & Customs

Responsibility for the care and management of both direct taxes and indirect taxes rests with the Chairman of the Board of Her Majesty's Revenue & Customs (HMRC). In simple terms this means that HMRC is responsible for the "collection and management" of tax. It has three strategic objectives:

- "maximise revenues due and bear down on avoidance and evasion
- transform tax and payments for our customers
- design and deliver a professional, efficient and engaged organisation".

The HMRC is a non-ministerial division within the Treasury Department, overall control of which rests with the Chancellor of the Exchequer. It consists of former high-ranking civil servants from various sections within HMRC, together with other non-executive personnel.

The HMRC Board is supported by several sub-committees, which include:

- the Audit and Risk Committee – is responsible for advising the Board and the principal accounting officer on financial statements and the risk management and control processes across HMRC;
- the Scrutiny Committee – addresses single issues in depth as and when circumstances require; and

■ the People, Nominations and Governance Committee – which, among other things, provides advice to the Board on HMRC's ability to meet its legislative responsibilities in relation to its people, including health and safety and equal opportunities.

The HMRC's Executive Committee is the executive decision-making body. Following the strategic direction provided by the Board, it oversees the whole breadth of HMRC's work and is also responsible for driving forward continuous improvement and change agendas. It meets every month in each of its three capacities:

1. Executive Committee;
2. Executive Committee (Performance); and
3. Executive Committee (Transformation).

The Executive Committee is supported by:

■ the Investment Committee – which makes "investment decisions on behalf of the Executive Committee, in line with HMRC's strategic direction and change initiatives";
■ the People Matters Committee – which plans ahead in respect of how HMRC will be structured and its use of resources, and helps make decisions on delegated issues with regard to people policies; and
■ the Portfolio Delivery Board – which reports directly to the Executive Committee (Transformation) and "acts as an additional decision-making body, helping others to implement change, offering support and advice as well as a challenge function".

Information on the structure, workings, policies, etc. of HMRC can be found at www.gov.uk/government/organisations/hm-revenue-customs.

The UK is divided into various tax regions, each headed up by Inspectors, who are assisted by their colleagues and other Revenue Assistants. They are referred to as Officers of HMRC. They are responsible for the efficient day-to-day operation of the tax system by issuing tax returns and other forms for completion, examining tax returns completed by taxpayers, issuing assessments where necessary and leading agreement of the taxpayers' liabilities.

The actual collection of taxes over the years has been centralised and, while the Board has overall responsibility, this has been delegated to collection offices. A specialised department, the Debt Management Unit, is responsible for following up amounts of unpaid tax referred to it from HMRC Accounts offices.

Interest, penalties and surcharges may be imposed to encourage the efficient collection of tax and to ensure that taxpayers comply in a timely fashion, e.g. daily penalties can be imposed where there is continued non-payment and/or requested information is not forthcoming.

1.6 Administration Procedures for Tax Assessment and Collection

HMRC operates a self-assessment system in the UK for income tax and VAT. For income tax, this system relies on individuals to register for income tax when they are required and to file their return and pay their tax on time. The self-assessment income tax return (SA100) must usually be filed by 31 October (if filed on paper) or 31 January (if filed electronically) following the end of the tax year. For example, for the 2016/17 tax year, if an individual files their 2016/17 SA100 online, the deadline for submission is 31 January 2018. Payments of self-assessed income tax should generally be made on 31 January and 31 July each year (see **Chapter 11** for further information).

It should be noted that many individuals receive a salary that has been taxed under the PAYE system only (see **Chapter 10**). Such individuals are not normally required to submit an income tax return under the self-assessment system unless they are a company director or have non-PAYE income (such as interest that cannot be adjusted for in their PAYE coding) in addition to their employment income.

For VAT purposes, an individual needs to register for VAT when they breach the VAT registration thresholds (currently £83,000, see **Chapter 13**). A VAT-registered individual will usually account for VAT on a quarterly basis. VAT returns must be submitted online within one month and seven days of the relevant quarter end. For example, the VAT return for the quarter ended 30 June 2016 must be filed by 7 August 2016. Any VAT liability due should also be paid electronically by this date.

The self-assessment system is supported by a penalty regime that can apply to individuals who are not tax-compliant. Interest may also be charged by HMRC on the late payment of taxes. In addition, HMRC will randomly select individuals and businesses to enquire into on an ongoing basis. HMRC will undertake enquiries and make discovery assessments on individuals and businesses. HMRC will also undertake campaigns targeted at specific sectors that it believes may have tax-compliance issues. Disputes may arise between an individual taxpayer and HMRC in respect of the tax treatment of a particular item or the level of penalty imposed. In such circumstances, an appeal may be made by the individual taxpayer. Details of the HMRC's investigation procedures and the penalty regime are covered in **Chapter 11**.

1.7   The Appeals System

Disputes may arise between an individual taxpayer and HMRC in respect of a decision or view taken by HMRC about a taxpayer's affairs. Where agreement cannot be reached, the taxpayer can appeal the decision and the case may be heard by the appropriate tax tribunal.

The Tribunals, Courts and Enforcement Act 2007, in conjunction with the Transfer of Functions Order, recast the whole system of tax appeals with effect from 1 April 2009. The new legislation streamlined the administration of appeals against Government departments across a wide range of both tax and non-tax areas. It created a two-tier system consisting of the First-tier Tribunal and the Upper Tribunal, which are further divided into various chambers. Thus there is the First-tier Tribunal (Tax) and the Upper Tribunal (Tax and Chancery Chamber).

The tax chambers have jurisdiction over all tax appeals and tax-related proceedings (except debt recovery). They deal with all the main taxes (tax heads), as well as PAYE notices, National Insurance contributions, statutory payments, other customs and excise duties, penalty enforcements, etc.

Under the Tribunal system, the appellant (the taxpayer) is the only party that can make a notification to list an appeal. Timeframes to lodge an appeal, however, must be strictly adhered to. For example, for direct taxes an appeal must be lodged within 30 days of a review conclusion.

The First-tier Tribunal is the starting point of the appeals process, after which appeals can be escalated to the Upper Tribunal then to the Court of Appeal and finally to the Supreme Court. The hierarchy of the appeals procedures is outlined in **Figure 1.1**.

1.7.1   The First-tier Tribunal (Tax)

The First-tier Tribunal (Tax) is comprised of full-time and part-time judges and non-legal members. It hears appeals made against decisions made by HMRC relating to tax. Appeals can be made by

FIGURE 1.1: THE APPEALS HIERARCHY FOR TAX MATTERS

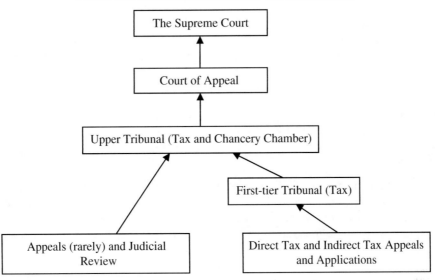

individuals or organisations, single taxpayers or large multinational companies. Appeals range from the relatively simple to complex areas across both direct and indirect tax.

The Tax Chamber is independent of HMRC and hears most of the appeals against decisions of HMRC in relation to tax. Appeals are heard by panels that are constituted according to the needs of the case and may be heard by legally qualified judges, non-legally qualified expert members or a mixture of the two. The jurisdiction of the tax tribunal is UK-wide, and hearings are held in tribunal service venues across the UK. Appeals may be brought against decisions of the First-tier Tribunal (Tax) to the Upper Tribunal (Tax and Chancery Chamber) on a point of law.

1.7.2   *The Upper Tribunal (Tax and Chancery Chamber)*

The Upper Tribunal comprises judges and other members (non-legally qualified experts). The main function of the Upper Tribunal (Tax and Chancery Chamber) is to hear appeals from the First-tier Tribunal (Tax) on points of law. However, there are occasions when cases may be referred directly to the Upper Tribunal without first going to the First-tier Tribunal. Typically, these would be matters giving rise to substantially complex issues regarding questions of law or judicial reviews.

1.7.3   *The Court of Appeal and The Supreme Court*

If the appellant disagrees with the decision of the Upper Tribunal and believes it made a mistake on a point of law, they may write to the Upper Tribunal to ask for permission to appeal. If permission is granted, the appeal moves to the higher court, i.e. the Court of Appeal. If permission is not granted, the appellant may ask the Court of Appeal directly for permission.

In a similar way, if the appellant disagrees with the decision of the Court of Appeal, they can obtain permission to appeal to the Supreme Court. Generally, permission will only be granted where there is an arguable point of law and it is of general public importance.

1.8   Chartered Accountants Regulatory Board *Code of Ethics*

The Chartered Accountants Regulatory Board *Code of Ethics* applies to all aspects of a Chartered Accountant's professional life, including dealing with issues in respect of income tax, corporation tax, capital gains tax, inheritance tax and stamp duty. The *Code of Ethics* outlines the principles that should guide a Chartered Accountant, namely:

- Integrity
- Objectivity
- Professional Competence and Due Care
- Confidentiality
- Professional Behaviour

As a Chartered Accountant, you will have to ensure that your dealings with the tax aspects of your professional life are in compliance with these fundamental principles. Set out in **Appendix 2** is further information regarding these principles and their importance in guiding you on how to deal with issues that may arise throughout your professional life, including giving tax advice and preparing tax computations.

1.9   Tax Evasion and Tax Avoidance

Tax evasion is illegal and is punishable by fines and/or imprisonment. For example, if a taxpayer deliberately provides false information to HMRC, such as reduced taxable profits, this would be regarded as tax evasion.

Tax avoidance involves a taxpayer organising their affairs in such a way so as to reduce their tax burden. For example, tax avoidance (or tax planning) could include an individual deciding to open a tax-exempt Individual Savings Account (ISA). By saving their money in an ISA and not in an ordinary bank account, the individual will be saving (avoiding) tax – the income earned as interest is generally not liable to income tax.

On the other hand, the term 'tax avoidance' can include schemes that are designed to achieve an unintended tax advantage for taxpayers. HMRC defines tax avoidance as "exploiting the tax rules to gain an advantage that parliament never intended". HMRC has a multi-faceted approach to tackling tax avoidance. In addition to having targeted anti-avoidance rules (TAARs), in 2011 the General Anti-Abuse Rule (GAAR) was introduced in the UK. The primary objective of the GAAR is to deter taxpayers from entering into abusive arrangements. In summary, the GAAR enables HMRC to challenge tax advantages arising from arrangements that are put in place for the main purpose of avoiding tax or obtaining a tax advantage.

Questions

Review Questions

(See Suggested Solutions to Review Questions at the end of this textbook.)

Question 1.1

(a) What is the deadline for filing a paper income tax return?
(b) What is the deadline for filing an electronic income tax return?
(c) When should self-assessed income tax be paid?

Question 1.2

Emma works in the tax department of a medium-sized practice. Yesterday she got a call from her friend, Jack. Jack is trying to buy a house at the moment and he is bidding against a local businessman. Jack knows that this businessman is a client of the practice where Emma works and he asks her to have a look at the businessman's tax file to see if he really does have the money to buy this house. Jack says to Emma, "Surely you have details of his income and bank balances." Jack tells Emma that he will owe her big time as this is the biggest investment decision he has ever made.

Requirement
What advice would you give to Emma about the request from Jack? You should make reference to the Chartered Accountants Regulatory Board *Code of Ethics*.

Introduction to the Computation of Income Tax

Learning Objectives

After studying this chapter you will understand:

- The general terms and definitions used when computing income tax.
- The tax bands and the associated tax rates for 2016/17.
- The standard personal allowance and the restriction on same if income exceeds £100,000.
- The steps involved in calculating income tax.
- How to prepare a simple income tax computation.

The Chartered Accountants Regulatory Board *Code of Ethics* applies to all aspects of a Chartered Accountant's professional life, including dealing with income tax issues. As outlined at the beginning of this book, further information regarding the principles in the *Code of Ethics* is set out in **Appendix 2**.

2.1   Introduction

Put simply, the purpose of the income tax computation is to enable us to calculate how much income tax an individual has to pay. The computation involves a number of stages and different calculations that follow in a logical sequence. In this chapter we will give an overview of each of the steps involved and introduce the basic terminology used.

In **Chapter 1, Section 1.4**, the important distinction between non-savings, savings and dividend income was noted, as was the classification of income depending on its source – trading income, employment income and so on. Each source of income has different rules and treatment for computing income tax, so recognising where an individual's income has come from is fundamental to the computation. For example, an individual's personal income tax computation may include:

- salary from employment;
- pension income;
- profits earned from a sole trade or partnership;
- rental profits;
- interest income from savings; and/or
- dividends from shares.

Before we look at the steps involved in assessing an individual's liability to income tax, it is important to be clear about the meaning of the key terms that you will encounter when studying income tax.

2.2   General Terminology and Definitions

The key terms and definitions that are used when discussing the computation of income tax include:

Income tax year – an individual's income tax computation brings together the income from all sources in a tax year. A tax year runs from 6 April to 5 April in the following year; so the 2016/17 tax year runs from 6 April 2016 to 5 April 2017.

Year of assessment – income tax is charged for a year of assessment.

Basis of assessment – refers to the way in which income is allocated to tax years for the purpose of assessing tax. There are a number of different types, for example: the cash basis (sometimes referred to as the receipts basis); the accruals basis or the current year basis. With the cash basis, income is assessable when it is received during the tax year; on the other hand, with the accruals basis assessable income includes amounts accrued during the tax year, regardless of whether it was actually received or not during the tax year. Under the current year basis, income earned in a tax year is assessable.

Self-assessment – this is the system by which taxpayers are responsible for self-assessing their own liability to income tax. They are responsible for reporting and paying the correct amount of income tax to HMRC.

The filing deadline for income tax self-assessment returns is 31 October for paper returns and, for returns filed online, it is 31 January following the end of the tax year. So, a paper tax return for 2016/17 must be filed by 31 October 2017, while an online return must be filed by 31 January 2018.

Taxable income – income that is liable to income tax after specified reliefs and allowances have been deducted (see **Section 2.5**).

Tax deducted at source – refers to tax that has already been deducted before an individual receives the income. Pay As You Earn (PAYE) is an example of tax deducted at source. PAYE may be deducted from gross employment earnings, for example, before it is received by an individual.

Tax relief – refers to an amount allowed as a deduction from an individual's total income. Examples of tax reliefs include: relief for trading losses (see **Chapter 5**); relief for pension contributions or relief for payments of eligible interest (see **Chapter 9**).

Allowances – most individuals are entitled to a certain amount of tax-free income each year. A number of different allowances may be available, including: a personal allowance, the level of which depends on an individual's income level; the age allowance or the blind person's allowance.

Tax reducers – refers to those reliefs that have the effect of reducing the tax due on taxable income. Examples of tax reducers include investments in venture capital trusts or enterprise investment schemes (see **Chapter 9**).

PAYE – Refers to the system used to collect income tax and National Insurance from employment earnings (see **Chapter 11**).

2.3   Income Tax Rates and Bands

UK income tax operates by using tax bands – ranges of taxable income – which correspond to different rates of income tax. Specific tax bands, or thresholds, and their corresponding tax rates apply to the three categories of income: non-savings, savings and dividend.

2.3.1 Non-savings Income

There are three tax rates for **non-savings** income:

- **Basic Rate** – the basic rate of tax for 2016/17 is 20% and applies to the first £32,000 of taxable income.
- **Higher Rate** – the higher rate of tax for 2016/17 is 40% and applies to taxable income from £32,001 to £150,000.
- **Additional Rate** – the additional rate of tax is 45% and applies to taxable income above £150,000.

2.3.2 Savings Income

For savings income the same tax bands and rates apply as for non-savings income, except that there is a "starting limit" of £5,000 for which a 0% rate applies, but only if the individual's **taxable non-savings income** is less than £5,000. If taxable non-savings income is greater than £5,000, then the savings income is subject to the basic rate (20%) up to the basic rate limit (£32,000).

Personal Savings Allowance

Finance Act 2016 introduced a new "personal savings allowance" for savings income earned from bank and building society accounts. The new provision allows up to £1,000 a year of a basic rate taxpayer's savings income to be tax-free; for higher rate taxpayers the annual threshold is £500. The personal savings allowance is not available to additional rate taxpayers.

The amount of personal savings allowance depends on an individual's adjusted net income (see **Section 2.5**).

The table below shows the amount of the personal savings allowance an individual is entitled to from 6 April 2016, depending on whether they are a basic, higher or additional rate taxpayer.

Tax Rate	Income Band (adjusted net income)	Personal Savings Allowance
Basic: 20%	Up to £43,000	Up to £1,000
Higher: 40%	£43,001–£150,000	Up to £500
Additional: 45%	Over £150,000	Nil

Income tax on savings income, prior to 6 April 2016, was a tax deducted at source (see definition above) by banks, building societies and National Savings. Finance Act 2016 removed this requirement, so that basic rate income tax is no longer deducted from interest paid to customers.

2.3.3 Dividend Income

Income tax on dividend income changed significantly from 6 April 2016. The previous system, complete with dividend tax credits, was abolished and replaced with a new system based on a "dividend allowance".

Dividend Allowance

From 6 April 2016, the dividend allowance was introduced that allows up to £5,000 of income earned from dividends to be tax-free. Dividend income in excess of the allowance is taxed at the following rates: 7.5% (dividend ordinary rate); 32.5% (dividend upper rate); and 38.1% (dividend additional rate).

2.3.4 Summary

The 2016/17 tax bands and tax rates are summarised in the table below.

Tax Year	Income Type	Rate	Tax Rate	Tax Band/Threshold
2016/17	Non-savings	Basic rate	20%	£0–£32,000
		Higher rate	40%	£32,001–£150,000
		Additional rate	45%	Over £150,000
	Savings	Starter rate	0%	£0–£5,000*
		Basic rate	20%	£0–£32,000**
		Higher rate	40%	£32,001–£150,000**
		Additional rate	45%	Over £150,000
	Dividend	Dividend allowance	0%	£0–£5,000***
		Dividend ordinary rate	7.5%	£5,000–£32,000
		Dividend upper rate	32.5%	£32,001–£150,000
		Dividend additional rate	38.1%	Over £150,000

*	Provided non-savings income is not greater than £5,000.
**	From 2016/17, the personal savings allowance is available: £1,000 to basic rate taxpayers; £500 to higher rate taxpayers. There is no personal savings allowance for additional rate taxpayers.
***	When calculating how much of a personal savings allowance a taxpayer is entitled to, dividends that are covered by the dividend allowance are to be included in the individual's taxable income amount to establish if the individual is a higher rate taxpayer (and entitled to £500 personal savings allowance) or an additional rate taxpayer (and not entitled to any personal savings allowance).

2.4 Standard Personal Allowance

An individual may be entitled to a number of allowances that will help reduce the amount of their income that will be subject to income tax.

All individuals are entitled to the standard personal allowance, which is simply the amount of income, from any source, that income tax is not payable on. For 2016/17 the standard personal allowance is £11,000.

The standard personal allowance is reduced for individuals with an "adjusted net income" (see **Section 2.5**) that exceeds £100,000. For every £2 above the £100,000 threshold, the personal allowance is reduced by £1. This calculation will continue until the personal allowance is reduced to nil – in other words, if an individual has adjusted net income of £122,000 or more they lose their entitlement to the personal allowance.

The personal allowance is also modified by age and eligibility to claim the marriage allowance or the blind person's allowance. Further details of all the allowances available are discussed in **Chapter 9**.

2.5 Income Tax Computation

The tax legislation, specifically the Income Tax Act 2007 (ITA 2007), details how income tax should be calculated. Section 23 ITA 2007 sets out the calculation in steps, while sections 24–30 ITA 2007 prescribe what eligible reliefs, deductions and reductions should be made at each step.

The calculation steps are outlined below as an overview of the whole process. Details of the calculation of the different sources of income, and the rules and restrictions around the various reliefs, allowances and reductions, are dealt with in subsequent chapters.

STEP 1	Identify "total income" for each source ("component") of income: non-savings, savings income and dividend income. The **gross** income from each component is added up separately in the personal income tax computation.
STEP 2	Deduct from the components of "total income" any **specified reliefs** (see **Chapter 9**) that the taxpayer is entitled to, such as various trade loss reliefs. This gives "net income".
STEP 3	Deduct from the components of "net income" any **allowances** that the taxpayer is entitled to, such as personal allowance and blind person's allowance. The personal allowance is deducted from the non-savings component of income first, then savings income and finally dividend income. These may need to be restricted (e.g. if income is greater than £100,000). This amount is referred to as "taxable income".
STEP 4	For each component amount calculated in Step 3, calculate tax at the applicable rates. Before calculating the tax on the savings income component, the personal savings allowance must be considered. The amount of the personal savings allowance depends on whether the individual is a basic rate taxpayer (£1,000 taxed at 0%) or higher rate taxpayer (£500 taxed at 0%). When calculating the tax on the dividend component, the dividend allowance covering the first £5,000 of dividends is taxed at 0%.
STEP 5	Add together the component amounts calculated in Step 4.
STEP 6	From the total calculated at Step 5, deduct any tax reductions that the taxpayer may be entitled to, such as married couples allowance (see **Chapter 9**).
STEP 7	To the amount calculated at Step 6, add additional tax charges that may apply, such as tax retained on annual payments (see **Chapter 9**).
STEP 8	Finally, income tax deducted at source (e.g. PAYE) is subtracted to get **tax payable**, which is the balance to be settled. The result is the taxpayer's income tax liability/(refund) – the income tax that is due to be paid or refunded for that particular tax year.

Steps 1–3

Steps 3–5

Steps 5–7

2.5.1   Pro Forma Income Tax Computation

A pro forma computation shows the layout of the calculation, indicating where the component amounts should be placed and systematically working through the computation.

	Non-savings Income £	Savings Income £	Dividend Income £	Total £
Gross income:				
Trading income	xx			xx
Property income	xx			xx
Employment income	xx			xx
Savings and investment income:				
Bank/building society interest		xx		xx
National Savings & Investment a/c interest		xx		xx
UK dividends			xx	xx

		Non-savings Income £	Savings Income £	Dividend Income £	Total £
Step 1	**Total income**	xxx	xxx	xxx	xxx
	Less: specified reliefs	(xx)	(xx)	(xx)	(xx)
Step 2	Net income	xxx	xxx	xxx	xxx
Step 3	Taxable income	xxxx	xxxx	xxxx	xxxx

		£
Step 4	**Income tax:**	
	Non-savings income:	
	£ × 20%	xxxx
	£ × 40%	xxxx
	£ × 45%	xxxx
	Savings income:	
	£ × 0% (Starting limit for savings income and personal savings allowance, if available.)	0
	£ × 20%	xxxx
	£ × 40%	xxxx
	£ × 45%	xxxx
	Dividend income:	
	Up to £5,000 dividend allowance × 0%	0
	£ × 7.5%	xxxx
	£ × 32.5%	xxxx
	£ × 38.1%	xxxx
Step 5	**Total**	xxxx
Step 6	**Less: tax reducers**	(xxx)
Step 7	**Add: additional tax**	xxx
Step 8	**Less: tax deducted at source**	(xxx)
Result	Income tax liability/(refund)	**xxx**

Having outlined the steps of the computation and the pro forma layout, let's now look at a simple worked example to illustrate the process.

Example 2.1

John is single, born 9 September 1962, and his sources of income for 2016/17 included income from employment of £15,000 (with PAYE deducted at source of £1,655), net property income of £3,650, income from occasional lectures of £600 and bank interest of £100.

John's income tax liability for 2016/17 will be computed as follows.

John's Income Tax Computation for 2016/17

	£ Non-savings	£ Savings	£ Dividend	£ Total
Employment income	15,000			
UK land and property income	3,650			
Miscellaneous income	600			
Savings and investment income	_____	100	_____	_____
Total income	19,250	100	0	19,350
Less: personal allowance	(11,000)	_____	_____	(11,000)
Taxable income	**8,350**	**0**	**0**	**8,350**

Income tax:	
Non-savings income:	
£8,250 @ 20%	1,650
Savings income:	
£100 × 0% (personal savings allowance)	0
Income tax due	1,650
Less: tax deducted at source:	
PAYE	(1,655)
Total tax due	5

Questions

Review Questions

(See Suggested Solutions to Review Questions at the end of this textbook.)

Question 2.1

Pat's employment income in the 2016/17 tax year is £15,000 (gross). He is married to Una, who is not employed but has interest income in the period of £40,000. Pat has paid PAYE of £3,000. Una has received £40,000 of interest income also in 2016/17.

Requirement

Compute both Pat and Una's income tax liabilities for the 2016/17 tax year.

Question 2.2

Paul and Jean are married. Paul had property income of £47,000 from a number of houses in Stranmillis in the 2016/17 tax year, as well as net employment income of £24,000 from his job with the council. PAYE suffered was £5,000. He also received interest income of £600 on a joint bank account he has with Jean.

Jean had self-employment income in the period of £41,000. Her neighbour also paid her £50 for cutting his grass when he was away for a week in the summer.

Requirement

Compute Paul and Jean's income tax liability for the 2016/17 tax year.

Question 2.3

M. Smyth lives alone. In 2016/17 he received property income of £10,000, net employment income of £23,000 (PAYE suffered of £4,000), dividend income from a UK company of £6,000 and bank interest of £20,000.

Requirement

Compute M. Smyth's income tax liability for the 2016/17 tax year.

3

Residence and Domicile

Learning Objectives

After studying this chapter you will understand:

- The concepts of residence and domicile in relation to income tax.
- The statutory residence test (SRT) and how it applies in practice.
- Determining an individual's residency status using the SRT.
- The tax treatment of individuals arriving and leaving the UK – split year treatment (SYT).
- The impact residence and domicile have on an individual's UK income tax liability.
- The impact residence and domicile have on an individual's eligibility to claim income tax allowances.
- The remittance basis, including the remittance basis charge, for non-UK domiciled individuals.
- The effect of double taxation relief and double taxation treaties (DTTs) on an individual's income tax liability.

3.1   Introduction

The extent to which an individual's income is liable to UK income tax depends on two criteria:

1. **residence**; and
2. **domicile**.

Residence is based on physical presence in the UK, whereas domicile is dependent upon an individual's permanent homeland. The concepts of residence and domicile are important because an individual's status will determine whether the person is liable to UK income tax in respect of the income he or she has earned in the tax year. The source of the income is also important, i.e. whether the income arises in the UK, such as rental income from a UK property, or whether it arises overseas, such as rental income from a property in Spain.

An individual can be either:

- UK resident and UK domiciled;
- UK resident and non-UK domiciled; or
- Non-UK resident.

The impact of the residence and domicile status on UK income tax liability is outlined below.

Status	UK Income	Overseas Income
UK resident and UK domiciled	Pay UK income tax on UK income arising in tax year.	Pay UK income tax on overseas income arising in tax year.
UK resident and non-UK domiciled	Pay UK income tax on UK income arising in tax year.	Pay UK income tax on overseas income – either "arising" or "remittance" basis.
Non-UK resident	Pay UK income tax on UK income arising in tax year.	Overseas income is exempt from UK income tax.

For tax purposes, the UK is England, Scotland, Wales and Northern Ireland, and includes its territorial waters and its designated continental shelf. It does not include the Isle of Man or the Channel Islands.

This chapter will explain what is meant by residence and domicile before outlining the tests that are used to determine whether someone is UK resident or non-UK resident for tax purposes. The residence and domicile status of an individual will then be examined to show how that status affects the amount of tax the individual will be due to pay in the UK.

3.2   Domicile

The concept of domicile is one of general and common law, having evolved through the court system and not being legislatively defined. In broad terms, unlike residency, an individual can only ever have one domicile at any one time. Domicile is distinct from nationality or residence and, as already noted, it is one half of the criteria used to determine UK income tax liability.

There are three kinds of domicile:

1.   domicile of origin;
2.   domicile of choice; and
3.   domicile of dependency.

Three general points regarding domicile require special attention:

1.   A person cannot be without a domicile.
2.   A person cannot possess more than one domicile at any time.
3.   An existing domicile is presumed to continue until it is proved that a new domicile of choice has been acquired.

The following factors can be relevant when considering an individual's domicile intentions; permanent residence; business interests; social and family interests; ownership of property; the form of any will made, burial arrangements and so on. This is not an exhaustive list, but it does illustrate the many different criteria that should be considered.

3.2.1   Domicile of Origin

An individual has a domicile that is acquired at **birth** and is known as the domicile of origin. It is either the domicile of the individual's father or, if the father is predeceased or the parents are not married, it is the domicile of the mother. Importantly, there need be no connection between an individual's place of birth and their domicile of origin.

As stated above, it is not possible to have more than one domicile. Thus the domicile of origin subsists until it is displaced by a new domicile, either of choice or of dependency. Domicile of origin is characterised by two main factors, namely: its permanence; and the large burden of proof required to displace it.

3.2.2 Domicile of Dependency

The domicile of dependency refers specifically to dependent persons, i.e. children less than 16 years old or incapacitated persons. The dependant's domicile is determined by the domicile of the person on whom they are dependent. If, before the age of 16, the domicile of the parent from whom the child has taken their domicile changes, then the child's domicile will also change and follow that of the parent.

3.2.3 Domicile of Choice

A domicile of choice is the domicile that any independent person, i.e. an individual of legal capacity not dependent for his or her domicile upon another person, may acquire for themselves by a **combination of residence and intention**.

To acquire a domicile of choice, an individual must establish a physical presence in the new jurisdiction and have an intention to reside there permanently. The individual must sever all ties with the country of his or her former domicile and settle in the new country with the clear intention of making his or her permanent home there indefinitely.

A domicile of choice can be abandoned; in which case the domicile of origin will be reinstated unless, and until, it is replaced by a new domicile of choice.

3.3 The Statutory Residence Test

In the 2011 Budget, the Government announced the introduction of the statutory residence test (SRT) to determine an individual's tax residence status. The SRT was formally legislated in Finance Act 2013.

3.3.1 Overview of the Statutory Residence Test

The SRT comprises three components:

1. the automatic overseas test;
2. the automatic UK test; and
3. the sufficient ties test.

The three tests are considered in the order given above. If, for a given tax year, an individual meets any of the automatic overseas tests, they will be treated as non-UK resident for the tax year in question. The automatic overseas test is therefore the first test to be considered.

If none of the automatic overseas tests are met, then the automatic UK tests are considered. An individual is deemed UK resident if any of the automatic UK tests applies.

If an individual does not satisfy either the automatic overseas tests or the automatic UK tests, recourse is made to the sufficient ties test. The individual will be considered UK resident if they have sufficient UK ties for the tax year.

It is therefore necessary to work through the tests systematically in order to determine whether an individual is non-resident or resident in the UK. In other words, where both the automatic overseas test and the automatic UK test apply, the automatic overseas test takes priority.

Note that an individual's residence is determined for **each tax year separately**, i.e. residency status must be re-assessed each tax year and an individual's status will depend upon the facts and circumstances in that tax year. An online tool is available on the HMRC website to enable individuals to assess their residence status under the SRT. Provided the correct details are inputted, the result of the online tool can be relied upon should the person's residence status be later enquired into by HMRC. However, HMRC will not be bound by the results where the information provided did not accurately reflect the facts and circumstances of the individual.

3.3.2   Automatic Overseas Tests

An individual will be treated as **non-resident** if any of the three automatic overseas tests are met.

1. **First automatic overseas test** – the individual was resident in the UK for one or more of the preceding three tax years but, in the relevant tax year, they have spent fewer than **16 days** in the UK.
2. **Second automatic overseas test** – the individual was not resident in the UK for any of the preceding three tax years and spends fewer than **46 days** in the UK in the relevant tax year.
3. **Third automatic overseas test** – in the relevant tax year the individual **works full time overseas** for "sufficient hours" without any "significant breaks" and, during that tax year:
    (a) has fewer than 31 UK "work days" (considered as working more than three hours per day in the UK); and
    (b) spends fewer than **91 days** in total in the UK.

    "Sufficient hours" is considered to be an average of at least 35 hours per week. "Significant break" is a period of more than 30 days during which the individual did not work for more than three hours, and this was not due to periods of annual leave, sick leave or parenting leave.

The tests require the individual to count the number of "days spent in the UK". These are explained in detail in **Section 3.3.6**.

If the individual does not meet any of the automatic overseas tests, the next step is to consider the automatic UK tests.

3.3.3   Automatic UK Tests

An individual will be considered **resident** in the UK if any of the three automatic UK tests are met.

1. **First automatic UK test** – the individual spends at least **183 days** in the UK in the tax year.
2. **Second automatic UK test** – this test applies if the individual **has a home in the UK** for all or part of the tax year. The conditions to be met are:
    (a) there is at least one period of **91 consecutive days** (at least 30 days of which fall within the tax year in question) when an individual has:
        (i) a home in the UK in which they spend a "sufficient amount of time" (at least **30 days** during the tax year), **and either**:
            I   no overseas home, **or**
            II   an overseas home or homes in each of which they spend no more than 30 days.
3. **Third automatic UK test** – the individual **works full time in the UK** for any period of **365 days** with no "significant break" and:

(a) all or part of that work period falls within the tax year;

(b) more than 75% of the 365-day period are UK work days (i.e. more than three hours work per day in the UK); and

(c) at least one day (which falls in both the tax year and the 365-day period) is a day on which they do more than three hours of work in the UK.

"Significant break" has the same meaning as for the third automatic overseas test (see above).

HMRC guidelines offer examples to illustrate the practical considerations of the tests.

Example 3.1: Second automatic UK residence test (adapted from HMRC example)
Stan has lived in Australia all his life. In June 2014 he takes a holiday in London and likes it so much he decides to emigrate to the UK. He spends the next few months preparing for the move. He sells his Australian house (his only home) on 10 January 2016 and arrives in the UK on 25 January 2016. He finds a flat in London and moves in on 1 February 2016. The London flat is now his only home and he lives there for a year.

There is a period of 91 consecutive days, falling partly within tax year 2015/16 (the period starting on 1 February 2016), when Stan has a home in the UK and no home overseas (it does not matter that the period when these conditions are met is in fact longer than 91 days). During tax year 2015/16, Stan is present in his UK home on at least 30 days. As Stan does not meet any of the automatic overseas tests, he is resident under the second automatic UK test for the tax year 2015/16.

Example 3.2: Third automatic UK residence test (adapted from HMRC example)
Henri travels to the UK on 1 July 2014 to start a new job on the following day. His posting finishes on 1 July 2015 and he leaves the UK on 6 August 2015. Over the 365-day period to 30 June 2015, Henri calculates that he worked full time in the UK and has not taken a significant break from his UK work during this period. Part of the period of 365 days falls within the tax year 2014/15 and part falls within the tax year 2015/16.

Over the period of 365 days ending 30 June 2015, Henri works for over three hours on 240 days, 196 (80%) of which are days when Henri worked for more than three hours in the UK. At least one day when Henri does more than three hours' work in the UK falls within the tax year 2014/15; therefore Henri is resident in the UK under the third automatic UK test for the tax year 2014/15.

There is also at least one day when Henri does more than three hours' work in the UK within the tax year 2015/16, so Henri also meets the third automatic UK test for that year.

3.3.4 The Sufficient Ties Test

If the individual does not meet any of the automatic overseas tests or any of the automatic UK tests, the "sufficient ties test" must be used to determine whether the individual is resident or non-resident in the UK. Essentially, the "sufficient ties test" is seeking to establish the level of connection (the number of ties) an individual has to the UK. If sufficient ties are recognised, then the individual is considered resident in the UK. The ties considered are:

- a "family tie";
- an "accommodation tie";
- a "work tie";
- a "90-day tie"; and
- a "country tie" (only applicable if an individual was UK resident for one or more of the preceding three tax years).

The test distinguishes between individuals who were resident in the UK in any of the three preceding tax years, and those who were not. Basically, if you were resident in one or more of the previous three tax years there is a greater chance of being classed as resident in the current tax year, compared to someone who was not resident in any of the three preceding tax years.

Number of Ties

Residency status is determined by the number of days spent in the UK (see **Section 3.3.6**) and the number of ties that must apply. **Table A** and **Table B**, taken from HMRC's *Guidance Note: Statutory Residence Test (SRT)* (December 2013), indicate the number of ties required to be UK resident.

TABLE A: UK TIES NEEDED IF RESIDENT IN ONE OR MORE OF THE PRECEDING THREE TAX YEARS

Days spent in the UK in the tax year under consideration	Number of ties to be UK resident
Less than 16 days	Automatically non-resident
16–45 days	At least 4
46–90 days	At least 3
91–120 days	At least 2
121–182 days	At least 1
183 days or more	Automatically resident

TABLE B: UK TIES NEEDED IF NOT RESIDENT IN ANY OF THE PRECEDING THREE TAX YEARS

Days spent in the UK in the tax year under consideration	Number of ties to be UK resident
45 or less	Automatically non-resident
46–90 days	All 4
91–120 days	At least 3
121–182 days	At least 2
183 days or more	Automatically resident

The more days an individual has spent in the UK, the fewer number of ties are needed to be treated as UK resident, and vice versa.

Definition of UK Ties

Family Tie

An individual will be considered to have a "family tie" for the tax year if any of the following are UK resident for tax purposes for that year:

- his or her husband, wife or civil partner (unless separated);
- his or her partner (if they are living together as husband and wife or as civil partners);
- his or her child, if aged under 18.

Accommodation Tie

An individual has an "accommodation tie" for a tax year if he or she has a "place to live" in the UK and "it is available to them for a continuous period of 91 days or more" during the tax year, and either:

- they "spend one or more nights there" during the tax year; or
- "if it is at the home of a close relative they spend 16 or more nights there".

"Place to live" can include a holiday home or a temporary retreat. "Close relative" includes parent, grandparent, brother, sister and children or grandchildren aged 18 or over.

Gaps of 15 days or fewer in the availability of the accommodation will count towards the continuous period of availability.

Work Tie

An individual will be treated as having a "work tie" if they work in the UK for "at least 40 days in the tax year (whether continuously or intermittently)". A work day is the same definition as used elsewhere in the SRT, i.e. where more than three hours of work is undertaken.

90-Day Tie

This tie is met if an individual spends more than 90 days in the UK in one or both of the preceding two tax years.

Country Tie

An individual has a "country tie" if he or she has spent more days in the UK than in any other country during the tax year. Remember, the country tie only applies to individuals who were resident in one of the previous three tax years.

Sufficient Ties Test – Examples

Example 3.3

Carmen, who is single and has no children, was born in Italy. Her mother was born in Belfast and so Carmen often comes to Belfast to visit her relatives.

She arrives in Belfast on 1 May 2015 and stays with her grandmother as she does not own a house in Northern Ireland. She has been asked to fill a full-time role teaching Italian for the period from 5 May 2015 to 31 August 2015. She will return to Italy on 8 September 2015 and will commence her final year at Rome University on 15 September 2015.

Carmen has not been UK resident in any of the previous three tax years and has spent less than 90 days in the UK in each of the previous two tax years.

Explain whether Carmen is UK resident for the tax year 2015/16.

1. **Consider the automatic overseas test** – Carmen has been in the UK for 130 days and therefore does not meet any of the automatic overseas tests.
2. **Consider the automatic UK test** – Although Carmen has been in the UK for over 30 days in the tax year, she does not have a home in the UK whereas she does in Italy. She does not meet any of the automatic UK tests.
3. **Consider the sufficient ties test** – Carmen has spent 130 days in the UK in the 2015/16 tax year and must meet the criteria for at least two ties to be considered UK resident.
    (a) *Family tie* – Carmen does not have a husband, civil partner, partner or child who is UK resident. The family tie is not met.
    (b) *Accommodation tie* – Carmen has a "place to live" in the UK. She stays at the home of a close relative (her grandmother) for 16 or more nights. Therefore the accommodation tie is met.

continued overleaf

(c) *Work tie* – Carmen is taking up a full-time post and will work for at least 40 days in the UK in the tax year. The work tie is also met.

(d) *90-day tie* – Carmen has not spent more than 90 days in the UK in one or both of the preceding two tax years, so this tie is not met.

(e) *Country tie* – As Carmen was non-UK resident for one or more of the preceding three tax years, we do not need to consider this tie.

So, Carmen meets two ties and will therefore be treated as UK resident in the 2015/16 tax year.

Example 3.4

Joe, a bachelor with no children, decided to take a year off work to travel the world. He finished work on 1 April 2015 and left the UK on 1 June 2015 to commence his travels with a tour of the Rockies.

He spent no more than 30 days in each country until he arrived in Austria, where he has an apartment. He spent two months there (February and March 2016) before continuing to tour Europe. He returned to the UK on 1 June 2016. While Joe was away he rented out his UK home.

Joe has always been UK resident, up to and including the 2014/15 tax year.

Explain whether Joe is UK resident for the 2015/16 tax year.

1. **Consider the automatic overseas test** – Joe has been in the UK for 56 days in the 2015/16 tax year. He is not going to work full time overseas. Therefore, he does not meet any of the automatic overseas tests.

2. **Consider the automatic UK test** – Although Joe has been in the UK for more than 30 days, he has a home in Austria where he has spent over 30 days. Joe does not meet any of the automatic UK tests.

3. **Consider the sufficient ties test** – Joe has spent 56 days in the UK in the 2015/16 tax year and must meet at least three ties to be considered UK resident.

    (a) *Family tie* – Joe does not have a wife, civil partner, partner or child who is UK resident. The family tie is not met.

    (b) *Accommodation tie* – Joe does have a "place to live" in the UK and has lived in it during the tax year; however, as he is renting it out while he is away it is not available for a continuous period of 91 days or more. Therefore the accommodation tie is not met.

    (c) *Work tie* – Joe does not work for at least 40 days in the UK in the tax year, meaning this tie is not met.

    (d) *90-day tie* – Joe has spent more than 90 days in the UK in both of the preceding two tax years. The 90-day tie is met.

    (e) *Country tie* – Joe has spent 56 days in the UK in the tax year, but he has spent more time in Austria (60 days). Therefore the country tie is not met.

Joe satisfies only one tie and is therefore treated as non-UK resident in the 2015/16 tax year.

3.3.5   The SRT – Summary

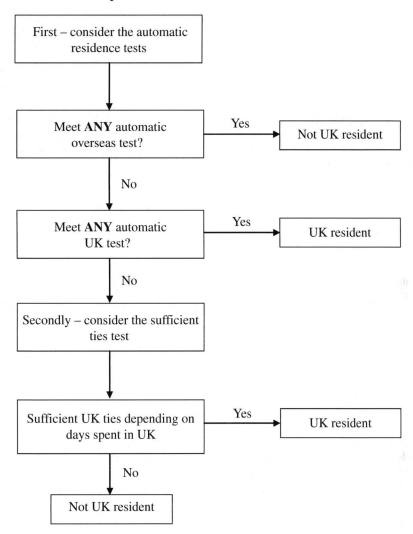

3.3.6   Meaning of "Day Spent in the UK"

All of the SRT tests require an individual to count the number of days they have spent in the UK in the particular tax year. The general rule is that if you are in the UK at the end of the day, i.e. midnight, then that is considered a day spent in the UK. However, there are clarifications to this general rule.

"Transit Days"
A "transit day" is the period between arrival in the UK as a passenger and departure the next day. Such days are not counted as days spent in the UK provided that, between arrival and departure, the individual does not engage in any activities that are "to a substantial extent unrelated to your passage through the UK".

HMRC guidance suggests that having dinner or breakfast at a hotel would be seen as "related to your passage"; while "enjoying a film at the local cinema or catching up with friends" would be "substantially unrelated", and would therefore be counted as a day spent in the UK for the SRT.

Example 3.5: Transit days (HMRC example)

Holly regularly visits the UK for work and social engagements. She also travels widely. She is planning to visit her aunt in Philadelphia, and will be flying in from Rome to connect with her continental flight at Heathrow.

Holly's flight lands at 23:05 on Monday evening. Her flight to Philadelphia does not depart Heathrow until 12:05 on Tuesday. Holly decides to stay at an airport hotel to catch some sleep, before returning to board the plane for her onward journey. She merely leaves the airport, catches a taxi to the hotel, sleeps, and snatches a quick coffee before returning to the airport.

At the end of the tax year when Holly is considering how many days she spent in the UK, this instance will not be counted as it qualifies as a "transit day".

"Exceptional Circumstances"

"Exceptional circumstances" normally apply where an individual has no choice concerning the length of time they spend in the UK or in coming back to the UK. **The situation must be beyond the individual's control**, and they **must intend to leave the UK as soon as circumstances permit**.

Examples of exceptional circumstances include:

- local or national emergencies, such as civil unrest;
- natural disasters;
- the outbreak of war;
- sudden serious or life-threatening illness or injury; and
- sudden life-threatening illness or injury to a spouse, person with whom they are living as husband and wife, civil partner or dependent child.

A limit of 60 days in any tax year may be disregarded due to exceptional circumstances. This limit applies if there is one event or several events in the same tax year. Any days spent in the UK over the 60-day limit are counted for the purposes of the SRT.

Again, HMRC offers examples to clarify the application of the rules.

Example 3.6: Exceptional circumstances (HMRC example)

Anna is returning to her home in Denmark having spent her seven-week summer holiday working in the UK. This was her first visit to the UK.

On the boat journey home there is an explosion in the engine room. Emergency rescue services attend the vessel and Anna is found unconscious and badly burned. The emergency services make the decision to airlift Anna to a specialist burns unit in the UK where she remains for five months. Anna returns to Denmark as soon as she is discharged from hospital.

Anna has been in the UK for 202 days.

This disaster would be considered to be exceptional circumstances. However, the maximum number of days that can be disregarded towards days spent in the UK is 60. So Anna has 142 days that count as days spent in the UK.

> **Example 3.7: Exceptional circumstances (HMRC example)**
> Claude is retired and came to the UK for the first time on 1 June for a five-month extended travelling holiday, intending to leave on 31 October.
>
> On 29 September, while travelling to Scotland, he is involved in a car crash and suffers multiple injuries. He is in hospital for a total of 14 weeks and arranges to travel back to his home in France on the day he is discharged.
>
> Claude has been in the UK for 220 days.
>
> The time Claude spent in hospital is an exceptional circumstance. The maximum number of days in the tax year that can be ignored is 60. Claude has 160 days counted as spent in the UK.

"Exceptional circumstances" do not include events that are within an individual's control, or where they could "reasonably have been foreseen or predicted". They include:

- "life events, such as birth, marriage, divorce and death";
- "choosing to come to the UK for medical treatment or to receive elective medical services, such as dentistry, cosmetic surgery or therapies"; and
- "travel problems, for example a delayed or missed flight due to traffic disruption, train delays or cancellations, or a car breakdown".

The Deeming Rule

The general rule states that if you are not present in the UK at midnight, then that day will not count as a day spent in the UK. However, this is subject to the "deeming rule". In essence, under the deeming rule an individual can be treated as being in the UK for a day even though they were not present in the UK at midnight.

The deeming rule will apply if the individual:

1. has at least three UK ties for the tax year (see **Section 3.3.4**); and
2. has been UK resident in one or more of the preceding three tax years; and
3. has been present in the UK on more than 30 days in the tax year but without being actually present at the end of that day. These are referred to as "qualifying days".

If all of these conditions are met, then all subsequent qualifying days (i.e. those after the first 30 qualifying days) will be treated as actual days spent in the UK and be counted in the SRT. So, when counting "days spent in the UK", these additional qualifying days over and above the 30-day threshold must be added to any days when the individual was present at the end of the day.

> **Example 3.8: HMRC example**
> Angharad does not meet any of the automatic UK or automatic overseas tests for the tax year. She spent 35 days in the UK where she was present at the end of the day, but was also present in the UK on 57 other days, leaving the UK before the end of the day. (She has three UK ties and was UK resident in the previous tax year.)
>
> Without the deeming rule, Angharad would be non-resident under the SRT sufficient ties test, as she has three UK ties but spent only 35 days here. However, Angharad will need to consider the deeming rule, as she was resident in the previous tax year and has at least three ties under the sufficient ties test.
>
> As Angharad was present in the UK on 57 other days she meets the deeming rule conditions, and therefore must include these further days in her day-counting. This gives her a total of 62 days spent in the UK (35 days where she was present at the end of the day, plus 27 qualifying days by virtue of the deeming rule); taken together with her three UK ties, this means that she will be resident under the sufficient ties test.

3.3.7 Split Year Treatment

Typically, if a person is deemed to be UK resident under the SRT they are treated as resident for the full tax year. However, in certain circumstances it is possible to split the tax year into two parts – one part where the individual is treated as UK resident, and the other where they are treated as non-UK resident.

HMRC identify eight circumstances, or cases, when this split year treatment (SYT) can apply.

- If leaving the UK:
  - Case 1 – Starting full-time work overseas;
  - Case 2 – Accompanying a partner overseas;
  - Case 3 – Ceasing to have a home in the UK.
- If arriving in the UK:
  - Case 4 – Starting to have a home in the UK only;
  - Case 5 – Starting full-time work in the UK;
  - Case 6 – Ceasing full-time work overseas;
  - Case 7 – Returning or relocating to the UK with your partner;
  - Case 8 – Starting to have a home in the UK.

Each case has specific and detailed criteria that need to be met. If the conditions of any of Cases 1–8 are met, SYT applies automatically. It is not possible to elect out of the SYT.

It should be noted that the split year rules do not apply to an individual who has been deemed to be non-UK resident (either under the automatic overseas tests or the sufficient ties test). If the individual is deemed to be non-UK resident, then they are non-UK resident for the whole of the tax year (and the application of the SYT is not relevant).

Leaving the UK

For those leaving the UK, SYT applies in the current tax year if the individual is:

- **UK resident** for the **current tax year** (i.e. the tax year being considered for SYT); and
- **UK resident** for the **previous tax year** (whether or not it is a split year); and
- **non-UK resident** in the **following tax year**; and
  - leaves part way through the current tax year for one of the reasons below.

Case	Reason	Conditions	Start of non-UK residence
1	Starting full-time work overseas	Individual starts to work **"sufficient hours"** (i.e. 35 hours or more a week over a period) **overseas** with no "significant breaks" (i.e. 31 or more continuous days). Individual must not spend more than a permitted number of days in the UK after leaving, i.e. the individual must spend less than 91 days per tax year in the UK after departure (reduced proportionately in the tax year of departure).	Date of starting overseas work.

Case	Reason	Conditions	Start of non-UK residence
2	Accompanying a partner overseas	The individual's **partner** (husband, wife or civil partner, or someone they are living with as husband, wife or civil partner) **meets the conditions for Case 1** for that year or the previous year. The individual and his/her partner must have been living together in the UK either at some point in the tax year or in the previous tax year. The **individual moves overseas** to continue to live with them. Individual must not spend more than a permitted number of days in the UK after leaving, i.e. the individual must spend less than 91 days per tax year in the UK after departure (reduced proportionately in the tax year of departure). After leaving, the individual has no home in the UK or, if the individual has homes in both the UK and overseas, he or she spends the greater part living in the overseas home.	Later of date: – partner starts overseas work, or – joins partner overseas.
3	Ceasing to have a home in the UK	The individual must have one or more homes in the UK at the start of the tax year and at some point in the year **cease to have any home in the UK** for the rest of the tax year. The individual must spend **fewer than 16 days in the UK** after ceasing to have a home in the UK.	Day on which the taxpayer ceases to have a home in the UK.

Example 3.9: SYT Case 1 (adapted from HMRC example)
Amanda has been living in the UK since she was born and is UK resident for tax purposes. She has worked in the media industry for five years and lands herself a job as a reporter on a three-year contract based in India. She moves there on 10 November 2015 and lives in an apartment provided by her new employer. She works full time overseas from 10 November 2015.

She returns to visit her family over the Christmas period for two weeks, and does not work while she is here.

Amanda remains working in India throughout the tax year 2016/17, again only returning for a two-week period over Christmas.

continued overleaf

Amanda is eligible for SYT for tax year 2015/16 because:

- she was UK resident for the current tax year (2015/16);
- she was UK resident for the previous tax year (2014/15);
- she is non-UK resident in the following tax year (2016/17); and
- she meets the Case 1 conditions, that is from 10 November 2015 until 5 April 2016 she:
  - works full time overseas;
  - spends 14 days in the UK, which is less than the permitted 37 days (being 91 days pro-rated for the tax year of departure, i.e. 5/12 months × 91 = 37 days rounded down (the month of departure is treated as a whole month)).

For Amanda, in 2015/16 she will be UK resident from 6 April 2015 to 9 November 2015 and non-UK resident from 10 November 2015 to 5 April 2016.

Example 3.10

Peter is Amanda's husband (see Example 3.9). He too had lived in the UK all his life and was resident in the UK for tax purposes. He travels with Amanda on 8 January 2016 to live with her in India, having given up his job. Amanda and Peter have let their flat in the UK for a three-year period, commencing on 9 January 2016.

Once in India, Peter spends his time following his lifelong hobby as a lepidopterist, cataloguing Indian butterflies. He spends all his time there, except for the Christmas trips to the UK with Amanda.

- Peter will receive SYT for tax year 2015/16 as he:
- is UK resident for the current tax year (2015/16);
- he was UK resident for the previous tax year (2014/15);
- he is non-UK resident in the following tax year (2016/17); and
- he meets the Case 2 conditions, i.e.:
  - his wife meets the conditions for Case 1;
  - he is moving overseas to live with her;
  - he has no home in the UK after 8 January 2016; and
  - from 8 January until 5 April 2016 he spends less than the permitted limit of 22 days in the UK, i.e. 91 days pro-rated for the tax year of departure (3/12 months × 91 = 22 days rounded down (the month of departure is treated as a whole month)).

For Peter in 2015/16 he will be UK resident from 6 April 2015 to 7 January 2016 and non-UK resident from 8 January 2016 (the day he joined Amanda to live with her in India) to 5 April 2016.

Arriving in the UK

For those arriving in the UK, SYT applies in the current tax year if the individual is:

- **UK resident** for the **current tax year** (tax year being considered for SYT);
- **non-UK resident** for the **previous tax year**; and
- arrives in the UK part way through the tax year for one of the reasons below.

Case	Reason	Conditions	Start of UK residence
4	Starting to have a home in the UK only	Individual meets the "only home test" at some point in the tax year (not necessarily at the start of the tax year) and continues to do so until the end of the tax year ("only home test" – the individual has only **one home** and it is **in the UK** or, if they have more than one home, all of them are in the UK).	Date of meeting "only home test".

Case	Reason	Conditions	Start of UK residence
		Individual does not meet the sufficient UK ties test for that part of the tax year before they first meet the "only home test".	
5	Starting full-time work in the UK	Individual must start to **work full time** in the UK at some point in the tax year for a **continuous period of at least 365 days**, with no significant breaks. Individual does not meet the sufficient UK ties test for that part of the tax year before the day he or she starts to work full time in the UK.	Date starts full-time work in UK.
6	Ceasing full-time work overseas	Ceases to satisfy the overseas work criteria at some point in the tax year (i.e. broadly, **ceases working full time overseas** (35 hours per week with no significant break) – see third automatic overseas test for overseas work criteria). Individual must be **UK resident** in the **following tax year**.	Date individual stops working overseas, i.e. no longer meets overseas work criteria.
7	Returning or relocating to the UK with your partner	**Individual's partner stops working overseas** and returns or relocates to the UK in the current or previous tax year (thus meeting the conditions for Case 6 SYT) and they decide to **join them**. Individual must be **UK resident** in the **following tax year**. **Before the start of UK residence** (i.e. later of date partner ceases working overseas or individual joins their partner in the UK), the individual has **no home in the UK** or, if the individual has homes in both the UK and overseas, he/she spends the greater part of the time living in the overseas home. Individual must not spend more than a permitted number of days in the UK before the start of UK residence, i.e. less than 91 days (reduced proportionately by reference to the number of complete months between the date of arrival and 5 April).	Later of date: – partner ceases overseas work, or – joins partner in the UK.

Case	Reason	Conditions	Start of UK residence
8	Starting to have a home in the UK	Individual must have no UK home at the beginning of the tax year but **start to have a UK home at some point during the tax year** and continue to have a UK home for the rest of the tax year and all of the following tax year. Individual must be **UK resident** in the **following tax year** (this must not be a split year). Individual does not meet the sufficient UK ties test for that part of the tax year before the day he or she starts to have a UK home.	Date individual starts to have a UK home.

Note: when considering whether there are sufficient UK ties in the part of the tax year before Cases 4, 5 and 8 are met, the individual must reduce the day-count limits in the sufficient UK ties tables on a pro rata basis by reference to the complete number of months between the date of arrival and 5 April.

Case 8 is very similar to Case 4. One of the main differences is that Case 8 only specifies that a home is in the UK (and not that the individual's **only** home is in the UK, as under Case 4). Therefore, it is possible that under Case 8 an individual will have both a UK home and an overseas home. Case 8 will allow such individuals (provided the other conditions are met) to split the year if they become UK resident in a tax year while still retaining an overseas home.

Example 3.11: SYT Case 4 (adapted from HMRC example)

Olan has been working for his employer in Germany for the last five years. He had no UK ties and was not resident in the UK. On 1 June 2015, Olan moves to the UK to look for work here. He rents out his flat in Germany on a two-year lease, from 27 May 2015.

He arrives in the UK and stays in temporary accommodation while he finds a flat to rent. He signs a 12-month lease on a flat in London on 1 July 2015.

He starts UK employment on 22 July 2015 and remains in the UK for a further two years.

Olan receives SYT for 2015/16 as:

- he is UK resident for the current tax year (2015/16);
- he is non-UK resident for the previous tax year (2014/15);
- he arrives part way through the current tax year; and
- he meets the Case 4 conditions, i.e.:
  - he meets the "only home test" during the tax year, i.e. he started to have his only home in the UK during the tax year and that continued until at least the end of the tax year; and
  - he had no UK ties from 6 April to 1 July 2015.

For Olan the overseas part of the tax year will end on 30 June 2015 and the UK part of the tax year will start on 1 July 2015, the day he started to have his only home in the UK.

Note: Olan might also meet the criteria for Case 5 or Case 8 split years, but priority is given to the case where the overseas part is the shortest.

Circumstances where More than One Case Applies

There may be times where more than one case for SYT can apply to the circumstances of an individual leaving or arriving in the UK. In such situations, there are rules to determine which case has priority.

Leaving the UK	Arriving in the UK
Case **1** has priority over cases 2 and 3	The case that results in the **shortest overseas**
Case **2** has priority over case **3**	**part** of the tax year has priority

3.4 Impact of Residence and Domicile

As we have seen, the whole question of whether an individual is liable to UK income tax, and to what extent, relies on their residence and their domicile. To recap, there are three possible situations:

1. UK resident and UK domiciled;
2. UK resident but non-UK domiciled; or
3. not UK resident.

3.4.1 UK Resident and UK Domiciled

An individual who is UK resident and UK domiciled is liable to UK income tax on his or her **worldwide personal income**, irrespective of where it is earned and whether or not it is remitted to the UK, i.e. all income is taxed on the arising basis.

3.4.2 UK Resident but Non-UK Domiciled

An individual who is resident but not domiciled in the UK can be taxed in one of two ways for UK income tax purposes:

1. their worldwide income is subject to UK tax (similar to individuals who are both resident and domiciled in the UK); or
2. they can be taxed on the "remittance basis", in which case their overseas income is subject to UK income tax only if it is actually remitted to the UK (i.e. it is brought in, used or enjoyed in the UK).

3.4.3 Non-UK Resident

An individual who is not resident in the UK is only liable to income tax on income that arises in the UK, e.g. UK property income, UK interest, dividends from UK shares. Overseas income is exempt from UK tax.

Non-UK Resident – Access to Allowances
In general, non-resident individuals are not entitled to allowances (such as personal allowance, blind person's allowance, married couples allowance and so on), but the following exceptions to the rule can claim allowances:

1. citizens of the European Economic Area (EEA), i.e. the European Union plus Iceland, Liechtenstein and Norway;
2. individuals resident in the Isle of Man and the Channel Islands;
3. current or former Crown servants and their widows or widowers;
4. former residents who have left the country for health reasons;
5. missionaries; and
6. nationals and/or residents of a country with which the UK has a double taxation treaty (DTT) (see **Section 3.6**).

The following table summarises the rules outlined above.

Status	UK Source Income	Overseas Source Income
UK resident and UK domiciled	Taxed – arising basis	Taxed – arising basis
UK resident and non-UK domiciled	Taxed – arising basis	Taxed – arising or remittance basis
Non-UK resident	Taxed – arising basis	Exempt

The "arising basis" means that the income that is subject to UK tax is the income that has arisen or accrued in the tax year.

The "remittance basis" means that the income that is subject to UK tax is the income that has been remitted to or brought into the UK in the tax year. Remittance income is always taxed as non-savings income.

Example 3.12

Anna has overseas property income of £25,000 per annum. She remits £10,000 of the overseas property income into the UK each tax year.

If she is taxed on the arising basis, she will include £25,000 in her UK income tax computation. If she is taxed on the remittance basis, she will include £10,000 in her UK income tax computation.

The legislation provides detailed provisions to identify what can be counted as a remittance. In essence, in this context a remittance is the "use or enjoyment" in the UK of income earned overseas. This covers overseas income spent in the UK or cash brought into the country, and includes property or services acquired in the UK with overseas income. Assets and personal effects, such as clothes, jewellery, etc. costing less than £1,000 are excluded.

An exemption was also introduced for remittances of foreign income or gains to the UK for the purposes of commercial investment in qualifying UK businesses. A qualifying investment is basically a purchase of shares (the purchase must be of newly issued shares in the company and not a purchase of shares from another existing shareholder) or where a loan is provided to a company. There is no limit to the amount of remittances that qualify for this relief.

3.5   Overseas Income – The Remittance Basis

As the table above shows, the overseas income of an individual who is **UK resident but non-UK domiciled** may be taxed either on the arising or the remittance basis. There are rules to determine what basis applies. These rules are set out below.

3.5.1   Overseas Income Automatically Taxed on the Remittance Basis

The remittance basis is automatically applied if the taxpayer has less than £2,000 unremitted overseas income in a tax year, i.e. less than £2,000 of the overseas income is effectively left overseas and is not "used or enjoyed" in the UK.

Example 3.13

Pierre is UK resident but French domiciled. He has lived in the UK for the past 10 years and earns property income of £12,000 from a property he rents out in France in tax year 2015/16. He has no other income or gains outside the UK and he remits all except £1,000 of the income into the UK.

Pierre will automatically be taxed on the remittance basis of tax, i.e. he will be taxed on the £11,000 he uses/enjoys in the UK rather than being taxed on the £12,000 that arises in the tax year. No formal claim is required for Pierre to have his overseas income taxed on the remittance basis.

In situations where the remittance basis is automatically applied, the taxpayer is allowed to keep their entitlement to UK personal tax allowances and is not required to file a tax return. They are also exempted from the remittance basis charge (RBC) (see **Section 3.5.4**).

3.5.2 Overseas Income Automatically Taxed on the Arising Basis

If a taxpayer has £2,000 or more of unremitted overseas income in a tax year, i.e. £2,000 or more is left overseas and is not used or enjoyed in the UK, they will automatically be taxed on the arising basis and will pay UK tax on all of their worldwide income, even if it remains outside the UK.

3.5.3 Overseas Income Taxed on the Remittance Basis but Formal Claim Required

As noted above, if the taxpayer has £2,000 or more of overseas income that is not remitted back to the UK, they will automatically be taxed on the arising basis. If they want to be taxed on the remittance basis, they will have to make a **formal claim** for that tax year. The formal application is made to HMRC using the self-assessment system.

Example 3.14

If Pierre, from Example 3.13, had overseas property income of £12,000 and had remitted only £3,000 into the UK, then he would automatically be taxed on the arising basis as he would have £9,000 of unremitted overseas income, i.e. greater than £2,000 unremitted. This means he would have £12,000 overseas property income in his UK income tax computation.

If he wanted to be taxed on the remittance basis and have only £3,000 of his overseas income subject to UK tax, he would have to make a **formal claim** to be taxed on the remittance basis.

Where a formal claim is made, certain personal tax allowances are withdrawn. They include: the basic personal allowance, age-related allowances, blind person's allowance, tax relief for married couples and civil partners and relief for life insurance premiums.

The withdrawal of allowances and reliefs is made under UK domestic law; however, if an individual is resident in the UK and is also resident in another treaty country (dual resident), then the treaty **may** provide that the individual retains the UK allowances/reliefs above. For example, the UK/Ireland double taxation treaty contains such a provision, whereas the UK/USA treaty does not.

3.5.4 The Remittance Basis Charge

When an individual has to make a formal claim in order to have their overseas income taxed on the remittance basis, they may be subject to the remittance basis charge. The remittance basis charge (RBC) is an annual tax charge in respect of overseas income and gains left outside the UK. It is in addition to any UK tax due on either UK income and gains or overseas income and gains remitted to the UK. The amount of the RBC depends upon how long the individual has been resident in the UK (see table below).

If a taxpayer has £2,000 or more in a tax year from overseas income that they have **not** remitted to the UK, they will pay the RBC if:

- they make a **claim** to use the remittance basis; and
- they are **resident in the UK** in the year that they make their claim for the remittance basis and are **aged 18 or over** at the end of the tax year; and
- they are long-term residents in line with the table below.

Long-term residence status	RBC
Individual has been resident in the UK for at least **7** of the previous **9** tax years	£30,000
Individual has been resident in the UK for at least **12** of the previous **14** tax years	£60,000
Individual has been resident in the UK for at least **17** of the previous **20** tax years	£90,000

When ascertaining the number of tax years an individual has been resident for this purpose, all the tax years when they were resident in the UK, even if they were under 18 years of age in those years, are counted. For example, an individual who is over 18 years of age during the tax year and has been **resident in the UK for seven out of nine years immediately preceding the year of assessment** will only be able to use the remittance basis if they pay the RBC of £30,000 for the year.

The charge will not apply in situations where the remittance basis is available without a formal claim, i.e. less than £2,000 of overseas income is left abroad/unremitted.

The RBC (whether £30,000, £60,000 or £90,000) is administered and collected through the self-assessment system. It should be noted that the full RBC applies irrespective of whether the individual was present in the UK for the whole of the year or only part of the year. In other words the RBC cannot be pro-rated for those entering or leaving the UK during a tax year.

If a taxpayer does not wish to pay the RBC, they can choose not to claim the remittance basis. They will then be taxed on the arising basis instead and will pay UK tax on their worldwide income. The decision is made on a year-by-year basis.

It is important to note that the remittance basis can only be claimed on overseas income – income earned in the UK is always taxable on the arising basis.

Example 3.15

Paulo is domiciled in Italy but has been resident in the UK since 2005/06. In 2015/16 he earned £50,000 from his UK employment and £20,000 gross interest from overseas investments. He remits £5,000 of the overseas interest into the UK in the tax year. Determine whether Paulo should claim the remittance basis or not (ignore any overseas tax paid).

Paulo has unremitted overseas income of £15,000. As this exceeds £2,000, he is automatically taxed on the arising basis. In order to be taxed on the remittance basis, he would have to make a formal claim.

Arising basis – automatic		Remittance basis – formal claim required	
Salary	£50,000	Salary	£50,000
Overseas interest	£20,000	Overseas interest	£5,000
Total income	£70,000	Total income	£55,000
Personal allowance	(£10,600)	Personal allowance	–
Taxable income	£59,400	Taxable income	£55,000
£31,785 × 20%	£6,357	£31,785 × 20%	£6,357
£27,615 × 40%	£11,046	£23,215 × 40%	£9,286
		RBC	£30,000
Tax liability	£17,403	Tax liability	£45,643

Note: if Paulo formally claims the remittance basis, he loses his entitlement to the personal allowance. The RBC of £30,000 applies because Paulo has been resident in the UK for more than seven of the previous nine tax years.

Paulo would be better off not making a formal claim to be taxed on the remittance basis.

Example 3.16

Martha is 42 years old and resident in the UK in 2015/16. Her unremitted foreign income for that year is £250,000. Martha's residence status for the preceding years was as follows:

2006/07 and 2007/08 – non-UK resident
2008/09 to 2014/15 – UK resident

Martha has been resident in the UK for seven of the preceding nine tax years and therefore has to consider whether to make a claim for the remittance basis. She will have to pay the £30,000 RBC if she decides to claim the remittance basis in 2015/16.

If, instead, Martha had been resident in the UK from the 2003/04 tax year (i.e. 12 out of the previous 14 tax years), the RBC would be £60,000 in the 2015/16 tax year.

The RBC represents tax paid in advance on income arising abroad but not yet remitted to the UK. When a taxpayer makes a claim for the remittance basis, they must nominate how much of their foreign income (and/or foreign gains for capital gains tax purposes) the RBC (whether £30,000, £60,000 or £90,000) is in respect of. This is known as their **"nominated" foreign income/gains**. When the "nominated" amounts are remitted, they are not taxed again; however, un-nominated income and gains are deemed to be remitted first.

3.6   Double Taxation Relief

As we have seen, UK income tax is liable on the worldwide income of UK residents, whether on the arising basis or the remittance basis, and on the UK income of non-residents. Due to domestic tax laws, income may, on occasion, be taxed in two countries:

- first, in the country where the income arises; and
- secondly, in the country where the taxpayer resides.

In order to eliminate this double tax charge, double taxation relief may be given. Relief can be obtained in one of three ways:

1. under the provisions of a double taxation treaty;
2. as credit relief (also known as "unilateral relief") under a double taxation treaty or in its own right; or
3. as deduction relief.

3.6.1   Double Taxation Treaties

Relief can be provided under a double taxation treaty (DTT) in two main ways:

- **Exemption relief** – where income is only taxable in the country of residence, e.g. the UK/ Ireland DTT states that interest income is taxable only where the individual is resident under the DTT.
- **Credit relief** – which reduces UK income tax by the amount of overseas tax paid. The maximum relief cannot exceed the UK tax on the same income.

3.6.2   Unilateral Relief

Where there is no DTT in place, relief for double taxation may be given as unilateral relief. The relief is the lower of:

- the overseas tax paid; or
- the UK tax on that source of income.

To determine the UK tax liability on overseas income, the overseas income is treated as the 'top slice' of income, i.e. considered after dividends. No refund can be given in the UK for any excess foreign tax paid.

Note that overseas income is always included gross in an income tax computation, i.e. inclusive of any foreign tax paid.

3.6.3 Deduction Relief

Deduction relief reduces overseas income in the tax computations by any overseas tax suffered. This is not usually as generous as credit relief and so is usually only claimed instead of credit relief if there is no UK tax liability (e.g. due to loss relief) to set off.

3.7 Coming to or Leaving the UK – Tax Registration

3.7.1 Coming to the UK

New arrivals to the UK are integrated into the UK tax system by registering their details with HMRC, depending on their status.

1. New employees – individual's details are included on the employer's Full Payment Submission as part of Real Time Information (RTI) for PAYE (see **Chapter 10** for additional details on the operation of RTI).
2. Self-employed – individual must complete and submit form CWF1, or register using the HMRC online service.
3. Individuals who are not self-employed but who need to complete a tax return must complete the SA1 registration process or register with HMRC online.

3.7.2 Leaving the UK

When leaving the UK an individual should complete Form P85 and submit it to HMRC. This allows HMRC to consider the individual's residence and domicile status in the future. It will also permit a refund of tax, if applicable.

Questions

Review Questions

(See Suggested Solutions to Review Questions at the end of this textbook.)

Question 3.1

Hank is a US citizen seconded to work in the UK for just over two years. He arrives on 19 May 2015 and leaves on 10 October 2017 and takes no significant breaks from his UK employment. During the secondment he does not leave the UK. On 11 October 2017 Hank returns to his employment in the US.

Hank returns to the UK for 10 days in November 2017 to see some friends he met during his secondment. He also visits London for six days in December 2017 to do some Christmas shopping.

Requirement
What is Hank's residence status for each tax year?

Question 3.2

Sheila is an Australian citizen. She is an architect but has been out of work for several months. Sheila's husband, Mark, has recently been seconded to London. The secondment is set to last for two years from March 2015. Mark will be UK resident during this time.

Sheila's brother, John, who lives in Edinburgh, has asked her to help him design the plans for his new house, which he hopes to build later that year. Sheila agrees to help John and travels to Edinburgh where she spends from 20 June to 25 September 2016 helping John with the plans for his house before returning home to Australia. Sheila lives with John and his family during her time in the UK.

Sheila has never been UK resident.

Requirement
What is Sheila's residence status for the tax year? (Assume that none of the automatic UK or overseas tests apply to Sheila in 2016/17.)

Question 3.3

Sean has lived in Belfast for several years and has been UK resident since his arrival. He runs a successful chain of internet cafés in Belfast and has plans to open several more cafés in the Republic of Ireland (RoI). In 2016/17, as part of his plans to expand into the RoI, he buys an apartment in Dublin and spends a lot of his time there overseeing the plans for the new cafés.

Sean's family are UK resident and remain resident in the UK while he is away setting up the new cafés. Sean travels back to Belfast once a month for the weekend and also returns for a few days in September, staying in his family home each time. His total time in the UK is 52 days.

Requirement
What is Sean's residence status for the tax year? (Assume that none of the automatic UK or overseas tests apply to Sean in 2016/17.)

Question 3.4

Mr Harris is an American citizen and is not resident in the UK. He is married to Sue-Ann and has the following sources of income in the 2016/17 tax year:

	£
Net UK property income (Note 1)	36,000
US dividends	4,000

Note:
1. £9,000 tax was deducted at source by the UK lessee. (Rental income paid to a non-resident landlord must have income tax at basic rate deducted.)

Requirement

Calculate Mr Harris's UK income tax liability for the 2016/17 tax year. Would the answer have been different if Mr Harris were a French citizen?

Question 3.5

Laura is UK resident and domiciled. She has the following income in 2016/17:

UK trading income	£35,000
UK bank interest	£400 (net)
Overseas bank interest	£1,000 (gross)

Overseas tax is paid at a rate of 15% in respect of the overseas interest.

Requirement

Calculate Laura's UK income tax liability for 2016/17.

Trading Income

Learning Objectives

After studying this chapter you will understand:

■ The identification of what constitutes a trade, profession or vocation by applying the "badges of trade" and relevant case law.
■ How to determine the trading profits for an accounting period, including in years of commencement, cessation and where there is a change of accounting date.
■ Inclusion of trading income as non-savings income in determining the appropriate rate of income tax to apply.
■ The format and layout of the income tax computation in arriving at the taxable profit from the net accounting profit.
■ The concept of "wholly and exclusively" for the purposes of the trade.
■ What are allowable and disallowable trading expenses in calculating tax-adjusted profits.
■ The difference between capital or revenue receipts and expenditure.
■ How to treat pre-trading and post-trading expenditure, and post-trading receipts.
■ The simplified process of calculating trading profits for smaller businesses.
■ How to calculate the apportionment of profits between partners.
■ How an overseas trade is subject to income tax.

4.1   Introduction

Income tax is charged on profits or gains arising from any **trade**, **profession** or **vocation**. The tax treatment and computational rules of each are practically identical and are, therefore, considered together.

Individuals liable to income tax are sometimes referred to as being self-employed (as opposed to being an employee). Some examples of individuals who are liable to income tax include:

■ shopkeepers, manufacturers and farmers – as they are carrying on a trade;
■ doctors, solicitors, architects and accountants – as they are carrying on a profession; and
■ dramatists and jockeys – as they are carrying on a vocation.

It is important to establish whether an activity constitutes a trade, as specific rules apply to the taxation of trading income, the deductibility of expenses and, in particular, to the ways in which trading losses can be relieved. In some instances, a profit or sale may be taxed as capital income (as opposed to trading income) and be subject to capital gains tax (CGT) rules. For example, a gain on a one-off sale of an investment property will be treated as capital income and be subject to CGT and not income tax. CGT is outside the scope of this text but will be relevant for your CA Proficiency 2 studies.

This chapter will begin by introducing you to the types of activities (trades, professions and vocations) that are subject to income tax. The specific tax rules for the commencement and cessation of a trade will be considered, in addition to the implications of a business changing its accounting date. The chapter will then discuss the rules for computing taxable trading income, including the simplified rules that have been recently introduced for smaller businesses. Finally, the chapter will discuss the specific tax rules that apply to partnerships and, in particular, to how a partnership's tax-adjusted profit/(losses) are calculated and apportioned.

4.1.1   Definition of "Trade", "Profession" and "Vocation"

Where the activity carried on by an individual falls within the definition of a trade, profession or vocation, then the income from that activity will be subject to income tax.

Trade
The term "trade" is not fully defined in tax legislation. Therefore, the interpretation of whether a trade exists or not is left largely to the courts. In the legislation, "trade" is taken to include "any venture in the nature of trade". This definition has caused much difficulty in the past, but it has, nevertheless, been adhered to.

The question of whether or not a trade is carried on is a **question of fact** rather than a point of law. The courts have held this definition to include profits or gains arising from trading in the normal sense of the word, but also from **isolated** transactions and activities.

Guidance as to what constitutes a trade can be taken from case law and this guidance is summarised in a collection of principles known as the "badges of trade". See **Section 4.1.2** below for further details on the badges of trade.

Profession
The term "profession" is not defined in tax legislation; therefore one must look at judgments from tax case law to help clarify the term. The following considerations are relevant in determining whether or not a profession exists:

1. Is the individual a member of a professional body?
2. Does the professional body:
   (a) Limit admittance or membership to persons who have successfully completed examinations and/or undergone a period of specified training?
   (b) Prescribe a code of ethics, breach of which may incur disciplinary measures against the member?
3. Does the occupation require mainly intellectual skill?
4. Is the individual operating as a self-employed individual? That is, they are self-employed as opposed to being an employee who is offering professional advice (see **Section 6.2.1**).

Examples of individuals regarded as carrying on a profession include teachers, doctors, opticians, accountants and journalists.

Vocation
In tax case law the word "vocation" has been compared with a "calling". Judgments in various tax cases have held that a bookmaker, dramatist, jockey and an author are all vocations.

4.1.2 "Badges of Trade"

The "badges of trade" are a set of six rules drawn up in 1955 by the **UK Royal Commission on the Taxation of Profits and Income**. They are used to help decide whether or not a trade exists.

1. "The subject matter of the realisation"
The general rule here is that an asset that does not give its owner an income or personal enjoyment merely by virtue of its ownership is more likely to have been acquired for the purpose of a trade. For example, an individual's principal private residence is more likely to have been bought for personal enjoyment rather than for the purposes of the individual's trade. A disposal of a residence, a disposal of shares and a disposal of a painting would all be capital transactions, and so any gain would not be subject to income tax. As noted above, gains from a capital transaction are subject to CGT.

In the case of *Rutledge v. CIR* (1929), in which 1,000,000 rolls of toilet paper were purchased in a single transaction and subsequently sold in a single transaction for a profit, it was held to be trading profit and not a capital gain; it was regarded as an "adventure in the nature of trade", there being no other justifiable reason to purchase such a large quantity of toilet rolls other than to sell them for a profit.

2. "The length of the period of ownership"
As a general rule, property acquired for a trading or dealing purpose is realised within a short time after acquisition. However, there may be many exceptions to this rule.

3. "The frequency or number of similar transactions by the same person"
If an individual completed a number of transactions involving the same type of asset in succession over a period of years, or if there had been several similar transactions around the same date, then a presumption arises that they were trading transactions.

In the case of *Martin v. Lowry* (1927), 34,000,000 yards of aircraft linen was sold. The size and frequency of the sales amounted to a trade. The subject matter, i.e. the aircraft linen, would not have been held as an investment asset and so on resale it gave rise to trading profits which would be subject to income tax.

In *Pickford v. Quirke* (1927), the individual purchased a mill and stripped and sold its assets in parcels. While this may be regarded as a capital transaction, where the individual repeated this exercise (i.e. the buying of a mill to strip and sell the assets) for a fourth time, he was viewed as carrying on a trade.

4. "Supplementary work on or in connection with the property realised"
If the asset is improved or developed in any way during the ownership so as to bring it into a more marketable condition, or if any special marketing efforts are made to find or attract purchasers, such as the opening of a sales office or a large-scale advertising campaign, then this would provide some evidence of trading. Where there is an organised effort to obtain profit, there is likely to be a source of taxable income. Likewise, if no work is done on or in connection with the property, the suggestion is that trading is not intended.

In *Cape Brandy Syndicate v. CIR* (1921), a group of accountants bought, blended and re-casked a quantity of brandy. They set up a phone line and information desk, and produced brochures in order to sell the product. As it was organised on a commercial basis, it was held that any profit on sale was trading profit.

5. "The circumstances that were responsible for the realisation"

This rule refers to possible circumstances that would eliminate the suggestion that the purchase was made deliberately for the purpose of a trade. For example, an asset may only be sold because of an emergency or "an opportunity calling for ready money".

Assets acquired by gift or inheritance are clearly not purchased with a trading motive, and so any future sale is unlikely to be trading.

6. "Motive"

Where a profit motive is evident, it is likely that the individual is trading. However, the absence of a profit motive will not necessarily be conclusive in establishing that a transaction is not trading.

When considering the "badges of trade", it is important to appreciate that the 'whole picture' needs to be taken into account, and that the weight given to the various factors may vary according to the circumstances. Furthermore, it should be recognised that any given factor may be present to a greater or lesser degree, and that the absence (or presence) of any single factor is unlikely to be conclusive in its own right.

Another rule not included in the "badges of trade", but one that can be of equal importance, is "intention". If the sale of an asset is clearly trading, then the individual's intentions are not relevant. However, it is possible that an individual could buy an asset for dual purposes. For example, an individual buys a premises intending to live on the ground floor and to convert the second and third floors into flats for resale. Therefore, the individual's intention for the second and third floors is to convert and sell the flats to make a profit. This intention is different to that of the ground floor of the premises, which will be kept as a capital asset.

Once it has been satisfactorily determined that an individual is carrying on a trade, profession or vocation and therefore has trading income, we then need to assess how much of this income is taxable and, importantly, when the tax is due to be paid.

4.2 Basis of Assessment of Trading Income

Each tax year runs from 6 April to 5 April; however, individuals who operate a trading business will not normally prepare their financial statements to 5 April each year. This would create a problem in terms of reporting income and hence the correct calculation of tax. To overcome this, a **basis period** is adopted to 'link' the "period of account" for a business (i.e. the accounting year/period end up to which the financial statements of the business are prepared) with the appropriate tax year. The basis period, for an ongoing trading business, will be **the 12-month period of account ending during the tax year**. Income, profits, etc. that fall in the basis period are considered when calculating income tax for the associated tax year.

Example 4.1

An individual running a trading business prepares the financial statements each year for the year ended 30 June.

What is the basis period for the tax year 2016/17? What would be the basis period for the tax year 2017/18?

For the 2016/17 tax year, the basis period will be the year ended 30 June 2016. For the 2017/18 tax year, the basis period will be the year ended 30 June 2017.

The basis period will be affected by the date of commencement (and cessation) of a trade and by any change in accounting date; each of these is subject to specific rules, which are outlined in **Sections 4.2.2–4.2.4**.

A summary of the key terms is outlined in the table below for easy reference.

Tax year or Year of assessment	6 April to 5 April
Period of account or Accounting year/period end	Refers to the date to which the financial statements or accounts of a trading business are prepared, e.g. accounting year end 30 June 2016 refers to the accounts that show the business profits from 1 July 2015 to 30 June 2016.
Basis period	The period that links the tax year to the period of account. Usually the basis period is the period of account ending in the tax year, but the commencement, cessation and change in accounting date rules should be considered.

The effect of the rules for taxing trading profits using tax years often means that some profits are taxable more than once, due to the profits in one accounting period overlapping two tax years. These are known as "**overlap profits**".

4.2.1 Overlap Profits

"Overlap profit" is the amount of profit in an accounting period that is taxed in two successive tax years. Overlap profits can occur:

- in the opening years of a business (see **Section 4.2.2**); or
- on a change of basis period following a change of accounting date (see **Section 4.2.3**).

To ensure that the business is taxed over its life on the actual profits made, "**overlap relief**" is provided. Basically this means that overlap profits are not actually taxed twice. Overlap profits may arise more than once over the lifetime of a business so, to ensure that overlap relief is received, a record should be kept of both the amount of the overlap profit and its overlap period. (See **Section 4.2.5** for details on overlap relief.)

Where the accounting period of a business coincides with the tax year throughout the life of the business, overlaps will not occur. To avoid short overlap periods, accounting dates ending on 31 March or on 1, 2, 3, 4 or 5 April are treated as ending on 5 April, unless the individual elects otherwise.

4.2.2 Commencement of a Trade

The date of commencement of a trade determines the accounting period for the business, which in turn determines the basis period of assessment for the business.

There are special provisions for the first three years after the commencement of the business.

First Tax Year
The first tax year is the tax year during which the trade commences. The basis period for the first tax year is the **profit from the date of commencement of the trade to the end of the tax year** (i.e. the following 5 April). If the period of account of the business does not coincide with the tax year, then the assessable profit is arrived at by time apportionment (see **Example 4.2** for the time-apportionment calculation).

> **Example 4.2**
> Mr Jones commenced to trade as a builder on 1 July 2016 and prepared accounts for 18 months to
> 31 December 2017.
>
> The 2016/17 tax year is the tax year in which Mr Jones commenced to trade. He will therefore be
> assessed as a trader for 2016/17 on the basis of the profits from 1 July 2016 to 5 April 2017. These
> will be arrived at by time apportioning the 18 months' results to 31 December 2017, i.e. the amount
> assessed for 2016/17 will be 9/18ths of the total profits for the period.
>
> If the calculation is performed using exact days, the time apportionment from 1 July 2016 to 5 April
> 2017 is 280/550 days. However, it is often more practical to apportion to the nearest month. Therefore,
> from 1 July 2016 to 5 April 2017 is nine months.

Second Tax Year

The basis period for the second tax year depends on the position in the second tax year. There are three possibilities:

1. If the accounting date falling in the second tax year is at least 12 months after the start of trading, the basis period is the **12 months to that accounting date**.
2. If the accounting date falling in the second tax year is less than 12 months after the start of trading, the basis period is **the first 12 months of trading**.
3. If there is **no** accounting date falling in the second tax year (because the first accounting period is a very long one that does not end until a date in the third tax year), the basis period **for the second tax year is the tax year itself (i.e. 6 April to the following 5 April)**.

> **Example 4.3: Accounting date ending in second year is at least 12 months after start date**
> Donna commences to trade on 1 January 2016. Accounts are prepared for the year ended
> 31 December 2016.
>
> Taxable profits for year ended 31 December 2016 = £24,000
> Accounts are prepared yearly to 31 December thereafter.
>
> | Tax Year | Period | Calculation | Profit |
> |---|---|---|---|
> | 2015/16 (1st year) | 01/01/16–05/04/16 | £24,000 × 3/12 | £6,000 |
> | 2016/17 (2nd year) | 01/01/16–31/12/16 | £24,000 | £24,000 |
>
> Note: the three-month period 01/01/16–05/04/16 is an "overlap period" where "overlap profits" of
> £6,000 have arisen. These will only be relieved on cessation of trade or on change of accounting date
> (see **Section 4.2.3**).

> **Example 4.4: Accounting date ending in second year is less than 12 months after start date**
> Lisa commences to trade on 1 October 2015. Accounts are prepared for the seven months ending
> 30 April 2016.
>
> Taxable profits for the seven months ending 30 April 2016 = £35,000
> Accounts are prepared yearly to end 30 April thereafter.
>
> | Tax Year | Period | Calculation | Profit |
> |---|---|---|---|
> | 2015/16 (1st year) | 01/10/15–05/04/16 | £35,000 × 6/7 | £30,000 |
> | 2016/17 (2nd year) | First 12 months: | | |
> | | 01/10/15–30/04/16 | £35,000 | £35,000 |
> | | 01/05/16–30/09/16 | £48,000 × 5/12 = £20,000 | £55,000 |
>
> Note: the periods 01/10/15–05/04/16 are "overlap periods" where "overlap profits" totalling £30,000
> have arisen.

> **Example 4.5: No accounting date ending in second tax year**
> Rose commences to trade on 1 March 2016. Accounts are prepared for the 15 months ending 31 May 2017.
>
> Taxable profits for the 15 months ending 31 May 2017 = £15,000
> Accounts are prepared yearly to end 31 May thereafter.
>
> | Tax Year | Period | Calculation | Profit |
> |---|---|---|---|
> | 2015/16 (1st year) | 01/03/16–05/04/16 | £15,000 × 1/15 | £1,000 |
> | 2016/17 (2nd year) | 06/04/16–05/04/17 | £15,000 × 12/15 | £12,000 |
> | No accounting date | | | |

Third Year

The basis of assessment for the third tax year depends on whether an accounting date falls in the second tax year.

1. If the accounting date does fall in the second tax year, the basis period for the third tax year is the accounting period ending in the third tax year.
2. If the accounting date does not fall in the second tax year, the basis period for the third tax year is the 12 months to the accounting date ending in the third year.

> **Example 4.6: Accounting date does fall in second tax year**
> Wilma commences to trade on 1 August 2015. Accounts are prepared for 2016, 2017 and 2018 as follows:
>
> | | Profit |
> |---|---|
> | Accounts for 11 months to 30 June 2016 | £44,000 |
> | Accounts for 12 months to 30 June 2017 | £60,000 |
> | Accounts for 12 months to 30 June 2018 | £30,000 |
>
> | Computation | Assessment |
> |---|---|
> | *First Year of Assessment 2015/16* | |
> | Profit for period 01/08/15–05/04/16, i.e. £44,000 × 8/11 | £32,000 |
> | *Second Year of Assessment 2016/17* | |
> | First 12 months (01/08/15–31/07/16), i.e. £44,000 + (£60,000 × 1/12) | £49,000 |
> | *Third Year of Assessment 2017/18* | |
> | 12-month accounting period ending 30/06/17 | £60,000 |
>
> *Note:*
>
> | | Overlap Profits |
> |---|---|
> | Overlap periods | |
> | 01/08/15–05/04/16 (assessed 2015/16 and 2016/17) (8 mths) | £32,000 |
> | 01/07/16–31/07/16 (assessed 2016/17 and 2017/18) (1 mth) | £5,000 |
> | | £37,000 |
>
> Overlap profit of £37,000 (9 mths).

Example 4.7: No accounting date ending in second tax year
Tanya commences to trade on 1 March 2016. Accounts are prepared for the 15 months ending 31 May 2017.

Taxable profits for the 15 months ending 31 May 2017 = £30,000.
Accounts are prepared yearly to end 31 May thereafter.

Tax Year	Period	Calculation	Profit
2015/16 (1st year)	01/03/16–05/04/16	£30,000 × 1/15	£2,000
2016/17 (2nd year)	06/04/16–05/04/17	£30,000 × 12/15	£24,000
No accounting date			
2017/18 (3rd year)	01/06/16–31/05/17	£30,000 × 12/15	£24,000

Note: the period 01/06/16–05/04/17 is an "overlap period" (10 mths) where "overlap profits" totalling £20,000 have arisen.

Fourth and Subsequent Years

For later tax years, apart from the year in which the trade ceases, the basis period for any particular tax year will be the accounting period ending during the tax year. This is known as the **current year basis of assessment**.

4.2.3   Change in Accounting Date

An individual may change the date to which they prepare the business accounts for a variety of commercial reasons: to align with the fiscal year-end; to align with the calendar year-end; to take account of seasonal variations and so on. On a change of accounting date, ending in that tax year, there may be either:

1.   one set of accounts covering a period of less than 12 months; **or**
2.   one set of accounts covering a period of more than 12 months; **or**
3.   no accounts; **or**
4.   two sets of accounts.

In the case of 1. and 2. above, the new basis period for the year will relate to the new accounting date. If the new basis period is less than 12 months, additional overlap profits may arise (see **Example 4.8** below). If the new basis period exceeds 12 months, a claim for overlap relief may be made (see **Example 4.9** below).

Example 4.8: New accounting period less than 12 months
Ms Ryan commenced trading on 1 January 2012, preparing accounts to 31 December each year. To coincide with a slack period, she changes her accounting year-end date to 30 June and prepares her first set of accounts to this date for the six months ending 30 June 2016. Her results were as follows.

	Profit
Year ended 31 December 2012	£12,000
Year ended 31 December 2013	£20,000
Year ended 31 December 2014	£32,000
Year ended 31 December 2015	£45,000
Six months ended 30 June 2016	£30,000

Computation	Assessment	Notes
2011/12 (01/01/12–05/04/12) = £12,000 × 3/12	£3,000	1
2012/13 (y/e 31/12/12)	£12,000	1

continued overleaf

Computation	Assessment	Notes
2013/14 (y/e 31/12/13)	£20,000	
2014/15 (y/e 31/12/14)	£32,000	
2015/16 (y/e 31/12/15)	£45,000	
2016/17:		
12 months to new accounting date (01/07/15–30/06/16)		
= (£45,000 × 6/12) + £30,000		
= £22,500 + £30,000	£52,500	2

Notes:
1. Overlap period of three months (01/01/12–05/04/12). Therefore £12,000 × 3/12 = £3,000 taxed in 2011/12 **and** 2012/13.
2. Overlap period of six months (01/07/15–31/12/15). Therefore £45,000 × 6/12 = £22,500 taxed in 2015/16 **and** 2016/17.

Therefore the total overlap profits **to be relieved** in the future stand at £25,500 for the nine months involved: £3,000 in 2011/12 and £22,500 in 2016/17.

Example 4.9: New accounting period more than 12 months
Mrs Nelson commenced trading on 1 January 2013, preparing accounts to 31 December each year. To coincide with her VAT quarters, she changes her accounting year-end date to 31 January and prepares her first set of accounts to this date for the 13-month period ending 31 January 2017. Her results were as follows:

	Profit
Year ended 31 December 2013	£20,000
Year ended 31 December 2014	£32,000
Year ended 31 December 2015	£45,000
13 months ended 31 January 2017	£65,000

Computation	Assessment
2012/13 (01/01/13–05/04/13) = £20,000 × 3/12	£5,000
2013/14 (y/e 31/12/13)	£20,000
2014/15 (y/e 31/12/14)	£32,000
2015/16 (y/e 31/12/15)	£45,000
2016/17:	
13 months to new accounting date of 31 January 2017:	
Profit for 13 months to 31/01/17	£65,000

See Example 4.14 to see how overlap relief reduces this profit for income tax purposes.

If there is no accounting date in the tax year, the basis period is the 12 months to the date that will be the new permanent accounting date. In this situation, overlap profits are created.

Example 4.10: No accounting date in the tax year
Will's business has been trading for many years and he has always prepared his accounts to 31 December each year. There are no overlap profits forward. Will has now decided to change his accounting period end to 30 April. His recent results are as follows:

	Profit
Year ended 31 December 2015	£19,000
16-month period ended 30 April 2017	£75,000
Year ended 30 April 2018	£65,000

continued overleaf

Computation
There is no accounting period ending in the 2016/17 tax year.

	Assessment
2015/16 (y/e 31/12/15)	£19,000
2016/17:	
Period end deemed to be y/e 30 April 2016	
£19,000 × 8/12 + £75,000 × 4/16	£31,417

Overlap profits of £12,667 (£19,000 × 8/12) are created.

If there are two accounting dates in the tax year, the basis period for the year ends on the new accounting date. It begins immediately following the previous basis period. In this situation overlap relief is available for months exceeding 12 months.

Example 4.11: Two accounting dates in the tax year
Sam's business has been trading for many years and there are eight months' overlap profits forward of £16,000. Sam always prepared his accounts to 30 April each year. However, he has now decided to change his accounting period end to 31 August. His recent results are as follows:

	Profit
Year ended 30 April 2015	£18,750
Year ended 30 April 2016	£20,000
4-month period ended 31 August 2016	£8,750
Year ended 31 August 2017	£17,500

Computation
There are two accounting periods ending in the 2016/17 tax year: y/e 30/04/16 and p/e 31/08/16.

	Assessment
2015/16 (y/e 30/04/15)	£18,750
2016/17:	
Period from 01/05/15 to 31/08/16 (16 mths)	£28,750
Less: overlap profits for 4 months (Note 1)	(£8,000)
	£20,750

Note:
1. As only four months' overlap arises as a result of the accounting date change, only four months of the eight months of overlap profits carried forward can be utilised in 2016/17. Four months of overlap profits of £8,000 remain to be relieved in the future.

4.2.4   Cessation of a Trade

Final Year
The cessation of a trade results in the application of rules that override those outlined above.

1. If the trade commences and ceases in the same (first) tax year, the basis period for that year is from the date of commencement to the date of cessation, i.e. the whole lifespan of the trade.
2. If the trade ceases in the second tax year, then the basis period for that year runs from 6 April at the start of the second tax year up to the date of cessation.

Example 4.12
Jim Johnson is a qualified electrician and starts to trade from 1 June 2016. However, on 31 May 2017 he decides he is not making enough money and ceases the business from that date. His profit for the year ended 31 May 2017 was £12,000.

Computation
Tax year 2016/17 – from 1 June 2016 to 5 April 2017: 10/12 × £12,000 = £10,000
Tax year 2017/18 – from 6 April 2017 to 31 May 2017: 2/12 × £12,000 = £2,000

3. If the trade ceases in the third or later tax year, the basis period runs from the end of the basis period for the previous year to the date of cessation.

Example 4.13
J. Jones, who traded as a butcher for many years, retired on 30 June 2016. The results for the last few years of trading were as follows:

	Profit
Year ended 30/09/2014	£36,000
Year ended 30/09/2015	£48,000
Nine months to 30/06/2016	£45,000

Computation

Tax year 2014/15 (y/e 30/09/14)	£36,000
Tax year 2015/16 (y/e 30/09/15)	£48,000
Tax year 2016/17 **(period from 01/10/15 to 30/06/16)**	**£45,000**
Less: any relevant overlap relief (deducted in 2016/17 year)	(X)

4.2.5   Relief for Overlap Profits

As stated earlier, the overriding thrust of how trade profits are taxed is that the business should be taxed over its lifetime on the cumulative total of the profits it has generated. On occasion, some profits can fall to be taxed in two or more basis periods, resulting in overlap profits.

Overlap Profits Relief on a Change of Accounting Date
Relief for overlap profits may be given on a change of accounting date (provided the new date is closer to 31 March/5 April; if the new date is further from 31 March/5 April, additional overlap profits can arise). The additional overlap profits will then be available for relief at a future change in accounting date or on the cessation of the trade (See **Example 4.8** above).

Example 4.14: Relief for overlap profits where there is a change of accounting date
Following on from Example 4.9 above, where Mrs Nelson changed her accounting year-end date to 31 January (previously 31 December) and prepared accounts for the 13-month period ending 31 January 2017, i.e. to her new accounting date. These accounts showed a profit of £65,000. Mrs Nelson also had incurred three months' overlap profits of £5,000 in her commencement years.
For 2016/17 her computation will include the 13 months to the new accounting date of 31 January 2017, but as the basis period exceeds 12 months, relief can be claimed for one month of the available overlap relief.

Profit for 13 months to 31/01/17	£65,000
Less: one month's overlap relief: (£5,000 × 1/3)	£1,667
	£63,333

Two months of overlap profits remain **to be relieved** in the future, a running total of £3,333 (£5,000 – £1,667).

Overlap Profits on the Cessation of a Trade
On the cessation of a trade any overlap profits that remain unrelieved are deducted from the profit falling to be taxed in that tax year (or they are added to any loss). In these circumstances other "loss reliefs" may be available; we will look at these in **Sections 5.12.3** and **5.12.7**.

Example 4.15

Mr James commenced trading on 1 September 2012, preparing accounts to 31 August each year. He ceased trading on 31 December 2016 and his results were as follows:

	Profit
Year ended 31 August 2013	£6,000
Year ended 31 August 2014	£15,000
Year ended 31 August 2015	£34,000
16 months ended 31 December 2015	£25,000

Computation		Assessment	Notes
2012/13 (01/09/12–05/04/13) = £6,000 × 7/12		£3,500	1
2013/14 (y/e 31/08/13)		£6,000	1
2014/15 (y/e 31/08/14)		£15,000	
2015/16 (y/e 31/08/15)		£34,000	
2016/17:			
Period from 01/09/15 to cessation	£25,000		
Less: overlap profits not already relieved	(£3,500)	£21,500	

Note:

1. Overlap profits of seven months (01/09/12–05/04/13). Therefore £6,000 × 7/12 = £3,500 taxed in 2012/13 **and** 2013/14.

Total profits earned in period:
£6,000 + £15,000 + £34,000 + £25,000   £80,000

Total profits assessed:
£3,500 + £6,000 + £15,000 + £34,000 + £21,500   £80,000

Before we move on to the next stage, work through **Questions 4.1–4.6** at the end of this chapter.

4.3   Computation of Taxable Trading Income

4.3.1   Overview

An individual, carrying on a trade or profession, will prepare accounts based on commercial and accounting principles to arrive at their net profit/(loss) for a particular year. However, the net profit/(loss) per the statement of profit or loss (SOPL) in the accounts **is not the taxable profit** – the Taxes Acts have their own set of rules for determining the taxable profit of a person carrying on a trade, profession or vocation. Accordingly, the net profit/(loss) will inevitably need **adjustment (i.e. amounts will need to be added and deducted)** to arrive at "**tax-adjusted**" profits/(losses) for income tax purposes. A pro forma of the adjustment needed for the net profit/(loss) per the SOPL is shown in **Figure 4.1** overleaf.

FIGURE 4.1: PRO FORMA FOR TAX-ADJUSTED PROFITS

Net profit/(loss) per the SOPL

ADD

1. Expenses included in the SOPL that are not allowable for tax purposes
2. Income that is taxable trading profits that is not included in the SOPL

DEDUCT

1. Profit/income included in the SOPL that is not taxable as trading income
2. Expenses not included in the SOPL that are tax deductible
3. Capital allowances

EQUALS

Tax-adjusted trading profit/(loss)

for income tax purposes

It is important to note some of the common terminology used in the adjustment process:

- Deductible expenditure can be referred to as "allowable expenditure" for tax purposes.
- Non-deductible expenditure can be referred to as "disallowable expenditure" for tax purposes.

The tax legislation provides that trading profits of a business are to be calculated in accordance with generally accepted accounting practice (GAAP). The majority of small and medium-sized businesses in the UK will apply FRS 102 (*The Financial Reporting Standard applicable in the UK and Republic of Ireland*) when preparing their annual financial statements.

4.3.2 The Adjustment of Profits – Allowable and Disallowable Items

When calculating tax-adjusted profit/(loss) for **income tax purposes**, there are two fundamental principles:

1. If an item is of a **capital** nature, it must be **disallowed**.
2. Even if an item is of a **revenue** nature, it may still be specifically disallowed by the legislation.

4.3.3 Capital versus Revenue Receipts

Capital receipts and expenditure (including profits and losses on the sale of non-current assets e.g. a property) are not subject to income tax as they are usually accountable under capital gains tax (CGT).

When deciding, for income tax purposes, whether a receipt is capital or revenue, the following general rules apply:

■ **Capital receipt** The sale of fixed capital (i.e. assets that form part of the permanent structure of a business or assets that have an enduring benefit to the business) is a capital receipt. For example, income from the sale of land, buildings, machinery or motor vehicles would be treated as capital.

■ **Revenue receipt** The sale of circulating capital (i.e. assets acquired in the ordinary course of a trade and sold) is a revenue receipt. For example, the groceries in a supermarket.

To further elaborate on the above rules, there are five basic principles:

1. Income from the sale of the **assets** of a business are, *prima facie*, **capital** receipts.
2. Income received as compensation for the destruction of the recipient's **profit-making apparatus** are capital receipts.
3. Income in lieu of **trading receipts** are of a revenue nature.
4. Income made in return for the imposition of substantial restrictions on the **activities** of a trader is a **capital** receipt.
5. Income of a **recurrent nature** is more likely to be treated as a **revenue** receipt.

Capital receipts (including income and gains) not taxable as trading income:

■ **Profits on sale of fixed assets** Profits or gains on the disposal of fixed assets or investments are exempt from income tax, but can be subject to CGT. Where capital allowances have been claimed on the purchase of an asset, the receipt of disposal proceeds may give rise to a balancing allowance or charge (see **Chapter 5**).

■ **Grants** Capital grants are exempt from income tax (but are taken into account for both capital allowances and CGT). Revenue grants are taxable.

■ **Investment income** Bank interest, dividends and other investment income are not part of the trading profits and are taxed under the category of savings and investment income (see **Chapter 7**).

■ **Rental income** Rental income is taxable as property income (see **Chapter 8**).

4.3.4   Capital versus Revenue Expenditure

Capital expenditure is **not** an allowable expense when calculating net trading profits/(losses) for income tax. Where capital expenditure or capital losses (e.g. loss on sale of fixed assets) have been included in the SOPL, they will be **disallowed** when arriving at taxable profits. Where the capital expenditure qualifies for capital allowances (see **Chapter 5**), the individual will receive tax relief for the expenditure by deducting the capital allowances for the period from the tax-adjusted profit.

The judicial statement of Lord Cave in the case of *Atherton v. British Insulated and Helsby Cables Ltd* (1925) is frequently used by the courts to assist them in resolving the problem of whether expenditure is of a revenue nature, and therefore allowable, or of a capital nature, and therefore disallowed:

> "When expenditure is made, not only once and for all, but with a view to bringing into existence an asset or an advantage for the enduring benefit of a trade . . . there is very good reason (in the absence of special circumstances leading to an opposite conclusion) for treating such an expenditure as properly attributed not to revenue but to capital."

The importance of the distinction is that, in the absence of a specific statutory disallowance (such as depreciation or political donations), revenue expenditure is an allowable expense of earning the profit, whereas capital expenditure is not. There are specific statutory provisions to allow some capital items to be deducted in arriving at tax-adjusted profit/(loss), e.g. the deduction of part of a short-lease premium spread over the term of the lease. Capital expenditure that does not qualify for capital allowances may form part of the allowable cost of an asset in arriving at the capital gain on a future disposal of the asset. However, on certain other assets (such as leases) the expenditure is deemed to waste away over the life of the assets and no tax relief is given.

Provisions

Once it has been decided that an item is revenue, it remains to be considered in which period it is to be relieved. As will be seen later, increases/decreases in general provisions are added back/ deducted from the accounting profits for tax purposes. International Accounting Standard 37 *Provisions, Contingent Liabilities and Contingent Assets* (IAS 37) sets out when such provisions should be made from an accountancy perspective. HMRC has stated that, in the main, it will follow the treatment in the financial accounts if it is in accordance with IAS 37. Thus a provision will be deductible if:

- it is a revenue amount;
- it is required by generally accepted accounting practice;
- it does not conflict with legislation; and
- it can be accurately quantified, i.e. it must be a specific provision and not a general provision.

Expenditure "wholly and exclusively" for the Trade

Unless it is covered by a specific statutory provision, expenditure is only allowable in computing profits if it is "wholly and exclusively" for the purposes of the trade. A payment that satisfies the general rule is not allowable if it is a criminal payment, such as a bribe or protection money to terrorists, or a payment made in response to threats, menaces, blackmail and other forms of extortion.

A distinction is also drawn between expenditure incurred in the capacity of a trader and the capacity of a taxpayer, the latter being an appropriation of profit (commonly called "drawings") and, therefore, not allowable.

Expenditure **not** wholly and exclusively laid out for the purposes of the trade includes the following:

- Any expenditure incurred on behalf of the trader or his or her family for private or domestic purposes.
- Rent of any dwelling house **not used** for the trade.
- Any sum expended **over and above** repairs to the premises, implements, utensils or articles employed for the purposes of the trade or profession.
- Any loss not connected with the trade.
- Any capital withdrawn from, or employed as capital in, the trade or profession or any capital employed in improvements to premises occupied by the trade or profession.
- Debts, other than the impairment of trade debts/receivables, or a **specific** estimation of an impairment loss.

Expenditure is, therefore, not tax deductible if it is not for trade purposes or if it reflects more than one purpose (duality of purpose). Note that any private proportions of expenses (e.g. light and heat, motor expenses, telephone, etc.) are not tax deductible. Relief is available for the business element of expenditure only. Note that where payments are to or on behalf of an employee, the full amounts are deductible, but the employee is taxed under the benefits-in-kind benefits code (see below).

4.3.5 Tax Treatment of Common Expenses

Expenses or Losses of a Capital Nature
Expenses or losses of a capital nature are disallowed and should be added to the net profit/(loss) per the SOPL. These costs include:

- depreciation;
- loss on sale of fixed assets;
- improvements to premises; and
- purchase of fixed assets.

Note: capital allowances may be claimed on certain qualifying assets (see **Chapter 5**).

Applications or Allocations of Profit
Applications or allocations of profit are disallowed and should be added to the net profit/(loss) per the SOPL:

- income tax;
- transfers to a general reserve; and
- drawings.

Payments from which Tax is Deducted
Payments from which tax is deducted are allowed if "wholly and exclusively" for trading purposes. For example, where an expense is incurred by a business in respect of patent royalties, the business should not have to add the expense back as long as it was incurred wholly and exclusively for the purposes of the trade.

Expenses not "wholly and exclusively" for the Business
Expenses not "wholly and exclusively" laid out for the purposes of the business are disallowed and therefore should be added to the net profit/(loss) per the SOPL. These will include:

- any private element of expenses;
- rental expenses;
- charitable (unless small and to local charities) and political donations and subscriptions (except where it can be shown that the political expenditure was incurred for the survival of the trade, in which case it may be deductible);
- life assurance premiums on the life of the individual or their spouse;
- fines and penalties (except parking fines for employees using their employer's car on business);
- subscriptions, unless professional or trade subscriptions.

General Provisions
In accordance with IAS 37, general provisions are allowed for tax purposes **if** the following conditions are satisfied:

- a present obligation (legal or constructive) has arisen as a result of a past event (the obligating event);
- payment is probable (i.e. it is more likely than not); and
- the amount can be estimated reliably.

Trade Debt Impairments
Trade debt impairments, i.e. the write-down in trade debtor balances that impact the SOPL, can be allowable or disallowable depending on their nature:

- an impairment loss is **allowable**, i.e. no adjustment required;
- a reversal of an impairment loss is **allowable**, i.e. no adjustment required;
- an increase in a specific impairment provision for bad debts is **allowable**, i.e. no adjustment required;
- a decrease in a specific impairment provision for bad debts is **allowable**, i.e. no adjustment required;
- an increase in a general impairment provision for bad debts is **disallowable**, i.e. it must be **added to the net profit/(loss)**; and
- a decrease in a general impairment provision for bad debts is **disallowable**, i.e. it must be **deducted from the net profit/(loss)**.

Write-off of Loans to an Employee
The write-off of a loan to an employee is generally tax deductible (so no adjustment needed) for the business and will be a benefit in kind for the employee.

Premiums on Short Leases
If an individual carries on a trade or profession in a premises leased for a period of less than 50 years, a proportion of any premium paid on the lease (as distinct from the assignment of a lease from one landlord to another) is allowable in computing the profits of a trade or profession. The applicable proportion is that part of the premium that is assessable on the landlord as additional rent, but spread over the period of the lease rather than as a single deduction.

The amount assessable on the landlord as additional rent is the total premium less 2% per annum for the number of years of the short lease, excluding the first year. The formula used is:

$$\text{Rental portion} = \text{premium} - \text{premium} \times \frac{(n-1)}{50}$$

where, n is the number of complete years of the lease.

The remainder will be subject to capital gains tax (CGT), which is covered at CA Proficiency 2.

Example 4.16
Joe Bloggs, a trader who has been in business for many years, makes up accounts to 30 September. He was granted a 21-year lease of business premises on 1 July 2016 at a premium of £105,000 and a rent of £25,000 per annum, payable quarterly in advance. Show the deductions to be made in respect of the lease in Joe Bloggs's accounts for the year to 30 September 2016.

Solution

	£
Premium payable 1 July 2016	105,000
Less: discount (2% × (21 − 1)) × £105,000	(42,000) (taxed under CGT)
Assessable on landlord as additional rent (property income)	63,000

Alternatively, the £63,000 can be calculated as follows:

£105,000 − (£105,000 × (21 −1)/50)

Therefore the annual amount allowable to Joe Bloggs is £3,000, being the £63,000, spread over the duration of the lease. That is £63,000/21 = £3,000 per annum.

continued overleaf

Thus in the year ended 30 September 2016, Joe Bloggs's deduction for the lease premium would be calculated on three months: 3/12 × £3,000.

	£
	750
Rent payable (one quarter) (£25,000 × 3/12)	6,250
Total	7,000

Entertainment Expenses

In general, entertainment expenses incurred are **completely disallowed** (this also applies to amounts reimbursed to employees for specific entertaining expenses, gifts and round-sum allowances which are exclusively for meeting such expenses). However, there are **exceptions to this rule**:

■ Gifts carrying a conspicuous advertisement for the trader, not consisting of food, drink or tobacco and not exceeding £50 per person per annum.

■ Expenditure for the benefit of **staff**, e.g. staff entertainment, annual parties, etc. is allowable, provided the entertainment is open to all staff generally and is not excessive. This includes employees' guests.

■ Gifts to charities (except under gift aid), provided they are wholly and exclusively for the purposes of the trade – it is usually very difficult to show a trading motive for a gift to charity.

Legal Expenses

Certain legal expenses are **allowable**, meaning that **no adjustment is required**:

■ debt recovery;

■ renewal of a short lease of less than 50 years;

■ product liability claims and employee actions;

■ expenses incurred defending the individual's title to fixed assets; and

■ expenses connected with an action for breach of contract.

Other legal expenses are **disallowable** and must be **added to the net profit/(loss) per the SOPL**:

■ expenses associated with the acquisition of capital assets;

■ the drafting of an original grant of a lease; and

■ expenses associated with acquiring a new asset.

Repairs

Replacement or redecoration repairs not involving material improvements are allowable. Expenditure on improvements/extensions, new assets, etc. is not allowable. As a general rule, expenditure incurred on repairs to buildings is deductible. The concept of repair is that it brings an item back to its original condition, and in this respect the following points are critical:

■ The expenditure must have actually been incurred. However, provisions for work to be done in the future will be allowable for tax purposes if the conditions for IAS 37 are met (see **General Provisions** above).

■ The term "repairs" does not include improvements and alterations to premises. In addition, it is not possible to claim a revenue deduction for the portion of the improvements or alterations that would represent the cost of repairs that could otherwise have been carried out.

■ The replacement of a capital asset or the "entirety" will not be treated as a repair. This would cover, for instance, the reconstruction of a trader's premises.

The test to be applied is whether or not the repair entails the renewal of a component part or of the entirety. If it is the former, it will be regarded as a repair; if it is the latter, i.e. the renewal of an entirety, it will be treated as a capital expenditure.

A separately identifiable portion of a building or structure may be regarded as an entirety in its own right and, accordingly, its replacement would be disallowed. A practical test is whether or not they are of sufficient size and importance to be regarded as an entirety. Examples of entireties from case law include the following:

● Replacement of a large chimney situated apart from other factory buildings (*O'Grady v. Bullcroft Main Collieries Ltd* (1932)).

● A ring in an auction mart (*Wynne-Jones (Inspector of Taxes) v. Bedale Auction Ltd* (1976)).

● A replacement of a stand in a football ground (*Brown v. Burnley Football & Athletic Ltd* (1980)).

● A barrier that protected a factory against the overflow from an adjoining canal (*Phillips v. Whieldon Sanitary Potteries Ltd* (1952)).

It appears that it is necessary to show that the item that has been replaced is ancillary to the complete building. In practice, the accounting treatment adopted and the total cost involved may also be important factors.

Repairs to Newly Acquired Assets

In *Odeon Associated Theatres Limited v. Jones* (1971), it was held that the expenditure on repairs to a newly acquired asset may be deductible, provided that:

■ the cost is properly charged to the revenue account in accordance with the correct principles of commercial accountancy; and

■ the repairs are not improvements; and

■ the expenditure is not incurred to make the asset commercially viable on its acquisition; and

■ the purchase price was not substantially less than it would have been if it had been in a proper state of repair at the time of purchase.

Leased Motor Vehicles

Where the CO_2 emissions of a leased motor car exceed 130g/km, 15% of the leasing costs are disallowed in calculating taxable profits (for leases entered into before 6 April 2013, the threshold was 160g/km).

Example 4.17
Joe, who is self-employed and prepares annual accounts to 30 September, leased a car on 20 April 2016. The car had CO_2 emissions of 135g/km. Lease charges of £6,000 are included in Joe's accounts for year-end 30 September 2016. Joe has agreed with HMRC that one-third of the usage is private.

Allowable lease cost is £6,000 × 85% = £5,100, less private element (1/3rd) = £3,400 for 2016/17.

Penalties and Interest on Late Payment of Tax

HMRC penalties and interest that have been incurred for late payment of income tax, VAT and most other tax heads are disallowed in computing tax-adjusted profits.

Intellectual Property

Any income or expenditure (excluding depreciation or amortisation) that is specifically associated with:

- intellectual property (including patents, copyrights and know-how);
- goodwill; and
- other intangible assets (including agricultural quotas and brands),

is, in general, taxable/deductible as trading income. Therefore, no adjustment is needed to the net profit/(loss).

Redundancy Payments

Statutory redundancy payments are specifically allowable. Redundancy payments made when a trade ends are deductible on the earlier of either the day of payment or the last day of trading.

The deduction extends to additional payments of up to three times the amount of the statutory redundancy pay on cessation of trade. Compensation for loss of office and ex-gratia payments are deductible if for the benefit of the trade.

Renewal or Registration of Trademarks

Expenses on renewal or registration of trademarks are specifically allowable for trades only. Copyright arises automatically and so does not have to be registered.

Patent royalties and copyright royalties paid "wholly and exclusively" in connection with a trade are deductible as trading expenses. They are paid with deduction of basic rate tax, which is then collected through self-assessment. Generally, copyright royalties are paid gross.

Accountancy and Tax Advisor Fees

Normal accounting, auditing and taxation compliance costs are allowable. Accountancy fees arising out of an enquiry are only permitted if no additional tax charges arise (the special costs regarding Tribunal appeals would also potentially be allowable if the appeal were found in favour of the individual). If accountancy fees are in connection with non-trade income, i.e. investment income or CGT), they are not deductible.

Pre-trading Expenses

An allowance may be claimed in respect of pre-trading expenses in the case of a trade or profession, provided that the expenses:

- were incurred for the purpose of the trade or profession; and
- were incurred within seven years of commencement; and
- are not otherwise allowable in computing profits.

Where an allowance is granted for pre-trading expenses, it is treated as if the expenditure were incurred **on the date** on which the trade or profession **commenced**.

Examples of qualifying pre-trading expenses include accountancy fees, market research, feasibility studies, salaries, advertising, preparing business plans and rent.

Key Person Insurance

Key person insurance is insurance taken out by an employer in their own favour against the death, sickness or injury of an employee (the "key person") whose services are vital to the success of the employer's business.

In general, premiums paid under policies insuring against loss of profits, consequent on certain contingencies, **are deductible** for tax purposes in the period in which they are paid. Correspondingly, all **sums received** by an employer under such policies are treated as **trading receipts** in the period in which they are received. Key person insurance policies qualify for this treatment where the following conditions are satisfied:

■ The sole relationship is that of employer and employee.
■ The employee does not have a major shareholding.
■ The insurance is intended to meet loss of profit resulting from the loss of the services of the employee, as distinct from the loss of goodwill or other capital loss.
■ In the case of insurance against death, the policy is a short-term insurance providing only for a sum to be paid in the event of the death of the insured within a specified number of years.

When the conditions are not met, key person insurance premiums are disallowed and any sums received are consequently not taxable.

Finance Leases

Assets leased under finance leases may be included as fixed assets in the accounts, and interest and depreciation for such assets included in the SOPL.

For tax purposes, capital allowances **may not** be claimed in respect of such assets. Instead a deduction can be given for **gross lease payments** made, i.e. interest plus capital. The adjustments to be made to the accounting profits would then be as follows:

■ add back interest and depreciation charged in respect of finance lease assets; **and**
■ give a deduction for gross lease payments made.

Alternatively, in line with the thrust of HMRC accepting financial statements prepared using generally accepted accounting standards, the deduction for finance leases can follow the accounting treatment and comprise a mixture of the finance charge element and the accounting depreciation. In this way no adjustment is required for leased assets in these circumstances (except if there was any private use of the asset or if the finance lease related to a motor vehicle with CO_2 emissions of more than 130g/km, see **Leased Motor Vehicles**). Provisions are included to counter leases with 'balloon payments' at the start or end of a lease.

Unpaid Remuneration

If earnings for employees are charged in the accounts but are not paid within nine months of the end of the period of account, the cost is only deductible for the period of account in which the earnings are **paid**.

National Insurance Contributions

Only employer's National Insurance contributions (NICs), i.e. its Class 1 secondary and Class 1A contributions, are tax deductible. A trader's self-employed Class 2 or Class 4 NICs are drawings and, as such, are not tax deductible. (See **Chapter 10** for full details on NICs.)

Incidental Costs of Obtaining Finance

Incidental costs of obtaining loan finance, or of attempting to obtain or redeem it, are deductible (e.g. bank fees/charges).

Pension Contributions

Ordinary annual contributions by an employer to a **Revenue-approved** pension scheme, for the benefit of employees, are **allowable** for tax purposes in the year in which they are **paid**. Thus, any **accruals** in respect of ordinary annual pension contributions due, which have been included in arriving at the accounts profit, will have to be disallowed.

'Spreading' (i.e. tax relief will be available over a number of years as opposed to the year in which the contribution is paid) will apply where the increase in contributions is more than 110% of the employer contributions paid in the previous period ('the excess') and the excess is £500,000 or more. The amount of the excess is the amount of the contribution in the current chargeable period that is more than 110% (or 1.1 times) of the contributions paid in the previous period. Relief will be spread over a two- to four-year period, depending on the size of the excess.

Amount of excess	Period over which relief is spread
Less than £500,000	No spreading
£500,000–£999,999	Spread over two years equally (i.e. this period and the following period)
£1,000,000–£1,999,999	Spread over three years equally
£2,000,000 or more	Spread over four years equally

Example 4.18

In the prior year an employer paid pension contributions of £400,000, and in the current year pays contributions of £1,200,000.

The increase in the contributions in the current year is 200% (i.e. (£1,200,000 – £400,000)/£400,000). The excess is £1,200,000 – (£400,000 × 110%) = £760,000.

Therefore, as the increase is more than 110% and the excess is greater than £500,000, we need to consider the pension spreading rules.

Relief for the excess will be spread over two years. Therefore, relief of £380,000 will be given in this period and £380,000 in the next period. Note that the remaining £440,000 of the £1,200,000 pension contributions paid in the current year will be able to receive tax relief in that year. It is only the excess element that is subject to the spreading rules. Therefore relief will be given as follows:

Current year: relief of £820,000 (in the tax computation this would be achieved by disallowing £380,000 of the £1,200,000).
Following year: relief of £380,000 (in the tax computation, an additional tax deduction of £380,000 would be given).

The pension spreading rules only apply to contributions that have actually been paid by the employer to a pension scheme. They do not apply to accrued pension contributions. When comparing the increase from the previous year to the current year, it will only involve a comparison of paid pension contributions.

Now that we have considered the allowable and disallowable items for tax purposes, let's look at a worked example to recap the calculation of tax-adjusted trading profits for income tax.

Example 4.19
Mr Bailey has operated a sports goods shop for 10 years. The statement of profit and loss for this business for the year ended 31 December 2016 is as follows:

Statement of Profit and Loss for the year ended 31 December 2016

	Notes	£	£
Sales			313,759
Less: cost of sales			(226,854)
Gross profit			86,905
Add:			
Bank interest received		1,300	
Profit on sale of equipment		580	1,880
			88,785
Less: expenses:			
Wages and NIC	1	45,000	
Rates	2	2,200	
Insurance	3	8,100	
Light and heat	2	850	
Telephone	4	970	
Repairs	5	3,400	
Motor and travel expenses	6	5,440	
General expenses	7	4,575	
Loan interest	2	9,000	
Bank interest and charges		3,260	
Depreciation		4,450	87,245
Net profit for the year			**1,540**

Notes:
1. Wages and NIC:

	£
Salary to self	20,000
Salary to wife	2,000
Own NICs	200
Bonus to staff	2,500

2. Rates, light and heat, loan interest
In March 1997, Mr Bailey purchased, for £100,000, the shop premises in which the business had been carried on for the previous three years. Since 1997, the top floor, which is a self-contained flat, has been occupied free of charge by Mr Bailey's elderly father, who takes no part in the business. One-fifth of the rates, property insurance, light and heat relate to the flat, which represents one-tenth of the value of the whole property.
The loan interest relates to interest paid on a loan taken out for the purchase of the premises.
3. Analysis of insurance charge

	£
Shopkeepers' all-in policy	1,400
Retirement annuity premiums for self	3,000
Permanent health insurance for self	2,400
Motor car insurance	800
Property insurance	500
	8,100

4. Telephone/home expenses
Telephone costs include Mr Bailey's home telephone and 25% of the total charge is for personal use. Mrs Bailey carries out most of her bookkeeping duties at home and a special deduction of £156 is to be allowed for costs incurred in carrying out these duties at home. This item has not been reflected in the profit and loss account.

continued overleaf

5. Repairs charge:

	£
Purchase of display stand	500
Repairs to shop front	600
Plumbing repairs in shop	800

6. Analysis of motor and travel expenses

Included in the motor and travel expenses is the cost of a trip to London to a sports goods wholesale exhibition. Mr Bailey attended the exhibition on two days and then spent a further five days visiting friends and relatives. Details of the expenses are as follows:

	£
Air fare	140
Hotel bill (for seven days)	400
Entertaining overseas exhibitor	100
	640

The remainder of the expenses relate to Mr Bailey's motor car, which had a market value of £25,000 and CO_2 emissions of 170g/km when first leased on 1 July 2011.

	£
Lease of car (12 payments × £240)	2,880
Running expenses	1,920
	4,800

Annual mileage:	
Personal mileage	6,000
Business mileage	12,000
Home to business mileage	2,000
Total mileage	20,000 miles

7. Analysis of general expenses

	£
Donation to church	405
Donation to church building fund (includes full-page advertisement in magazine – £200)	1,000
Subscriptions to trade association	350
Accountancy fee	1,100
Branded sponsorship of "open day" at local golf club	900
Entertainment – customers	520
Entertainment – staff Christmas party	300
	4,575

Computation of Tax-adjusted Profits

	Notes	£	£
Net profit per accounts			1,540
Add:			
Depreciation		4,450	
Wages and NIC	1	20,200	
Rates (1/5th)		440	
Insurance	2		5,500
Light and heat (1/5th)		170	
Loan interest (1/10th)		900	
Telephone (25%)		242	
Repairs	3		500
Motor and travel expenses	4		3,139
General expenses	5	1,725	37,266
			38,806

continued overleaf

Deduct:

Bank interest received	1,300	
Profit on sale of equipment	580	
Mrs Bailey's business telephone	156	(2,036)
Adjusted profits (prior to calculation in respect		
of capital allowances – see Chapter 5)		36,770

Notes:

1. Wages and NIC

	£
	£
Salary to self	20,000
Own NIC	200
Disallowed, as these are drawings	20,200

2. Insurance

	£
	£
Retirement annuity premiums for self	3,000
Permanent health insurance for self	2,400
Property insurance (1/5th)	100
Disallowed	5,500

The restriction in respect of the motor car insurance is included in Note 4.

3. Repairs

    Display stand is capital expenditure – disallowed.

4. Motor and travel

Leasing charges	£2,880
Running expenses	£1,920
Motor car insurance	£800
Cost per accounts	£5,600
Total mileage	20,000 miles
Personal mileage	(6,000)
Home to business	(2,000)
Business mileage	12,000 miles (60%)

Disallow – Car Restrictions:

(a) Lease restriction

    CO_2 g/km of car 170g/km (when first leased the CO_2 limit was 160g/km; therefore the 15% restriction applies)

Payments £240 × 12 =	2,880	
15% restriction	(432)	
	2,448	
Lease hire restriction		£432

(b) Private car element

Disallowable element 40% × £2,448	£979

(c) Private running expenses and motor car insurance

Disallowable element 40% × £2,720	£1,088

(d) Air fare and hotel bill (none allowable because of

duality of purpose*)	£540
Business entertainment	£100
Motor and travel disallowed	£3,139

* The strict position is that because the expenditure was not incurred "wholly and exclusively" for the purpose of the trade, none of the expenditure is allowable. In practice, however, it would normally be acceptable to claim a deduction for a proportion of the total expenditure equal to the business element, e.g. 2/7ths.

continued overleaf

5. General expenses

Donation to church	£405
Donation to church building fund (excluding magazine advertisement)	£800
Entertainment – customers	£520
Disallowable	£1,725

The sponsorship of the "open day" at the local golf club would be allowable as advertising.

The donations to church could potentially be allowable if it could be shown they were provided for the purposes of the trade, or if the business obtained a benefit from it (e.g. advertising in the church's newsletter). It has been assumed this is not the case here.

Before we move on to the next stage, try **Questions 4.7-4.11** at the end of this chapter.

4.3.6   Special Rules for Small Businesses: Cash Basis of Accounting and Simplified Expenses

Finance Act 2013 (FA 2013) introduced two measures that simplified the process of calculating tax-adjusted profits for small businesses: the cash basis of accounting and simplified expenses.

Cash Basis of Accounting

The cash basis of accounting is a simpler tax system designed for businesses that do not need, or want, to prepare accounts on an accruals basis. Introduced in Finance Act 2013, it allows small businesses to be taxed on their receipts (i.e. money received) less payments of allowable expenses, rather than having to make accounting adjustments and other calculations that are designed for larger or more complex businesses.

It is important to note that the cash basis scheme is only open to unincorporated businesses – companies must continue to prepare accounts on an accruals basis, regardless of their size.

The key aspects of the cash basis are as follows:

■   It is optional and must be elected into. In the case of a partnership, the election for the cash basis must be made by the person responsible for making the partnership's tax return (the "nominated partner"). If an election is made for the cash basis to apply, it applies for both income tax and Class 4 NIC purposes (see **Chapter 10**).

■   Businesses can enter into the cash basis if their receipts for the year do not exceed the VAT registration threshold (currently £83,000), or twice this limit (currently £166,000) for those in receipt of the universal tax credit. In subsequent years businesses can continue to use the cash basis even though they exceed these limits, but once their receipts exceed twice the amount of the VAT registration threshold (£166,000) then, for the following tax year, the business must stop using the cash basis and return to using the accruals basis.

■   Businesses can leave the cash basis if their commercial circumstances change and it is no longer appropriate or desirable for them. Examples of such changes include a business that is expanding and wishes to claim more than £500 interest deductions (see later), a business that wishes to claim "sideways" loss relief or a business that decides to register for VAT.

■   Certain trades are excluded from using the cash basis, such as dealers in securities and waste disposal.

Electing into the cash basis has a number of tax implications. These include:

■   Expenses are only allowable when they are paid.

■   Allowable payments are those made "wholly and exclusively" for the purposes of the trade, subject to a small number of specific rules and exceptions.

- Motoring expenses for motorcycles and goods vehicles may be calculated using either actual expenditure or the simplified expense mileage rates, i.e. rather than taking relief for actual expenditure, relief is claimed by multiplying business mileage in the period by the approved mileage rates (see **Section 6.4.2** and **Motoring Expenses** below).
- The typical adjustment for trading stock taken for a trader's own use when calculating tax-adjusted profits is not applied to a business using the cash basis, i.e. when a trader takes items from the business for his or her own use, an adjustment is made to taxable trading profit to account for any profit that would have been recorded in the accounts had the sale been made to a third party. This adjustment is not required when using the cash basis.
- Interest on cash borrowing is only allowable up to £500. It is not necessary to establish that the borrowing is financing capital employed in the business because it is not a condition of this deduction that the interest is "wholly and exclusively" for business purposes.
- Capital expenditure (excluding cars) is an allowable deduction for the business (provided it would qualify for capital allowances).
- As relief is given as a deduction from income for the cost of purchasing plant and machinery (other than cars), it follows that if the plant and machinery is sold while using the cash basis, then the proceeds must be included as trading income.
- For a disposal of business assets while in the cash basis, the disposal does not give rise to a chargeable gain or allowable loss.
- Business losses may be carried forward to set against the profits of future years but cannot be carried back or set off "sideways" against other sources of income (see **Chapter 5**).

Entering the Cash Basis

Since tax year 2013/14, any new unincorporated businesses can decide whether or not to use the cash basis when calculating their taxable profits. For an existing business that decides to start using the cash basis, certain adjustments are required.

1. **Capital allowances** (see **Chapter 5**) The amount of any unrelieved qualifying capital expenditure carried forward from the previous basis period – effectively the written down value (WDV) of the capital allowance pools – is brought in as an expense in the year of the transition to the cash basis. This is because businesses electing to use the cash basis do not claim capital allowances (other than on cars), but are instead allowed a deduction from profits for certain capital expenditure that would otherwise qualify for plant and machinery allowances.

    As noted, the above rules will not apply to any capital allowances that relate to cars. It is still possible to claim capital allowances on cars under the cash basis. If a car has been included in the main pool, the amount to be carried forward for capital allowances purposes in respect of the car must be determined on a "just and reasonable" basis.
2. **Income adjustment** An adjustment expense needs to be calculated by the trader so that income and expenses are not double counted as a result of the change in basis of calculating taxable profits (i.e. from following the accounting treatment (accruals basis) to using the cash basis).

    The overall effect is to treat the value of debtors plus stock (accounted for as closing stock under GAAP) less the value of creditors as an expense against trading profits.

Leaving the Cash Basis

Similarly, adjustments are required if leaving the cash basis.
1. **Capital allowances** If a business moving out of the cash basis is in the process of buying plant and machinery on hire purchase (HP), there are transitional rules that deal with the balance of

any payments due under the HP contract. The balance of the total purchase price, which will automatically not have been available as actual expenditure during the cash basis, can be brought in as the start of a capital allowance pool. A claim under the annual investment allowance would be permitted.

Any new expenditure that qualifies for capital allowances would be treated as normal under the typical rules for businesses not within the cash basis.

2. **Income adjustment** A similar calculation to that used when entering the cash basis must be carried out if the business leaves and goes back to using an accruals basis (under UK GAAP) to calculate its taxable profits. If the adjustment relates to taxable income, this income can be spread over each of the six tax years, beginning with the year a business leaves the cash basis, 1/6th being treated as arising and charged to tax in each year.

    It is possible to elect for the adjustment income to be brought forward and taxed earlier if required (for example, this may be beneficial if there are losses available).

Simplified Expenses

Certain items of expenditure, such as motoring expenses, often have both a business and a private element. Previously, in order to claim the relevant deduction, the taxpayer had to calculate the actual expenditure incurred and then apportion it between business and non-business use, supported by detailed records (e.g. appropriate mileage records). This was an administrative burden for the taxpayer, the business and the Government.

Finance Act 2013 therefore introduced the simplified expenses measure as an alternative method to claim for particular items of business expenditure. It allows all **unincorporated businesses**, irrespective of size, to choose to use flat-rate expenses for particular items of business expenditure, namely:

- business use of cars, motorcycles and goods vehicles;
- business use of home; and
- private use of business premises.

A separate claim can be made for each relevant category of expenditure, meaning that the taxpayer can claim using the flat-rate deduction (the simplified expenses measure) for one category and the apportionment method for another. For example, a business may decide to claim the flat-rate expense for motor expenses, while claiming relief on the business use of the home by apportioning actual expenses.

It is important to note that this measure only applies to unincorporated businesses. Companies must continue to prepare accounts on an accruals basis, regardless of their size.

Motoring Expenses

Car, van or motorcycle expenses can be calculated using a flat rate for mileage instead of the actual costs of buying and running the vehicle, e.g. insurance, repairs, servicing and fuel. The flat-rate amount depends on the type of vehicle and the level of business mileage.

Vehicle type	Rate	
	First 10,000 business miles	**Over 10,000 business miles**
Car	45p per mile	25p per mile
Goods vehicle		
Motorcycle	24p per mile	

> **Example 4.20**
> Michael uses his car for his business and he travelled 11,000 business miles in the year to 31 March 2017. In arriving at his taxable trading profits for the 2016/17 tax year, the allowable deduction for motor expense would be £4,750, where he claims the flat-rate mileage expense.
>
> His £4,750 flat-rate expense claim is calculated as follows:
>
> 10,000 miles × 45p = £4,500
> 1,000 miles × 25p = £250

The rates are the same as the approved mileage rates for payments made to employees in respect of the business use of their own car (see **Chapter 6** on employment income).

There are a number of conditions to using the flat-rate deduction:

- Once claimed, no other relief is allowed in respect of that vehicle. For example, no capital allowances (see **Chapter 5**) or lease rental payments deductions (see **Section 4.3.5**) can be claimed.
- Once claimed, it must continue to be claimed for as long as the asset is used in the business. A trader cannot subsequently switch to claim the business element of the actual costs in a later accounting period.

In addition, the flat-rate deduction cannot be claimed for:

- vehicles on which capital allowances (see **Chapter 5**) have already been claimed; and
- goods vehicles or motorcycles where any expenditure incurred on acquiring the vehicle has been deducted in calculating the profits under the cash basis.

Business Use of a Home

A business owner, i.e. a sole trader or partner, can claim expenses, such as rent or mortgage interest and household utilities, for any time spent working at home. As mentioned above, prior to Finance Act 2013 the business proportion of the expenses had to be apportioned and verified to make a claim.

The simplified expenses measure allows instead a simple monthly deduction based on the number of hours worked at home.

Number of hours worked at home	Rate
25–50 hours per month	£10 per month
51–100 hours per month	£18 per month
101 hours or more per month	£26 per month

> **Example 4.21**
> Angela is self-employed and she prepares her accounts to 31 March 2017. In the year ended 31 March 2017, she worked 40 hours from home for 10 months and 60 hours during two months.
>
> In arriving at her taxable trading profits, the allowable deduction for tax purposes would be £136 (10 months x £10 + 2 months x £18 = £136).

The amount of hours per month relates to the hours spent working in the home "**wholly and exclusively**" for the purposes of the trade.

Unlike the flat-rate deduction for vehicle expenses, an individual can decide each tax year whether to claim the flat-rate deduction or to make a claim for the business proportion of actual expenses incurred.

Private Use of Business Premises

A business can only claim those expenses that relate solely to the running of the business. In circumstances where a business premises is also used for non-business purposes, the private expenditure must be excluded.

Rather than having to recognise and apportion the private-use element of the expenditure, the simplified expenses option allows businesses to claim relief for the full costs, i.e. business and non-business, with a flat-rate deduction to cover the private element.

The adjustment is made based on the number of occupants using the premises as a home each month.

Number of occupants	Reduction in claim
1	£350 per month
2	£500 per month
3 or more	£650 per month

Example 4.22

A husband and wife own a pub in which they also live. They incurred total expenses of £20,000 for the tax year and make a claim under the simplified expenses measure. The husband's aunt comes to stay with them for one month during the tax year.

In arriving at their taxable trading profits, the allowable deduction would be £13,850, being:

£20,000
Less: 11 months × £500 (when only husband and wife live in the pub)
Less: 1 month × £650 (when the aunt also stays, i.e. three occupants)

4.3.7 Partnerships

A partnership is regarded as a single unit for the purposes of determining tax-adjusted profits. However, for the purposes of tax assessment, each partner's share of the joint profits is treated as personal to that partner, as if they arose from a **separate trade or profession**. As a consequence, commencement and cessation rules apply to each partner **individually** when they enter or leave the partnership.

The Partnership Act 1890 defines "partnership" as "**the relationship which subsists between persons carrying on a business in common with a view of profit**".

For taxation purposes, a partnership continues no matter how many partners are admitted or leave, provided one of the old partners continues after the change.

Once the partnership's profits for a period of account have been computed, they are shared between the partners according to the profit-sharing arrangements for that accounting period. Partners' salaries, commissions and interest on capital accounts are not deducted in arriving at taxable profits; they are treated instead as a prior share and are allocated to the partners concerned. The balance of profits is allocated in accordance with the profit-sharing ratios in operation. This allocation cannot create or increase a loss for a partner. Any "notional" loss calculated in this way must be re-allocated to the other partners.

The general approach is to calculate the partnership's profit, then to tax each partner as if they were a sole trader running a business equal to their share of the partnership (e.g. 50% of the partnership).

Example 4.23
Andrew and Charlotte are partners in AC Partnership. They agree to share profits equally after paying a salary of £8,000 to Andrew. The tax-adjusted trading profits for AC Partnership in respect of the year ended 31 December 2016 are £4,000.

What is the allocation of profits between Andrew and Charlotte for the year ended 31 December 2016?

	Andrew £	Charlotte £	Total £
Salary	8,000	–	8,000
Balance (split 50:50)	(2,000)	(2,000)	(4,000)
Partnership profit	6,000	(2,000)	4,000
Re-allocation of "notional loss"	(2,000)	2,000	–
Allocation of profits	4,000	Nil	4,000

A partnership may have **non-trading income**, such as dividends on shares or interest on a partnership bank account (see **Chapter 7**) or partnership rental income (see **Chapter 8**). Such items are kept separate from trading income, but they (and any associated tax credits) are shared between the partners in a similar fashion as trading income on the basis of the profit-sharing agreements. For income (excluding income taxed at source and dividends), the accounting period for trading profits is also applied to the source of income, and commencement and cessation rules equally apply. However, for income taxed at source, the basis period is the actual tax year (6 April–5 April).

A partnership **ceases** to exist when:

■ the business ceases; or
■ only one partner remains (i.e. the partnership becomes a sole trader); or
■ a completely different set of partners takes over from the old partners.

The "nominated partner" is responsible for ensuring the partnership's tax return is prepared and submitted to the partnership's tax office.

Allocation of Partnership Profits/Losses
There are two steps in calculating each partner's share of the tax-adjusted trading profits/losses.

Step 1: allocate salaries, interest on capital, etc. to each partner first. (Note: pro rata for periods less than 12 months.)
Step 2: divide profit/losses between the partners according to profit-sharing ratio in the accounting period.

Example 4.24: No change in partnership members or profit-sharing ratios
John and Kate are in partnership. Trading profits (after tax adjustments) for the year to 31 October 2016 are £120,000. As per the profit-sharing agreement, profits will be shared in the ratio 70:30 between John and Kate, but this is after paying a salary of £7,000 per annum to John because he puts in longer hours each week into the partnership. Interest on capital of £3,000 per annum is paid to John and £5,000 per annum is paid to Kate (Kate has a higher capital account; therefore her interest on capital is higher).

continued overleaf

During the year John drew £50,000 and Kate drew £48,000 on account of their profit shares. Partners' drawings are shown as a reduction in their capital account and will be reflected on the partnership balance sheet.

Solution

Year ended 31 October 2016	Total (£)	John (£)	Kate (£)
Trading income	120,000		
Partner's salary	(7,000)	7,000	
Interest on capital	(8,000)	3,000	5,000
Residual profit	105,000		
Shared 70:30	(105,000)	73,500	31,500
		83,500	36,500

The information on drawings is irrelevant as far as the tax computations are concerned. When and how John and Kate draw these profits has no bearing on their tax liabilities. Drawings are simply the amount that partners draw on account in advance of their profit share being determined. (This is understandable, as partners do not know how much they have earned until the end of the accounting year, but they may not be able to afford to wait until the end of the accounting year to take money.)

The amount determined in relation to John and Kate will be entered into their respective tax returns (in this case for the tax year 2016/17).

Example 4.25: Change in partnership and in profit-sharing ratios
Mike and Phil are in partnership, sharing profits in the ratio 60:40. A salary of £10,000 per annum is paid to Mike.

Stephen is admitted to the partnership on 1 February 2016 and the profits are shared 40:40:20 between Mike, Phil and Stephen from that date. With effect from that date, Mike's salary is to be reduced to £8,000 per annum. Tax-adjusted profits for the year to 31 July 2016 are £130,000. The estimated profits for the year ended 31 July 2017 are £155,000.

Solution
When Stephen comes into the practice on 1 February 2016, the ratios will change. We need to approach the calculation by looking at the period up to the introduction of Stephen and then the period after he is admitted as a partner.

	Total (£)	Mike (£)	Phil (£)	Stephen (£)
1 August 2015 to 31 January 2016				
Adjusted profit (i.e. 6/12 × £130,000)	65,000			
Partner's salary (i.e. 6/12 × £10,000)	(5,000)	5,000		
Residual profit	60,000			
Shared 60:40	(60,000)	36,000	24,000	
1 February 2016 to 31 July 2016				
Adjusted profit (i.e. 6/12 × £130,000)	65,000			
Partner's salary (i.e. 6/12 × £8,000)	(4,000)	4,000		
Residual profit	61,000			
Shared 40:40:20	(61,000)	24,400	24,400	12,200
		69,400	48,400	12,200

These values will be entered into Mike, Phil and Stephen's tax returns. Note that Stephen will be subject to the trade commencement rules (see **Section 4.2.2**). Under the opening year rules, Stephen's profits will be taxed as follows:

continued overleaf

> **2015/16:** 1 February to 5 April 2016: 2/6 × £12,200 = £4,067
> **2016/17:** First 12 months to 31 January 2017: £12,200 + 6/12 × (20% of (£155,000 – £8,000)) = £26,900
> **2017/18:** Year ended 31 July 2017: £29,400 (i.e. 20% of (£155,000 – £8,000))
>
> Stephen will have overlap profits of £18,767, being:
>
> - the first two months (taxed in 2015/16 and 2016/17): £4,067; and
> - the period from 1 August 2016 to 31 January 2017 (taxed in 2016/17 and 2017/18): 6/12 × £29,400 = £14,700.
>
> As a check, the amounts taxed less overlap relief should match what Stephen will receive from the partnership for the periods ending 31 July 2016 and 31 July 2017 (i.e. £4,067 + £26,900 + £29,400 less £18,767 = £41,600, which is the same as £12,200 + £29,400).

Interest on Capital

Interest on capital is a distribution of profit and is, accordingly, a drawing. It is therefore a disallowable expense in computing the partnership's profits or losses for a period. Interest on capital must, however, be carefully distinguished from interest paid by the partnership in respect of a loan made to the partnership by an individual partner. Such interest, provided the funds borrowed have been used for the partnership business, will be an allowable trading deduction.

For periods of less than 12 months, interest on capital should be allocated to the respective partner on a pro rata basis.

Salaries

Salaries paid to a partner are treated in the same manner as drawings taken out of a business by a sole trader, i.e. they are disallowed for computation purposes. However, in reaching the residual profit share they must be included in the calculation. And again, for periods of less than 12 months, they should be allocated on a pro rata basis to the respective partner.

Rent Paid to a Partner

If a partner beneficially owns the premises from which the partnership is operated and lets the premises on an arm's length basis to the partnership, then the rent will be allowed as a deduction in computing the partnership profits and the landlord partner will be assessed personally on the net profit rents (see **Chapter 8** on property income for more details).

Change in Profit-sharing Ratios/Partnerships

Profits for an accounting period are allocated between the partners according to the profit-sharing agreement. If the salaries, interest on capital or profit-sharing ratio change during the accounting period, the profits are split in proportion to the periods before and after the change and allocated accordingly. The constituent elements are then added together to give each partner a share of profits for the period of account.

Limited Liability Partnerships

A limited liability partnership (LLP) is a special form of partnership in the UK. It is taxed on virtually the same basis as a normal partnership, but special rules apply for restricting loss relief to all the partners. The difference between an LLP and a normal partnership is that, in an LLP, the liability of the partners is limited to the capital they contributed. In practice, this structure gives commercial protection (similar to a limited liability company) to the partners of the business.

Apportionment of Tax-adjusted Profits

Partnerships prepare an annual profit and loss account, which is the basis of a tax-adjusted profits computation. Trading income rules regarding allowable and disallowable expenses are applied in arriving at the partnership's tax-adjusted profit or loss figure. The only unusual feature is that partners' **salaries/drawings/wages** are **not allowable** as they are an **appropriation of profit** (i.e. effectively the same as the **drawings** of a sole trader). Similarly, **interest paid on partners' capital accounts** is not an allowable deduction in arriving at the tax-adjusted profit.

The tax-adjusted profits of a partnership are divided among the partners in accordance with:

- the specific terms of the partnership agreement regarding **guaranteed salaries and interest on capital**; and
- the **profit-sharing ratio** that existed during the accounting period.

Example 4.26

Smith and Jones are in partnership as engineers for many years, sharing profits 60:40. The statement of profit and loss for the year ended 30 April 2016 is as follows:

Statement of Profit and Loss for the year ended 30 April 2016

	Notes	£	£
Gross fees			200,000
Less:			
Overheads		50,000	
Salaries paid to partners	1	41,000	
Interest paid on partners			
Capital accounts	2	13,000	
Rent paid to Smith for partnership premises		35,000	
Entertainment expenses (all client related)		15,000	154,000
Net profit for the year			**46,000**

Notes:

1. Salaries	£
Smith	18,000
Jones	23,000
	41,000

2. Interest paid on capital accounts	£
Smith	6,000
Jones	7,000
	13,000

Computation of Taxable Profits

	£	£
Net profit per accounts		46,000
Add back:		
Salaries paid to partners	41,000	
Interest paid on partners' capital accounts	13,000	
Disallowed entertainment expenses	15,000	69,000
Assessable profit		**115,000**

Apportionment of Assessable Profit 2016/17	Total	Smith	Jones
	£	£	£
Salaries	41,000	18,000	23,000
Interest paid on capital accounts	13,000	6,000	7,000
Balance (apportioned 60 : 40)	61,000	36,600	24,400
Taxable profits	115,000	60,600	54,400

Before we move on to the next stage, try **Questions 4.12** and **4.13** at the end of this chapter.

4.3.8   Overseas Trades

Profits of an overseas trade are computed under the same rules as for UK trades. However, the remittance basis may apply for non-UK domiciled individuals (see **Chapter 3**).

If a trader who is UK resident has a business that is conducted wholly or mainly overseas, the trade profits are chargeable to UK income tax on either the arising basis or the remittance basis. An individual who is not UK resident is not liable to UK tax on the profits of trades carried on wholly abroad unless they have a "permanent establishment" in the UK.

A permanent establishment would include a fixed base, e.g. a shop, a place of management, a branch office or a construction site lasting over six months (as per the UK/Ireland double taxation agreement (DTA), although Ireland's DTA with other countries may include construction sites lasting over 12 or 18 months). For example, if a Republic of Ireland resident individual owns a shoe shop in the centre of Belfast, they will be taxed in the UK on profits from the permanent establishment, i.e. the shoe shop, but they will also be taxed on this income in the Republic of Ireland as that is where they are resident. Relief will be available under the UK/Ireland DTA to reduce the Irish income tax liability by any UK income tax suffered on the same profits from the shoe shop.

A loss sustained in a trade (or profession or vocation) carried on abroad can only be relieved against overseas trade profits, overseas pensions and overseas earnings. Overseas trades are kept separate to a UK trade.

Questions

Review Questions

(See Suggested Solutions to Review Questions at the end of this textbook.)

Question 4.1

Ms Lola commenced trading on 1 June 2014 and makes up accounts to 31 May. Her trading results are as follows:

	£
01/06/2014–31/05/2015	48,000
01/06/2015–31/05/2016	39,000
01/06/2016–31/05/2017	37,200

Requirement
Calculate Ms Lola's taxable profits from her sole trade for the tax years 2014/15 to 2017/18, and any overlap profits arising.

Question 4.2

Mr Charlie commenced trading on 1 May 2015 and makes up accounts to 31 October. His trading results are as follows:

	£
01/05/2015–31/10/2015	44,800
01/11/2015–31/10/2016	54,400
01/11/2016–31/10/2017	53,600

01/11/2017–31/10/2018   46,400

He had no other income in each relevant tax year.

Requirement

Calculate Mr Charlie's taxable profits from his sole trade for the tax years 2015/16 to 2017/18, and any overlap profits arising.

Question 4.3

Jim commenced practice as a solicitor on 1 May 2015. Tax-adjusted profits for the opening years were as follows:

	£
1 May 2015 to 30 April 2016	48,000
Year ended 30 April 2017	60,000
Year ended 30 April 2018	9,600

Requirements

(a) Calculate Jim's taxable profits for the first four tax years, and any overlap profits arising.
(b) Do these taxable profits arise from a trade, profession or vocation?

Question 4.4

Donna Ross is a new client of the office. She resigned from her job at Northern Bank on 31 March 2016 to sell children's clothing full time on eBay.

She tells you that she has traded on eBay part-time for a "few" years. She sold only household items or sale bargains picked up while shopping. She estimates that her sales were £5,000 in 2015/16 and her costs were minimal since the items sold were "lying about the house" and had been used by her family until they grew tired of them. She used the family computer and packed the items in her garage. In June 2016, she spotted a market opportunity when she bought a job lot of designer children's clothes for £10,000 and sold them on eBay individually for £20,000 in just one month! This prompted her to try to ramp up her selling on eBay from 1 September 2016. Her tax-adjusted profit for the year ended 31 August 2017 was £79,400.

Donna is a 32-year-old single parent.

Requirements

(a) Compute the income tax payable by Donna for 2016/17 and 2017/18, and any overlap profits arising. (Assume the same rates/allowances apply to 2017/18 as they do for 2016/17.)
(b) Write a letter to Donna explaining, with reasons, if her eBay activity for 2015/16 and 2016/17 is taxable, and how her overlap profits can be relieved.

Question 4.5

Ms Dora ceases trading on 31 December 2016. She made up her accounts annually to 31 May. Her trading results were as follows:

	£
Year ended 31/05/2015	72,000
Year ended 31/05/2016	9,600
Period ended 31/12/2016	12,000

She has unused overlap relief of £5,000.

4. *Trading Income* **79**

Requirement
Calculate Ms Dora's taxable profits for the 2015/16 and 2016/17 tax years.

Question 4.6

In 2016, J. Cog changed his accounting date to 30 September, having previously always made up accounts for the year to 31 October. His tax-adjusted profits for recent periods were as follows:

	£
Year ended 31 October 2015	64,000
11 months to 30 September 2016	24,000

He had unrelieved overlap profits of £15,000.

Requirement
Calculate J. Cog's assessable profits for the 2015/16 and 2016/17 tax years, and overlap relief available going forward.

Question 4.7

Joseph Murphy is a trader. He prepares accounts annually to 31 December. His profit and loss account for the year ended 31 December 2016 was as follows:

Expenditure	Notes	£	Income	£
Salaries	1	61,864	Gross profit	112,500
Travelling	2	17,512	Discounts received	7,349
Commissions		7,236	Dividends from URNO Co.	2,813
Interest on late payment			Interest on National Loan Stock	2,250
of VAT		1,121		
Interest on late payment			Deposit interest	170
of PAYE		1,238		
Depreciation		13,793	Profit on sale of fixed assets	5,063
Bank interest		4,008		
Subscriptions	3	1,225		
Repairs	4	6,480		
Bad debts	5	2,475		
Legal fees	6	1,069		
Accountancy fees		2,250		
Net profit		9,874		
		130,145		130,145

Notes:
1. Salaries include salary to Mr Murphy of £7,500 and a salary paid to his wife of £5,000 for her work as secretary.
2. Travelling expenses include £1,000 for a holiday trip by Mr and Mrs Murphy.
3. Subscriptions

	£
Political party	75
Local football club	50
Traders' association	500
Trade papers	200
Old folks' home	150

	Sports club	250	
		1,225	

4. Repairs account

	DR £	CR £
Opening provision for repairs		855
Expenditure during period	2,335	
New extension to office	3,000	
Charge to profit and loss account		6,480
Closing provision	2,000	
	7,335	7,335

The opening and closing repairs provisions represent general provisions that do not conform with IAS 37.

5. Bad debts account

	DR £	CR £
Opening provision – general		5,100
Bad debts recovered		2,675
Bad debts written off	2,275	
Charge to profit and loss account		2,475
Closing provision – general	7,975	
	10,250	10,250

6. Legal fees

	£
Bad debts recovery	60
Sale of freehold	1,009
	1,069

Requirement

Compute Joseph Murphy's taxable trading profits for 2016/17.

Question 4.8

Andy Reilly operates a consultancy business providing technical advice. He has been in business for many years and makes up annual accounts to 31 December. His profit and loss account for the year to 31 December 2016 is set out below.

	£	£
Fees charged		178,000
Less: Direct costs		
Technical salaries and employment expenses	64,000	
Stationery and printing	4,000	
Repairs to equipment	980	
Professional indemnity insurance	370	
Motor vehicle expenses (Note 1)	6,250	
Depreciation – Equipment	2,500	
– Motor vehicles	3,000	(81,100)
Deduct: overheads		96,900
Rent, rates and property insurance	11,000	

	£	£
Repairs to premises (Note 2)	6,500	
Light and heat	1,100	
Office salaries	7,200	
Telephone and postage	400	
Advertising	800	
Entertaining (Note 5)	390	
Bad debts (Note 3)	550	
Defalcations (theft) (Note 4)	6,000	
Successful claim by client not covered by insurance	2,500	
Andy Reilly's drawings	10,000	
Depreciation – office equipment and fittings	900	(47,340)
Net profit before taxation:		49,560

Notes:

1. £4,000 of the total motor vehicle expenses relate to the lease of Andy Reilly's car. The car cost £24,500 in January 2013, had CO_2 emissions of 189g/km and 40% of Andy's total mileage is business mileage. The other motor expenses relate to the lease of sales representatives' cars, all of which cost £19,000 when purchased in March 2013 and have CO_2 emissions of 150g/km.
2. Repairs to premises include the charge for constructing two additional garages adjoining the firm's buildings for the sales representatives' cars. This amounted to £3,150.
3. The bad debts charge includes a credit for the recovery of a specific debt amounting to £350 and the creation of a general bad debt reserve amounting to £275.
4. The defalcations were traced to staff and were not covered by insurance.
5. The charge for entertainment comprises:

	£
Private holiday for Andy Reilly (June 2016)	120
Tickets for Andy Reilly and his friend to	
All-Ireland football final	30
Staff Christmas party	120
Business meals with customers	120
	390

Requirement

Compute Andy Reilly's taxable trading profits for 2016/17.

Question 4.9

Tony set up business as a car dealer/garage proprietor on 1 October 2015. His first accounts were made up for the 15-month period ended 31 December 2016 and subsequently to 31 December each year. The first two sets of accounts show the following results:

	15 months to 31/12/2016	Year ended 31/12/2017
	£	£
Sales – cars	250,000	200,000
Sales – workshop	100,000	90,000
	350,000	290,000

	15 months to 31/12/2016 £	Year ended 31/12/2017 £
Direct Costs		
Cost of cars sold	211,500	168,300
Salesman's salary and commission	15,000	13,000
Workshop labour and parts	62,500	66,000
	289,000	247,300
Gross profit	61,000	42,700
General and Administrative Costs		
Accountancy	1,500	1,250
Advertising	900	1,100
Bad debts (Note 1)	2,500	400
Depreciation	3,000	2,400
Drawings	15,000	12,000
Entertaining (Note 2)	1,500	700
Insurance	5,000	4,000
Interest (Note 3)	18,000	14,000
Legal fees (Note 4)	400	600
Light and heat	2,250	1,800
Office staff salaries	10,600	8,500
Postage, telephone and stationery	1,500	1,200
Sundries (Note 5)	1,250	650
Travel expenses (Note 6)	1,950	1,500
	65,350	50,100
Net loss	(4,350)	(7,400)

Notes:	15 months to 31/12/2016 £	Year ended 31/12/2017 £
1. Bad debts		
General provision	2,500	–
Bad debt written off	–	900
General provision no longer required	–	(500)
	2,500	400
2. Entertaining	£	£
Hospitality for representatives of car manufacturer during negotiations for supply of cars	–	800
Entertaining customers	700	700
	1,500	700
3. Interest	£	£
Interest on loan from car manufacturer to buy stock	9,500	7,000
Interest on bank loan to establish business	8,500	7,000
	18,000	14,000

4.	Legal fees	£	£
	Advice on supply agreement with car manufacturer	250	200
	Recovery of outstanding debts	–	200
	Defending customer claim re. faulty car	150	200
		400	600

5.	Sundries	£	£
	Security	500	300
	Drinks at staff Christmas party	150	150
	Subscription to trade association	200	200
	Political donation	100	–
	Charitable donation	50	–
	Interest on late payment of VAT	250	–
		1,250	650

6. Travel expenses   These expenses contain no disallowable element.

Requirements
(a) Compute the adjusted trading profits for the 15 months ended 31 December 2016 and the year ended 31 December 2017.
(b) Calculate Tony's taxable trading profits for the 2016/17 tax year.

Question 4.10

John Smith commenced trading on 1 May 2015. The profit and loss account for 1 May 2015 to 30 April 2016 shows the following information:

	Notes	£	£
Sales			201,230
Less: cost of sales			(140,560)
			60,670
Interest received	1		390
Gross profit			61,060
Expenses:			
Wages	2	23,500	
Motor expenses	3	1,860	
Depreciation		1,250	
Rent and rates		12,800	
Leasing charges	4	4,300	
Repairs	5	3,900	
Telephone		800	
Bank interest and charges		3,800	
Sundry expenses	6	3,400	
Insurance	7	2,630	58,240
Profit for period			2,820

Notes:

		£
1.	Interest received	390

2. Included in wages charges are: £

Wage to Mrs Smith (wife), as bookkeeper	1,800
Wages to self	5,200
Accrued bonus for sales assistants (paid on 1 July 2016)	500
Own NICs	200

3. Motor expenses relate solely to Mr Smith's own motoring and include a £100 fine for careless driving; 60% of total mileage is for business purposes. Motor insurance has been included under the insurance charge.

4. Analysis of leasing charges (all operating leases): £

Lease of till	300
Lease of shelving	1,200
Lease of Mr Smith's car	2,800
	4,300

The motor car had a market value of £25,000 and CO_2 emissions of 135g/km when first leased on 1 May 2015.

5. Repairs: £

Painting outside of premises	1,000
Repairing shop front damaged in accident	1,300
Insurance claim re. above accident	(900)
Extension to shop	1,500
General provision for repairs	1,000
	3,900

6. Sundry expenses: £

Trade subscriptions	250
Interest on the late payment of income tax	120
Donation to church	970
Christmas party for staff	560
Accountancy	1,500
	3,400

7. Insurance: £

Business 'all-in' policy	1,370
Motor car	300
Life assurance	460
Key person life assurance on salesman	500
	2,630

Requirement

Compute John Smith's tax-adjusted trading profits.

Question 4.11

Polly Styrene has been in business for many years manufacturing shoes, and she makes up her accounts to 31 December each year. Her profit and loss account for the year ended 31 December 2016 was as follows:

	£	£
Gross profit		170,000
Less:		
Wages and salaries (Note 1)	90,000	
Depreciation	20,000	
Light, heat and telephone (Note 2)	6,000	
Postage and stationery	500	
Repairs and renewals (Note 3)	5,000	
Legal and professional fees (Note 4)	3,000	
Bad debts (Note 5)	2,000	
Travel and entertainment (Note 6)	2,500	
Bank interest (Note 7)	3,500	
Royalties (Note 9)	25,000	
Insurance	3,000	
Freight	4,000	
Sundries (Note 8)	3,000	167,500
Net profit		2,500

Notes:

1. Wages and salaries – includes £8,000 for Polly Styrene.

2. Light, heat and telephone – includes £1,500 for light, heat and telephone at the residence of Polly Styrene. One-sixth is business-related.

3. Repairs and renewals	£
Painting and decorating	1,600
Extension to shop	1,400
General provision for future repairs	2,000
	5,000

4. Legal and professional fees	£
Debt collection	1,200
Accountancy	1,500
Surveyor's fees re. abortive purchase of premises	300
	3,000

5. Bad debts	£
Trade debts written off	2,800
Bad debt recovered	(200)
Decrease in general reserve	(600)
	2,000

6. Travel and entertainment   £

Car expenses (Note)	1,500
Christmas drinks for employees	400
Entertaining customers	600
	2,500

Note: the car cost £32,000, has CO_2 emissions of 155g/km and was bought in February 2015. Private use is one-third.

7. Bank interest   £

Bank interest	1,500
Lease interest	2,000
	3,500

Polly leased plant and equipment through ACC Commercial Finance, under a three-year finance lease. The total repayments for the year were £18,600. Depreciation charged in the year on the asset was £15,000.

8. Sundries   £

Advertising	1,051
Trade protection association	100
Political party subscription	1,000
Parking fines	49
Rubbish disposal	300
Donation to Cancer Focus (registered charity)	500
	3,000

9. Royalties – Polly pays royalties of £25,000 (gross) for the use of specialised equipment to manufacture her shoes.

Requirement
Calculate the trading taxable profits for 2016/17.

Question 4.12

A and B have traded as partners for many years, sharing profits equally. They prepare accounts each year to 30 September. On 1 October 2012, C was admitted as a partner and from that date profits are shared as follows:
A: 2/5ths
B: 2/5ths
C: 1/5th

Tax-adjusted trading profits were as follows:

	£
Year ended 30/09/2012	20,000
Year ended 30/09/2013	25,000
Year ended 30/09/2014	30,000
Year ended 30/09/2015	30,000
Year ended 30/09/2016	35,000

On 30 September 2014, A left the partnership. Since that date, B and C have shared profits and losses equally.

Requirement

Calculate the taxable trading profits for A, B and C for the years 2012/13 to 2016/17.

Question 4.13

Jack and John are in partnership as accountants for many years. The SOPL for the year ended 30 April 2016 was as follows:

	£	£
Gross fees		200,000
Less: Overheads	100,000	
Jack's salary	20,000	
John's salary	21,000	
Jack's interest on capital	6,000	
John's interest on capital	7,000	154,000
		46,000

Disallowable expenses included in general overheads amount to £26,000. The profit-sharing ratio for year ending 30/04/2016 was 50:50.

Requirement

Adjust the trading profit for tax purposes and allocate the profits to the partners in the profit-sharing ratio.

Capital Allowances and Loss Relief

Learning Objectives

After studying this chapter you will understand:

Capital Allowances

- How to calculate capital allowances on items of plant and machinery and their position in the tax computation.
- What items qualify for plant and machinery allowances based on tax legislation and case law.
- The different rates that apply and the nature of qualifying expenditure.
- The impact on the capital allowance claim for specific assets, such as motor cars, short-life assets and those with private use.
- How to determine the capital allowances available on the commencement and cessation of a business.
- The main features of the business premises renovations allowance (BPRA).

Loss Relief

- Calculation of the trading loss for a basis period and the various methods of utilising those trading losses tax efficiently.
- The interaction of capital allowances and losses.
- How trading losses may be set off against other income and gains.
- How to calculate the new cap on income tax reliefs.

5.1 Capital Allowances: Introduction

In essence, income tax is a tax solely on income (revenue), which means that capital expenditure is not deductible for income tax purposes. This, therefore, denies the individual a tax deduction for depreciation or amortisation, which represents capital amounts written off in the accounts. In other words, when arriving at the tax-adjusted trading profits of a business, depreciation, for accounting purposes, is specifically disallowed and is added to the net profit/(loss) per the statement of profit or loss (SOPL). Instead, businesses can claim capital allowances on certain types of asset. The basic objective of capital allowances is to allow the business a **deduction** against tax-adjusted business profits for the **net cost of certain capital assets employed** for the purpose of the business.

The main types of capital allowance are:

■ annual investment allowance (AIA)
■ first year allowance (FYA)
■ writing down allowance (WDA)
■ balancing allowance/balancing charge
■ business property renovation allowance (BPRA).

Capital allowances are operated through the use of "pools". The cost of the asset is allocated to a specific "pool", depending on the nature of the asset. The "main pool" is where most assets meeting the definition of plant and machinery will be allocated.

The "special rate pool" is where specific assets, such as "integral features", will be allocated. A "single asset pool" may also be needed where assets are used partly for private purposes by the individual, e.g. the sole trader or the partner.

A business obtains relief for its capital expenditure by reducing the value of the pool in accordance with specific rates and rules. The reduction in the pool value (i.e. the capital allowance) is included as a deduction from taxable trading profits.

For unincorporated businesses (such as sole trades and partnerships), capital allowances are calculated for accounting periods.

This chapter will begin by looking at what assets can qualify for capital allowances. Once the type of assets that can qualify for capital allowances is understood, we will then move on to look at the main pool for capital allowances. It is into this pool that the vast majority of assets will fall. However, certain assets will fall into the special rate pool. The various types of capital allowance available on assets in the main and special rate pools will be discussed: the AIA, the FYA and the WDA. Special rules apply to assets that are used partly for private use and also assets that are categorised as "short-life assets". Finally, this chapter will look at the special business premises renovation allowance that is available for expenditure incurred on renovating or converting a premises.

5.2 Capital Allowances: Plant and Machinery

5.2.1 Meaning of "Plant"

Before we look at the capital allowances available for plant and machinery, we need to understand what is meant by "plant and machinery". There is no statutory definition of plant and machinery for the purposes of capital allowances. Therefore we must look to case law for various tests which must be satisfied if an item of expenditure is to qualify as "plant" for the purposes of capital allowances.

The question of whether an item is "plant" is considered a matter of fact and will be decided according to the circumstances of each particular case. The most quoted definition of the word "plant" is from *Yarmouth v. France* (1887), in which Lord Justice Lindley said:

"There is no definition of plant in the Act, but in its ordinary sense, it includes whatever apparatus is used by a businessman for carrying on his business – not his stock-in-trade, which he buys or makes for sale; but all goods and chattels, fixed or moveable, live or dead, which he keeps for permanent employment in the business."

The principal test suggested by case law is whether the asset in question is **functional** to the operation of the business, as distinct from the **setting** in which the business is carried on. Other tests suggested by case law are:

- Is the expenditure incurred directly on the provision of plant and not, for instance, on the provision of finance, which is used to acquire plant?
- Does the expenditure replace an item previously regarded as plant?
- Is the expenditure related to an entire unit or is it merely expenditure on part of a larger, non-functional unit?

The most significant tax cases used in deciding the various aspects of what is and is not considered plant are outlined below.

Jarrold v. John Good & Sons Ltd (1963)
It was held in this case that purpose-built partitioning, although forming part of the setting of the business, was an essential part of the equipment necessary for the operation of the business, i.e. it was functional, and should therefore be regarded as plant. The partitions were moveable and it was contended that they were specifically designed to enable employees to carry out their duties according to the state of the company's business and were moved as required by the volume of the company's activities.

CIR v. Barclay Curle & Co. Ltd (1969)
This case, taken by the Revenue, concerned expenditure on construction of a dry dock. The main facts of the case were as follows.

Barclay Curle and Co. Ltd (the defendant), a shipbuilding company, constructed a dry dock that involved the excavation of some 200,000 tons of earth and rock, which was then lined throughout with 100,000 tons of concrete. The installations included a dock gate, pump and valves, piping, electrical machinery, etc. The dock acted like a hydraulic chamber in which a volume of water, variable at will, could be used to lower a ship so that it could be exposed for inspection and repair and to raise it again to high-tide level. The defendant contended that the dock was a single and indivisible entity, performing the function of a large hydraulic lift-cum-vice, and that the expenditure on both the excavation and concrete work was incurred under the provision of plant and machinery.

The House of Lords found in favour of the defendant and the following quote from Lord Reid is important in considering the test to be applied:

> "It seems to me that every part of the dry dock plays an essential part in getting vessels into a position where work on the outside hull can begin and that it is wrong to regard either the concrete or any part of the dock as a mere setting or part of the premises in which the operation takes place. The whole dock is, I think, the means by which, or plant with which, the operation is performed."

This decision stressed the **functional** test as opposed to the **setting** test.

Schofield v. R. & H. Hall Ltd (1974)
In this case, R & H Hall Ltd (the defendant), claimed capital allowances on expenditure it incurred on the construction of two silos, which were used to take grain from ships and to dispense it to customers. The silos consisted of large concrete structures into which concrete bins were built, a smaller structure, the workhouse containing machinery and plant, and machinery consisting of

gantries, conveyor belts, mobile chutes, etc. The defendant claimed that all of the expenditure qualified for capital allowances as plant and machinery. It was held that, considering the function of the silos in relation to the company's trade, they seemed an essential part of the overall trade activity. Their function was to hold grain in a position from which it could be conveniently discharged in varying amounts. Accordingly, they found that the silos were plant and qualified for capital allowances.

An important aspect of the case was the **detailed description of plant** given by the company by way of documentation and evidence.

Dixon v. Fitch's Garage (1975)

In this UK case, it was claimed that the forecourt canopy of a petrol filling station constituted plant for capital allowances purposes. It was held that the canopy provided no more than shelter and light to the customers while the commercial process of delivering fuel was carried on; therefore it was not plant. The judge ruled that the canopy did not help to supply the petrol but only made the motorist and staff more comfortable. It has later been commented that this approach was unduly narrow and in fact has been criticised in future cases where it is acknowledged that an asset can play a part in the conduct of a trade without being directly involved at the point of sale. In recent UK and Irish cases there is a recognition that the bringing in of custom in itself represents an important trading function.

S. Ó Culachain (Inspector of Taxes, RoI) v. McMullan Brothers (1995)

In a similar case in the Republic of Ireland, the defendant claimed that forecourt canopies at petrol filling stations were essential to provide advertising, brand image and attractive surroundings, and therefore created an ambience and had a function in carrying on the business.

Likewise, the Irish Revenue Commissioners argued that the canopies provided no more than shelter from the rain and wind and played no part in the trade of selling petrol. However, it was held that the canopies did perform a function in the actual **carrying out** of the trade and therefore qualified for capital allowances as an item of plant.

Hampton v. Fortes Autogrill Ltd (1980)

It was held that a false ceiling is not plant on the basis that it simply provided a covering, which was not functional, to the actual carrying on of the catering business by the individual.

JD Wetherspoon plc v. The Commissioners for Her Majesty's Revenue & Customs (2012)

The Upper Tribunal published a decision in 2012 in relation to the fit-out of several restaurants and pubs owned by JD Wetherspoon plc. The decision followed on from the First-tier Tribunal's decision (2009) and the Special Commissioner's decision (2007). The 2012 ruling focused on those areas that were still in contention: the treatment of building alterations incidental to the installation of plant and machinery; and the treatment of "preliminaries" (project overheads) and professional fees.

In terms of the incidental building alterations, the Tribunal stated: "if plant is installed in an existing building rather than in a purpose-built new building, it is entirely possible that something will not fit, and that this will lead to alterations having to be made to the existing building". An example provided was the strengthening of a kitchen floor for the purposes of installing plant (such expenditure would qualify as plant under section 25 Capital Allowances Act 2001).

"Preliminaries" generally refer to contractors' costs that are not reflected in finished work costing. In capital allowance claims, these items are usually apportioned among the various work items (which will be either qualifying or ineligible for capital allowances purposes). HMRC argued that any apportionment should be performed on a much more specific basis and that certain items should be excluded before any apportionment. However, the court rejected this line of argument and confirmed that a pro rata apportionment would be allowable if done on a reasonable basis.

5.2.2 Expenditure on Buildings/Structures

The general rule is that expenditure on buildings/structures or on any asset that is incorporated into a building/structure, or that is of a kind normally incorporated into buildings/structures, does not qualify as expenditure on "plant". For example, expenditure on the walls and floors of a building would not be regarded as plant. Similarly, expenditure on a structure such as a bridge would not be regarded as plant.

However, over the years case law has made exceptions to this rule in certain instances. For example, the following have been ruled as qualifying expenditure on plant for capital allowance purposes:

- Cookers, washing machines, refrigeration or cooling equipment, sanitary ware and furniture and furnishings.
- Sound insulation provided mainly to meet the particular requirements of the trade.
- Computer, telecommunications and surveillance systems.
- Sprinkler equipment, fire alarm and burglar alarm systems.
- Partition walls, where moveable and intended to be moved.
- Dry docks and jetties.
- Silos provided for temporary storage and storage tanks, slurry pits and silage clamps.

This list is not exhaustive. All of the above items have been the subject of case law and are now enshrined in legislation at section 23, List C, Capital Allowances Act 2001 (see **Appendix 3** for items included in List C).

Having identified what is and is not plant and machinery – and so what can and cannot be claimed as a capital allowance – we can now move on to look in detail at the main types of capital allowance.

5.3   Annual Investment Allowance

The annual investment allowance (AIA) is available to all businesses, and offers 100% capital allowances, up to a specified annual limit, on plant and machinery. It can be claimed against the main pool additions (see **Section 5.5**) and special rate pool additions (see **Section 5.6**).

There are some instances when the AIA cannot be claimed:

- cars;
- plant and machinery previously used for another purpose, e.g. a computer used at home and introduced into the business;
- plant and machinery gifted to the business;
- on a sale and leaseback where the leaseback is a long-funding lease; or
- expenditure incurred in the accounting period in which the business ceases.

The AIA limit has changed frequently in recent years. A summary of the changes is set out below.

Accounting period	AIA limit for a 12-month accounting period
	£
6 April 2010–5 April 2012	100,000
6 April 2012–31 December 2012	25,000
1 January 2013–5 April 2014	250,000
6 April 2014–31 December 2015	500,000
1 January 2016–	200,000

If the accounting period of the business is greater than or less than 12 months, the AIA is proportionately reduced or increased. For example, if the accounting period was for the six months to 31 December 2016, the AIA available would be £100,000 (i.e. £200,000 × 6/12).

5.3.1   Accounting Periods that Straddle AIA Limits

The frequent changes in the AIA limit in recent years has meant that accounting periods can often straddle one or more of a change in the AIA limit. To address this, special transitional rules apply to calculate the amount of the AIA available for the accounting period.

With reference to the table above, we will consider two scenarios:

1. periods that span 6 April 2014 (i.e. the date of the increase in AIA from £250,000 to £500,000); and
2. periods that span 1 January 2016 (i.e. the date of the decrease in AIA from £500,000 to £200,000).

Periods Spanning 6 April 2014
Where a business has an accounting period that spans 6 April 2014, the maximum allowance for the period is the sum of:

1. the AIA entitlement based on the previous £250,000 annual cap for the portion of a year falling before the relevant operative date; **plus**
2. the AIA entitlement based on the new £500,000 cap for the portion of a year falling on or after the relevant operative date.

In relation to that part of the period falling **before** 6 April 2014, no more than a maximum of £250,000 of the business's actual expenditure would be covered by its transitional AIA entitlement.

Example 5.1
With reference to the table above, for a trade with a year-end of 30 June 2014, the AIA would be calculated as follows:

the proportion of the accounting period prior to 6 April 2014, i.e. 9/12 × £250,000 = £187,500

PLUS

the proportion of the accounting period after 6 April 2014, i.e. 3/12 × £500,000 = £125,000

Therefore the company's maximum AIA that can be claimed is £312,500.

However, if the trader incurred £270,000 of "main pool" expenditure in the first nine months to 5 April 2014, the AIA would be restricted to the maximum for that period, i.e. only £250,000 could be claimed.

If, instead, the £270,000 expenditure had all been incurred in the final three months to 30 June 2014, there would be no restriction and the full AIA could be used (in this case the £270,000 would be covered by the AIA of £312,500).

Periods Spanning 1 January 2016

Where a business has an accounting period that spans 1 January 2016, the maximum allowance for the period is the sum of:

1. the AIA entitlement, based on the previous £500,000 annual cap, for the portion of a year falling before the relevant operative date; **plus**
2. the AIA entitlement, based on the new £200,000 cap, for the portion of a year falling on or after the relevant operative date.

In relation to that part of the period falling **after** 1 January 2016, the pro rata AIA calculation represents the maximum of the **actual** expenditure in this period that would be covered by AIA.

Example 5.2

For a trade with a year-end of 31 March 2016, the AIA would be calculated as follows:

> proportion of the accounting period prior to 1 January 2016, i.e. 9/12 × £500,000 = £375,000

> PLUS

> proportion of the accounting period after 1 January 2016, i.e. 3/12 × £200,000 = £50,000

Therefore the company's maximum AIA that can be claimed is £425,000.

However, if the trader incurred £390,000 of "main pool" expenditure in the period from 1 January 2016 to 31 March 2016, the AIA would be restricted to £50,000.

Instead, if that expenditure had all been incurred in the first nine months of the period, the restriction would be £425,000 (i.e. the same as the maximum entitlement for the whole period to 31 March 2016).

The balance of expenditure that cannot be covered by the AIA is transferred immediately to the main pool (see **Section 5.5.1** for writing down allowance available) or special rate pool (see **Section 5.6**), and will be eligible for writing down allowances in the same period.

Example 5.3

An established trader who prepares his accounts up to 31 March each year, incurs expenditure in the year to 31 March 2016 of machinery purchased for £280,000 in June 2015, and other various pieces of equipment purchased for £85,000 in February 2016.

Step 1 – calculate maximum AIA

Period to 31 December 2015: 9/12 × £500,000 = £375,000

Period from 1 January 2016–31 March 2016: 3/12 × £200,000 = £50,000

Total maximum AIA is £425,000.

Step 2 – maximum expenditure which **potentially** qualifies for AIA is £365,000 (being the total machinery and equipment purchased as these would all be main pool additions).

Step 3 – £280,000 falls into the period to 31 December 2015.

Step 4 – as this is less than the maximum AIA calculated for the whole accounting period (i.e. £425,000), AIA can be claimed on the full amount.

continued overleaf

Step 5 – £85,000 falls into the period from 1 January 2016 to 31 March 2016.

Step 6 – as this is more than £50,000 (from Step 1), only £50,000 of the expenditure can be considered for AIA. A claim for £50,000 will not breach the maximum limit for the whole accounting period (i.e. £280,000 + £50,000 = £330,000, which is below the maximum limit of £425,000).

Step 7 – the remaining expenditure of £35,000 will be added to the main pool where a WDA at 18% can be claimed (see **Section 5.5.1**).

The total AIA claim for the period is £330,000 (i.e. £280,000 + £50,000).

5.4   First Year Allowance

If an asset is purchased and it qualifies for the first year allowance (FYA), then the full cost of the asset can be deducted in arriving at the tax-adjusted trading profits of a business.

The **100%** FYA is available in relation to the following:

1. New cars that are electronically propelled or cars with CO_2 emissions less than 75g/km acquired on or after 1 April 2015. (Previously, for cars acquired between 1 April 2013 and 31 March 2015, the CO_2 emissions limit was less than 95g/km, and 110g/km for cars acquired prior to 1 April 2013.)
2. Natural gas, biogas and hydrogen refuelling equipment.
3. **New** energy-efficient and **new** water-saving (environmentally beneficial) technologies – 100% allowance, but only if the item is on the Energy Technology Product List or the Water Efficient Technologies Product List issued by the Government.
4. Zero-emissions goods vehicles.

The 100% first year allowance on energy-saving plant and machinery, low emission cars and zero-emissions goods vehicles is only available if these assets are acquired unused and are not second-hand.

Where the FYA is not claimed in full, the balance of expenditure is transferred to the main pool (see **Section 5.5**). An FYA is not reduced pro rata in a short period of account, unlike AIAs and annual writing down allowances (WDAs).

The AIA and the FYA **cannot** be claimed in respect of the same expenditure. Where both allowances are possible, the taxpayer can choose which, if any, to claim, with any excess being treated as noted above.

5.5   The Main Pool

The majority of plant and machinery expenditure will fall into the main pool. The main pool comprises all items of plant and machinery, including cars with CO_2 emissions of 130g/km or less, but it does not include assets that should form part of the special rate pool (see **Section 5.6**), assets that are used for both business and personal use (see **Section 5.7**) and assets that have been elected as short-life assets (see **Section 5.8**).

When an individual buys assets that fall into the main pool, the additions will increase the size of the pool. When assets are disposed of from the main pool, the value of the main pool is decreased.

5.5.1   Writing Down Allowance

The writing down allowance (WDA) is an annual allowance to reflect the wear and tear of plant and machinery (new or second-hand) in use for the purpose of a trade, profession or employment at the end of an accounting period. Unlike the AIA and the FYA, which are applied to the cost price of the equipment, WDAs are applied on a reducing balance basis. The WDA is calculated on the cost price of the plant and machinery **less any capital grants** received in the first period. The WDAs in subsequent periods are calculated based on the opening tax written down values (i.e. cost less previous WDA claimed) plus current period additions less current period disposals.

For assets acquired since 6 April 2012 the WDA is 18%.

To qualify for WDA, an asset must be **owned** by the individual and in use "wholly and exclusively" for the purposes of the individual's trade, profession or employment.

Example 5.4

Regina, a sole trader in business for many years, prepares accounts to 5 April each year. During the year ended 5 April 2017 she bought the following assets:

		£
		£
10/05/2016	Office equipment	1,000
01/04/2017	Printer	3,500

The tax written down value (TWDV) on the main pool at 6 April 2016 was £56,000.

Regina's capital allowances computation for the year ended 5 April 2017 is as follows:

	AIA/FYA Pool	Main Pool	Allowances Claimed
	£	£	£
TWDV b/fwd		56,000	
Additions		–	
Disposals		–	
Additions qualifying 100% AIA	4,500		
AIA	(4,500)		4,500
Remaining TWDV (transfer to main pool)	0	0	
		56,000	
Allowances @18%		(10,080)	10,080
TWDV c/fwd at 5 April 2017		45,920	
Total capital allowances claim			14,580

Businesses can claim a WDA of up to £1,000 in the case of either the main pool or the special rate pool (see **Sections 5.5** and **5.6**) provided the unrelieved expenditure is £1,000 or less. If the maximum WDA is claimed, then the pool (main or special rate) will have a nil tax written down balance forward.

When plant is sold, the proceeds (limited to the original cost) are removed from the main pool. Where the trade is continuing, the pool balance remaining will continue to be written down on an annual basis by WDAs, even if there are no assets left.

Example 5.5

Rory, a sole trader in business for many years, prepares accounts to 5 April each year. During the year ended 5 April 2017 he did not buy any assets. However, he did dispose of a machine for £16,000 (it originally cost £15,000). The TWDV on the main pool at 6 April 2016 was £15,900.

Rory's capital allowances computation for the year ended 5 April 2017 is as follows:

	AIA/FYA Pool £	Main Pool £	Allowances Claimed £
TWDV b/fwd		15,900	
Additions		–	
Disposals (limited to cost)		(15,000)	
		900	
Allowances @ "small pool"		(900)	900
TWDV c/fwd at 5 April 2017		0	
Total capital allowances claim			900

For long or short periods of account, the WDA is pro-rated.

Example 5.6

A business had a tax written down value carried forward in its main pool of £12,000. The accounting period was for 10 months and there were no additions or disposals during this period.

The WDA claimed would be:

$$£12,000 \times 18\% \times 10/12 = £1,800$$

5.5.2 Balancing Allowances and Balancing Charges

Profits and losses on the disposal of non-current assets (such as property, plant and equipment) are **not included** in the tax-adjusted profits of a business. In order to adequately capture these profits and losses, the capital allowances system uses balancing charges and balancing allowances to reflect any profit or loss on the disposal (i.e. sale) of an asset.

A **balancing allowance** arises when the **sales proceeds of an asset are less than its tax written down value (a loss on disposal)**.

A **balancing charge** arises when the **sales proceeds of an asset are greater than its tax written down value (a profit on disposal)**. However, if the sales proceeds exceed the original cost, the sales proceeds in the capital allowances computation are restricted to the original cost.

Note that the tax-adjusted profit/(loss) will not be the same as the profit/(loss) on disposal in the accounts. This is due to the differing rates and rules between depreciation and capital allowances.

In essence, the aim is to ensure that the allowances potentially available to the taxpayer equate to the cost to them of the equipment.

Balancing allowances and charges can arise when one of the following occurs:

- the trade or profession ceases;
- the assets are no longer "in use" for the trade;
- an asset, on which capital allowances were previously claimed, is sold/scrapped; or
- an asset permanently ceases to be used for the purposes of the trade, profession or employment.

Where the sale proceeds are **not** at 'arm's length' (as they would be in a sale between unrelated parties) or where there are no sale proceeds (e.g. due to a takeover or to the gifting of a business asset for personal use), the market value is used to calculate the balancing allowance/charge.

Generally, on the disposal of an asset from the main pool or special rate pool, no balancing allowances or charges arise, except on the cessation of a trade. For this reason there is an option to treat certain assets as "short-life" assets (see **Section 5.8**). Short-life assets are kept in a separate asset pool, which means that relief will be obtained for any balancing allowances that may arise on the disposal of the asset (see **Example 5.9**).

Limitation of Balancing Charges

The balancing charge **cannot exceed** the aggregate of the capital allowances **already claimed** on the asset.

5.6   Special Rate Pool

The special rate pool contains capital expenditure on:

- thermal insulation;
- long-life assets (see **Section 5.6.1**);
- integral features of a building (see **Section 5.6.2**);
- Solar panels; and
- cars with CO_2 emissions greater than 130g/km (160g/km prior to 6 April 2013).

The WDA applied to the special rate pool is, since 6 April 2012, 8%.

The AIA can apply to all assets in the special rate pool except for cars. An individual can decide how to allocate the AIA in the most tax-efficient manner. For example, where there is **expenditure on assets in both pools in the period**, it will be **more tax efficient to set the allowance against special rate pool expenditure (where the WDA is 8%) rather than to main pool expenditure (18% WDA rate)**. Expenditure in excess of the AIA is added to the special rate pool and will be eligible for WDA in the same period in which the expenditure is incurred.

Like the main pool, the 8% rate is per annum; therefore, a pro rata adjustment is required for long or short periods of account (see **Example 5.6**).

5.6.1   Long-life Assets

Long-life assets are assets with an expected working life of 25 years or more. In order for expenditure to fall within the long-life asset rules (and so be categorised as a special rate pool asset), total expenditure on assets with an expected working life of 25 years or more in a basis period must be more than £100,000.

If an individual spends less than £100,000 on long-life assets in a basis period, the long-life assets rules do not apply and the asset may fall into the main pool; if they spend more than £100,000 on long-life assets in a basis period, the long-life asset rules apply and all the expenditure falls into the special rate pool.

For shorter basis periods, the £100,000 should be reduced proportionately.

5.6.2   Integral Fixtures and Fittings

"Integral features" are certain features that are seen as essential to a building and which, in HMRC's view, have a longer average economic life than other plant and machinery and should therefore be written down using a lower capital allowance rate.

Expenditure on integral features therefore attracts a WDA rate of 8%. Integral features include:

- electrical systems (including lighting systems);
- hot and cold water systems;
- space-heating systems, powered systems of ventilation, air cooling or air purification, and any floor or ceiling comprised in such systems;
- lifts, escalators and moving walkways; and
- external solar shading.

Example 5.7

Danielle runs a bakery/café in the centre of Belfast. She makes up her accounts to 31 March each year. The TWDV of her main pool as at 1 April 2016 was £100,000. In the tax year 2016/17, Danielle had the following costs:

Date	Cost	General description
14 April 2016	£400,000	General plant and machinery, e.g. new shelving, new cooler machine, new refrigerators, etc.
19 August 2016	£50,000	New lighting system for the inside and outside of the shop/café
30 September 2016	£55,000	Lift installed
5 February 2017	£22,000	New car (CO_2 145 g/km) – 100% business use
5 February 2017	£12,000	New delivery van and signage

What is the maximum capital allowances claim that Danielle can make for the tax year 2016/17?

Y/e 31 March 2017	AIA £	Main Pool £	Special Rate Pool £	Claim £
TWDV b/fwd		100,000		
Additions qualifying for AIA only:				
Lighting, lift, P&M, van	517,000			
AIA	(200,000)			200,000
T/f to main rate pool	317,000	317,000		
Additions not qualifying for AIA:				
Plant and machinery + van				
Car (>130g/km)			22,000	
Additions qualifying for WDA		417,000	22,000	
WDA @ 18%		(75,060)		75,060
WDA @ 8%			(1,760)	1,760
TWDV c/fwd		341,940	20,240	
Total capital allowance claim for period				276,820

Note: the AIA would first be set against the integral features (the lift and lighting system), leaving the remainder to be offset against the main pool additions. The maximum AIA for the period is £200,000.

Acquisition of Property that Includes Fixtures

Special rules apply where a business acquires a property that includes existing fixtures: part of the purchase price of the property will relate to the fixtures, and the purchaser may be able to make a capital allowances claim on these fixtures.

Since 6 April 2012, where fixtures were acquired and the previous owner had claimed capital allowances, the purchaser must agree (usually by completing a section 198 CAA 2001 election) a value for the fixtures within two years of the transfer of the property. The value cannot exceed the seller's original cost or the actual sale price.

Since 6 April 2014, the purchaser can only claim capital allowances on fixtures where the seller has previously claimed either the FYA or the AIA on those fixtures, or where the cost of the fixtures has been allocated to a capital allowance pool. Basically, unless a capital allowance claim has been made by the seller, the new purchaser cannot make a claim.

5.7 Single Assets Pool: Private Use Assets

An asset that has mixed use and is used privately by a trader is dealt with in a **single asset pool** and the capital allowances are restricted. The allowance is calculated as normal and is then reduced by the private element. Only the business use proportion of the WDAs is allowed as a deduction from trading profits; however, the **full annual allowance is deducted** when arriving at the tax written down value at the end of each period. This restriction applies to the AIAs, FYAs, WDAs, balancing allowances and balancing charges.

An asset with some private use by an employee suffers no such private use restriction. The employee may be taxed on the benefit in kind (see **Chapter 6**) instead, so the business receives capital allowances on the full cost of the asset.

When an asset in a single asset pool is sold, a balancing allowance/charge arises, depending on the proceeds received. This differs from the disposal of an asset from the main rate or special rate pool where the tax written down value of the pool is reduced by the lower of the cost or the sale proceeds (thereby reducing the WDA available to claim in the future). (See **Examples 5.8** and **5.9**.)

5.7.1 Motor Cars: Recap

Cars acquired since 1 April 2015 are categorised in accordance with their CO_2 emissions:

1. CO_2 emissions over 130g/km – expenditure is added to the special rate pool (WDA @ 8%).
2. CO_2 emissions between 76 and 130g/km – expenditure is added to the main pool (WDA @ 18%).
3. CO_2 emissions of 75g/km or less – expenditure is eligible for 100% first year allowance (FYA @ 100%). If FYA is not claimed in full, the excess may be added to the main pool (WDA @ 18%).

Cars that have an element of private use by the taxpayer must be kept in **single asset pools**. The WDA on the special rate pool will be 18% if CO_2 emissions range from 76–130g/km; and 8% if CO_2 emissions are over 130g/km.

Note, in the legislation, lorries, vans and trucks are not defined as cars. Cars do not qualify for AIA.

Example 5.8

Kieran started to trade Kieran's Kitchens on 1 October 2016, making up accounts to 31 March 2017 and each 31 March thereafter. On 1 November 2016 he bought a car for £19,000 with CO_2 emissions of 125g/km. The private-use proportion is 20%. The car was sold in October 2019 for £6,000.

Calculate the capital allowances, assuming:

1. the car was used by an employee; or

2. the car was used by Kieran.

Assumption 1

	Main Pool (18%) £	Allowances £
Six months to 31 March 2017		
Purchase price	19,000	
WDA 18% × 6/12 × £19,000	(1,710)	1,710
	17,290	

continued overleaf

	Single Asset Pool	Allowances

Y/e 31 March 2018
WDA 18% × £17,290 (3,112) 3,112
14,178

Y/e 31 March 2019
WDA 18% × £14,178 (2,552) 2,552
11,626

Y/e 31 March 2020
Proceeds (6,000)
Balancing allowance **5,626** 5,626

The private use of the car by the employee has no effect on the capital allowances due to Kieran's Kitchens (see **Section 6.4.3** for details of the benefit in kind calculation for the employee's private use, which will be subject to income tax). The car would be included in the main pool and WDAs at 18% apply. The first accounting period was only six months in length; therefore, the WDA was reduced proportionately.

Assumption 2

	Single Asset Pool (WDA 18%) £	Private Use (20%) £	Allowances £
Six months to 31 March 2017			
Purchase price	19,000		
WDA 18% × 6/12 × £19,000	(1,710)	342	1,368
	17,290		
Y/e 31 March 2018			
WDA 18% × £17,290	(3,112)	622	2,490
	14,178		
Y/e 31 March 2019			
WDA 18% × £14,178	(2,552)	510	2,042
	11,626		
Y/e 31 March 2020			
Proceeds	(6,000)		
Balancing allowance	**5,626**	1,125	4,501

The private use is by the proprietor of Kieran's Kitchens, therefore only 80% of the WDAs and balancing allowance are available.

Example 5.9
Joe, who is self-employed and prepares annual accounts to 5 April, purchased a new car on 1 June 2016, which cost £20,000, with CO_2 emissions of 125g/km. His annual mileage is 20,000 miles, of which 5,000 are private.

Joe's sales director, Sarah, also has a business car, purchased on 30 September 2016 for £15,000, with CO_2 emissions of 120g/km. Sarah's mileage is 35,000 miles, of which 28,000 miles are business-related. Joe previously had a BMW, which he purchased for £20,000. The TWDV at 05/04/15 was £11,000. Joe sold this car for £9,500 during the tax year 2016/17. Joe used this car 50% for business purposes. The TWDV of the main pool on 5 April 2016 was £10,000.

WDA	Pool £	Joe's Car 1 (50% private use) £	Joe's Car 2 (25% private use) (WDA 18%) £	Private Use £	Allowance £
TWDV @ 06/04/16	10,000	11,000			
Additions	15,000		20,000		
	25,000	11,000	20,000		
Disposal proceeds		(9,500)			
Balancing allowance		1,500		(750)	750
WDA @ 18%	(4,500)		(3,600)	900	7,200

continued overleaf

TWDV @ 05/04/17	<u>20,500</u>	<u>nil</u>	<u>16,400</u>
Total capital allowance claim			**7,950**

Joe sold his previous car, which was included in a single asset pool. A balancing allowance arises of £1,500. However, as only 50% of use of the car was business use, its balancing allowance is restricted to 50%.

Joe's new car is included in a single asset pool under new rules because there is private use (25%). The WDAs are restricted by 25% private use. Sarah's car is included within the main pool as the CO_2 is less than 130g/km, and there is no private use element as Sarah is an employee. WDA at 18% applies. No AIA can be used as the additions relate to cars.

5.8 Short-life Assets

Where an asset is acquired and is likely to be disposed of within eight years from the end of the accounting period in which it was bought, it is considered a "short-life" asset. Provided an election is made to treat the asset in a single asset pool instead of the main pool, a balancing charge or allowance arises on its disposal.

If the asset is not disposed of within this time period, its tax written down value is added to the main pool at the end of that time.

The AIA and the FYA can be claimed for short-life assets. It will be more tax-efficient to set the AIA or FYA allowances against main pool expenditure in priority to short-life asset expenditure. The reason for this is that tax relief is more likely to be received quicker for assets elected to be short-life assets than for assets in the main pool where the writing down allowance is at a rate of 18% on a reducing balance method.

Short-life asset treatment cannot be claimed for motor cars or plant used partly for non-business purposes.

5.9 Disclaim of Capital Allowances

Where the capital allowances claim for a particular year of assessment exceeds the assessable profits from the trade or profession, it will give rise to a trade loss. In this situation an individual does not have to claim the full capital allowances to which they are entitled and can make a partial claim instead. This would reduce any trade loss and result in a higher tax written down value brought forward (increasing the WDA in future years).

A trader should therefore consider whether it is beneficial to claim capital allowances in the period and, if so, whether a full or partial claim should be made. Issues to consider include whether the individual has sufficient income in the period to utilise the trade loss without wasting their personal allowance (which is £11,000 for the 2016/17 tax year, see **Chapter 2**).

5.10 Treatment of Purchases, Capital Grants, Hire Purchase, Finance Leases, Lessors and VAT

5.10.1 Date of Purchase of Assets

For capital allowances purposes, expenditure is generally deemed to be incurred when the obligation to pay becomes unconditional (provided this is within four months). This will usually be the date of the contract, e.g. where payment is due a month after delivery, then the date of delivery is relevant.

However, if the amount is due more than four months after the obligation to pay becomes unconditional for capital allowance purposes, then the expenditure is instead deemed to be incurred when paid.

Assets acquired under a hire-purchase contract are deemed to be incurred at the time they are brought into use, i.e. the four-month rule does not apply.

5.10.2 Capital Grants

The qualifying cost for capital allowance purposes is the **net cost**, i.e. total cost minus grant receivable. Capital grants are increasingly rare in today's economic environment.

5.10.3 Hire Purchase

Capital allowances are available on assets acquired under hire-purchase (HP) agreements. The key features of capital allowances under HP agreements are:

- The appropriate allowance can be claimed in the period for which the asset is put into use.
- The qualifying cost for the purposes of computing the writing down allowance is limited to the cost of the asset, **exclusive** of hire-purchase charges, i.e. interest.
- The timing of the actual hire-purchase instalments is not relevant, provided the agreement is **executed** during the period.
- The individual will be able to claim the interest charges as a tax-deductible trading expense over the term of the contract.

5.10.4 Finance-leased Assets

Where an individual leases an asset on a finance lease, no capital allowances can be claimed on the capital expenditure.

However, in the accounts of the business the asset will be depreciated over its life. In accordance with general accounting practice, the depreciation as well as the interest being charged by the lessor will be debited to the statement of profit or loss for the period. Both the interest and the depreciation can be treated as allowable expenses. This is the only time that an individual will get a tax deduction for depreciation.

5.10.5 Qualifying Cost and VAT

The qualifying cost of plant and equipment for capital allowance purposes is the **actual expenditure incurred** on the plant or equipment. This will be the cost of the plant or equipment **exclusive** of VAT, where the VAT paid on acquisition is recoverable by the individual because they are VAT registered. If, however, a business that is not registered for VAT acquires plant or equipment outright, then the VAT element of the purchase price represents a cost and the **total cost, including VAT**, could be claimed as a capital allowance.

5.11 Business Premises Renovation Allowance

The business premises renovation allowance (BPRA) was introduced by Finance Act 2005. Under the scheme, a 100% allowance is available on the costs of renovation or conversion of a "qualifying business premises". A qualifying business premises is one that:

- has been vacant for at least one year;
- is in a designated disadvantaged area of the UK, which includes the entire area of Northern Ireland;
- was last used for the purpose of a qualifying trade or profession or as an office; and
- was not used wholly, or partly, for residential purposes.

"Qualifying expenditure" means any capital expenditure, including fixtures, used for the repair, conversion or renovation of the building into a qualifying business premises. Qualifying business premises are those that are used for the purposes of a qualifying trade, profession or vocation or as offices. Qualifying trades exclude fisheries, shipbuilding, coal and steel, synthetic fibres and the production of certain agricultural and milk products.

Since 6 April 2014, the categories of costs that qualify for BPRA have changed. From this date, the BPRA is limited to the actual costs of construction and building works, as well as certain specified activities (such as architectural fees, planning applications and surveying services). The BPRA on other associated but unspecified activities, such as project management, is limited to 5% of the actual costs

In addition, BPRA is no longer available where other State aid has been, or will be, received. The scheme is due to finish on 5 April 2017.

The 100% allowance need not be taken in full. Where the full allowance is not taken, writing down allowances of 25% per annum on a straight-line basis will be available on the unclaimed residue of expenditure.

Example 5.10

In August 2015 (i.e. the 2015/16 tax year), Michael, a self-employed mechanic, purchased a vacant premises in Belfast that had previously been a sweet-making factory. He converted the premises into a garage with office space, from which he intends to carry on his trade. The total cost incurred in 2015/16 for renovation work was £500,000.

The premises is eligible for BPRA at the 100% rate, i.e. the full amount of £500,000 can be claimed back.

However, say Michael decided to claim only £200,000 of the total cost under the BPRA in 2015/16. The remaining cost of £300,000 would be available as a writing down allowance of £125,000 (£500,000 x 25%) in each of the next two years (i.e. 2016/17 and 2017/18). The remaining £50,000 would be claimed as a writing down allowance in 2018/19.

5.11.1 Balancing Allowance/Charge and BPRA

Where there is a "balancing event", e.g. the premises is sold, let on a long lease, demolished or destroyed or otherwise ceases to be a qualifying premises, or if the individual who incurred the qualifying expenditure dies, then a balancing allowance or balancing charge can arise.

No balancing adjustments will be made if the balancing event occurs more than five years from when the premises was first brought back into use or made suitable and available for letting.

5.12 Loss Relief

This section will discuss the tax implications of a tax-adjusted trading loss being incurred by an individual and how such a loss-suffering individual can use their trading loss to reduce their tax liability.

5.12.1 Introduction: Income Tax Loss Relief

As stated previously, businesses prepare accounts based on commercial and accounting principles to arrive at their net profit/(loss). This net profit/(loss) per the statement of profit or loss will then be adjusted in accordance with the tax legislation to arrive at the tax-adjusted profit/(loss) (see **Chapter 4**). It should be noted that a trading loss is computed in exactly the same way as a profit. When a tax-adjusted trading loss (hereafter referred to as a trading loss) is calculated for a business, which is traded by an individual alone or in a partnership, income tax relief may be available for trading losses in the following ways:

1. by offsetting the losses against other (general) income in the same year and/or the previous tax year (subject to the cap on income tax reliefs (see **Section 5.12.8**));
2. by carrying forward the losses against subsequent (future) profits of the **same** trade;
3. where the losses occur in the early years of a trade, by carrying them back against other income from previous years (subject to the cap on income tax reliefs (see **Section 5.12.8**));
4. by offsetting the losses against capital gains (which may arise on the sale of a property, for example) of the same or preceding tax year; or
5. by carry back in a "terminal loss" situation, i.e. where a trade ceases.

5.12.2 Effect of Capital Allowances

Capital allowances for a year of assessment may be used to create or augment (i.e. increase) a trading loss, provided that such allowances are **first** offset against any **balancing charges** arising in the tax year to which they relate and which are not covered by capital allowances brought forward.

This is a useful planning tool that individuals may utilise to try to preserve their personal allowance, for example. In addition, where the effective rate of tax for the individual is likely to be higher in future years, then it may be advisable from a tax point of view to defer claiming capital allowances to future years (i.e. by not claiming in the current tax year so that the balance carried forward to next year's capital allowances computation is higher).

5.12.3 Trade Loss Relief against General Income

Offsetting trade losses against other general income is provided for by section 64 of the Income Tax Act 2007 (ITA 2007), hence it is sometimes referred to as "section 64 relief". The trading loss is relieved by way of deduction from **any other income** chargeable to tax **in that tax year** or the prior tax year.

The loss is deducted from the **total income**, i.e. before deductions (personal allowances or other reliefs). The loss must be set-off first against non-savings income (i.e. trading income, employment income, property income and miscellaneous income), then from savings income and finally from dividend income.

One of the conditions of section 64 relief is that the business is conducted on a commercial basis with a view to the realisation of profits.

In addition, partial claims are not permitted under section 64. The relief must be for either the **full amount** of the loss available, or the total income, whichever is less. This means that by claiming the relief there could be a loss of personal allowances.

Example 5.11

Sandra is a self-employed beautician. She also works part time at a local spa and earns a gross salary of £15,000 annually. Sandra has incurred a lot of expenditure in her beautician business during the year ended 31 March 2017. As a result, she incurred a tax-adjusted trading loss of £28,000. Sandra had £5,000 of tax-adjusted trading profits for the year ended 31 March 2016.

In the 2016/17 tax year, Sandra's trade was loss-making. If Sandra claims to offset this trading loss in 2016/17 against her general income in 2016/17 and 2015/16, her position will be as follows:

	2015/16	2016/17
	£	£
Trading income	5,000	0
Employment income	15,000	15,000
Total income	20,000	15,000
Less: loss relief against general income	(13,000)	(15,000)
Net income	7,000	0
Less: personal allowance	(10,600)	(11,000)
Taxable income	0	0

As you can see, in the 2016/17 tax year, if Sandra claims to offset her trading loss against her employment income she will be fully wasting her personal allowance of £11,000. Similarly, if she carries the remaining trading losses back to 2015/16 for offset against general income, she will waste £3,600 of her 2015/16 personal allowance.

Sandra's options in respect of the 2016/17 trading loss are:

1. Set it against general income in 2016/17 only and carry forward the balance against same trade profits in future years (see **Section 5.12.3**).
2. Set it against general income in 2015/16 only and carry forward the balance against same trade profits in future years.
3. Set it against general income in 2016/17 and 2015/16 (as shown above).
4. Carry forward the loss against same trade profits in future years.

Section 64 loss relief is subject to the cap on income tax relief introduced by Finance Act 2013 (see **Section 5.12.8**).

Where a trading loss is unrelieved, it will be carried forward to set against the first available profits of the same trade.

5.12.4 Carry Forward of Trading Losses

Any trading losses not relieved under section 64 can be carried forward and offset against profits (after deduction of capital allowances) of the same trade or profession in subsequent years (section 83 ITA 2007).

The loss must be set-off against the **first** subsequent year's trading profits, then against the second year's profits, and so on. Losses may be carried forward indefinitely, provided the trade that incurred the loss continues to be carried on.

Example 5.12

Alex has been trading as an accountant for a number of years and has his own accountancy practice, which is his only source of income. His tax-adjusted trading profits/(losses) for the last few years are:

Year to 31 July 2014	(£12,000)
Year to 31 July 2015	£9,000
Year to 31 July 2016	£15,000

continued overleaf

	2014/15	2015/16	2016/17
	£	£	£
Trading income	0	9,000	15,000
Less: carry-forward loss relief	0	(9,000)	(3,000)
Trading income after relief	0	0	12,000

In respect of the tax-adjusted loss of £12,000 incurred in the 2014/15 tax year, Alex claims carry-forward loss relief:

5.12.5 Early Trade Loss Relief

Section 72 ITA 2007 provides for relief of trading losses that arise in the first four years of a trade. These losses may be offset against general income for the three tax years preceding the year of loss, taking the earliest year first. Thus a loss arising in 2016/17 may be offset against income from 2013/14, 2014/15 and 2015/16, in that order.

Example 5.13

John, a trader, started in business on 1 July 2014 and makes up annual accounts to 30 June. In the first and second years of trading, he incurred losses of £16,000 and £20,000 respectively.

What losses are available to John to carry back under section 72 ITA 2007? (Assume the losses are not restricted under the cap on income tax reliefs.)

Tax year 2014/15
Loss: 01/07/14–05/04/15 = £16,000 × 9/12 = £12,000
This loss can be carried back and set against total income for the tax years 2011/12, then 2012/13 and then 2013/14.

Tax year 2015/16
Loss: year ended 30/06/15 = £16,000 less amount assessed re. 2014/15 of £12,000 = £4,000
This loss can be carried back and set against total income for the tax years 2012/13, then 2013/14 and then 2014/15.

Tax year 2016/17
Loss: year ended 30/06/16 = £20,000
This loss can be carried back and set against total income for the tax years 2013/14, then 2014/15 and then 2015/16.

A single claim is required and the loss must be offset to the maximum extent possible against the income of all three years. In other words, an individual cannot choose a specific amount to relieve. However, the loss could be reduced by claiming less capital allowances for that tax year, which would also mean that higher capital allowances could be claimed in future years.

When considering early trade loss relief, care should be taken to ensure no double counting of loss relief where basis periods overlap. For loss relief purposes, a loss in the overlap period is treated as a loss in the earlier tax year (see **Example 5.13**).

Relief is not available unless the trade is operated on a commercial basis, in such a way that a profit could be expected within a "reasonable timeframe". In practice, this may be difficult to prove in the case of a new business and a viable business plan may be necessary to support a carry-back claim.

Early trade loss relief is subject to the cap on income tax reliefs that was introduced by Finance Act 2013 (see **Section 5.12.8**).

5.12.6 Offsetting Trade Losses against Capital Gains

Where an individual makes a claim for trading losses against general income in a tax year and some trading losses remain unrelieved, an individual can then make a further claim to have the unrelieved trading losses set against any capital gains in the year. Capital gains tax is covered in the CA Proficiency 2 syllabus.

5.12.7 Terminal Loss Relief

Where a trade ceases, terminal loss relief can be claimed in respect of a loss incurred in the **final 12 months** of trading. This loss can be offset against trading profits in the tax year of cessation and **carried back** against profits for the previous **three tax years** (later years first).

The losses must be carried back against taxable trading profits of the same trade. The terminal loss for the final 12 months of trading must be calculated. It comprises:

1. The trading loss incurred from 6 April (at the beginning of the tax year of cessation) to the date of cessation (including any unrelieved overlap profits).
2. The trading loss for the 12 months prior to the date of cessation until the end of the penultimate tax year.

1. and 2. added together will give you the total terminal trading loss. However, it is important to note that if either 1. or 2. is a profit, then it is treated as zero for the purposes of adding 1. and 2. together to the total terminal trading loss.

Example 5.14

Andy has been trading as an architect for many years but he decides to cease trading on 31 May 2016 due to ill health. He has overlap profits from his years of commencement of £10,000. Until recently Andy had always made a profit. His tax-adjusted profits/(losses) for recent years are:

	£
Year to 30 June 2013	40,000
Year to 30 June 2014	16,000
Year to 30 June 2015	(7,000)
11 months to 31 May 2016	(33,000)

Andy has other non-savings income of £15,000 per year.

Andy ceases to trade in the 2016/17 tax year. His terminal loss for the last 12 months is:

Trading loss incurred from 6 April (beginning of the tax year of cessation) to the date of cessation (including any unrelieved overlap profits)	£33,000 × 2/11 + £10,000	£16,000
Trading loss for the 12 months prior to the date of cessation until the end of the penultimate tax year, i.e. 1 June 2015 to 5 April 2016	£7,000 × 1/12 + £33,000 × 9/11	£27,583
Terminal loss		£43,583

continued overleaf

Andy can relieve this terminal loss as follows:

	2013/14 £	2014/15 £	2015/16 £	2016/17 £
Adjusted profit	40,000	16,000	nil	nil
Less: terminal loss relief	(27,583)	(16,000)		
Total income	12,417	–	–	–
Other non-savings income	15,000	15,000	15,000	15,000
Total income	27,417	15,000	15,000	15,000

Special Relief where Trade is Ceasing because of Incorporation
If a business is transferred to a company, any unrelieved loss of the sole trader/partnership can be carried forward and set-off against the first available income received from the company by way of salary, dividends, interest, etc. The sequence is to offset the loss against non-savings income, savings income and then dividend income. The consideration for the transfer of the business must be wholly or mainly in the form of shares (at least 80%), which must be retained by the seller throughout any tax year in which the loss is relieved.

5.12.8 Cap on Income Tax Loss Reliefs

Finance Act 2013 introduced a cap on certain income tax reliefs. The cap limits the relief available to the **greater** of:

- £50,000; or
- 25% of the individual's "adjusted total income" for the tax year.

Adjusted Total Income
"Adjusted total income" (ATI) is the income calculated specifically for the purposes of the cap on income tax loss reliefs – it is not a term that is used in any other context. There are three steps to calculate ATI:

1. Aggregate all income sources, i.e. trading income, employment income, savings income, etc., to give **total income**.
2. Deduct any relevant pension contributions, i.e. gross amounts of personal pension contributions (see **Chapter 9, Section 9.3.1**).
3. Add back any charitable donations made through payroll giving (see **Chapter 6, Section 6.4.2**).

The purpose of the adjustments is to ensure that the income calculated, and on which the cap will be based, takes into account deductions made before or after tax has been paid. **Chapter 6 Employment Income** explains the income tax treatment of pension contributions and charitable donations, but for now it is enough to know that they are used to calculate ATI. The cap is applied to the year of the claim and any earlier or later year in which the relief claimed is allocated against total income.

Example 5.15
In 2016/17 Cathy's income is £650,000 from employment and £100,000 of trading losses from her share of the losses from a partnership in which she is a partner. Cathy does not have an occupational pension with her employer, but does contribute to a personal pension scheme. In 2016/17 she makes gross contributions of £40,000 to her personal pension.

continued overleaf

Cathy makes a claim for loss relief for 2016/17.

Her individual relief cap in 2016/17 is £152,500. This is calculated as follows:

Cathy's adjusted total income is £610,000 (i.e. £650,000 less the gross personal pension contributions of £40,000). Therefore her total loss relief claim cannot exceed the greater of:

1. £50,0000
2. £610,000 × 25% = £152,500 (take this amount as greater)

Summary of Reliefs Impacted on by the Restriction

Reliefs Affected by the Cap
To the extent that they can be relieved by individuals against **general income**, those reliefs affected include the following:

- trade loss relief against general income;
- early trade losses relief; and
- qualifying loan interest – available for interest paid on certain loans, including loans to buy an interest in certain types of company or to invest in a partnership (see **Chapter 9, Section 9.2.1**).

It is important to note that trading losses that have been generated by overlap relief will not be subject to the cap. In addition, there is no restriction on losses that are carried back and set against profits of the same trade. Similarly, no restriction applies to trading losses carried forward against profits of the same trade.

Other deductions against total income that have **not** been affected by the cap are pension contributions and charitable donations.

Trading Loss Relief over Multiple Tax Years
Section 64 relief and early trade losses relief can be claimed against income of an earlier tax year than the year in which the loss was incurred. To make this claim, the adjusted total income (ATI) must be **recalculated for each relevant tax year**.

For example, if a trading loss arose in the 2015/16 tax year, the trader could offset this loss against general income in the 2016/17 tax year, but could then also carry back some of the loss and offset it against general income in the 2015/16 tax year. The mechanics of the claim would be to:

1. Determine the amount of relief available for the 2016/17 tax year, i.e. either 25% of the trader's ATI for the 2016/17 tax year or £50,000, whichever is the greater.
2. Determine the amount of relief available for the 2015/16 tax year, i.e. either 25% of the trader's ATI for the 2015/16 tax year or £50,000, whichever is the greater.

Example 5.16
John, a local builder who is self-employed, has trade losses in the 2016/17 tax year of £180,000 and trading profits in 2015/16 of £70,000. He has other income of £120,000 in 2016/17 and £140,000 in 2015/16.

The cap for 2016/17 is equal to the greater of:

- £50,000; or
- 25% of £120,000 (i.e. £30,000).

continued overleaf

Therefore the cap for 2016/17 is £50,000. So his relief against general income is capped at £50,000. This limit (which is based on his income in the year of the loss) will apply only to 2016/17.

The limit for 2015/16 is the greater of £50,000 or 25% of £210,000 (i.e. £52,500).

John makes a claim to set £50,000 of the trade losses against his 2016/17 general income. He can also claim to carry back £52,500 of the losses against his general income in 2015/16. John also claims to carry back £70,000 against 2015/16 profits from the same trade (unrestricted).

	2015/16	2016/17
	£	£
Trading income	70,000	Nil
Section 64 loss relief (unrestricted)	(70,000)	
Other income	140,000	120,000
Section 64 loss relief		
(capped at limit, or the available loss if less)	(52,500)	(50,000)
Net income	87,500	70,000

The remaining £7,500 of trading losses can be carried forward and offset against future trading profits from the same trade.

Practical tip: an individual should choose whichever loss relief saves tax at the highest tax rate – but they need to be careful and consider the potential loss of other reliefs, such as personal allowances, etc.

Questions

Review Questions

(See Suggested Solutions to Review Questions at the end of this textbook.)

Question 5.1

Barney Connor is a self-employed accountant who has been in business for many years and prepares accounts to 5 April each year. During the year ended 5 April 2017 he purchased the following assets:

		£
		£
29/12/2016	Computer	8,000
30/12/2016	Car (CO_2 125g/km)	11,500
08/03/2017	Desks	1,800
20/03/2017	Filing cabinets	2,300 (not delivered until 15/04/2017 but paid for before 5 April 2017)
		23,720

The tax written down value on the main pool at 6 April 2016 was £20,000.

Requirement
Prepare the capital allowances computation for the year ended 5 April 2017, and calculate the TWDV carried forward at 5 April 2017.

Question 5.2

Bobby Robson is a self-employed sports goods retailer who has been in business for many years and prepares accounts to 31 August each year. In the year ended 31 August 2016, he purchased the following assets:

		£
10/10/2015	Cash registers	7,000
31/12/2015	Air-conditioning unit	6,900
		13,900

The tax written down value on the main pool at 1 September 2015 was £100,000. In the same period he also purchased a car for use by an employee for £40,000 with CO_2 emissions of 165g/km, and a second car for use by another employee for £10,000 with CO_2 emissions of 130g/km.

Requirement

Prepare the capital allowances computation for the year ended 31 August 2016, and calculate the TWDV carried forward at 31 August 2016.

Question 5.3

Jim, a sole trader, has been in business for many years and prepares accounts to 31 August each year. The tax written down value on the main pool at 1 September 2015 was £120,000.

He bought a printing press, with an expected useful life of 50 years, on 30 September 2015 for £110,000. The following assets were also purchased in the period: a car for £20,000 (CO_2 emissions 125g/km) on 21 September 2015; a van for £15,000 (CO_2 emissions 135g/km) on 14 March 2016; and miscellaneous plant and machinery for £30,000 in May 2016.

Requirement

Prepare the capital allowances computation for the year ended 31 August 2016, and calculate the TWDV carried forward at 31 August 2016. The car is 100% for business purposes.

Question 5.4

Joan O'Reilly is a bookbinder who prepares accounts to 5 April each year. She made a profit on sale of some plant and machinery of £5,000 in the year to 5 April 2017. The net book value (NBV) of the assets sold was £10,000 (original cost £18,000). She also purchased machinery in June 2016 costing £10,000.

The tax written down value on the main pool at 6 April 2016 was £20,000.

Requirement

Prepare the capital allowances computation for the year ended 5 April 2017, and calculate the TWDV carried forward at 5 April 2017.

Question 5.5

Cormac Molloy, a self-employed farmer, has been in business for many years and prepares accounts to 31 December each year. His motor vehicle details are:

Motor car cost 01/06/2014	£26,000 (CO_2 emissions 155g/km)
Total estimated annual mileage	20,000 miles
Total estimated private mileage	5,000 miles (i.e. 3/4 of total mileage is business)

Requirement
Calculate the deductible capital allowances for the 2016/17 tax year and the TWDV carried forward at 31 December 2016. Assume no assets other than the motor car.

Question 5.6

Joseph Ryan is a shopkeeper who has been in business many years and prepares accounts to 5 April each year. On 10 November 2014 he bought a car for £13,000 with CO_2 emissions of 165g/km. The private use is one-third.

Requirement
Calculate the deductible capital allowances for the 2016/17 tax year and the TWDV carried forward at 6 April 2017. Assume no TWDV brought forward as of 6 April 2014.

Question 5.7

Louise Kenny is a clothes designer and commenced business as a sole trader on 1 January 2016. In the period ended 30 September 2016, she purchased the following assets:

	Cost £	Purchase date
Sewing machines	8,000	2 February 2016
Dummies	7,500	7 April 2016
Computer and laser printer	6,900	10 June 2016
Car (CO_2 emissions 127g/km)	11,000	10 June 2016

In the year ended 30 September 2017 she purchased the following assets:

	Cost £	Purchase date
Cutting table	2,000	18 August 2017
Cash register	1,500	21 September 2017

Requirement
What capital allowances will be deductible in calculating trading profits for the periods ended 30 September 2016 and 2017? Assume the same rates and allowances as for 2016/17 apply to the 2017/18 tax year.

Question 5.8

Joe is a butcher who prepares annual accounts to 5 April (he has traded for many years). He has a TWDV brought forward at 6 April 2016 on his main pool of £10,000. He sells plant in December 2016 with a net book value in his financial statement of £10,000 and realises a profit of £30,000. The plant had cost £35,000 originally. He did not purchase any assets in the year to 5 April 2017.

Requirement
Calculate the available capital allowances. What would the consequences be if Joe did not buy any plant in the year to 5 April 2018 but sold more plant for £3,000?

Question 5.9

Fitzroy runs a construction company in Northern Ireland. He has been in business for many years and prepares annual accounts to 31 March. During the year ended 31 March 2017 the following transactions took place:

1. Purchased an asset used in the business with a life of 28 years for £200,000.
2. Purchased a car for £11,000 (CO_2 emissions 120 g/km).
3. Purchased a van for £14,000.
4. Purchased partition walls for his office for £5,000, toilets for £4,000, doors for £2,000 and a desk for £1,000. He also purchased a portacabin, which he used as an office when his other head office was being refurbished, for £15,000. He purchased some portable toilets for £8,000 for use by employees on his various building sites in Northern Ireland.

Fitzroy has no other assets in respect of which capital allowances were claimed.

Requirement
Calculate the capital allowance available in the year to 31 March 2017.

Question 5.10

Joe Bloggs has operated a newsagent/tobacconist/confectionery shop for many years. He has previously dealt with his own income tax affairs and supplies the following details relating to his business for the year ended 31 March 2017:

	£	£
Gross profit	26,880	
Sale proceeds of old equipment	1,500	
Building society interest received	210	28,590
Wages to self	5,200	
Motor expenses	1,750	
Light and heat	1,200	
Wages to wife as bookkeeper and assistant	1,500	
Wages to other employees	7,600	
Advertising	270	
Christmas gifts to customers (bottles of whiskey)	300	
Depreciation		
Motor car (CO_2 emissions 125g/km)	500	
Fixtures and equipment	400	
Rates	800	
Charitable donation	105	
Repairs to yard wall (June 2016)	200	
Painting of shop	450	
New cash register (purchased April 2016)	380	
Deposit on new shelving (paid July 2016)	1,000	
New display freezer (purchased August 2016)	600	
Insurance	375	
Insurance on contents of flat	100	
New shelving (purchased August 2016)	1,920	
Payment to self in lieu of rent	2,000	
Sundry expenses	2,250	(28,900)
Loss for year		(310)

Mr Bloggs owns the property, which consists of the shop and the flat above the shop where he and his wife live. He estimates that one-quarter of the heat and light costs relate to the living accommodation.

The motor car cost £14,000 on 1 January 2012. Mr Bloggs has advised you that business mileage accounts for three-quarters of his annual motoring. Note that the main rate WDA in 2011/12 and 2012/13 was 20%.

TWDV brought forward in the main pool at 1 April 2016 is £12,750.

Requirement

Compute:

(a) Joe Bloggs's taxable trading income for 2016/17; and
(b) his capital allowance claim for 2016/17.

Question 5.11

Linda's income for 2016/17 is as follows:

	£
Trading loss y/e 30 September 2016	(60,000)
Salary for 2016/17 tax year	80,000

Requirement

Compute her assessable income for 2016/17.

Question 5.12

Mr Jones's income for 2016/17 is as follows:

	£
Trading profit (loss) y/e 30 June 2016	(30,000)
Salary	50,000
Interest on Government securities	25,000

Mr Jones has possessed the above sources of income for many years. He is single and was born in 1975.

Requirement

Compute his assessable income for 2016/17.

Question 5.13

Mr Fool, who has traded for many years, has the following profits and capital allowance:

	£
Profit y/e 31/12/2016	20,000
Capital allowance entitlement	(37,000)

He also had a balancing charge of £10,000 arising in the year.

Requirement

What is Mr Fool's taxable income (if any) for 2016/17?

Question 5.14

John has been in business for many years and prepares annual accounts to 30 September. He has the following sources of income:

	Tax Year		
	2014/15	**2015/16**	**2016/17**
	£	**£**	**£**
Rents	20,000	30,000	25,000
Interest (gross)	1,000	1,200	1,200
Trading profit/(loss)	30,000	(187,000)	45,000

Requirement

(a) What is John's net income in each period? (Assume he is claiming loss relief as soon as possible.)
(b) Prepare a loss memorandum.

Question 5.15

Jim's only source of income is his travel agency business, which he has carried on for many years. He prepares annual accounts to 30 June. Recent tax-adjusted results are as follows:

	£
Y/e 30/06/2014 tax-adjusted loss	(8,000)
Y/e 30/06/2015 tax-adjusted profit	7,000
Y/e 30/06/2016 tax-adjusted profit	30,000

Requirement
Calculate Jim's taxable income for all years.

Question 5.16

Basil Bond has the following income:

	Tax Year		
	2014/15	**2015/16**	**2016/17**
	£	**£**	**£**
Rents	20,000	30,000	25,000
Interest (gross)	1,000	1,200	1,200
Trading profit (loss) y/e 30/09 in tax year	80,000	(37,000)	45,000

Requirement
Calculate the assessable income for 2014/15 to 2016/17, claiming optimum relief for losses.

Employment Income

6.1   Introduction

In **Chapter 5** we saw how the taxable trading income of a self-employed individual is calculated. Important distinctions exist between the tax treatment of an individual who is an employee versus someone who is operating a business in a self-employed capacity. In this chapter we will look at the key differences and the guidance available to help decide whether an individual is an employee or not.

Employment earnings are generally understood in monetary terms, i.e. as salary or wages received on a weekly or monthly basis, but they can also include benefits or 'perks'. For income tax purposes, such non-monetary benefits must be converted to a cash equivalent. Any income tax computation must also take account of expenses incurred by an employee in the performance of their work and subsequently reimbursed by the employer – there are rules established to decide if such expenses are deductible from employment income. Each of these areas will be looked at in detail in this chapter.

However, first it is important to understand the distinction between general employment income (sometimes referred to as "general earnings") and "specific employment income". The distinction is recognised in the Income Tax (Earnings and Pensions) Act 2003 (ITEPA 2003).

General earnings are an individual's employment earnings plus the cash equivalent of any (taxable) non-monetary benefits. That is, "benefits in kind" or "perquisites" ('perks'). General earnings assessable for income tax include:

■ salary/wages;
■ directors' fees (i.e. income from office holders);
■ bonuses and commission;
■ non-monetary remuneration, i.e. benefits in kind and perquisites, such as:
  ● use of a company vehicle;
  ● provision of rent-free or subsidised accommodation to an employee;
  ● holiday vouchers (say from a local travel agent to pay for employee's summer holiday);
  ● preferential loans;
■ Round sum expense allowances, e.g. where an employer gives an employee £100 extra per month, in addition to their agreed salary, to cover personal expenditure that does not have to be employment related;
■ Payments on commencement of employment, e.g. inducement payments;
■ Payments on termination of employment (subject to possible relief up to £30,000, see **Section 6.4.6**), e.g. non-statutory redundancy payments and ex-gratia payments; and
■ holiday pay, sick pay and maternity/paternity and adoption pay.

Specific employment income includes:

■ payments on termination of employment, such as:
  ● non-statutory redundancy payments;
  ● ex-gratia or compensation payments on retirement or dismissal; and
■ share-related income.

Throughout this chapter reference is made to "net taxable earnings" or "net earnings". The terms are interchangeable and are defined as employment income less any allowable expenses or deductions, e.g. statutory mileage allowances or contributions to registered occupational pension schemes.

The tax treatment of general earnings and specific employment income will be dealt with in greater detail as we work through the chapter, but first we need to understand the basis of assessment – what income is assessed, and when and how it is assessed.

6.2   Employment Status

The distinction between an **employee** and a **self-employed** person is not set out in tax legislation. Whether an individual is employed or self-employed is an important question for tax purposes as there are many differences in the way in which they are taxed.

Employees are taxed under the Pay As You Earn (PAYE) system with income tax and Class 1 National Insurance contributions (NICs) being deducted from payments made to them. Class 1 NICs are also payable by their employers. By contrast, the self-employed pay income tax and Class 4 NICs directly to HMRC under self-assessment and they are also liable to Class 2 NICs. (See **Chapter 10** in relation to the PAYE system generally, and **Section 10.5** for NICs.)

Some important consequences that arise from the above are:

1. the NIC liability of a self-employed individual is much lower than that of an employee (especially if the employer's liability is also taken into account);
2. the rules allowing tax relief for expenses are generally more relaxed for the self-employed – expenses incurred by the self-employed are allowable business expenses when they are incurred "wholly and exclusively" for the purposes of the trade, whereas employees can only obtain tax relief for expenses that are incurred "wholly, exclusively and necessarily" in the performance of their employment duties;
3. the self-employed have a cash-flow advantage in the timing of their payments compared with employees who are taxed at source (either weekly or monthly); and
4. if there has been an incorrect classification, the employer may find that he has additional income tax, NIC, penalties and interest to pay.

6.2.1   *Contract of Service versus Contract for Service*

As mentioned, there is no legislation to distinguish between employment and self-employment, but numerous cases decided in the courts provide guidance as to the indicating factors. Case law has determined that an employee is a person who has a **contract of service** with his employer; a self-employed person will provide services under a **contract for services**. A contract can be written, oral, implied or a combination of these.

Sometimes, the distinction between an employee and a self-employed person is not entirely clear, and accordingly the issue has been the subject of a number of cases. Initially, one should try to establish the terms and conditions of the engagement, which can normally be determined from the contract between the person and the client or employer. Next, any other relevant facts should be considered. No one single factor is decisive in itself; it is necessary to look at the circumstances as a whole. Where the evidence is evenly balanced, the intention of the parties may then decide the issue. HMRC provides an online tool, the Employment Status Indicator (ESI), to check the employment status of an individual or a group of workers (see www.gov.uk/guidance/employment-status-indicator). If used correctly, HMRC will now recognise the decision given by this online tool.

From case law, the main factors to be taken into account in determining whether a person is an employee or self-employed are:

1. **The terms of the contract**   If, under the terms of the contract the individual providing the service is entitled to holiday pay, sick pay, pension entitlements, company car or other benefits, they are more likely to be an employee than self-employed. If the contract provides that the individual is required to work fixed hours on particular days, then they are more likely to be an employee, although this is not always the case.
2. **The degree of integration of the individual into the organisation to which their services are provided**   The greater the degree of integration into the organisation, the more likely the person is to be regarded as an employee.
3. **Whether the individual can subcontract the work**   If the individual is free to hire others to undertake the work, and under terms that they have set, this is more indicative of self-employed rather than employee status.
4. **Whether the individual provides his own equipment**   If the individual provides their own equipment to carry out the work, this is also indicative of self-employed rather than employee status.
5. **The extent of control exercised over the individual**   Generally, a self-employed person will have more control in terms of how, when and where the work is to be carried out than an employee would.

6.   **The degree of responsibility for investment and management**   A person who is responsible for running a business, who uses their own capital and who is responsible for determining the running and expansion of a business, is clearly a self-employed person.

7.   **The degree of financial risk taken**   Individuals who risk their own money (for example by buying assets, bearing their running costs, paying for overheads and large quantities of materials) are more likely to be self-employed. Financial risk could also take the form of quoting a fixed price for a job, with the consequent risk of bearing the additional costs of unforeseen circumstances. However, there must be a real risk of financial loss to be considered self-employed.

8.   **Opportunity to profit from sound management**   A person whose profit or loss depends on his capacity to reduce overheads and organise his work effectively is likely to be self-employed.

To determine between employment and self-employment, the following questions can be considered:

■   Is there a mutual obligation between the parties to offer and accept work? If there is an obligation, then this indicates employment.

■   Has the person been integrated into the business, e.g. own desk, own e-mail address, wears company uniform, etc.? A 'yes' to this question would indicate employment.

■   What control is placed over the activities of the individual, e.g. working hours, do they have to report back to a manager on a daily basis, is the work reviewed, is the individual told where to work and what work to undertake, etc.? A high level of control indicates employment.

■   What equipment does the individual require to carry out the activities and do they supply these themselves? If an individual's own equipment is used then this would suggest self-employment.

■   What financial risk is undertaken by the individual should a job overrun or be performed poorly? Will the individual have to suffer the financial loss in remedying this work? Also, does the individual have their own insurance? A higher financial risk indicates self-employment.

■   How many paymasters does the individual have, e.g. does the individual supply their services to a number of different persons? A higher number of paymasters would indicate self-employment.

■   Is the individual able to provide a substitute should they not be able to attend and undertake the work themselves, e.g. are they able to arrange another subcontractor or are they able to arrange for an employee who works for them to undertake the work? If 'yes', this indicates self-employment.

6.3   Basis of Assessment of Employment Income

There are three main determinants in assessing how an individual's employment income is treated for income tax purposes:

1.   residency status;
2.   employment status; and
3.   nature of the earnings.

The relevance of an individual's employment status has been discussed above and, as we have seen, employment income can be divided into general earnings and specific employment income. Different rules apply to the taxation of each. In addition, the various types of general earnings can also have different rules.

6.3.1   Residency Status

As discussed in **Chapter 3**, an individual's residency status can be either UK resident and UK domiciled, UK resident but non-UK domiciled or non-UK resident. Establishing an individual's residency status is the first step in assessing their liability to income tax. In addition, a UK resident and domiciled individual may have an employment that is based overseas; hence it would be taxed overseas. Such overseas employment income may also be subject to UK taxation (see **Section 6.3.4**).

6.3.2   General Employment Income

A **UK tax resident individual's general earnings**, excluding non-monetary remuneration (benefits in kind), are taxed in **the year of receipt, i.e. when the income is "received"**. Assessment is therefore on the "arising basis", i.e. in the tax year in which the income is earned; this is also sometimes referred to as the "receipts basis".

General earnings are treated as "received" on the earlier of:

- the date the payment is actually paid; or
- the date the employee becomes entitled to the payment.

For example, an individual is due to receive a cash bonus for their performance in 2016/17. If the bonus is paid on 20 May 2017 it will be treated as being received in 2017/18 for income tax purposes.

Directors' General Earnings

In the case of directors, general earnings are "received" on either the earlier of the dates as above, or on the earlier of:

- the date the director's remuneration is credited in the company's accounts; or
- the end of the accounting period during which the director's remuneration is determined; or
- the date the director's remuneration is determined, if that is after the end of the accounting period.

Benefits in Kind

Non-monetary remuneration, i.e. benefits in kind, is "received" in the **tax year in which it is provided to the employee**. However, as we will see shortly, a monetary value needs to be calculated. These rules will be considered later in this chapter.

> **Example 6.1**
> Sally is a director of Tully Ltd. In 2016/17 she receives a salary of £55,000. In addition, she is provided with a company car, the monetary value of which is £6,500. Due to her strong sales performance, the board of directors at a meeting on 1 April 2017 decide that Sally should receive a bonus of £12,000 for the year ended 31 January 2017. Sally's bonus was credited to the accounts of Tully Ltd on 2 April 2017, but she did not receive the bonus until 1 May 2017.
>
> Sally's taxable employment income for 2016/17 is £73,500. Sally's bonus is determined by the board of directors on 1 April 2017 (i.e. in the 2016/17 tax year); hence it forms part of her taxable employment income for 2016/17.

Pensions and Social Security Benefits

Those social security benefits, including the State pension, that are taxable are assessed on the total amount received (or accrued) in the tax year, irrespective of the date when the payment is received.

6.3.3 Specific Employment Income

Specific employment income, for example payments on termination of employment and share-related income, is subject to special taxation rules. These particular areas will be considered in more detail in **Section 6.4** when we look at the computation of taxable employment income.

6.3.4 Overseas Employment Income

Overseas employment income arises where the duties of employment are performed outside of the UK, whether wholly or partly. The basis of assessment of this overseas income will depend on the residency status of the individual.

1. If the individual is UK resident and UK domiciled – all employment income is taxable (on the arising/receipts basis). It does not matter where the duties of employment are carried out.
2. If the individual is UK resident but non-UK domiciled – the overseas earnings portion of the income **may** be taxed on the remittance basis (see **Section 3.5**). The availability of the remittance basis will depend on factors such as whether the employer is a foreign employer and the residence status of the individual in the previous five tax years.
3. If the individual is non-UK resident – only the UK portion of the income is taxable (on the arising/receipts basis); overseas earnings are not taxable in the UK.

This information is summarised in **Table 6.1**.

TABLE 6.1: OVERSEAS EMPLOYMENT INCOME

Residency status	Duties performed wholly or partly in the UK		Duties performed wholly outside the UK
	In the UK	*Outside the UK*	
UK resident and domiciled	Taxable on a receipts/arising basis	Taxable on a receipts/arising basis	Taxable on a receipts/arising basis
UK resident but non-UK domiciled	Taxable on a receipts/arising basis	Taxable on a receipts/arising basis unless remittance basis (automatic or claimed)	Taxable on a receipts/arising basis unless remittance basis (automatic or claimed)
Non-UK resident	Taxable on a receipts/arising basis	Not taxable	Not taxable

Before we move on to the next stage, try **Question 6.1** at the end of this chapter.

Having outlined the basic rules around what, when and how employment income is assessed for income tax purposes, we will now look at the computation of taxable employment income.

6.4 Computation of Taxable Employment Income

In simple terms, an individual's general earnings – the salary or wage they are paid, plus any bonus, commission or lump sum that they may have received – is subject to income tax on an arising/receipts basis, i.e. in the year it was received.

This general rule applies for most individuals in ordinary circumstances; however there are particular types of earnings or circumstances that require clarification on the terms of their treatment.

6.4.1 General Earnings: Tax Treatment of Lump Sum Payments

Lump sum payments fall under the "general earnings" category, and as such are taxed on the arising/receipts basis. There are a variety of lump sum payments, the terms of which need to be understood.

Restrictive Covenant Payment
A restrictive covenant is a lump sum payment made in return for an undertaking by an employee to restrict their conduct or activity in some way. For example, an employee may agree to not set up in competition for a certain length of time or to not behave in any manner that would be detrimental to the employer's (or former employer's) business. Such payments are fully taxable as general earnings.

Commencement or Inducement Payments
Payments made to an individual as an incentive to take up an employment, often known as 'golden hellos' or 'golden handcuffs', are generally treated as **advance pay** for future services of employment and are therefore taxable as general earnings.

A payment by one employer to induce an employee to take up employment with another employer is also taxable in full. The case of *Shilton v. Wilmshurst* (1991) involved a taxpayer who was transferred from one football club to another. He was paid £75,000 to persuade him to move. It was held that this payment was taxable as general earnings.

"Gardening Leave"
If a payment is made to an employee where notice has been given but not worked, the employee continues to be employed until the end of the notice period and the payment is taxable as general earnings.

6.4.2 General Earnings: Allowable Deductions from Employment Income

In order for an expense to be deductible from an employee's or director's employment income, it must be shown that it was incurred for "qualifying travel" or "wholly, exclusively and necessarily in performing the duties of the office or employment". The latter test is extremely difficult to satisfy in practice as:

1. the employee or director must be necessarily obliged to incur the expense;
2. the expense must be wholly, exclusively and necessarily incurred; and
3. the expense must be incurred in the actual performance of the duties.

It should be noted that all three criteria must be satisfied. The difficulty with this was expressed by Judge Vaisey, in *Lomax v. Newton* (1953), when he observed:

"An expenditure may be necessary for the holder of an office without being necessary to him in the performance of the duties of that office: It may be necessary in the performance of those duties without being exclusively referable to those duties: It may perhaps be both necessarily and exclusively and still not be wholly so referable. The words are indeed stringent and exacting".

Consequently, in *Smith v. Abbott* (1994), it was decided that journalists cannot claim a deduction for buying newspapers or journals to keep themselves informed as they merely prepare them to perform their duties better. They are not costs earned "wholly, exclusively and necessarily" for the performance of their duties.

Qualifying Travel Expenses
Income tax relief is not available for an employee's normal commuting costs, i.e. those incurred in travelling between the workplace and home. However, employees are entitled to relief for travel

expenses, at full cost, incurred while travelling in the performance of their duties or to or from a place they have to attend in the performance of their duties (so long as their attendance at a particular workplace does not last, or is not expected to last, more than 24 months). Tax relief is available for travel accommodation and subsistence expenses incurred by an employee who is working at a temporary workplace on a secondment expected to last up to 24 months.

Other Allowable Deductions

Certain other expenditure is specifically deductible in computing net taxable earning:

- Contributions to registered occupational pension schemes.
- Subscriptions to professional bodies (HMRC-approved) if relevant to duties.
- Certain liability costs relating to the employment and insurance against them.
- Payroll giving, i.e. payments to charity through the payroll deductions scheme.
- Mileage allowance relief, i.e. where an employee uses his or her own car for business travel.

Mileage Allowance Relief

Where an employee uses their own private car for business purposes, the employer can pay approved mileage allowance payments (AMAPs) up to prescribed limits. The rates per mile that can be claimed are shown **Table 6.2**.

TABLE 6.2: MILEAGE ALLOWANCE RELIEF RATES

Vehicle	Flat rate per mile
Cars and goods vehicles: first 10,000 business miles	45p
Cars and goods vehicles: after 10,000 business miles	25p
Motorcycles	24p

Payments may be made tax-free by the employer and are not taxable in the hands of the employee. No Form P11D (see below for further details) is required in relation to such payments. If the employer's policy is to pay less, the employee may claim tax relief up to that level. If employers pay in excess of these levels, the excess is a taxable benefit (Form P11D).

Round Sum Expense Allowance

In general, a round sum expense allowance advanced to an employee to be disbursed at their discretion is regarded as taxable general earnings. The employee can then make a claim for deduction against their general earnings in respect of actual expenses incurred in the performance of their duties, including capital allowances (for example, where an employee must buy a computer for the purpose of performing their employment duties, but the employer does not reimburse them for the cost of the computer.

Expenses not Reimbursed by Employer

If an employee incurs legitimate allowable expenses, i.e. those which were incurred wholly, exclusively and necessarily in the performance of their employment duties, for which they are not reimbursed by their employer, tax relief can still be available. Some examples of this may be fees and subscriptions to professional bodies, work-related books, allowable training and travel expenditure (see **Section 6.4.4** for further details).

Administration Issues regarding Expense Payments to Employees

Until 5 April 2016, where an employee or director received payment to cover expenses or was reimbursed for expenses that were incurred, then these were treated as the employee's/director's general earnings. This was the case irrespective of whether the payment was made by way of a round sum allowance or on foot of the submission of an expenses claim.

The employee could then generally make a claim for tax relief in respect of expenses which had been incurred "**wholly, exclusively and necessarily" in the performance of their duties**. In many situations, and to ease the overall administrative burden, the employer would have applied for a "dispensation" from HMRC so as to avoid having to record these types of business expenses on Form P11D by 6 July the following tax year (2015/16, due by 6 July 2016) and to save the employee from having to claim the relief. Note that, in this latter situation, the employer has to maintain adequate records to demonstrate to HMRC that the expenses meet the very broad test laid down in the legislation.

From 6 April 2016, the dispensation regime will be replaced with an exemption for paid and reimbursed expenses. No further dispensations can be applied for from this date. Expenses that are covered by an exemption include: business travel; phone bills; business entertainment expenses; uniforms and tools for work.

To qualify for an exemption, the employer must be either:

1. paying a flat rate to an employee as part of their earnings – this must be either a benchmark rate or a special ('bespoke') rate approved by HMRC; or
2. paying back the employee's actual costs

There is no need to apply for an exemption if the employer is paying HMRC's benchmark rates for allowable expenses. An exemption only needs to be applied for if an employer wants to pay bespoke rates to employees. Where bespoke rates are applied for, HMRC will require evidence from the employer that the bespoke rates are based on employees' actual expenses before they will provide the exemption.

If an employer had dispensation from HMRC that was agreed between 6 April 2011 and 5 April 2016, the employer should have applied to HMRC to carry on using this dispensation post-5 April 2016.

An employer can only use the bespoke rates for up to five years from the date they were agreed and an employer must have a system in place to check payments made at the benchmark or bespoke rates. Employees are not allowed to check their own expenses. The employer needs to do this to make sure the expenses are legitimate.

6.4.3   General Earnings: Tax Treatment of Benefits in Kind

As noted previously, benefits in kind (BIK) are treated as received in the tax year in which they are provided.

General Rule

Some expense payments and benefits are treated as taxable remuneration. The main benefits that are taxable on all employees and directors include:

- non-exempt vouchers (e.g. gift vouchers, travel season tickets) – taxed on cost of providing;
- loans written off;
- living accommodation;
- costs charged to the employer's credit card for personal (i.e. non-business) expenditure;
- assets transferred by employer at below market value;
- gifts;
- payments made on the employee's behalf;

- payments made in respect of expenses payments other than those wholly for business purposes;
- cars/vans made available by the employer for private use;
- car fuel supplied for private motoring;
- private medical insurance;
- interest-free or low-interest loans;
- goods or services provided at less than their full cost;
- use of the employer's assets; and
- taxable excess mileage allowance.

Benefits provided to an individual (including his or her family or household members) are taxed on the cash equivalent of the benefit.

The cash equivalent is generally the cost to the employer of providing the benefit, less any amounts made good by the employee. Note, however, that there are special rules for valuing certain benefits, such as share options, company cars, fuel for private use in company cars, living accommodation, etc.

If benefits are provided in-house, the value for tax purposes is generally the additional marginal cost to the employer.

Non-taxable payments and benefits include:

- Free car-parking facilities at or near the place of work.
- Work bus/minibus with seating capacity of nine or more.
- Mobile telephones (restricted to business mobile and only one per employee) and can include smartphones.
- Free canteen meals (provided they are open to all staff).
- Childcare facilities (if provided by employer). Otherwise up to £55 a week of childcare vouchers are tax-free (must be available to all employees and be a regulated/approved childcarer). The tax-free amount is £55 for basic rate taxpayers, £28 per week for higher rate taxpayers and £25 per week for additional rate taxpayers.
- Sporting facilities provided in-house (must be offered to all employees).
- Bicycles or cycle safety equipment for travel to/from work (available to all employees).
- Gifts of goods from third parties not costing more than £250 (including VAT) per year from any one donor.
- Qualifying relocation/removal expenses and benefits up to £8,000 per annum.
- Job-related accommodation – living accommodation provided in the performance of employee's duties or due to a threat to the employee's security.
- Christmas and other parties, dinners, etc., provided the total cost to the employer for each person attending is not more than £150 per year, including VAT.
- Late-night taxis in certain circumstances.
- Contributions by employer to an approved occupational scheme or to an employee's personal pension scheme.
- Non-cash long-service and suggestion scheme awards (conditions apply).
- Retraining expenses and courses to help an employee to find another post.
- Emergency vehicles for employees required to take vehicles home in order to respond quickly to emergencies when on-call.
- Vans provided by the employer for business travel, provided any private use is insignificant.
- Personal incidental expenses of employee while working away from home of up to £5 per night if in the UK (£10 per night if abroad).
- Certain other benefits (e.g. office supplies) provided for the employee's work, where private use is insignificant.

- Awards under staff suggestion schemes.
- A health screening assessment or medical check provided by an employer.
- Cheap loans that do not exceed £10,000 **at any time in** the tax year.
- Employer contributions towards additional household costs incurred by an employee who works partly at home. Payments up to £4/week (£18 per month for employees paid monthly) may be made without supporting evidence.

Further details on some of the above taxable and non-taxable benefits are outlined below.

Provision of Living Accommodation

In general, if an employee is provided with free or subsidised living accommodation by their employer, the employee is liable to income tax to the value of the accommodation. The "value" of the accommodation depends on whether it is **owned** by the employer, or whether it is **rented** by the employer for use by the employee.

Where the accommodation is rented, the annual value charge is the **higher** of:

- the rent paid by the employer, or
- the annual value of the property (i.e. its rateable value),

less any sum paid by the employee.

Where the property is **owned by the employer**, the annual value charge is the rent that would have been payable if the premises had been let at an amount equal to its annual value.

An additional charge may also apply where the "cost of providing accommodation" exceeds £75,000. The "cost of providing" the accommodation is the aggregate of the purchase cost of the property and the cost of any improvements made **before** the start of the tax year. The additional charge is calculated as:

1. the excess cost of providing the accommodation over £75,000, multiplied by the official rate of interest (currently 3%), less
2. the amount by which any rent paid by the employee exceeds the annual value.

Example 6.2

Harry, a senior manager, is provided with a house by his employer by reason of his employment. He is required to pay a rental value of £1,500 per annum. The house cost his employer £175,000 in January 2011. The gross rating value of the property is £1,000 per annum. Harry occupies the property throughout the tax year 2016/17 and we shall assume an official rate of interest of 3%.

The benefit in kind assessable on Harry will be as follows:

No annual value charge arises because the annual rental value of £1,500 payable by Harry is more than the annual rating value of £1,000.

However, one must consider the potential additional charge as the cost of providing the accommodation exceeds £75,000.

	£
Cost of providing accommodation	175,000
Less	(75,000)
Excess	100,000
£100,000 × 3%	3,000
Less: (excess of rent paid over rating value)	(500)
Cash equivalent	2,500

The BIK value is £2,500

If the accommodation is not provided for the whole of the tax year, then the value (whether calculated on the rented or owned basis) is pro-rated.

If the property was acquired more than six years before being provided to the employee, then the cost of providing the accommodation is calculated on the "market value" when the accommodation is first provided, plus the cost of subsequent improvements made before the start of the tax year. The market value rule only applies if the actual cost of providing the accommodation (including only those improvements made before the start of the tax year) is in excess of £75,000.

Exemptions

There is an exemption to the benefit where the provision of accommodation is 'job-related' and one of the following applies:

1. it is necessary for the employee to reside in the accommodation (e.g. caretaker, clergy);
2. it is customary for the employee to be provided with accommodation (e.g. pub landlord); or
3. the accommodation is provided by reason of security (e.g. Government minister, police officer).

Directors of a company do not qualify for the exemption under categories 1 and 2 unless:

- they have no "material interest" (broadly more than 5% of the ordinary share capital) in the company, and
- they are a "full-time working director" or the company is non-profit-making or is a charity.

Provision of Accommodation: Related Expenses

In addition to the benefit of the accommodation itself, employees are also liable to income tax on the property's related expenses that are paid by the employer. Related expenses include:

- heating, lighting or cleaning the premises;
- repairing, maintaining or decorating the premises; and
- the provision of furniture (the annual value is 20% of the cost).

The full cost of such ancillary services (excluding structural repairs) is taxable as general earnings.

"Job-related" accommodation, although exempt from the cost of providing the accommodation itself, is still liable to tax on the ancillary services, although it is restricted to a maximum of 10% of the employee's "net earnings".

Provision of Company Vehicles

Company Cars

Where a company car is available for an employee's **private** use (which includes "normal commuting"), the employee is taxable on the value of the benefit.

Since 6 April 2002, the tax liability is calculated based on the car's carbon dioxide (CO_2) emissions and its list price when new. As the table below shows, the lower the car's CO_2 emissions, the lower the rate to be applied.

CO_2 emissions band	Percentage of car's list price taxed
Up to 50g/km	7% of the list price
Between 51–75g/km	11% of the list price
Between 76–94g/km	15% of the list price
Between 95–99g/km	16% of the list price
Above 100g/km	Additional 1% per every 5g/km over (rounded down to nearest multiple of five) Rate is capped at 37% of the list price

There is a 3% supplement for all diesel cars (subject to the 37% cap) and no discounts are available for cars using alternative fuels and technologies.

Where a car has been registered with no CO_2 emission figures (now very rare), including those powered solely by electricity, the rate is now set at 7% (since 6 April 2016).

The value of the benefit is calculated by reference to the "**cash equivalent**" of the company car, **less** amounts made good by the employee to the employer.

If the employee is provided with the car for only part of the particular tax year, the value of the benefit is proportionately reduced. This is also the case if the car is incapable of being used for a period of at least 30 days.

A car's list price is its retail price at first registration, **including** charges for delivery and standard accessories, **plus** the price (including fitting) of all optional accessories supplied when the car was **first provided** to the employee (excluding mobile phones and equipment needed by a disabled employee) plus the price (including fitting) of all optional accessories **fitted after** the car was provided to the employee and costing at least £100 each (excluding mobile phones and equipment needed by a disabled employee; replacement accessories are ignored.)

There is a special rule for classic cars, i.e. those at least 15 years old at the end of the tax year: if the car's market value at year end is over £15,000 and is greater than its list price, then the market value is used instead of the list price. The market value takes account of all accessories.

The list price is reduced by capital contributions made by the employee in that tax year and previous years for the same car up to a maximum of £5,000. These are payments in respect of the price of the car or car accessories.

The benefit in kind is reduced by any payment the user must make for the **private use** of the car. (Note, this is different from the capital contributions element, which reduces the list price of the car.) Also note that payments for insuring the car are ignored and are not taken into account.

Example 6.3

Niall was given a petrol company car by his employer on 1 January 2017. The car has a list price of £30,000 and Niall contributed £5,000 to the cost of the car. The CO_2 emissions of the car are 250g/km and Niall pays his employer £200 per month to be able to use the car for private journeys.

Niall's company car BIK (for three months in 2016/17) is calculated as follows:

List price of car	£30,000
Less: capital contribution (max.)	(£5,000)
	£25,000
£25,000 × 37% × 3/12 =	£2,313
Less: 3 months paid at £200/month	(£600)
2016/17 BIK	£1,713

Fuel Benefit Charge

The company car fuel charge is operated on the same basis as the car benefit charge. The same percentage rate, based on CO_2 emissions, is applied to a single set figure for all cars (currently £22,200; £22,100 in 2015/16) to arrive at the chargeable amount.

Fuel charges are reduced to nil if the employee is required (and actually does) make good all fuel provided for private use, including journeys between home and work (normal commuting). Note that all private fuel costs must be met in order to affect the benefit in kind. For example, if only half of private fuel is met by the employee, the full fuel benefit in kind charge is payable. Contrast this to payments made for private use of a car.

The fuel charge for private fuel provided with company cars is proportionately reduced where an employee stops receiving fuel partway through a year (unless he starts to receive fuel again in the same tax year, then the reduction does not apply). It is also proportionately reduced where a car is not available for any part of the year (provided this is at least 30 consecutive days).

Advisory fuel rates for company cars are produced by HMRC and periodically updated when fuel prices change significantly. These charges can be used by employers to calculate the payment/reimbursement due to employees in respect of business mileage where private fuel is not provided with the company car. The HMRC rates, per mile, from 1 March 2016 are as follows:

Engine Size	Petrol	LPG
1400cc or less	10p	7p
1401cc to 2000cc	12p	8p
Over 2000cc	19p	13p

Engine Size	Diesel
1600cc or less	8p
1601cc to 2000cc	10p
Over 2000cc	11p

Example 6.4

Tim was provided with a new company car costing £15,000 for 2016/17. It is a petrol vehicle with CO_2 emissions of 196 g/km. During the year Tim paid £270 for the private use of the car and £150 towards the fuel. His employer paid insurance of £800, repairs of £320, tax of £180 and all fuel costs. What is the taxable benefit to Tim?

CO_2 emissions of 196g/km, rounded down to 195g/km
Additional 1% for every 5g/km above 95g/km: (195 – 95) = 100/5 = 20%
Taxable percentage: 16% + 20% = 36%

Car: £15,000 × 36%	£5,400
Fuel: £22,200 × 36%	£7,992
	£13,392
Less: contributions for private use	(270)
	£13,122

Note: the £150 payment for fuel by Tim is ignored, as only payments for private use are taken into account. The insurance and repairs costs and the motor tax are not treated as benefits. Therefore, Tim's BIK is £13,122.

Company Vans

Where a company van is made available to an employee for his **private** use, the employee is taxable on a flat-rate benefit charge. The van benefit charge is currently £3,170 per annum (for 2016/17). **For these purposes only, normal commuting is not treated as private use**. Normal commuting means the journey the employee takes between their home and permanent workplace. The van benefit charge covers insurance, servicing, etc.

Note that an **additional** fuel charge of £598 will apply for fuel supplied for unrestricted private use.

The taxable amount is reduced by any payments made by the employee for private use (only if made during the relevant tax year) and is proportionately reduced if the van is not available throughout the whole of the tax year.

Example 6.5

On 6 October 2016, Denis was provided with a company van. His employer also provides him with all fuel for the van.

Denis will have a BIK of:

Van benefit charge	£3,170
Fuel charge	£598
	£3,768
Van and fuel for six months	£1,884

Car and Van Pool Exemption

Where a company car or van is in a "pool", i.e. available for all employees generally, no benefit is assessed on any individual employee. A company car or van is treated as belonging to a pool where:

- it has been made available to, and actually used by, **more than one** employee and is not ordinarily used by any one of the employees to the exclusion of others; **and**
- any private use of the company vehicle by any employee is incidental to its business use; **and**
- it is not normally kept overnight at the home of any of the employees.

Provision of "Preferential Loans"

A "preferential loan" means a loan made by an employer to an employee, a former employee or a prospective employee, or their spouses, in respect of which no interest is payable, or that interest is payable at a rate **lower** than the "specified rate".

It does **not include** any loan made by an employer to an employee where:

- in the course of his trade, on an arm's length basis where normal commercial rates of interest are charged (e.g. a bank employee getting a loan from their employer at the same rate as any other customer); or
- if the total of all beneficial loans made to an individual employee did not exceed £10,000 at any time in the tax year.

The official rate of interest is set each year. The rate for 2016/17 as at 6 April 2016 is 3%.

Calculating the Taxable Benefit

The taxable benefit of a preferential loan is determined by considering the difference between the interest actually paid during the particular tax year and the amount of interest calculated at the official rate.

There are **two alternative ways** of calculating the taxable benefit: the 'average' method or the 'strict' method.

1. The **'average' method** averages the balances at the beginning and end of the tax year (or the dates on which the loan was made and discharged if it were not in existence throughout the tax year) and applies the official rate of interest to this average. If the loan was not in existence throughout the tax year, only the number of complete tax months (from the 6th of the month) for which it existed are taken into account.
2. The **'strict' method** is to compute interest at the official rate (currently 3%) on the actual amount outstanding on a daily basis.

Example 6.6

Tom's employer loans him £7,000 interest-free on 8 June 2016 for personal use. He repays £2,000 on 1 December 2016. The remaining balance is still outstanding at 5 April 2017. The official rate of interest is 3%. What is the taxable benefit of the loan?

Average method

The maximum amount outstanding at commencement of the loan was £7,000.

The maximum amount outstanding at the end of the tax year was £5,000.

The average amount, therefore, is £6,000 ((£7,000 + £5,000)/2).

The number of whole months the loan is outstanding is nine. (Months run from the 6th to the 5th, so the loan was not outstanding for the whole month 6 June–5 July.)

Interest at official rate, i.e. taxable benefit, is £6,000 × 3% × 9/12 mths = £135

Strict method

Period	No. of days	Loan balance	Interest rate	Taxable benefit
8 June 2016 to 1 December 2016	177	£7,000	3%	£102
2 December 2016 to 5 April 2017	126	£5,000	3%	£52
Total				£154

As the strict method gives the higher figure, you would expect HMRC to apply that method.

Tax is charged on the amount written off any loans, whether or not the recipient is still employed and regardless of the amount of the loan written off.

6.4.4 General Earnings: Miscellaneous

Medical Insurance

Medical insurance provided by an employer is a taxable benefit, the taxable amount being the gross premium, i.e. the cost to the employer. However, since 1 January 2015, where an employer pays for recommended medical treatment in order to help an employee return to work and it is less than £500 per year, no BIK is considered to have arisen.

Employee's Subsistence Allowances

Where an employee performs the duties of their employment while temporarily away from their normal place of work or while working abroad on a foreign assignment, the employer may reimburse the employee for actual expenses incurred or, alternatively, may pay the employee a flat-rate subsistence allowance to cover costs incurred by the employee.

Where the employee pays all subsistence expenses and is reimbursed for these expenses by a flat-rate subsistence allowance in line with HMRC guidelines (civil service rates), then such an allowance may be paid **tax-free** by the employer and is not taxable in the hands of the employee, provided HMRC is satisfied that the allowance does no more than reimburse the costs incurred.

Removal/Relocation Expenses

An employer may pay or reimburse, free of tax, certain removal/relocation expenses incurred by an employee in moving house to take up employment. To qualify, the change of residence must satisfy a number of conditions, the most important being that the employee must change his or her only, or main, residence as a result of:

- starting a new employment;
- a change in the duties of the current employment; or
- changing the place where the duties are usually performed.

Expenses that can be reimbursed free of tax are those incurred **directly** as a result of the change of residence and include such items as:

- auctioneer's and solicitor's fees and stamp duty arising from moving house;
- removal of furniture and effects, and insurance on items in transit or in storage;
- storage charges;
- travelling expenses on removal;
- temporary subsistence while looking for accommodation at the new location; and
- temporary living accommodation.

The amount reimbursed or borne by the employer may not exceed expenditure **actually incurred**. There are no reporting requirements or income tax and NICs on amounts up to £8,000.
Qualifying expenses include the following:

- Disposal expenses and benefits – such as legal and advertising expenses in connection with the disposal of an accommodation, penalty for redemption of mortgage, estate agent's fees, disconnection of utilities, etc.
- Acquisition expenses and benefits – such as legal expenses, loan fees and mortgage insurance on new accommodation, stamp duty, connection of utilities, etc.
- Transportation of domestic belongings.
- Travelling and subsistence expenses and benefits – such as for temporary visits to new residence before relocation, travel from old residence to new.
- Bridging loan expenses and beneficial bridging loans – such as relief on any charge to interest at the official rate.
- Expenses in respect of the new residence – replacement of domestic items, etc.

Canteen Meals
Where free or subsidised meals in staff canteens/or at the workplace are provided and **available to all employees**, a taxable benefit **does not** arise. If the facility is not available to all employees, the running costs of the canteen must be apportioned between those employees entitled to use the canteen and the apportioned costs are a taxable benefit for those employees.

Childcare and Childcare Vouchers
A BIK exemption applies to the provision of qualifying childcare contracted by the employer, and on employer-provided childcare vouchers. An employee can receive vouchers for registered or approved childcare worth up to £55 per week free of income tax and NICs, provided certain conditions are met.

Finance Act 2011 introduced measures for individuals joining the scheme after 9 April 2011 that mean higher rate and additional rate taxpayers only receive the same tax relief as a basic rate taxpayer. Higher rate taxpayers can receive up to £28 per week and additional rate taxpayers up to £25 per week.

> **Example 6.7**
> Emma is an employee and earns £600 (gross) per week. She is married with one child. Emma is a basic rate taxpayer (assuming this is her only income).
>
> Emma could ask her employer to split her salary into cash and childcare vouchers. That is, she could be taxed on £545 gross pay per week, plus £55 of childcare vouchers. On this basis, Emma would only pay income tax at 20% and NICs on £545. The childcare vouchers can be received free of income tax and NICs.

From April 2018, no new entrants will be able to join the childcare vouchers scheme.

From 2017, a new scheme, Tax-Free Childcare, will be launched. At the time of writing, no specific date had been given by the Government for implementation of the scheme. Under the new scheme, eligible families will get 20% of their annual childcare costs (up to certain limits) paid for by the Government. For example, if the childcare cost for one child is £10,000 per annum, the Government will contribute £2,000 towards the cost.

Professional Subscriptions
Where an employer pays a subscription to a professional body on behalf of an employee, or reimburses the employee who has paid such a subscription, a taxable benefit **does not arise**, providing membership of that professional institute is **relevant** to the business of the employer. Membership of a professional body is regarded as relevant where:

- it is **necessary** for the performance of the employee's or director's present or prospective duties of the office or employment; or
- it **facilitates** the acquisition of knowledge, which is **necessary** for, or directly related to, the performance of the duties of the office or employment.

Course or Exam Fees
Where an employer pays or reimburses an employee for the cost of any course or exam fee that is relevant, necessary or directly related to the employee's duties (or prospective duties), this is not treated as a taxable benefit.

Staff Suggestion Schemes
Awards made under most staff suggestion schemes are tax-free. For example, financial rewards offered by an employer to encourage staff members to suggest ways to reduce costs, improve efficiency, add revenue and so on can be given tax-free. The scheme must be available to all employees and the maximum award is £5,000.

Long-service Awards
A taxable benefit will **not arise** in respect of long-service awards where the following conditions are satisfied:
- the award is made as a testimonial to mark long service of **not less** than 20 years;
- the award takes the form of a tangible article of reasonable cost;
- the cost does **not exceed £50 for each year of service**; and
- no similar award has been made to the recipient within the previous 10 years.

This treatment **does not apply** to awards made in cash or in the form of vouchers, bonds, etc. Such awards are fully taxable.

Use of Employer's Assets

Tax is chargeable on the annual rental value of land and for other assets (apart from those specifically excluded above) at **20% of the market value when they are first provided or the rental charge to the employer, if higher**. If provided for only part of a year, then there is a need to time-apportion. The benefit is reduced by any contributions made by the employee that are exempt BIK. There is a special rule for bicycles, which are exempt benefits.

Assets given to Employees

If the asset given is new, tax is chargeable on the cost to the employer (market value in the case of lower paid employees). If it is a used asset, tax is chargeable on the greater of:

(i)   the market value at the date of transfer less the price paid by the employee; or
(ii) the market value when first provided to the employee **less** amounts charged to tax previously.

6.4.5   General Earnings: State Pension and Social Security Benefits

The main **taxable** social security benefits are:

- Bereavement allowance
- Widow's pension, paid to widows whose entitlement arose pre-9 April 2001 (thereafter replaced by bereavement allowance)
- Carer's allowance
- Incapacity benefit (except first 28 weeks)
- Jobseeker's allowance
- State pension
- Statutory adoption pay (see **Section 6.5**)
- Statutory maternity pay and statutory paternity pay (see **Section 6.5**)
- Statutory sick pay (see **Section 6.5**)
- Widowed parent's allowance
- Contributions-based employment and support allowance
- Pensions payable under the Industrial Death Benefit Scheme
- Graduated retirement benefit.

The main **non-taxable** social security benefits are:

- Attendance allowance
- Child benefit (if adjusted net income is less than £50,000, see note below)
- Guardian's allowance
- Back to work bonus
- Income support (unless paid to individuals who are striking or involved in a trade dispute, which is taxable)
- Incapacity benefit (short-term, first 28 weeks)
- Maternity allowance (where statutory maternity pay (SMP) is not available)
- Severe disablement allowance
- Disability living allowance
- Working tax credit and child tax credit
- Winter fuel payment
- Pensioner's Christmas bonus
- Universal tax credit.

With regard to child benefit, legislation was introduced in Finance Act 2012 whereby recipients of child benefit who have (or their partner has) "adjusted net income" of greater than £50,000 in a tax year, are liable to income tax on the child benefit income. That is, the child benefit income is included as general earnings when calculating the income tax liability. Adjusted net income is defined in the same way as the restriction of the personal allowance (see **Chapter 2**).

The tax liability depends on the actual income and is split into two bands:

1. Adjusted net income between £50,000 and £60,000 – the income tax rate is 1% of the child benefit award for each £100 of income greater than £50,000.
2. Adjusted net income greater than £60,000 – the income tax is a rate equal to the amount of child benefit received, i.e. the child benefit is effectively lost.

Example 6.8

An individual's adjusted net income is £55,000 and they are in receipt of child benefit of £400.

Income over £50,000 = £5,000
Income tax rate: £5,000/£100 = 50%
Income tax due: 50% × £400 = £200

If the individual's adjusted net income had been £70,000, the tax charge would have been equal to the child benefit and the child benefit would be lost in full.

If both the individual and their partner have adjusted net income greater than £50,000, then the partner with the higher income is the one liable.

Individuals claiming child benefit can decide not to receive the benefit if they (or their partner) do not wish to pay the income tax charge.

6.4.6 Specific Employment Income

Specific employment income (as opposed to "general earnings" discussed above) includes payments on the termination of employment and share-related income.

Specific Employment Income: Tax Treatment of Termination Payments

Lump sum payments made on the termination of employment, often known as 'golden handshakes', are taxable under the normal general employment income rules, where they are considered as payment for employment services rendered (e.g. payments for work carried out prior to termination or a terminal bonus based on work carried out for employer as an employee). Where the payment does not fall within those general rules, it is taxable under special rules, subject to an exemption for the first £30,000 (section 401 ITEPA 2003), i.e. specific employment income.

Generally, where the employee is contractually entitled to receive the payment (whether implicit (by custom or practice) or explicit (actual written documentation)), it is taxable under PAYE as earnings. Where a payment is made by way of compensation for breach of the employment contract, it falls under the special rules (i.e. first £30,000 exemption).

Example 6.9

Nuala Casey, a director of a company, was discharged from her employment contract and received £90,000 compensation for breach of contract, i.e. it was not a contractual entitlement.

As Ms Casey's compensation payment was entirely ex-gratia, the £30,000 exemption is available. Therefore income tax would only be liable on £60,000 of the payment.

Payment in Lieu of Notice and Compensation for Loss of Office

If an employer is contractually obliged to make a payment where due notice is not given, then the payment arises under the contract and is taxable as general employment income in the normal way. If the contract provides only for notice to be given, i.e. there is no associated payment, failure to give notice is a breach of contract and the payment is thus compensation for breach of contract rather than arising under the contract. In this case the payment would be taxable under the 'special rules' (£30,000 exemption), provided that it was not the employer's normal practice to make such payments and there was no understanding or expectation that such a payment would in fact be made.

Redundancy Payments

Payments in respect of genuine redundancy (where the post originally held no longer exists, etc.) are taxable under the "special rules" and the first £30,000, including any statutory redundancy, is exempt from income tax. As noted before, although statutory redundancy itself is not taxable, it does use part of the exempt £30,000 threshold.

Exempt Payments

Certain termination payments may be completely exempt (and not just up to the £30,000 limit). Such payments include payments on termination of employment, on the accidental death of the employee or on account of injury or disability. Lump sum payments to an approved pension scheme relating to employment, which included an element of foreign service, may be wholly or partly exempt, depending on the period and timing of the overseas service.

Example 6.10

Helena was made redundant in May 2015. She received £5,000 statutory redundancy pay and £18,000, under the terms of her contract, as payment in lieu of notice (PILON). She also received £36,000 as compensation for loss of office; this was not a contractual entitlement.

Confirm the treatment of each type of income and calculate the total taxable income.

1. The statutory redundancy payment of £5,000 is exempt.
2. The PILON of £18,000, a contractual payment, is fully taxable.
3. The compensation for loss of office is entirely ex-gratia, meaning that the £30,000 exemption is available – although it will be reduced by the statutory redundancy payment.

Total taxable income is:

	£	£	£
PILON			18,000
Compensation for loss of office	£36,000		
Less: exemption	£30,000		
Less: statutory redundancy	(£5,000)	(25,000)	
		11,000	11,000
			29,000

Payments and other benefits provided in connection with the termination of employment (or a change of terms of employment) are taxable in the year in which they are **received**. For this purpose, "received" means when it is paid or when the recipient becomes entitled to it (for cash payments) or when it is used or enjoyed (for non-cash benefits). Non-cash benefits are taxed by reason of their cash equivalent.

HMRC regards payments notionally made as compensation for loss of office, but which are made on retirement or death (not accidental death, which is exempt), as lump sum payments under the unapproved pension scheme regime and, therefore, taxable in full. An employee may, on leaving or at some later date, accept a limitation on his future conduct in return for a payment (restrictive covenant). In these circumstances, the payment is taxable in full as general earnings.

However, the provision of counselling for unemployment or to help an employee leaving to find new employment or self-employment is not a taxable benefit and nor is the reimbursement of the cost of such counselling.

It should be noted that a payment accepted as full and final settlement of any claims the employee may have against the employer may not be automatically taxable. In the case of *Mairs v. Haughey* (1993), it was held that a payment to an employee as compensation for the loss of rights under a redundancy scheme was not taxable. Also, a payment to compensate for loss of rights under a share option scheme, following a management buyout of the subsidiary for whom the employee worked, was held not to be taxable (*Wilcock v. Eve* (1994)).

If the termination package is a partly exempt one and exceeds £30,000, then the exempt limit is allocated to earlier benefits and payments. In any particular year the exemption is allocated to cash payments before non-cash payments.

Unfair dismissal payments are eligible for the £30,000 exemption. Employees have an obligation to report termination settlements to HMRC by 6 July following the end of the tax year. No report is required if the settlement is entirely cash.

Specific Employment Income: Share-related Income

Shares and share options are a way of remunerating, rewarding or incentivising employees and directors. Share options arise when employees or directors are granted an option to acquire shares in their employer's company or its parent company, at a fixed price, at some time in the future.

The ownership of shares in an employing company may lead to an income tax liability in the following circumstances:

1. If, while the director or employee has a beneficial interest in the shares, a "**chargeable event**" occurs (e.g. when the rights associated with the shares increase), then there is a charge on the increase in the value of the interest caused by the chargeable event as specific employment income.
2. If an employee, having obtained shares by reason of his being an employee or director, receives any special benefit as a result of owning the shares, he is taxable on the benefit as specific employment income, unless certain conditions apply.
3. If a director or employee receives shares that may be **forfeited** (and the forfeiture relates to the first five years from the date the shares were awarded), there is no income tax charge when the shares are acquired (a different treatment applies if the date of forfeiture is five years or more from the date of award). There is, however, an income tax charge on the earlier of when the risk of forfeiture is lifted or when the shares are sold. The specific employment income is the difference between the market value of the shares less the cost of the shares.
4. If shares received as a result of employment are subsequently **converted** to shares of another class, then there may be an income tax charge on conversion.

Share Schemes

When directors and employees acquire shares (and securities) in their employing company, income tax may be chargeable as specific employment income, for example, where:

- a director or an employee is given shares, or is sold shares for less than their market value, the **employee is liable to tax on the difference between the market value and the amount (if any) which the individual paid for the shares**; or
- the employee has an option to acquire shares – the employee is liable to tax on the difference between the market value of the shares when the option is exercised and the cost of the shares when the option is granted (plus any amount paid for the shares).

Example 6.11

Malcolm works for Sparks plc. He is granted a share option in consideration of services in his employment at a time when the shares are worth £1 per share. The option entitles Malcolm to acquire 1,000 shares at £2 per share. Four years later Malcolm exercises the option, pays £2,000 and acquires 1,000 shares which, at the time he acquires them, have a market value of £5,000 (£5 per share).

There is no liability to income tax in respect of the grant. However, Malcolm will be subject to income tax on £3,000 when the option is exercised. That is, he will be liable to tax on the difference between the market value of the shares when the option is exercised (£5,000) and the cost of the shares to him (£2,000).

To minimise or avoid the liability to income tax, there are a range of tax-efficient schemes under which an employer may be able to give employees a stake in the business.

SAYE (Save As You Earn) Option Scheme

In an SAYE option scheme, an employer enables employees to make regular monthly investments into special bank or building society accounts called "sharesave accounts". The main features of the scheme are as follows:

- Employees can save a fixed monthly amount of between £5 and £500.
- The investments are made for three or five years and a tax-free bonus is added to the account by way of interest.
- At the withdrawal date, the employee can take the money in cash or can choose to buy ordinary shares in the employing company under options granted when the employee started to save. The price that will have to be paid to exercise the options is fixed from the start and the option price must be at least 80% of the market value of the shares at the date the option is granted.
- There is no income tax charge on the purchase of the shares using the employee's savings.
- The scheme must be open to all employees and all full-time directors on similar terms. Part-time directors may be included or excluded. Discretionary criteria may be imposed.

Example 6.12

Sinead works for Spencer plc and is offered the opportunity to take part in its HMRC-approved SAYE option scheme. The share price was £4.25 at the time the SAYE scheme launched and the maximum discount of 20% was applied, so the option price was set at £3.40.

Sinead decides to save £8.50 a week and after three years in the SAYE scheme she has saved £1,224. She has the opportunity to buy Spencer plc shares at the option price of £3.40, despite the fact that the current share price is £10 per share.

Sinead, as a result of her savings, can now buy 360 shares. No income tax is due on the purchase of the shares.

Company Share Option Plans

An employer may offer a company share option plan (CSOP) under which employees are granted options on shares. The main features of the scheme are as follows:

■   There is no income tax on either the grant of the option or on the profit arising from the exercise of the option between three and 10 years after the date of grant of the option or on the disposal of the shares.

■   There are a variety of conditions that must be satisfied in order to obtain the tax advantages available for CSOPs. For example, there must be no discount offered on the shares; therefore, the share price must equal the market value at the time of the granting of the options.

■   The tax exemption is lost in respect of an option if it is exercised earlier than three years or later than 10 years after the grant.

■   The scheme can be altered so that, if the company concerned was taken over, employees may exchange their options for equivalent options in the acquiring company.

■   The scheme does not have to be open to all employees/directors; therefore key employees can be rewarded.

■   No options may be granted that take the total market value of shares an employee holds above £30,000.

Enterprise Management Incentives

Enterprise Management Incentive (EMI) schemes are intended to encourage experienced people to 'take the plunge' and leave established careers in large companies for riskier jobs in similar start-up or developing firms.

No income tax or NICs are chargeable on either the grant or exercise of the options under an EMI scheme, provided that the exercise takes place within 10 years of the grant and the exercise price is the market value of the shares at the date of the grant.

Key employees can be selected and granted options over shares worth up to £250,000 (effective for grants of option on or after 16 June 2012) at the time of the grant, subject to a maximum of £3 million in total share value under EMI options to **all** employees. If options are granted at a discount, the discount is subject to income tax at the date of exercise.

EMI is a very flexible way of incentivising employees, as targets can be set that employees must achieve before options can be exercised.

Share Incentive Plans

In share incentive plans (SIPs), employers can give up to £3,600 of 'free shares' a year to employees without any income tax or NIC liability. In addition, employees can purchase up to £1,800 worth of "partnership shares" at any time in the year and the employers can 'match' this latter purchase in the ratio of 2:1, i.e. they can provide another £3,600 worth of shares. Only employees who purchase partnership shares can be awarded matching shares.

Employers offering free shares must offer a minimum amount to each employee on "similar terms". This scheme must be open to all full- or part-time employees (but can exclude employees with "insufficient" service, e.g. the employer may specify a minimum employment period of 18 months). Criteria can be established to reward these employees, such as individual or team performance targets.

Normally, **free and matching shares** must be held in the SIP for at least three years; **partnership shares** can be withdrawn at any time.

If any of the shares are withdrawn within three years, an income tax liability and an NIC charge may arise. Holdings of more than three years but less than five years attract a reduced rate of income tax and NIC charges. Dividends on shares in the plan are tax-free, provided the dividends are used to acquire additional shares in the company, which are then held in the SIP for a further three years. There is no limit on the amount of dividend that can be reinvested. Other conditions apply, but once the shares are held for five years the dividends are no longer liable to income tax or NIC charges.

Administration Changes – Share Schemes

Since 6 April 2014, it is no longer necessary to obtain HMRC approval in order to use tax-advantaged share schemes. Instead, businesses must self-certify that they meet the relevant legislative requirements. It also became necessary to register all existing and new employee share schemes and arrangements (including EMI) online using the new Employment Related Securities (ERS) online service. The ERS is part of the PAYE Online for employers service. To use the service, a company must be registered for HMRC taxes and signed up as an organisation for online services. Businesses had to register their schemes by 6 July 2015 if they wanted them to remain tax-advantaged for 2014/15 and subsequent years. The following had to be registered:

- unexercised EMI options;
- new grants of EMI options;
- non-tax-advantaged arrangements previously recorded on Form 42; and
- CSOP schemes, SAYE option schemes and SIPs.

The interests of SIP and SAYE participants who were awarded shares or granted options prior to 6 April 2014 were protected. There was, however, no comparable protection for options granted to CSOP participants prior to 6 April 2014 in cases where the 6 July 2015 deadline was missed.

For new schemes set up after 6 April 2014, or for schemes set up but not approved by HMRC prior to 6 April 2014, the business must self-certify by 6 July following the end of the tax year in which the first award of shares is made.

From April 2015, all annual information returns for employment-related securities must be filed online. Automatic penalties will apply for late filing.

6.5 Statutory Payments

6.5.1 *Statutory Sick Pay*

Statutory sick pay (SSP) is a mandatory payment made by employers to qualifying employees who are unable to work through sickness. SSP is paid, and fully funded, by the employer (as of 6 April 2014, employers can no longer recover from HMRC any of the amount paid as SSP).

The current rate of SSP is £88.45 per week, payable up to a maximum of 28 weeks. To qualify the employee must:

- have an employment contract and have worked under that contract;
- earn above the "**lower earnings limit**" (**LEL**) of £112.00 (gross) per week;
- have been unable to work due to sickness for at least four consecutive days (referred to as a "period of incapacity for work" (PIW);
- have informed the employer of their sickness within the specified time limit; and
- have provided proof of sickness, i.e. a "fit note" from their doctor.

A **"period of incapacity for work"** (PIW) includes non-qualifying days, a "qualifying day" being a day that an employee is required to work. The first three days of the PIW are called "waiting days", and SSP is paid from the fourth qualifying day. If an employee is in work and leaves work due to sickness, this day is not counted as a qualifying day.

PIWs can be linked and treated as one PIW if the gap between them is eight weeks or less. Where PIWs are linked and all three waiting days have been served in the first PIW, there will be no waiting days in any later linked PIW. Therefore SSP will be paid from and including the first qualifying day of the second PIW.

If SSP runs out (i.e. is paid for 28 weeks) or the employee is no longer entitled to it, the employee can apply for **Employment and Support Allowance** using form SSP1 provided by the employer. An employee cannot receive SSP at the same time as Employment and Support Allowance.

6.5.2 Statutory Maternity Pay

Statutory maternity pay (SMP) is paid to pregnant employees by their employer in the same way that wages are paid. It is paid for up to 39 weeks (the "maternity pay period") and is liable to income tax and NICs.

To be eligible for SMP the employee must:

■ be on the employer's payroll in the "qualifying week" (the 15th week before the baby is due);
■ have worked for the employer continuously for at least 26 weeks up to the qualifying week;
■ have gross average weekly earnings (AWE) above the "lower earnings limit" (LEL) of £112 (gross) per week. AWE is calculated from the pay received for the eight weeks (up to and including the qualifying week) before the baby is due;
■ inform the employer within at least 28 days of when she would like SMP to start; and
■ provide proof of pregnancy (a doctor's letter or a MATB1 certificate).

The amount of SMP paid is based on the employee's AWE as follows:

■ the first six weeks at 90% of gross AWE;
■ the remaining 33 weeks at the lower of:
  ● 90% of gross AWE, or
  ● £139.58.

The employee can choose when to start receiving SMP, providing the 28-day notice has been given. The start date can be changed, but 28 days' notice must still be given. The earliest it can start is from the 11th week before the week the baby is due; the latest is from the day following the day the baby is born. If the employee has stopped work before the baby is born, SMP will generally start from the following Sunday.

If the baby is born before the beginning of the 11th week or before the date chosen for SMP to start, then the SMP will start from the day following the day the baby is born.

If the baby is born early, before the employee has had an opportunity to tell the employer, SMP is still payable, provided the employer is informed of the birth within 28 days.

If the employee is off work sick for a pregnancy-related reason in the four weeks before the week the baby is due, then SMP will start automatically on the day following the first day she is off sick in that four-week period.

If the employee qualified for SMP and leaves the employment after the qualifying week, i.e. the 15th week, then the employer must still pay the SMP.

6.5.3 Statutory Paternity Pay

Statutory paternity pay (SPP) is a payment to an employee who is taking time off to care for a baby or support the mother in the first weeks after the birth. SPP is available for either one or two weeks to employees who are:

- the biological father of a baby;
- adopting a child; or
- having a baby through a surrogacy arrangement.

The qualifying conditions for SPP are broadly similar in intent to those for SMP, but with an obvious need for modification. Thus the employee must:

- be employed by the employer up to the date the child is born;
- have worked for the employer continuously for at least 26 weeks up to the "qualifying week" (the 15th week before the baby is due);
- earn above the "lower earnings limit" (LEL) of £112 (gross) per week for an eight-week period before the baby is due;
- inform the employer within at least 15 weeks of when the baby is due;
- be looking after the child or the child's mother during the SPP period; and
- be responsible for the child's upbringing.

As with SMP, SPP is based on the employee's gross average weekly earnings (AWE). It is the lower of:

- 90% of gross AWE; or
- £139.58.

SPP is paid by the employer and is liable to income tax and NICs.

6.5.4 Statutory Adoption Pay

Statutory adoption pay (SAP), like statutory maternity and paternity pay, is a payment for employees who are adopting a child or having a child through a surrogacy arrangement. It is operated in the same way as SMP and SPP, i.e. paid by the employer and liable to income tax and NICs. Similar employment and earnings conditions must be met by the employee. Thus, the employee must:

- have worked for the employer continuously for at least 26 weeks by the week they were 'matched' with the child;
- be on the employer's payroll and earn above the "lower earnings limit" (LEL) of £112 (gross) per week for an eight-week period before the 'match' was made;
- inform their employer within at least 28 days of when they would like the SAP to be paid; and
- provide proof of the adoption or surrogacy.

SAP is only available to one of the adopting parents, or to the single parent if adopting on their own. The payment of SAP is much the same as for SMP. Thus:

- it is available for a maximum of 39 weeks;
- the first six weeks is paid at 90% of gross average weekly earnings (AWE); and
- the remaining 33 weeks at the lower of either 90% of AWE or £139.58.

Questions

Review Questions

(See Suggested Solutions to Review Questions at the end of this textbook.)

Question 6.1

How much of the following income would be taxable in 2016/17?

1. £100,000 wholly ex-gratia payment received on termination of your job with the Civil Service.
2. £2,000 statutory sick pay.
3. £5,000 received due to legal claim when you were hit by a passing car.
4. £50,000 paid by employer's health insurance when you lose an arm in a factory accident and cannot return to work.
5. £2,400 of shares given to you by your employer.
6. £2,400 of shares given to you by your employer via a HMRC-approved share incentive plan (SIP).

Question 6.2

Nuala Casey, a director of a company, was discharged from her 35-year contract on 30 September 2016 with four-and-a-half years of her contract still to run.

She received £90,000 compensation for breach of contract (this was not a contractual entitlement) and her salary from 6 April 2016 to date of discharge on 30 September 2016 was £33,750 gross (PAYE paid £7,300).

In the 2016/17 tax year, she also received £50,000 from exercising her Enterprise Management Incentive scheme share options and immediately selling the shares. The options had cost £42,000.

Requirement
Calculate Ms Casey's income tax liability for the tax year 2016/17.

Question 6.3

Mr Houghton, a single person aged 60, retired from Liver Ltd on 30 June 2016 after 18 years' service. As a token of their appreciation, the board of directors of Liver Ltd voted him a lump sum of £65,000. This was not provided for in his contract of employment, but every employee who had previously retired from the company in the last six years had received a similar payment.

Mr Houghton had been paid a salary of £20,000 net of PAYE of £7,000 up to the date he retired in the tax year.

He was also able to exercise 20,000 tax-advantaged/approved share options that had been granted to him four years ago under a HMRC-approved scheme (net gain arising was £30,000) and 5,000 tax-advantaged/approved share options that had been granted to him 18 months ago under the same scheme (net gain arising £5,000).

Requirement
Calculate Mr Houghton's income tax liability for the tax year 2016/17.

Question 6.4

Dermot O'Donnell, a single man, is an employee of Super McBurgers, a fast-food restaurant chain. He has been employed by the company for 15 years and eight months. He was made redundant on 1 October 2016. The following information is provided.

1. As part of the redundancy package he received:

Lump sum from approved pension fund	£8,000
Pay in lieu of notice	£1,200
Company car worth	£22,500
Compensation payment	£40,500

2. In the period from April 2016 to 30 September 2016, Dermot earned a gross salary and benefits in kind on his company car of £37,000. PAYE deducted was £9,500.
3. He was also provided with a mobile phone when he was employed by Super McBurgers. All calls on the phone were paid for by the company. The personal element of the calls cost £2,000 as his sister lived in Japan for a year.
4. He commenced new employment in Burger Palace on 1 November 2016 and his gross earnings in the period to March 2017 were £14,200 (PAYE deducted was £2,900). He also received a commencement incentive of £4,000 when he started this employment as a number of fast-food outlets were keen to have him as an employee.
5. He received dividends on shares he holds in a share incentive plan of £1,000, which were reinvested in shares in the relevant company.

Requirement
Calculate Dermot's final liability to income tax for the year 2016/17.

Question 6.5

Sid Harvey is an employee of General Services Ltd. His gross basic salary for 2016/17 amounted to £40,000. His employer also gives him £100 every month by way of a round sum expense allowance to meet incidental outlay. He is not obliged to provide his employer with receipts to account for this expenditure.

Sid is supplied with a company car (petrol), which was bought by General Services Ltd, second-hand, in July 2009, for £15,000. The car is a 2004 model and originally cost £36,000 (after 10% cash discount) when first registered. General Services Ltd pay all the outgoings in respect of the running of the car. However, Sid is required to reimburse the company for all private fuel used. The CO_2 emissions are 145g/km.

In recognition of the fact that he has the car available to him during leisure hours, Sid is also obliged to make a monthly contribution of £100 to his employer. This is deducted from his salary. Sid's total mileage in the tax year 2016/17 amounted to 25,000 miles, of which 16,500 miles were in the course of the performance of his duties. Sid spends approximately 50% of his working time away from the premises of General Services Limited.

General Services Ltd also provides a free apartment to Sid. The current market value of the apartment is estimated at £110,000. It was worth £80,000 when first made available to Sid in 2010. General Services Ltd pay the annual management charge and light and heat costs of the apartment, which, for 2016/17, amounted to £890. The apartment was purchased for £55,000 in 1995. The annual value of the apartment is £600.

Sid receives free meals in the staff canteen on the days he is located at his head office. The cost of providing these meals by his employer amounted to approximately £300. The staff canteen is available to all staff and all meals are provided free.

On 1 November 2013, General Services Ltd provided Sid with a £1,000 interest-free loan to enable him to go on his annual holidays. On 6 August 2016 the board of directors of General Services Ltd decided to waive repayment of the loan.

Sid is not married and paid £13,900 PAYE in the tax year 2016/17.

Requirement

Calculate Sid's taxable benefits assessable for 2016/17. (Assume official rate of interest of 3%.)

Question 6.6

Terry is considering an employment offer from Rich Bank plc, with a proposed start date of 6 April 2016. In addition to an attractive salary of £70,000, Rich Bank plc has offered to take over his mortgage loan of £125,000, which he used to purchase his first main residence in January 2005. The rate of interest payable on the loan is 2%. Such loans are not available to the public.

Rich Bank plc will also provide an interest-free loan of £4,000 to pay Terry's affiliation fees at the Posh Golf and Country Club, and will pay annual membership of £3,500 on his behalf.

He would also be provided with a new diesel VW Passat car, with a list price of £30,000 and CO_2 emissions of 158g/km. Rich Bank plc intends to pay all associated expenses. There is no business mileage.

Terry is married and will earn £75,000 with no benefits if he stays in his current job in 2016. He pays 5.5% on his mortgage and estimates that his car costs £10,500 per annum. He is not a member of any golf club and has no business mileage in his current job.

Requirement

(a) Calculate the taxable benefits assessable for 2016/17 from his new employer. (Assume official rate of interest of 3%.)
(b) Prepare income tax computations for both his current job and the new employment offer and advise which leaves him better off.

Question 6.7

Philip Stodge is employed as a commercial representative. Details of his income for the tax year 2016/17 are as follows:

	£
Gross salary	43,600
Sales commission	6,000
Pension contributions made by employer	10,000

The following additional information is available:

1. PAYE deducted amounted to £7,900.
2. The sales commission of £6,000 earned was paid directly to his wife.
3. He receives a monthly round sum expense allowance of £50 to meet routine incidental expenses, such as telephone calls, tips that he gives for food/beverages when travelling on business, etc. In addition, his employer pays his hotel accommodation costs directly. He is away on business in the UK 10 nights each month.
4. Philip runs an Audi A4 car (list price £27,000). He drove 10,000 business miles, but his fuel expenses are not reimbursed by his employer. CO_2 emissions are 150g/km.
5. He is provided with a free parking space in a public car park beside his work. This costs his employer £1,000 a year.
6. In addition to car expenses, the following expenses (vouched with receipts) are not reimbursed by his employer:

	£
Work-related telephone charges	180
Cost of new suit	450
Cost of advanced commercial correspondence course	150
Taxi/train fares while on business	130
	910

7. He pays a professional subscription of £400 per year.

Requirement

(a) Compute Philip Stodge's income tax liability for the tax year 2016/17.
(b) You are aware that Philip plays at the same golf course as your father and have heard that he had disposed of a number of share options in April 2016 for a significant profit. However, there is no mention of this in the information provided by Philip for his 2016/17 tax return. How should you approach this situation in line with ethical standards?

Question 6.8

Frank, a sales representative who is single, received a salary of £50,000 in 2016/17 and the following benefits in kind:

1. Company Ferrari (over 2000cc) with a list price of £120,000. CO_2 emissions are 300g/km. He had to pay £35,000 towards the cost of the car.
2. All fuel was paid for by the employer.
3. 15,000 share options, with an exercise price of £1 each, granted on 6 April 2016. It is anticipated that they will be worth £50,000 in five years' time when he can exercise them.
4. He paid professional subscriptions of £800.

Requirement

Calculate Frank's gross income tax liability (before credit for PAYE deducted) for the tax year 2016/17.

7

Savings and Investment Income

Learning Objectives

After studying this chapter you will understand:

■ The identification of income classified as savings and dividend income, and whether it is taxable or non-taxable.
■ The calculation of the effective tax rate for individuals in receipt of dividend income.
■ Whether an individual's savings and investment income is assessed on an accruals basis or a receipts basis.
■ The separation of savings and dividend income when determining the appropriate rate of income tax to apply.
■ The income tax treatment of overseas savings and investment income.
■ The tax benefits and conditions of various Government savings incentive schemes, including individual savings accounts (ISAs) and new individual savings accounts (NISAs), Help to Buy ISAs and Lifetime ISAs.

7.1 Introduction

In the previous chapters we have learned how an individual's taxable trading income and/or taxable employment income are classified as non-savings income for the purpose of the overall income tax calculation. However, non-savings income is not the only type of income that an individual may earn in a tax year. For example, where an individual has money on deposit in a bank, savings income, i.e. interest, may be earned on the money invested. Similarly, an individual may have purchased shares in a company and if that company decides to pay a dividend to its shareholders, dividend income will have been earned and will need to be taxed accordingly.

Throughout this chapter you will be introduced to the various types of UK savings and dividend income and the various tax rates that apply to each. The calculation of the income tax liability of an individual who earns interest income and/or dividend income changed significantly from 6 April 2016. The 2016 Budget announced new measures such as the personal savings allowance and the dividend allowance, which will be looked at in detail. As UK resident individuals may hold money in non-UK bank accounts and/or hold shares in overseas companies, this chapter will address the differing tax treatment of overseas income. Finally, we will consider a number of saving incentives that were introduced in Budget 2016 to encourage individuals to save to buy their first home or for their retirement. The various rules and regulations surrounding such savings incentives will be discussed.

7.1.1 Types of Savings and Investment Income

Savings Income
In simple terms, savings income is interest. It includes:

- interest from a bank account;
- interest from a building society account;
- interest from a credit union account;
- interest from National Savings and Investment Accounts;
- interest from gilt-edged securities – that is, British Government stock; and
- interest from debentures issued by companies (sometimes referred to as company loan stock).

Dividend Income
When an individual owns shares in a company, they may receive dividends from the company throughout the year. Such income is taxed as dividend income.

Companies can pay dividends either as a cash dividend or as a scrip (or stock) dividend. A scrip dividend is an issue of new shares to existing shareholders in place of a cash dividend, and is sometimes referred to as "shares received in lieu of dividends". For taxation purposes, scrip dividends must have a cash-equivalent value, which is determined by reference to the "market value" of the shares:

1. If the new shares (those received as the scrip dividend) have a market value (on the first day of dealing) that is within 15% of the original market value, then the original market value is taken as the cash equivalent.
2. If the market value (on the first day of dealing) is more than 15% of the original market value, then the current market value is the cash equivalent.

Example 7.1
Jenny owns 100 shares in Market plc. Market plc intends to declare either a cash dividend of 10p per share or a scrip dividend of one new share for 50 existing shares. The company's shares are currently quoted at £5 each.

Jenny, as a holder of 100 shares, will receive either £10 as a cash dividend or two new shares worth £5 each (i.e. a total of £10) as a scrip dividend.

If the market value of the shares on the first day of dealing were £5.80, then the dividend income liable to income tax would be £5.80 × 2 = £11.60. This is because the current market value (£5.80) is more than 15% of the original market value (£5 + 15% = £5.75).

If the market value of the shares on the first day of dealing were £5.10, then the dividend income liable to income tax would be £10 (the original market value), because it is within the 15% limit.

7.2 Basis of Assessment and Computation of Savings and Investment Income

7.2.1 General Rules

Generally, the amount of savings and investment income taxable for a tax year is the amount arising in that year. Income arises when it is paid or credited. Accrued income not yet paid or credited is ignored.

Savings and investment income is generally 'pure' income profit, i.e. it is unusual for there to be any deductions to be accounted for, e.g. expenses or costs. This makes the income tax computation of savings and dividend income a relatively straightforward calculation – in essence it is to determine the amount of taxable income and to then apply the necessary tax rate.

7.2.2 Savings Income

Personal Savings Allowance

In **Chapter 2, Section 2.3.2**, you were introduced to the new personal savings allowance, which is available from 6 April 2016. The amount of personal savings allowance depends on an individual's "adjusted net income". Adjusted net income is total taxable income before deducting the personal allowance (**Chapter 2**) and after certain other tax reliefs, such as:

- trading losses (**Chapter 5**);
- donations made to charities through Gift Aid (**Chapter 9**);
- pension contributions paid gross, i.e. before tax relief (**Chapter 9**); and
- pension contributions where the pension provider has already given tax relief at the basic rate (**Chapter 9**).

Example 7.2

For the 2016/17 tax year, Maeve's total taxable income is £30,000, made up of £15,000 employment income, £5,000 bank interest and £10,000 of dividends. In 2016/17, Maeve also made a trading loss of £2,500.

Maeve's adjusted net income is £27,500 (£30,000 less £2,500).

The table below shows the amount of the personal savings allowance an individual is entitled to from 6 April 2016, depending on whether they are a basic, higher or additional rate taxpayer.

Tax Rate	Income Band (adjusted net income)	Personal Savings Allowance
Basic: 20%	Up to £43,000	Up to £1,000
Higher: 40%	£43,001–£150,000	Up to £500
Additional: 45%	Over £150,001	Nil

There is an important interaction between the personal savings allowance and the new dividend allowance (**Section 7.2.3**). When determining the amount of the personal savings allowance, it is necessary to consider if the adjusted net income includes dividend income. If dividend income is included, that income is treated as if it is chargeable at the higher or additional rate, even if it is within the £5,000 dividend allowance, when calculating the personal savings allowance.

Example 7.3

Frank has the following income in 2016/17:

Employment income	£34,000
Savings income	£1,000
Dividend income	£10,000
	£45,000

Frank's adjusted net income is £45,000. His dividends will be taxed as the highest part of income with the first £5,000 of dividends being covered by the new dividend allowance (**Section 7.2.3**), chargeable at 0%. Despite the fact that £5,000 of his dividends will be chargeable at 0%, for the purpose of considering the personal saving allowance the dividends are treated as if they are chargeable at the higher rate. Therefore, Frank's adjusted net income is £45,000, i.e. he is a higher rate taxpayer, and so will receive a personal savings allowance of £500.

Income tax on savings income, prior to 6 April 2016, was a tax deducted at source by banks, building societies and National Savings. Finance Act 2016 removed this requirement, so that basic rate income tax is no longer deducted from interest paid to customers.

Rates of Tax

As outlined in **Chapter 2** and in the table above, the same rates of tax that apply to non-savings income also apply to savings income. That is, the basic rate at 20%, the higher rate at 40% and the additional rate at 45%. In addition, a "starter rate" also applies to savings income only. The starter rate is 0% for savings income up to £5,000, i.e. it is tax-exempt. For the starter rate to apply, an individual's savings income must fall wholly or partly below the £5,000 limit and, importantly, the individual must not have non-savings income of £5,000 or more in the tax year. The table below outlines the rates of tax applicable to savings income:

	Rate	**Adjusted Net Income**
Savings income starter rate*	0%	Up to £5,000
Basic rate	20%	Up to £32,000
Higher rate	40%	£32,001 to £150,000
Additional rate	45%	Over £150,001

*The personal savings allowance is available in addition to the savings income starter rate, increasing the amount of savings income that could be received tax-free to £6,000.

To illustrate how the different rates are applied, let's look at a few examples.

Example 7.4

Beth earns employment income of £15,000 in the 2016/17 tax year. She also earns £250 interest from her building society account.

Beth is a basic rate taxpayer. As Beth's savings income of £250 is covered by her personal savings allowance she will not pay any tax on her savings income.

Example 7.5

James has property income profits of £25,000 in 2016/17 and he also earns £1,500 in interest income.

James is a basic rate taxpayer. He will not pay income tax on £1,000 of his interest income as this is covered by his personal savings allowance. He will pay basic rate tax of 20% on the £500 interest over his personal savings allowance.

Example 7.6

Lisa earns employment income of £80,000 in 2016/17. She also earns £400 of interest income in 2016/17.

Lisa is a higher rate taxpayer. As Lisa's savings income of £400 is covered by her personal savings allowance (of £500), she will not pay any tax on her savings income.

Example 7.7

Edward has taxable trading profits of £60,000 in the 2016/17 tax year. He also earns £1,200 of interest income in 2016/17.

Edward is a higher rate taxpayer. He will not pay income tax on £500 of his interest income, as this is covered by his personal savings allowance. He will pay the higher rate tax of 40% on the £700 interest over his personal savings allowance.

Example 7.8

Jacqui has employment income of £170,000 in the 2016/17 tax year. She also earns £1,500 of interest income in 2016/17.

Jacqui is an additional rate taxpayer, and as such she is not entitled to the personal savings allowance. She will pay additional rate tax of 45% on the £1,500 interest income.

7.2.3 Dividend Income

Dividend Allowance

From 6 April 2016, the 10% dividend tax credit was replaced by the new tax-free dividend allowance. The dividend allowance means that individuals will not have to pay tax on the first £5,000 of their dividend income, regardless of their levels of earnings.

Rates of Tax

An individual will pay the following rates of tax on dividends received over £5,000:

- 7.5% on dividend income within the basic rate band (£5,000– £32,000);
- 32.5% on dividend income within the higher rate band (£32,001–£150,000);
- 38.1% on dividend income within the additional rate band (over £150,001).

As noted above, dividend income covered by the dividend allowance will still count towards an individual's basic or higher rate bands, and will therefore affect the rate of tax that is payable on dividends received in excess of the £5,000 allowance.

Again, some examples will help to illustrate the application of the rates.

Example 7.9

Megan receives £4,000 of dividends in 2016/17.

She will not have to pay any tax on her dividends as they are covered by the dividend allowance.

Example 7.10

Ryan earns £7,000 employment income and £15,000 dividend income in 2016/17.

Ryan will be entitled to a personal allowance of £11,000, so £4,000 (i.e. £11,000 – £7,000) of his dividends will be covered by his remaining personal allowance. A further £5,000 comes within the dividend allowance, leaving tax to pay at the basic rate (7.5%) on £6,000.

Example 7.11

Nicole has taxable trading profits of £20,000 and £22,000 dividend income in 2016/17.

Nicole will be entitled to a personal allowance of £11,000, which will be fully used against her non-savings income. Nicole will not need to pay tax on the first £5,000 of dividends due to the dividend allowance, but will pay tax on £17,000 of dividends at the basic rate (7.5%) as her dividend income falls within the basic rate band.

> **Example 7.12**
> Anna has employment income of £40,000 and dividend income of £12,000 in 2016/17.
>
> Of the £40,000 employment income, £11,000 is covered by her personal allowance, leaving £29,000 to be taxed at the basic rate. This leaves £3,000 of income that can be earned within the basic rate limit before the higher rate threshold is crossed.
>
> The dividend allowance covers this £3,000 first, leaving £2,000 of the dividend allowance to use in the higher rate band. All of this £5,000 dividend income is therefore covered by the dividend allowance and is not subject to tax. The remaining £7,000 of dividends will all be taxed at the higher rate (32.5%).

7.2.4   Overseas Savings Income

Overseas savings income is interest received from a non-UK bank, building society or other financial institution.

If the **arising basis** applies, overseas savings income is taxed in the same way as UK savings income, i.e. at 0% for the starter rate band, 20% for the basic rate band and so on.

Where the **remittance basis** applies, all income from the relevant source is treated as if it were non-savings income. It is then taxed in the same way as other non-savings income, i.e. at 20% for the basic rate band, 40% for the higher rate band and 45% for the additional rate band.

7.2.5   Overseas Dividend Income

Overseas dividend income is dividend income from non-UK resident companies. Its treatment is similar to overseas saving income, with the distinction being between the arising basis and the remittance basis.

Thus, if the arising basis applies, then the income is taxable in the year in which it arises, and it is taxed in the same way as UK dividend income, i.e. at 7.5% if it falls within the basic rate band; at 32.5% for the higher dividend rate band; and at 38.1% for the additional rate band. The dividend allowance applies in all instances.

Where the remittance basis of tax applies, the overseas dividends are taxed as non-savings income and the 20% basic rate, 40% higher rate or 45% additional rate applies instead.

Whether the arising basis or the remittance basis applies, if the overseas dividend income is subject to dividend withholding tax (DWT) in the company's 'home' country, it should be considered whether a double taxation agreement (DTA) exists between the UK and that country. If a DTA does exist, any DWT that has been paid will be deducted from the UK liability, up to the limit of the UK tax suffered. Some DTAs have provision whereby an individual can apply for an exemption to the DWT before it is deducted. For example, the Republic of Ireland (RoI) has a DWT of 20% on the gross dividend at the time of payment. However, residents in other EU Member States or residents of a country with a DTA with the RoI can apply for exemption from this Irish DWT. As the UK has a DTA with the RoI, no Irish DWT should be suffered by a UK resident receiving RoI dividends.

Example 7.13

A UK resident but non-domiciled individual (who claims the remittance basis) receives an overseas net dividend of £25,000 in the 2016/17 tax year. The dividend is received net of withholding tax paid at 20%. The individual remits the £25,000 dividend to his UK bank account. The individual is a 40% taxpayer.

The overseas dividend that is remitted would be taxed as follows:

	£
Dividend remitted to the UK	25,000
Add: withholding tax suffered	5,000
Gross dividend for UK purposes	30,000
UK dividend income tax @ 40%	12,000
Less: withholding tax (Note 1)	(5,000)
Tax payable	7,000

Note:
1. Full relief on the overseas DWT paid is available as the overseas rate is lower than the UK rate.

7.2.6 Exempt Savings and Investment Income

Certain investment and savings income is exempt for investors resident and domiciled in the UK. Exempt income includes the following:

1. Interest and dividend income from individual savings accounts (ISAs) and new individual savings accounts (NISAs). See below for more information.
2. Accumulated interest on National Savings Certificates issued by National Savings and Investments (NS&I).
3. Interest and terminal bonuses under Save As You Earn (SAYE) schemes.
4. Interest awarded as part of an award of damages for personal injury or death.
5. Dividends on ordinary shares in a venture capital trust (VCT) (see **Section 9.5.1**).
6. Interest on tax-exempt special savings account (TESSAs), unless the account closes within five years – no new TESSAs can now be opened.
7. Income from personal equity plans (PEPs) – no new PEPs can now be opened.
8. Betting and premium bond prizes.

New Individual Savings Accounts

New individual savings accounts (NISAs) were introduced in July 2014 as a simpler form of the ISA. From 1 July 2014, all existing ISAs became NISAs. NISA savings can be held either as cash or as stocks and shares, or in combination of the two. NISAs are exempt from income tax (and capital gains tax). Withdrawals can be made at any time.

Up to a maximum of £15,240 can be saved in a NISA in the 2016/17 tax year. This limit will be increased to £20,000 from April 2017. Individuals can only open one cash NISA and one stocks and shares NISA each tax year. The annual limit of £15,240 can be split in whatever way the individual prefers between cash NISAs or stocks and shares NISAs.

Finance Act 2015 enabled savers to be able to withdraw money from their cash NISA and replace it without it counting towards the annual subscription limit for that year, providing the repayment is made in the same tax year as the withdrawal.

Individuals can receive an additional NISA investment allowance where their spouse or civil partner dies on or after 3 December 2014. The additional allowance will be set at the value held in the deceased person's NISA on the date of their death.

7.3 Savings and Investments Incentives

In an attempt to get individuals to save, a number of savings and investment incentives have been introduced. Generally, these incentives offer individuals the ability to save money and earn interest tax-free, up to certain limits. More recently, some of the incentives offer a tax-free cash bonus to be paid by the Government if certain conditions are met. We will now look at a number of these savings and investment incentives.

7.3.1 Help to Buy ISA

Finance Act 2016 introduced the Help to Buy ISA to allow individuals saving for their first home to save up to £200 a month into the account, with the Government topping up the amount by 25%. The Government bonus will be capped at a total of £3,000 on savings of £12,000, and will be paid at the time the individual is ready to buy their first home. Only cash can be held in this type of ISA.

New accounts can be opened by individuals who are over 18 years old until April 2019, and the government contribution is available until April 2029.

7.3.2 Junior ISA

The junior ISA has an annual contribution limit of £4,080 and can only be held in the name of a child under 18 years old. Cash or stocks and shares can be held in funds. Money contributed can only be accessed by the child from age 18, and the money will be in their sole control.

7.3.3 Lifetime ISA

The Lifetime ISA, another incentive introduced by Finance Act 2016, will be available from April 2017. It will allow individuals under the age of 40 to save £4,000 each year into either cash or stocks and shares. This forms part of the overall £20,000 ISA limit that will be available from April 2017.

The benefit of investing in a Lifetime ISA is that the Government will add an extra 25% to an individual's contribution from any year, but the individual will only benefit from this top-up if the money is used to buy a house (up to the value of £450,000) or if they withdraw it after their 60th birthday. Withdrawals before this date will result in not only the Government bonus being lost, but also a 5% charge being incurred.

Questions

Review Questions

(See Suggested Solutions to Review Questions at the end of this textbook.)

Question 7.1

Maeve, who is widowed and 56 years of age, is in receipt of the following UK-source income in the 2016/17 tax year:

	£
Dividend income received	
Tyson Limited	17,520
Holyfield Manufacturing Limited	3,724
	21,244
Deposit interest received	
National Savings Bank account	6,300
Credit Union interest	1,200
Nationwide ISA interest	720
	8,220
Personal pension	7,800

Requirement

Compute Maeve's 2016/17 income tax liability.

Question 7.2

David Lee, a single person aged 44, works for a travel agency. In 2016/17 he had the following income and outgoings:

	£
Income	
Salary (gross)	42,000
Ordinary bank interest	625
Interest on Government loans	1,130
Ordinary building society interest	175
National Savings Certificates interest	100
Gift from neighbour for getting her shopping when she had a cold	30
Outgoings	
PAYE deducted	4,900
NIC deducted	2,255
Post Office (Note 1)	1,200

Notes:

1. David buys £100 worth of premium bonds each month. He received £10,000 from the bonds in the tax year.
2. David also won £40,000 on the National Lottery in January 2017.

Requirement

Calculate David Lee's income tax liability for the 2016/17 tax year, stating clearly the amount payable by, or refundable to, him.

Property Income

8.1   Introduction

Property income is a non-savings income. A taxpayer with UK property income is treated as if they are operating a UK property business, and as such the considerations and calculations for income tax purposes are broadly the same as for trading income (see **Chapter 4**). That is, all property/rental income (hereafter referred to as 'property income') and property expenses are consolidated to give a single profit or loss figure on which income tax is assessed on an accruals basis. An overseas rental property is regarded as an overseas property business and the same rules apply as for a UK property business. However, they are treated as two different and separate property businesses. Property income, although similar to trading income, is subject to specific rules relating to the taxing of property income and to the property expenses allowable as deductions.

In this chapter, we will first look at the computation of taxable profits (or losses) for a property business, looking in detail at how the rental income amount in a tax year is established and the expenses that can be deducted. It may be the case that the expenses incurred by a landlord in a tax year exceed the rental income in that year, i.e. a property business loss arises, so we will look at how such losses can be 'utilised'.

We will then look in detail at some of the special schemes and reliefs available in respect of property income, such as the rent-a-room scheme, the non-resident landlord scheme and furnished holiday lettings.

8.2 Basis of Assessment of Property Income

8.2.1 UK Property Income

The profits of UK property income are computed for each tax year and each tax year's profit is taxed in that year. That is, for the 2016/17 tax year, property income profits from 6 April 2016 to 5 April 2017 are taxed. Property income profits or losses are computed on the accruals basis.

8.2.2 Overseas Property Income

An individual who receives rents and other property income from abroad is treated as carrying on an overseas property business. This is liable to income tax in the same way as income from a UK property business and is calculated in the same way. If an individual had both UK and overseas property income, they would be treated as two separate property businesses. 'Overseas' refers to any country or territory outside the UK, as defined in **Chapter 3**. It would therefore include the Isle of Man, the Channel Islands and the Republic of Ireland.

The only difference in the taxation of UK and overseas property income profits is the extent to which they are taxed in the UK. A UK property business is always taxable in the UK on an arising basis, whereas an overseas property business depends on the domicile status of the landlord and whether an election for remittance basis applies (see **Chapter 3**).

If a loss arises in an overseas property business and the remittance basis of taxation is not claimed by the landlord, the loss can be carried forward and set against future income from the overseas property business as soon as it arises. It cannot be set off against income on a UK property business because they are kept separate.

8.3 Computation of Taxable Property Income

8.3.1 Computation of Profits

We have established that a landlord with property income is treated as if he or she is running a 'property business' and, as such, property income is essentially treated in the same way as trading income, with the calculation of profit or loss, i.e. income minus costs or expenses. Property income includes not only the agreed rents (whether weekly, monthly, quarterly or annual), but also the taxable portion of any premium paid (see **Section 8.3.2**). Many expenses are allowed as a deduction from property income, which will be covered in detail in **Section 8.3.3**.

An individual's property income profit or loss for the tax year is calculated in the same way as trading profits, i.e. on an accruals basis. If more than one property is being let, the income and expenses for each property are pooled together to calculate a total profit or loss for the tax year.

The pro forma computation overleaf shows the layout of the property income calculation. It does not include all potential expenses that are allowable as deductions against property income, but it does include the most common.

FIGURE 8.1: PRO FORMA PROPERTY INCOME COMPUTATION

	£	£
Rental income	X	
Lease premium received	X	
		X
Less: expenses:		
Rent payable	X	
Rates/council tax	X	
Gas/electricity/waste disposal costs paid by landlord and not reimbursed by tenant	X	
Accountancy fees	X	
Legal fee re. lease renewal	X	
Travel costs to and from the property	X	
Replacement furniture relief (where a dwelling house is let)	X	
Capital allowances (where a commercial property is let)	X	(X)
Property income profit/(loss)		X

8.3.2   Premiums on Short Leases

As stated above, a landlord is taxed not only on the rents received but also on a proportion of the "premium" of the "short lease". A lease premium is a non-refundable lump sum payment made by the tenant to the landlord on the signing of a lease. A "short lease" is one that does not exceed 50 years.

The landlord is treated as receiving a proportion of the premium **by way of rent** (in addition to the actual rent received) and is also liable to income tax on this amount. It is calculated using the following formula:

$$\text{Premium} - \left(\text{Premium} \times \frac{(\text{Duration of lease}) - 1}{50}\right)$$

Note: this does not apply to assignments of leases, i.e. to the transfer or sale of leases to another party. The remainder of the premium is taxable as a capital gain (which will be relevant for the CA Proficiency 2 syllabus).

Example 8.1
On 1 June 2016, Mr White rented premises to Mr Blake for 25 years at a rent of £2,000 per month, subject to a premium of £20,000.
Taxable portion of premium:

	£
Premium	20,000
Less: £20,000 × $\frac{25 - 1}{50}$	(9,600)
Additional rent	10,400
2016/17	
Taxable portion of premium	10,400
Rent receivable (£2,000 × 10)*	20,000
Total property income assessable	**30,400**

* Only rented for 10 months during the tax year.

Where a trader pays a premium for the lease of a premises that will be used for their trade, a deduction in respect of the premium is allowed against taxable trading profits for each year of the lease (see **Section 4.3.5**).

8.3.3 Allowable Deductions from Property Income

As property income rules broadly follow trading income rules, any qualifying costs incurred by the property business can be deducted to reduce the tax liability. The "wholly and exclusively" rule is the main rule applied to property income. The following costs are deductible from the gross rents receivable:

- Rent payable on the property. For example, where a landlord is renting a property and is in turn renting part of that property to others, i.e. subletting.
- Rates, council tax and ground rent payable on the property.
- The cost of goods or services that the landlord is obliged to provide and for which no separate consideration is received, e.g. gas, electricity, waste disposal.
- Cost of insurance, maintenance and management of the property.
- Interest on any loan (e.g. mortgage) associated with the purchase of the property. Capital repayments in respect of loans are not deductible, only the interest portion is deductible.
- Accountancy fees incurred in drawing up rental accounts and keeping rental records.
- Legal fees regarding the **renewal** of a short lease (apart from the first letting, unless it is for a lease of less than one year). A short lease is one lasting 50 years or less.
- For **commercial** property, capital allowances may be claimed on plant and machinery (see **Chapter 5**).
- Travel costs to and from let properties, unless the trip is partly for private purposes.
- Irrecoverable rent, i.e. bad debts, can be relieved as an impairment loss.
- Replacement furniture relief applies to the replacement of furnishings. The initial cost of furnishing a property is not allowable but, under the replacement furniture relief, landlords of all dwelling houses (excluding furnished holiday lettings, see **Section 8.3.7**) are able to claim a deduction for the capital cost of replacing furniture, furnishings, appliances and kitchenware provided for the tenant's use. This includes:
  - movable furniture or furnishings, such as beds, sofas, etc.;
  - televisions;
  - fridges and freezers;
  - carpets and floor coverings;
  - curtains;
  - linen; and
  - crockery or cutlery.
  The amount of replacement furniture relief available depends on the cost incurred in respect of the replacement item. If the replacement item is substantially the same as the old item, then its full cost can be claimed. If the replacement item is of a higher or improved quality, then the amount of relief is limited to the cost that would have been incurred if replacing 'like with like'.
- Fixtures that are considered 'integral' to the property, i.e. those that would not normally be removed if the property were to be sold, are not allowable under replacement furniture relief, but can instead be claimed as a deductible expense as a repair to the property itself. They include items such as:
  - baths, washbasins and toilets;
  - boilers;
  - fitted kitchen units; and
  - repair of a windowpane, electric light fittings, door locks, etc.

Pre-letting Expenses

As property income rules broadly follow trading income rules, expenses incurred in the seven years prior to commencement of the property business (i.e. before the first lease is entered into) are treated as having been incurred on the first day of the business. Pre-letting expenses are subject to the same rules as allowable deductions, that is, they must be incurred wholly and exclusively for the property business and they must not be capital in nature. In addition, two other conditions must be met:

- the property was in a fit state to be rented (subject to furnishing, cleaning and the setting up of a tenancy agreement); and
- the landlord (taxpayer) was actively and genuinely trying to find tenants.

Common expenses that normally qualify as pre-letting expenses include:

- interest on any loan associated with the property;
- costs of advertising for tenants; and
- telephone and travel expenses associated with tenant viewings.

Expenses between Lettings

During periods of vacancy, where the landlord is seeking to re-let the property, expenses incurred should still be tax deductible. The difficulty arises when there is a significant period of vacancy between lettings; the question then is whether it constitutes a resumption of the old business or the creation of a new property business. HMRC normally accept a vacancy period of up to three years where the landlord was clearly trying to continue the property business; and property business is usually considered ceased when the last let property is sold or starts to be used for some other purpose, e.g. private or trading purpose.

The consideration is important because expenses continue to be deductible and, typically, the landlord would be treated as carrying on the same property business as before, meaning any losses from earlier years could be carried forward and set against future property profits. The merits of each case would have to be considered. Typical expenses that can be claimed between lettings include:

- interest on a loan associated with purchasing or renovating the property;
- management company fees;
- gas and electricity safety inspections and certificates;
- costs of advertising for new tenants;
- telephone and travel expenses associated with tenant viewings.

Now that we have considered the types of property income an individual can receive and the expenses that are allowed to be offset against that property income, let's look at a worked example to recap the property income computation for income tax purposes.

Example 8.2

John Black has owned rental properties for several years. You are given the following information about the properties owned during the tax year 2016/17.

Property A	£
Rent receivable per annum	40,000
Expenditure incurred:	
Insurance (for period 06/04/16–05/04/17)	1,200
Repairs (incurred December 2016)	400
Interest on loan to acquire the property	36,000

This property is let on a 10-year lease, which commenced on 1 July 2016. A premium of £20,000 was payable on commencement of the lease. The property was acquired on 6 April 2016 for £450,000 with a bank loan taken out on the same date.

continued overleaf

	£
Property B	
Rent receivable per annum	9,600
Expenditure incurred:	
Insurance	280
Painting exterior	740
Repairs to door and alarm following burglary	1,250

Property B is a residential property that was let at £800 per month on a two-year lease that commenced on 1 January 2016. The tenant left suddenly in December 2016, leaving rent owing for the month of November and December. Mr Black subsequently found out that the tenant had emigrated to Australia and has written-off the rent owing as a bad debt. The property was re-let to another tenant on 1 January 2017 at the same annual rent.

	£
Property C	
Rent received	6,000
Expenditure incurred:	
Insurance	500
Construction of conservatory (May 2016)	12,400
Interest	15,000

Property C had been let until 30 November 2016. It was vacant until re-let on a one-year lease from 1 March 2017.

	£
Property D	
Rent received	30,000

Mr Black acquired property D from his wife in 2006 for £450,000. Mrs Black had inherited the house from her mother in 2006. Mrs Black used funds from the sale of property D to Mr Black towards the cost of a new house purchased by Mr and Mrs Black as their principal private residence.

Rental Assessment	Prop. A	Prop. B	Prop. C	Prop. D
	£	£	£	£
Rent received/receivable (Note 1)	30,000	8,000	6,000	30,000
Income element of premium (Note 2)	16,400	0	0	0
Gross rent	46,400	8,000	6,000	30,000
Deduct:				
Insurance (Note 3)	1,200	280	500	0
Repairs/painting	400	1,990	0	0
Loan interest (Note 4)	36,000	0	15,000	0
Total deductions	37,600	2,270	15,500	0
Net profit/(loss)	8,800	5,730	(9,500)	30,000
Rental income assessable 2016/17 – total				**35,030**

Notes:

1.
Property A	£	*Property B*	£
Rent receivable*	40,000	Rent receivable	9,600
Less: amount for period un-let	(10,000)	Less: amount written-off as bad debt	(1,600)
Total rent	30,000	Total rent	8,000

   * Three-month period, i.e. 3/12 x £40,000.

2. *Property A*
   Taxable portion of premium: £20,000 − (£20,000 × 18%) = £16,400.
3. *Property A*
   Expenses incurred before first letting are allowed, provided incurred wholly and exclusively for the property business and are not capital in nature.
   Insurance allowed £1,200.
4. *Property A*
   Expenses incurred before first letting are allowed, provided incurred wholly and exclusively for the property business and are not capital in nature.
   Property C
   Interest incurred between lettings is allowable.
5. Transactions between Mr and Mrs Black on property D and subsequent purchase of principal private residence are not applicable to rental profits of property D.

8.3.4   Losses on Property Income

In general, losses from a UK property business can be carried forward indefinitely to be used against **future UK property profits** for the same property business. For a property business that has more than one property, the net profit or loss is computed for each one **separately** for the particular tax year. The profits/losses are then aggregated to arrive at the total UK profit/loss for the tax year.

Losses on overseas property businesses are ring-fenced and can only be used against current year overseas property profits and the excess carried forward against further overseas property income only.

Losses on favoured lettings, i.e. properties let at less than market value, are not allowed. Expenses are only permitted up to the level of income on such lettings. For example, if an individual lets an apartment to their friend for £1,000 per annum (whereas the market rent would be £5,000 per annum) and the management company fee for the apartment block is £1,500 per annum, as this is a favoured letting the £500 loss will not be permitted and the rental computation will be £1,000 of rental income less £1,000 of allowable expenses.

Furnished holiday homes letting (see **Section 8.3.7**) losses have their own specific rules and should be kept separate from property income losses.

8.3.5   Rent a Room Scheme

Under the Rent a Room Scheme, where an individual rents out a furnished room (or rooms) in a "qualifying residence" and the **gross** income received, including an amount for food, laundry or similar goods and services, **does not exceed £7,500 per year (previously £4,250)**, this income is automatically **exempt** from income tax. Expenses and capital allowances are ignored under the scheme.

A "qualifying residence" is a residential premises occupied by the landlord as their sole or main residence during the year of assessment. If more than one person owns the residence, then the threshold is split accordingly.

If the £7,500 limit is exceeded, then the landlord has two options:

1.   opt into the scheme and claim the £7,500 threshold as an allowance; or
2.   ignore the scheme and be assessed in the normal way for a property business.

Under option 1, the landlord is taxed on gross receipts less £7,500 but with no deductions for expenses and capital allowances. An election to opt into the scheme remains in force until withdrawn or until a year when gross rents do not exceed the £7,500 limit.

Under option 2, the landlord can elect to ignore the exemption and claim expenses and capital allowances to generate a rental loss that can then be carried forward (see **Sections 8.3.3–8.3.4**). An election to ignore the exemption applies only for the current year.

Example 8.3

Clive rents out a spare room in his own home. The rent is £180 a week, which includes the cost of heating and electricity. Clive estimates that renting out a room means he pays an extra £80 in home insurance and his electricity and heating bills have increased by £400 per year.

If Clive were to claim the £7,500 as an allowance (Option 1), he would pay tax on:

Rental income	£9,360
Less: expenses	(£7,500)
	£1,860

If Clive were to use his actual profit (Option 2), he would pay tax on:

Property income	£9,360
Less: expenses	(£480)
	£8,880

It is therefore much more beneficial for Clive to claim rent-a-room relief and be taxed on £1,860.

Example 8.4

Matthew is a self-employed building contractor. He purchased a commercial premises a number of years ago, which has been let to a tenant since the purchase. He made a loss on his property income in 2015/16 of £10,000. During the 2016/17 tax year he invested in two new properties. Matthew has supplied you with the following information for the year to 5 April 2017:

Existing commercial premises

The premises was originally purchased for £1,500,000 in 2011, funded by a bank loan. Interest payable on the loan in the year ended 5 April 2017 was £65,000. The original tenant rented the property for £18,000 per month, but vacated the premises on 30 June 2016 when the lease ended. A new tenant rented the property from 1 August 2016 and the agreed rent was £210,000 per annum, payable annually in advance. During the period when the property was vacant, routine maintenance and decorating was carried out at a cost of £12,500. The insurance premium for the year ended 5 April 2017 was £2,200 and Matthew paid rates of £15,750 for the year.

New property 1

On 1 May 2016 Matthew bought a residential property for £550,000. Before letting, a small extension was added to the property at a cost of £35,000 and £8,000 was spent on new furniture and appliances. The property was let, fully furnished, from 1 July 2016 at an annual rent of £48,000, payable on a monthly basis in advance. The following expenses were paid during the year ended 5 April 2017:

■ Rates (from 1 May 2016 to 31 March 2017)	£1,985
■ Insurance (from 1 May 2016 to 30 April 2017)	£640
■ Legal fees to collect unpaid rent in January 2017	£440
■ Repairs to broken toilet and boiler in November 2016	£3,577

New property 2

On 1 August 2016, Matthew purchased another residential property for £375,000, partially funded by a £200,000 bank loan with 3% interest payable annually. The property was immediately advertised for rent and new tenants moved in on 1 October 2016. The annual rent is £26,400, payable annually in advance. The property is let furnished and the following expenses were paid during the year ended 5 April 2017:

■ Rates (from 1 August 2016 to 31 March 2017)	£1,300
■ Insurance (from 1 August 2016 to 31 July 2017)	£470
■ Legal fees for purchase of property	£2,100
■ General repairs and maintenance	£330
■ Replacement of a bed and fridge (similar standard)	£3,500

Matthew also lets a room in his own private residence to a tenant and in the 2016/17 tax year he received £9,000 and had £735 of allowable expenses.

Calculate Matthew's property business income for 2016/17.

	£	£
Commercial Property		
Rental income – original tenant (£18,000 × 3)		54,000
Rental income – new tenant (£210,000/12 × 8)		140,000
		194,000
Less: expenses:		
Loan interest	65,000	
Maintenance & decorating	12,500	
Insurance	2,200	
Rates	15,750	
		(95,450)
Rental profit for commercial property		98,550

continued overleaf

New Property 1

Rental income – new tenant (£48,000/12 × 9)		36,000
		36,000
Less: expenses:		
Extension & furniture (not allowable)	0	
Rates	1,985	
Insurance (£640/12 × 11)	587	
Legal fees re. unpaid rent	440	
Repairs	3,577	
		(6,589)
Rental profit for new property 1		29,411

New Property 2

Rental income – new tenant (£26,400/12 × 6)		13,200
		13,200
Less: expenses:		
Loan interest (£200,000 × 3% × 8/12)	4,000	
Rates	1,300	
Insurance (£470/12 × 8)	313	
Legal fees for purchase of property (not allowable)	0	
Repairs	330	
Replacement furniture relief	3,500	
		(9,443)
Rental profit for new property 2		3,757

Rent-a-room relief

Choice of being taxed on:

Option 1	
Income	9,000
Less: exempt amount	(7,500)
Taxable profit	1,500

Or

Option 2	
Income	9,000
Less: allowable expenses	(735)
Taxable profit	8,265

Matthew would choose to be taxed on the basis of rent-a-room relief (Option 2).

Total property income for 2016/17	**133,218**
Less: loss forward from 2015/16	**(10,000)**
Taxable property income for 2016/17	**123,218**

8.3.6 Non-resident Landlord Scheme

Non-UK residents (under the statutory residence test (SRT)) who receive rental income from a UK property are treated under the non-resident landlord (NRL) scheme. Basically, under the scheme the rental income is taxed at source at the basic income tax rate of 20% and the landlord's property income is received net.

To operate the NRL scheme, a non-resident landlord has a representative, either their tenant or collecting agent, designated as the "prescribed person" by HMRC. The prescribed person is required to make the requisite payments (20% income tax on rental payments to the non-resident landlord) direct to HMRC. A tenant who pays more than £5,200 per year (or the proportionate equivalent for a shorter period) is automatically the prescribed person; tenants who pay less than that amount do not have to operate the scheme unless requested to do so by HMRC.

The prescribed person is entitled to be indemnified by the landlord for such payments and to retain from the payments sufficient sums to meet their obligations to HMRC. The income tax due, less certain allowable expenses and deductions (see **Section 8.3.3**), must be paid on a quarterly basis. HMRC's prescribed person must provide the non-resident landlord with an **annual certificate** showing details of tax deducted and paid, **by 5 July after the year end**.

Non-resident landlords will then set the tax deducted against their UK tax liability through their self-assessment.

Non-resident landlords can apply to HMRC to be excluded from the scheme and to receive their UK property income gross. HMRC must be satisfied that the non-resident landlord will comply fully with the self-assessment provisions, and that the following points are met:

1. their UK tax affairs are up to date;
2. they have never had any obligations in relation to UK tax or they do not expect to be liable to UK income tax; and
3. they undertake to comply with all their future UK tax obligations.

The landlord has the right to appeal against a refusal of their application or a withdrawal of previous approval.

Example 8.5

Derek is Irish tax resident and lets out an apartment in Belfast. He lets the apartment through a letting agency, which deducts tax on his quarterly rental income under the non-resident landlord scheme. Derek has agreed a quarterly rental amount of £4,500. The letting agency charges a 10% fee on the gross rents.

Under the NRL scheme, how much will be paid in income tax?

Rental income per quarter	£4,500
Less: letting agent fee	(£450)
Net rental income	£4,050
NRL scheme (20% of net rents)	£810

Annual amount paid by the letting agent to HMRC: £810 × 4 = £3,240

When Derek prepares his property income computation for inclusion in his self-assessment tax return, he will calculate his tax liability as follows:

Rental income		£18,000
Less: expenses:		
Letting agent fee	£1,800	
Mortgage interest	£7,000	
Accountancy fees	£1,200	
	(£10,000)	
Property income profits	£8,000	

The £8,000 property income profit will be fully covered by the personal allowance of £11,000. Therefore no income tax will be due.

Derek will be due a refund of £3,240 from HMRC as he will be able to claim a credit in respect of the tax already paid by the letting agent.

8.3.7 Furnished Holiday Home Lettings

Furnished holiday homes (FHH) lettings are subject to favourable tax rules whereby the letting is treated as if it were a **trade** rather than under property income rules. This means that although the income is taxed as income from a property business, the more generous provisions that apply to actual trades also apply to FHHs. The original legislation on FHHs only applied to UK-situated properties; however, this was ruled in breach of EU law and HMRC therefore extended the relief to qualifying FHHs located in the EEA, i.e. the 28 EU Member States plus Iceland, Liechtenstein and Norway.

The income tax rules for FHHs are:

1. loss relief may only be offset against income from the same FHH business;
2. capital allowances are available on furniture, equipment and fixtures;
3. the income qualifies as relevant earnings for pension relief (see **Chapter 9**);
4. capital gains tax rollover relief, entrepreneurs' relief and relief for gifts of business assets are available (although outside the scope of CA Proficiency 1, they are relevant for CA Proficiency 2); and
5. the basis period rules for trades do not apply, and the profits or losses on an FHH must be computed for actual tax years (6 April–5 April).

To qualify as an FHH, the property must be **furnished** accommodation and run on a **commercial basis with a view to the realisation of profit**. The property must also satisfy the following three conditions:

1. *Availability condition* – the accommodation is available for commercial letting as holiday accommodation to the general public for at least 210 days in the year.
2. *Letting condition* – the accommodation is commercially let as holiday accommodation to the public for at least 105 days in the year.
3. *Pattern of occupation condition* – during a 12-month period, not more than 155 days fall during periods of longer-term occupation. "Longer term" is a continuous period of more than 31 consecutive days during which the accommodation is in the same occupation, unless there are abnormal circumstances.

If a landlord has both FHH lettings and other lettings, it is necessary to keep separate rental accounts to reflect the fact they are two separate property businesses. This is so that the profits and losses treated as trade profits and losses can be clearly identified.

Landlords can currently choose whether to be taxed under the FHH rules or under the normal rules for property businesses. A claim for FHH is made on the property income supplementary pages of the UK tax return.

A grace period of one or two years was also introduced to allow businesses/taxpayers that do not meet the occupancy threshold (i.e. the letting condition), but genuinely intend to do so, to elect to continue to qualify throughout that period. The election must be made within one year of 31 January following the first tax year in which the failure to meet the letting condition occurs.

8.3.8 Real Estate Investment Trusts

Property companies can choose to operate as real estate investment trusts (REITs). In an REIT, distributions paid to shareholders are not treated as normal company dividends but instead are taxed as property income. This property income has the basic rate (currently 20%) deducted at source from the distribution paid.

Distributions by REITs out of other income (i.e. not property income or gains) are taxed as dividends in the normal way.

Questions

Review Questions

(See Suggested Solutions to Review Questions at the end of this textbook.)

Question 8.1

Mr O'Reilly owns five properties that he lets. Details of his income from these properties and the letting terms are as follows.

Property A (residential property) Acquired in November 2012 and let on a five-year lease, expiring in November 2017, at a monthly rent of £500, payable monthly in advance. The rent due on 28 February 2017 was not received until 10 April 2017. Interest of £5,500 was incurred during the year on a bank loan taken out to acquire the property.

Property B (commercial property) Acquired on 1 April 2015 and let for the first time on 1 August 2016, on a 21-year lease at a full annual rent of £12,000, payable monthly in advance. A bank loan was raised to help purchase the property and interest of £3,600 was paid on 30 June 2016 and £3,600 on 31 December 2016. A premium of £10,000 was also received under the terms of the new lease.

Property C (residential property) Let at a full annual rent of £6,000 under a seven-year lease, which expired on 30 April 2016. The property was vacant until 1 November 2016, when it was let again on a five-year lease at a full rent of £9,000 per annum.

Property D (residential property) Let to Mr O'Reilly's brother on a 21-year lease from 1 May 2003, at an annual rent of £52 (not a full rent).

The landlord is responsible for repairs on all properties, except for Property A, in respect of which there is a "tenants's repairing" lease. During the tax year 2016/17, the following additional expenses were incurred:

		£
Property B		
30 April	Dry rot repairs	950
30 June	Window broken by vandals	80
31 December	Storm damage	1,400
Property C		
20 May	Blocked drains	90
31 July	Painting	700
31 October	Advertising for tenant	130
Property D		
28 September	Roof repairs	1,600

Requirement
Compute Mr O'Reilly's UK property business income for the tax year 2016/17.

Question 8.2

Sonya, a widow aged 47, has recently brought you details of her property income, which will be needed to prepare schedules supporting her tax return. All properties are non-residential properties. Relevant information is as follows.

- Property 1 is let on a 10-year lease. The lease was granted in December 2013 at an annual rent of £16,000, payable monthly in arrears, subject to review every three years.
- Property 2 is let at a rent of £8,000 per annum, payable monthly in advance.
- Property 3 is let at a rent of £9,600 per annum, payable monthly in advance. The instalment of rent due on 1 December 2015 was never received. This property was first let some years ago.
- Property 4 was first let on a 15-year lease on 30 June 2016 and a rent of £9,000 per annum payable quarterly in arrears on 30 September, 31 December, 30 March and 30 June, subject to review every three years.
- Property 5 is let on a 15-year lease, expiring June 2017, at a nominal rent of £10 per month, payable annually in advance on 30 June. The tenant is Sonya's sister.

The expenses (all allowable) paid in 2016 by Sonya for each property were:

	£
Property 1	4,300
Property 2	1,200
Property 3	800
Property 4	NIL
Property 5	10

In addition, mortgage interest of £1,400 was paid on a loan to finance the purchase of Property 3.

Requirement
Prepare a schedule summarising Sonya's UK property business income assessable in 2016/17.

Deductions on Income, Allowances and Reliefs

Learning Objectives

After studying this chapter you will understand:

- The relief available on total income for qualifying reliefs, such as eligible loan interest and gifts of quoted shares/land to charity.
- The tax relief available for an individual's:
  - pension contributions; and
  - gift aid donations.
- The rules and conditions for personal allowances, including:
  - standard personal allowance (including restrictions);
  - blind person's allowance; and
  - marriage allowance.
- The rules and conditions for each of the following tax reducers:
  - the venture capital trust (VCT) scheme;
  - the Enterprise Investment Scheme (EIS) and Seed Enterprise Investment Scheme (SEIS);
  - social investment tax relief (SITR);
  - maintenance payments; and
  - married couple's allowance (MCA).
- The entitlement and operation of Child Tax Credit, Working Tax Credit and Universal Tax Credit.

9.1 Introduction

In **Chapter 2** the income tax computation pro forma was outlined, which provided an overview for the steps and calculations required to calculate income tax liability. In each of the subsequent chapters dealing with the specific types of income, the pro forma layout has been used first to determine "total income", then to calculate "taxable income" and finally to compute the income tax. In doing so we have encountered some of the more universal reliefs and allowances that are available to reduce a taxpayer's income tax liability. In this chapter we will consider all the various deductions, allowances and reliefs in greater detail.

To refresh, the pro forma income tax computation is shown below (**Figure 9.1**). There are four areas of the computation that we will look at in turn:

1. "qualifying reliefs" – which are deducted from total income to give "net income";
2. "pension contributions and gift aid donations" – which are tax reliefs at the marginal rate;
3. "personal allowances" – which are deducted from net income to give "taxable income"; and
4. "tax reducers" – which reduce the tax suffered.

FIGURE 9.1: PRO FORMA INCOME TAX COMPUTATION

		Non-savings Income £	Savings Income £	Dividend Income £	Total £
Gross income:					
Trading income		xx			xx
Property income		xx			xx
Employment income		xx			xx
Savings and investment income:					
Bank/building society interest			xx		xx
National Savings & Investment a/c interest			xx		xx
UK dividends				xx	xx
Step 1	**Total income**	xxx	xxx	xxx	xxx
	Less: specified reliefs	(xx)	(xx)	(xx)	(xx)
Step 2	**Net income**	xxx	xxx	xxx	xxx
	Less: personal allowance	(max.11,000)			(max.11,000)
Step 3	**Taxable income**	xxxx	xxxx	xxxx	xxxx
Step 4	**Income tax:**				**£**
	Non-savings income:				
	£ × 20%				xxxx
	£ × 40%				xxxx
	£ × 45%				xxxx
	Savings income:				
	£ × 0% (starting limit for savings income and personal savings allowance, if available)				0
	£ × 20%				xxxx
	£ × 40%				xxxx
	£ × 45%				xxxx

continued overleaf

	£
Dividend income:	
Up to £5,000 dividend allowance × 0%	0
£ × 7.5%	xxxx
£ × 32.5%	xxxx
£ × 38.1%	xxxx

		£
Step 5	**Total**	xxxx
Step 6	**Less: tax reducers**	(xxx)
Step 7	**Add: additional tax**	xxx
Step 8	**Less: tax deducted at source**	(xxx)
Result	Income tax liability/(refund)	**xxx**

9.2 Qualifying Reliefs

In the income tax computation, total income has qualifying reliefs deducted to arrive at "adjusted net income".

9.2.1 Relief for Eligible Interest

Interest charged on certain loans is eligible for income tax relief. As with the other qualifying reliefs, it operates by deducting the qualifying amount (the interest paid) from total income to give net income for a particular tax year (the tax year in which the interest has been **paid**).

The following loans are eligible for this relief:

- Loan to purchase an interest in a partnership.
- Loan to buy ordinary shares in, or to lend money to, a close company that the taxpayer manages, or in which they own more than 5% of the ordinary shares.
- Loan for the purchase of shares in an employee-controlled company, where the taxpayer is an employee.
- Loan for the purchase of plant and machinery for a partnership by one of the partners (interest allowable for a period of three years from the end of the tax year in which a loan was taken out).
- Loan for the purchase of plant and machinery by an employee for use in their employment (allowable for a period of three years from the end of the tax year in which loan was taken out).
- Loan to pay inheritance tax (allowable for a period of one year).
- Loan to invest in a co-operative, provided the taxpayer spends the greater part of his or her time working in the co-operative.

It is important to note from the list above that an eligible loan can be for business (trading) purposes, for investment purposes or, in the case of a loan to pay inheritance tax, for individual reasons. The purpose of the loan will determine from what class of income the interest paid should be deducted and, in some cases, on what basis it is assessed. For example, a taxpayer paying interest "wholly and exclusively" for business purposes can deduct interest against trading profits and it is tax deductible on an **accruals** basis, not on a **paid** basis.

Interest on an eligible loan is deducted from non-savings income first; then, if there is any interest amount remaining, it is deducted from savings income; and, lastly, any remaining amount will be deducted from dividend income.

Example 9.1
Janice has employment income of £50,000 and savings income of £5,000 in 2016/17. She also paid interest of £2,000 on a loan for the purchase of an interest in a partnership.

	Non-savings income £	Savings income £
Income sources		
Employment income	50,000	
Savings income		5,000
Total income	50,000	5,000
Less: qualifying reliefs	(2,000)	–
Net income	48,000	5,000
Less: personal allowances	(11,000)	
Taxable income	37,000	5,000

Tax relief for eligible interest is one of the reliefs affected by the cap on loss relief (see **Section 5.12.8** for further details).

9.2.2 Annual Payments

An annual payment is a payment made that is "pure income profit" in the hands of the recipient. Therefore, the person in receipt of the annual payment usually does not have any expenses against this income.

A deduction of income tax at the basic rate (20%) is required to be made by the individual paying the qualifying annual payments and patent royalties. Basic rate tax is deducted from annual payments by the payer where the annual payment is made for genuine commercial reasons in connection with the individual's trade, profession or vocation.

The principal annual payments include:

- purchased life annuity payments;
- distributions from unauthorised unit trusts;
- royalties, etc. from intellectual property; and
- annual payments not otherwise charged.

In practice, few such payments are likely to be made by individuals who are not traders and, as noted, annual payments made for genuine commercial purposes must deduct tax.

Annual payments do **not** include:

- dividends;
- interest;
- qualifying charitable donations;
- gift aid;
- exempt patent royalties, etc.

Copyright/design royalties are annual payments, but they are subject to special treatment. They are **paid gross of tax unless the recipient is resident abroad**.

Relief for annual payments is on a **paid basis** only and not on an accruals basis.

The additional tax to be paid to HMRC (i.e. the amount that was withheld by the payer) is collected through self-assessment, but is not taken into account for payment on account purposes.

Example 9.2

Ryan has employment income of £20,000 in 2016/17. He agreed to pay a patent owner £1,000 per annum for use of the patent. Ryan will therefore have only paid the patent owner £800, 20% of the payment having been withheld to be paid to HMRC.

Ryan's income tax computation will be as follows:

	Non-savings income £
Income sources	
Employment income	20,000
Total income	**20,000**
Less: qualifying reliefs	(1,000)
Net income	19,000
Less: personal allowances	(11,000)
Taxable income	8,000
Income tax non-savings income:	
£8,000 × 20%	1,600
Add tax deducted on patent royalty	200
Tax liability	1,800

9.2.3   Gifts of Shares or Land to Charity

Gifts of qualifying investments to a UK charity are eligible for income tax relief as a qualifying relief. The following categories of investment qualify for the relief:

■ shares or securities that are listed on any recognised stock exchange, e.g. the London Stock Exchange and the New York Stock Exchange;

■ shares and securities dealt on any designated market in the UK, e.g. the Alternative Investment Market (AIM) of the London Stock Exchange; and

■ a qualifying interest in land.

As with the other qualifying reliefs, it operates by deducting the qualifying amount (the amount gifted) from total income to give net income for a particular tax year (the tax year in which the gift is made). The value of the gift of qualifying assets that is eligible for relief is deducted first from non-savings income; then, if there is any amount remaining, it is deducted from savings income; and lastly, any remaining amount will be deducted from dividend income.

9.3   Pension Contributions and Gift Aid Donations

Relief for pension contributions and gift aid donations are given at an individual's marginal rate of tax. An individual's marginal rate of tax is the highest rate of tax they pay.

9.3.1   Pension Contributions

Introduction

The Government aims to incentivise saving through pensions. It does this by offering tax relief to individuals who pay contributions to their pension schemes, allowing the pension schemes to grow tax-free. Each year an individual is limited on the amount that they can invest in a pension and a breach of these limits will mean that a tax charge will be incurred.

The size to which a pension fund can grow to be tax-free is also restricted. Where an individual is an employee, they will pay into their work/occupational pension scheme. Their employer will normally also contribute to the pension scheme on the employee's behalf. Where an individual is self-employed (or where an employee finds that their employer does not offer an occupational scheme), they can contribute to a personal pension scheme.

In the UK, the normal minimum pension age rose from 50 to 55 from 6 April 2010. Pensions are normally accessed by the age of 75 at the latest.

A pension scheme may be either a defined benefits scheme or a defined contribution scheme. In a defined benefits pension scheme (also known as a final salary scheme) the benefits payable to members are usually based on final salary (or career-average salary) and length of service. In a defined contribution scheme (also known as a money purchase scheme), the benefits payable to members are based on the size of the pension fund built up during a member's working life.

In addition, pension schemes can be either registered, i.e. formally approved by HMRC in accordance with tax legislation, or unregistered. Income tax relief is only available on registered pension schemes (see below for more details); unregistered schemes are liable to income tax.

Registered pension schemes include:

- occupational pension schemes (including workplace pension schemes) – schemes set up by an employer for its employees;
- public service pension schemes – schemes set up by Government, e.g. the civil service pension scheme; or
- personal pension schemes – schemes set up by a financial institution for an individual's private contributions.

As already noted, registered pension schemes enjoy certain tax advantages. For example, they are exempt from income tax (and from CGT on capital gains arising on the disposal of investments). Tax relief is available in relation to contributions made by members and employers. Tax-free lump sums may be paid to members.

Income Tax Relief on Registered Pension Schemes

Income tax relief on an individual's contributions to a registered pension scheme is dependent on the rate of income tax paid by the individual: a basic rate taxpayer will receive relief at 20%; a higher rate taxpayer's relief will be 40%; and an additional rate taxpayer's relief will be at 45%.

Basic rate tax relief is generally deducted at source, i.e. net of tax; it is then 'repaid' by HMRC into the individual's pension scheme. Higher rate relief operates by increasing the upper limit of the basic rate tax band (£32,000) by the individual's **gross** contributions and applying the higher rate tax relief. The proportion of the relief applicable to the basic rate is deducted at source, i.e. net at 20% tax; the remaining relief, the higher rate, is claimed by the individual through their year-end tax return.

Example 9.3

Sara pays a personal pension contribution of £8,000 (net) to her private pension scheme. What is the position if Sara is:

1. a basic rate taxpayer?
2. A higher rate taxpayer?

1. The £8,000 contribution is net, the basic rate tax of 20% having been paid at source. Sara's gross contribution is £10,000 (100/80 × £8,000), so HMRC re-pays the 20% (£2,000) into the scheme on her behalf.
2. Sara's basic rate band is increased by the gross pension contribution: £32,000 + £10,000 = £42,000. Overall 40% income tax relief is available, 20% deducted at source (£2,000) and 20% through Sara's year-end tax return.

For occupational pension schemes only, an alternative method of administering the relief is available whereby the individual's (the employee's) gross contributions are deducted from their gross pay, i.e. before PAYE is deducted. This arrangement is referred to as a "net pay arrangement". The individual therefore obtains tax relief on the pension contributions at their marginal rate of tax without having to make a claim.

Example 9.4

Sara has an occupational pension scheme into which she pays £10,000 under a net pay arrangement. Her gross salary is £60,000.

Under the net pay arrangement the contribution to the pension fund is deducted from gross pay to give taxable pay of £50,000 on which PAYE is operated.

	£
Employment income	60,000
Less: pension contributions	(10,000)
Net income	50,000
Less: personal allowance	(11,000)
Taxable income	39,000

Income tax: non-savings income	
£32,000 × 20%	6,400
£7,000 × 40%	2,800
	9,200

Sara is therefore saving tax at the marginal rate (40%) as, instead of having £17,000 taxable at 40%, she has £7,000 only.

If Sara was a basic rate taxpayer, the relief would have been 20%. No separate claim would be required to obtain this relief (and there would be no need to extend the basic rate band).

Annual Allowance

The annual allowance is a 'ceiling' on the amount of pension contributions (an individual's and an employer's, if applicable) that can benefit from the tax relief. It does not restrict the amount of tax relief; instead it applies a charge, the "**annual allowance charge**", when the annual allowance has been exceeded. In effect, the charge reverses the relief on the excess amount over the annual allowance. What this means is that if the amount paid into a pension exceeds the annual allowance, this does not mean that the relief is restricted to the annual allowance. Rather, the relief available is the greater of either:

- an individual's "**relevant UK earnings**" (subject to the annual allowance); or,
- if an individual does not have any relevant UK earnings in a tax year, £3,600.

"Relevant UK earnings" includes income from self-employment, employment and furnished holiday lettings (see **Section 8.3.7**). Investment and property income do not qualify as relevant earnings and therefore cannot increase a taxpayer's capacity to make pension contributions.

The annual allowance for tax years 2006/07 to 2016/17 are:

2006/07	£215,000
2007/08	£225,000
2008/09	£235,000
2009/10	£245,000
2010/11	£255,000
2011/12	£50,000

2012/13	£50,000
2013/14	£50,000
2014/15	£40,000
2015/16	£40,000
2016/17	**£40,000**

If an individual's gross contributions in a tax year (including any from an employer) exceed the annual allowance, the excess contributions are liable to income tax. This is known as the **annual allowance charge** and is calculated on the individual's marginal tax rate (i.e. top rate).

Example 9.5

Joseph had employment income of £140,000 in 2016/17. He made gross pension contributions of £60,000 in 2016/17 and has no unused annual allowance brought forward from earlier years.

Joseph's income tax position is as follows:

	£
Total income	140,000
Personal allowance	
(as income over £122,000. See **Section 9.4**)	Nil
Taxable income	140,000
Income tax on savings income:	
£32,000 × 20%	6,400
£60,000 × 20%	12,000
£48,000 × 40%	19,200
£140,000	37,600
Add excess pension contribution	
£20,000 × 40% (Note 1)	8,000
	45,600

Note:
1. Excess pension contribution is £20,000 (£60,000 – £20,000 = £40,000 annual allowance amount).

Where the individual is an employee, if the **employer contributes to the pension scheme, these are exempt benefits**. There is no limit to the amount of the contributions that may be made by an employer, but they will count towards the individual's annual allowance (see below). An employer can contribute into an occupational scheme or into an individual's personal pension scheme but, in either case, the contributions will always be made **gross**. This is a tax-deductible expense for the employer if made **wholly and exclusively** for business purposes. On some occasions, the employer may have to **spread** the tax relief on large contributions over a number of accounting periods.

An individual may have more than one pension scheme at a time, e.g. an occupational scheme and a private pension; however, the maximum limit on contributions applies to all the pension contributions made, **not** to each of them separately.

Any unused annual allowance in a tax year can be carried over and added to the next tax year's annual allowance, up to a maximum of three tax years. For example, if gross pension contributions of £30,000 were made in 2015/16, the unused £10,000 can be carried forward to 2016/17 and, if still unused, can be carried forward to 2017/18 and, finally, to the 2018/19 tax year. If there is unused annual allowance from a previous year, the current year annual allowance is used first, then the unused annual allowance from the prior year.

Example 9.6

In 2014/15 an individual joined a pension scheme and made gross contributions of £30,000. In 2015/16 they made contributions of £50,000 and in 2016/17 they made gross contributions of £30,000.

The amount of unused allowance in 2014/15 was £10,000. The £10,000 can be carried forward from 2014/15 and used in 2015/16 (i.e. added to the £40,000 allowance in that year). The £10,000 unused allowance in 2014/15 will be used in 2015/16 as the amount of gross contributions was £50,000. That is, £10,000 more than the £40,000 annual allowance in 2015/16.

If there is unused annual allowance from more than one previous tax year, relief from the earlier year is used first (the first in, first out (FIFO) basis).

Example 9.7

In 2014/15 an individual joined a pension scheme and made gross contributions of £20,000. In 2015/16 they made contributions of £30,000 and in 2016/17 they made gross contributions of £60,000.

In 2014/15, the unused annual allowance was £20,000. In 2015/16, the unused annual allowance was £10,000.

In 2016/17, pension contributions of £60,000 were made. The excess of £20,000 contributions will be covered by the unused annual allowance of £20,000 for 2014/15. The unused allowance of £10,000 from 2015/16 will carry forward to 2017/18.

If an unused amount from one of the three previous tax years could have been utilised before the current year, it cannot be carried forward.

In addition, when calculating the annual allowance for 2015/16, it is assumed that the carry-forward rules also applied in the three previous tax years. This means that if any of the unused allowance could have been used up by the gross contributions made in the three previous tax years, it will not be possible to carry forward the unused allowance to the current year.

Example 9.8

Helen runs a clothes shop. She has been trading profitably for a number of years, but 2016/17 is a particularly profitable year and she wishes to make a large personal pension contribution. Her gross pension contributions for the last few years are:

2012/13	£25,000
2013/14	£30,000
2014/15	£25,000
2015/16	£15,000

The maximum gross tax relievable pension that Helen can make in 2016/17 is:

2016/17 annual allowance	£40,000	
2013/14 unused annual allowance	£20,000	(£50,000 – £30,000)
2014/15 unused annual allowance	£15,000	(£40,000 – £25,000)
2015/16 unused annual allowance	£25,000	(£40,000 – £15,000)
	£100,000	

The 2012/13 unused annual allowance cannot be used in 2016/17, as unused allowances can only be carried forward three years.

As noted above, contributions in excess of annual allowance will be liable to tax at the individual's marginal rate (basically, the excess contribution is added to their taxable income). The overall position is to remove any tax relief on the pension contribution. It is, therefore, still possible to contribute to a pension in excess of the annual allowance, but no tax relief will be given on the excess contribution.

Lifetime Allowance

There is no limit on the amount of benefits an individual can be paid from a pension scheme; however, the amount that can be received without suffering income tax is subject to the lifetime allowance. Like the annual allowance, the lifetime allowance operates by applying a charge (the **lifetime allowance charge**) for payments received that exceed the limit.

The lifetime allowance for tax years 2006/07 to 2016/17 are:

2006/07	£1,500,000
2007/08	£1,600,000
2008/09	£1,650,000
2009/10	£1,750,000
2010/11	£1,800,000
2011/12	£1,800,000
2012/13	£1,500,000
2013/14	£1,500,000
2014/15	£1,250,000
2015/16	£1,250,000
2016/17	**£1,000,000**

The lifetime allowance is 'used' when a "benefit crystallisation event" occurs. The most common examples of such an event are the payment of a lump sum to a member or the commencement of pension benefits.

The value of the crystallised benefit is compared with the unused proportion of the lifetime allowance and any excess is charged to income tax. Whenever a benefit crystallisation event occurs, it is necessary to compare the value of the benefits that have crystallised with the proportion of the individual's lifetime allowance that remain unused after any previous such events. On the first occasion that a benefit crystallisation event occurs, the value of the benefits that have crystallised is compared with the lifetime allowance as it stands on the date of the event. On a subsequent event, the value of the crystallised benefits is compared with the proportion of the lifetime allowance (if any) that remains after previous events. However, this proportion is applied to the lifetime allowance as it stands on the date of the subsequent event.

The lifetime allowance charge is either 55% or 25% of the excess amount received, depending on whether it has been taken as a lump sum (55%) or as pension income (25%). The charge falls jointly upon the scheme administrator and the member concerned. In practice, it will usually be paid by the scheme administrator and then deducted from the benefits paid to the individual.

Example 9.9

Jeff is 60 years old in 2016/17 and decides to access his pension on retirement. His pension fund was valued at £1,800,000 on retirement. He receives a lump sum of £250,000 tax-free and buys an annuity for £750,000 to provide him with pension income. The remaining £800,000 over the lifetime allowance of £1,000,000 is taken as a lump sum.

Jeff will be subject to a lifetime allowance charge of £800,000 × 55% = £440,000.

Retirement Benefits

Unless retiring due to ill health, pensions will not normally be allowed to be paid out of a pension scheme until the individual member reaches normal pension age – 50 years for members who reach this age on or before 5 April 2010, 55 years thereafter.

All or part of the pension fund can be taken to provide pension benefits at any time from age 55 onwards. It is therefore possible to receive a pension and still continue to work.

As noted above, if the fund value exceeds the lifetime allowance, the excess is charged to income tax at differing rates, depending on how the excess is used, as explained above.

A tax-free lump sum payment of up to 25% of the lower of the fund value or the lifetime allowance can be paid out of the scheme; but a tax-free lump sum cannot be taken and recycled into future pension contributions to obtain double tax relief.

Defined Contributions Pension Schemes

Individuals with defined contribution pension savings have three main options when accessing their pension benefits. From age 55, individuals can choose any one option or a combination of them.

1. Individuals can purchase an annuity – a tax-free lump sum of 25% of the pension pot can be taken, with the remainder being used to purchase an annuity that will provide income for the rest of the person's life (subject to income tax on receipt).
2. Individuals can draw down funds – a tax-fee lump sum of 25% of the pension pot can be taken at the same time the funds are put into drawdown. The drawdown funds are invested and the individual can decide how much to take each year (taxed as income).
3. Individuals can take multiple lump sum payments from the pension pot – 25% of each lump sum will be tax-free, with the remainder being taxed as income. The lump sums are referred to as "uncrystallised funds pension lump sum" (UFPLS).

In addition, from April 2015, if an individual dies before the age of 75 they can now pass on their unused defined contribution pension savings free of income tax.

Defined Benefits Pension Scheme

The benefits from a defined benefit scheme depend upon length of service, pensionable earnings, etc. and are received in line with the rules set out by the scheme. Therefore individuals with defined benefit pension savings do not have the same options with regard to accessing their benefits. However, from 5 April 2015, individuals can transfer from a defined benefit scheme to a defined contribution scheme to avail of the greater flexibility (although, traditionally, defined benefit schemes tend to provide valuable benefits and any transfer should be carefully considered).

Pension income is taxable as non-savings income. A pension provider will provide each pensioner with a Form P60 (see **Chapter 10**), showing details of their gross pension and the tax deducted at source.

9.3.2   Gift Aid Donations

Charitable donations made under gift aid are paid net of basic rate tax. This has the effect of giving basic rate tax relief when the payment is made.

Example 9.10

Nigel would like to give his local charity £1,000; to do so he need only donate £800. The charity can reclaim Nigel's tax relief on the £800 donation (20% = £200) from HMRC.

Gift aid donations attract relief at the donor's highest, or marginal, rate of tax. This is done by extending the taxpayer's basic rate band by the grossed-up amount for higher rate taxpayers; and by extending both the basic rate and higher rate bands if they are an additional rate taxpayer (i.e. similar to the way tax relief on pension contributions is given, see **Section 9.3.1**). No additional tax relief is due for basic rate taxpayers. As shown in the example, the charity will claim a basis rate taxpayer's tax relief.

Gifts can be once-off or part of a series of donations, and there is no minimum or maximum amount that can be donated. The donor must give an appropriate declaration to the charity concerned either in writing, by telephone, by fax or via the internet.

Example 9.11
Jean is 71 years old. In 2016/17 she receives income from property of £44,750. She also pays a copyright royalty of £500 during the year and makes a gift aid donation of £100. Calculate the tax payable by Jean.

Income Tax Computation 2016/17		£
Property income		44,750
Less: copyright royalty (paid)		(500)
Net income		44,250
Less: personal allowance		(11,000)
Taxable income		33,250
Income tax due:		
Basic rate:	£32,000 @ 20%	6,400
Extended basic rate (Note 1)	£125 @ 20%	25
Higher rate	£1,125 @ 40%	450
		33,250
Tax liability		6,875

Note:
1. The gift aid donation is paid net of £25 tax (£100 × 20/80) and higher rate tax relief is given by extending the basic rate band by the grossed-up donation.

Note: **sufficient tax must be paid by the donor to cover the basic rate repayment to the charity**. If a donor pays insufficient tax, it may be necessary to restrict their personal allowance or to raise an assessment to ensure that the tax paid to the charity has been paid by the individual.

The donor may elect that gift aid donations made on or before 31 January in a tax year be treated as if **paid** in the previous tax year, so long as these donations are made before the tax return for the previous tax year is submitted (i.e. extend the basic rate band for the previous tax year).

Gift Aid Small Donation Scheme
On cash donations of £20 or less, charities may be able to claim 25% tax relief even if the charity doesn't have a gift aid declaration. This is called the Gift Aid Small Donation Scheme. There is no relief for the donor for these small donations. Relief for the charity is capped at £8,000 per annum from April 2016.

If the donor, or persons connected to them, receives benefit (such as a lapel sticker, a pen or a keyring) from making the gift, it must not exceed:

- 25% of the amount of the gift, if the gift does not exceed £100;
- £25 if the gift exceeds £100 but does not exceed £1,000;
- 5% of the amount of the gift, if the gift exceeds £1,000; or
- an overall cap on benefits of £2,500.

Payroll Giving Scheme

Charitable donations may be deducted from gross employment earnings before tax is calculated. The employer must obtain HMRC approval to operate the scheme. The employer passes the donation on to the approved charity.

The donation made by an employee under a payroll giving scheme is an allowable deduction from the employee's earnings for income tax purposes. The tax relief is given at source as the employee will only pay tax on their salary, less the donations. Under the payroll giving scheme, if an individual is a basic rate taxpayer, then they need to give £0.80 from their wages for the charity to receive £1.

Example 9.12
Anne is a higher rate taxpayer, with employment income of £80,000 in 2016/17. Anne wishes to donate £50 via her employer's payroll giving scheme to her favourite charity. Anne's employer pays all the administration costs associated with running the payroll giving scheme.

Anne will have £30 deducted from her wages before tax. By having this amount deducted from her wages, her favourite charity will receive £50. That is, £30 from Anne and £20 from the HMRC.

9.4 Personal Allowances

When all an individual's income has been aggregated and the qualifying reliefs have been deducted, the result is the individual's net income from which personal allowances are deducted (see pro forma in **Section 9.1**).

9.4.1 Standard Personal Allowance

A personal allowance of £11,000 for 2016/17 can be claimed by any individual who is in receipt of any income and who is UK resident (whether UK domiciled or not); and by some non-UK residents, e.g. citizens from the European Economic Area (EEA), Isle of Man or Channel Islands (see **Section 3.4** for further details). The personal allowance is deducted from net income, first from non-savings income, then from savings income and lastly from investment income (dividends).

In year of death, separation or divorce, full personal allowances are awarded. Therefore no apportionment is required.

Restriction on Standard Personal Allowance

The standard personal allowance is abated (reduced) where an individual's "adjusted net income" (see **Section 9.1**) is in excess of £100,000. For every £2 above £100,000, the standard personal allowance is reduced by £1. So, for example, adjusted net income of £110,000 would mean that the standard personal allowance would be reduced to £6,000. This restriction applies until the allowance is removed entirely; therefore, if your income is £122,000 or more, your personal allowance is zero.

It is for this reason that financial planning, such as pension contributions, is particularly important in reducing tax liability – by bringing adjusted net income below the £100,000 threshold, thus preserving personal allowances.

9.4.2 Blind Person's Allowance

If a taxpayer is registered as blind, the blind person's allowance can be claimed. This is in **addition** to the standard personal allowance and is £2,290 for 2016/17. A claim can also be made in the tax year before registration if blindness can be proved in that year.

The allowance is set against the taxpayer's net income and gives tax relief at the marginal rate (i.e. the highest rate at which the taxpayer pays tax). If all or part of the blind person's allowance cannot be fully used by one spouse/civil partner, then the unused portion can be transferred to the other spouse/civil partner, even if they are not a registered blind person.

9.4.3   Marriage Allowance

The marriage allowance lets an individual transfer £1,100 of his or her personal allowance to their husband/wife/civil partner. The marriage allowance can reduce an individual's tax by up to £220 (i.e. £1,100 × 20%) in the 2016/17 tax year.

For a couple to benefit from the marriage allowance, the lower earning spouse/civil partner must have an income of £11,000 or less. The higher earning spouse/civil partner must have income between £11,001 and £43,000 (i.e. he/she must be a basic rate taxpayer). In addition, both spouses/civil partners must be born on or after 6 April 1935 to be eligible for the marriage allowance.

9.4.4   Summary: Personal Allowances Rates and Thresholds

	2015/16 £	2016/17 £
Standard personal allowance	10,600	11,000
Age allowance		
Born between 6 April 1938 and 5 April 1948	10,600	11,000
Born before 6 April 1938	10,660	11,000
Income limit for the allowances for those born before 6 April 1938	27,700	27,700
Income limit for personal allowances	100,000	100,000
Marriage allowance	1,060	1,100
Blind person's allowance	2,290	2,290

9.5   Tax Reducers

The key point to note with tax reducers is that they do not directly impact on income, they reduce the tax on income. They entitle the taxpayer to a maximum fixed percentage reduction, rather than providing tax relief at the taxpayer's marginal rate. Another key point to note is that tax reducers can only reduce a tax liability to zero, they cannot create a refund.

Tax reducers include:

- venture capital trust (VCT) scheme;
- the Enterprise Investment Scheme (EIS);
- the Seed Enterprise Investment Scheme (SEIS);
- social investment tax relief (SITR);
- maintenance payments; and
- married couple's allowance.

When computing the income tax payable, the relief granted by tax reducers must be applied in the order in which they are listed above.

The VCT scheme and EIS and SEIS are broadly aimed at promoting investment in target companies. SITR is aimed at promoting investment in social enterprises.

9.5.1 Venture Capital Trust Scheme

The VCT scheme is designed to encourage individual investment in unquoted trading companies. The scheme offers generous tax reliefs (both income tax and capital gains tax) to individual investors who invest directly in a VCT company that invests in high-risk, unquoted companies. The individual investor therefore spreads the risk.

Individuals can invest a maximum of £200,000 per annum, attracting income tax relief at 30% on their taxable income, providing the shares are held for five years. VCT relief is always given in the tax year in which the investment is made; there is no carry-back facility. Tax relief can be claimed on the individual's tax return.

Dividends received from VCT shares are exempt from income tax in respect of shares acquired within the permitted maximum of £200,000.

Example 9.13

Jonathan subscribed £100,000 for shares in a VCT company in May 2016. His maximum tax reducer would be £30,000.

If his tax liability in the 2016/17 tax year was £50,000 before his VCT was taken into consideration, then his tax liability will be reduced to £20,000.

To avail of the generous tax reliefs, stringent conditions must be met by the VCT and the company it invests in. The conditions to be met by the VCT itself are:

- it must be listed on a regulated EU market;
- its income must come "wholly or mainly" from shares or securities;
- at least 70% of its investment must be shares in "qualifying holdings" (broadly unquoted companies carrying on qualifying trades in the UK);
- no single holding can amount to more than 15% of its total investment shares; and
- it must distribute (i.e. pay out in dividends to shareholders) at least 85% of its income from shareholdings and securities.

HMRC's approval of the VCT for the scheme may be withdrawn if it ceases to satisfy these conditions.

The conditions for the company invested in by the VCT are:

- it must have fewer than 250 full-time employees at the date of issue;
- its gross assets must not exceed £15 million prior to, nor £16 million after, the investment;
- it must not have raised more than £5 million in venture capital schemes in the 12 months ending on the date of the investment.

In addition, the money invested by the VCT must be used by the recipient company wholly for the purpose of the company's qualifying trade within two years.

Withdrawal of the Relief

The income tax relief can be withdrawn if:

- the shares in the VCT are disposed of within five years of issue (this only applies to the 30% relief; the exemption on dividends is not subject to the minimum holding period); or
- if the VCT's approval is withdrawn by HMRC within five years of issue.

Where the income tax relief is withdrawn, the additional tax now due will need to be paid to HMRC.

9.5.2 Enterprise Investment Scheme

The Enterprise Investment Scheme (EIS) is broadly similar to the VCT scheme except that it targets **direct** investment in high-risk, unquoted trading companies. As with the VCT scheme, generous reliefs (income tax and capital gains tax) are available that recognise the commercial risk involved in such investments.

An individual investor can invest up to £1 million in a tax year and obtain relief at 30% against their taxable income, providing that the shares are held for at least three years. Unlike the VCT scheme, the investment can be carried back and treated as if invested in the prior tax year. The carry back is subject to the caveat that the amount carried back plus any amount already subscribed in that prior year does not exceed the threshold for that earlier year. For example, if £40,000 is subscribed in 2016/17, this could be carried back to 2015/16. However, if £990,000 had already been subscribed in 2015/16, only £10,000 can be carried back from 2016/17.

As with the VCT scheme, extensive conditions are required to be met in order for a company and an individual investor to qualify for EIS relief. The main conditions for the investor to qualify are:

■ they must subscribe in cash for new shares in the company;
■ they cannot be "connected" to the company, i.e. they cannot be an employee or own more than 30% of the ordinary share capital, voting rights or rights available on winding up the company. With regard to connection, rights owned by a spouse or "other connected person" are included.

For the company being invested in, the main conditions are:

■ it must be an unquoted trading company (which can include companies listed on the Alternative Investment Market (AIM), the London Stock Exchange's international market for smaller, growing companies);
■ the funds raised must be used by the company (or by a 90% subsidiary) in carrying out "qualifying trading activities". Activities such as dealing in land, financial services, legal and accountancy services and property-backed activities do not qualify. Other trading companies will qualify where they are conducted on a commercial basis with a view to the realisation of profit;
■ it must not be a 51% subsidiary (or be under the control) of another company;
■ it must have fewer than 250 full-time employees on the date of issue;
■ its gross assets must not exceed £15 million prior to, nor £16 million after, the investment; and
■ it must not have raised more than £5 million in Venture Capital Schemes (the VCT scheme, EIS or SEIS) in the 12 months ending in the date of investment.

In addition, the money raised by the EIS share issue must be used for the purpose of the trade either within two years of the issue of the shares or within two years from the commencement to trade.

Withdrawal of Relief

As with the VCT scheme, the relief can be withdrawn if the shares are disposed of within three years of their issue. As the relief is a tax reducer relief, the withdrawal of the relief must be made at the same rate of tax as when it was provided. Where the relief is clawed back, additional tax will be due for the tax year in which the relief was originally claimed.

Although the company must be unquoted when the EIS shares are issued, there is no withdrawal of relief if the company subsequently becomes listed (unless there were arrangements in place for the company to cease to be listed at the time of issue).

9.5.3   Seed Enterprise Investment Scheme

Finance Act 2012 introduced the Seed Enterprise Investment Scheme (SEIS) to incentivise investment in new, small start-up companies by offering substantial tax breaks. SEIS will typically apply to relatively new companies that are in need of investment in order to kick-start their businesses. The increased inherent risk in investing in new start-up companies is reflected in a higher rate of relief than for the EIS – 50% rather than 30%. Likewise, the maximum investment is reduced to £100,000 per annum. As with EIS, the investment can be carried back to the previous year. However, the carry back amount, in addition to the amount already subscribed in that prior year cannot exceed the threshold for that earlier year.

The operation of the scheme is also very similar to the EIS, though it is designed for much smaller companies. The conditions for the SEIS are largely the same as for the EIS, just that the scale is reduced. Thus, the company must:

- have less than 25 full-time employees;
- the total value of its assets must not exceed £200,000 before the share issue;
- the maximum it may raise under the scheme is £150,000;
- be less than two years old; and
- must carry on a genuine new trade.

As with the EIS, an SEIS company must not be controlled by another company; and an individual investor must not be "connected" to the company, i.e. be an employee or own a 30% share of the company.

The money invested must have been used for the purposes of the trade by the company (or by a 90% subsidiary of the company) within three years of the share issue (two years under EIS).

The SEIS only applies to shares issued after 6 April 2012, and the company must not have previously raised money under either the EIS or VCT schemes, i.e. SEIS relief must be claimed as the priority.

Once a company has claimed SEIS, it can only seek EIS or VCT investment if at least 70% of the SEIS funds have been spent in its qualifying business.

Withdrawal of Relief
The SEIS relief can be withdrawn if the shares are disposed of within three years of their issue. As the relief is a tax reducer relief, the withdrawal of the relief must be made at the same rate of tax as when it was provided. Where the relief is clawed back, additional tax will be due for the tax year in which the relief was originally claimed.

9.5.4   Social Investment Tax Relief

Social investment tax relief (SITR) is designed to support social enterprises seeking external finance by offering a range of tax reliefs to individual investors who invest in new shares or new "qualifying debt investments" in those enterprises. A "social enterprise" is defined as a community interest company, a community benefit society or a charity (either a company or a trust). SITR can be claimed for investments made on or after 6 April 2014.

The broad details of SITR are very similar to EIS, thus:

- relief is 30% of the amount invested (against taxable income);
- the maximum annual investment is £1 million;

- there is a carry-back facility, allowing all or part of the amount invested in one tax year to be treated as though the investment had been made in the preceding tax year (subject to the same caveat, see **Section 9.5.2**); and
- the investment must be held for a period of three years from the date the investment is made.

SITR cannot be claimed on any investment in which the investor has already obtained relief under EIS or SEIS. However, a claim can be made up to five years after the 31 January following the tax year in which the investment was made.

If it is disposed of within that three-year period, or if any of the qualifying conditions cease to be met (e.g. the investor obtains 30% of the share capital) during that period, relief will be withdrawn or reduced.

Qualifying Conditions
The conditions attached to the scheme largely mirror those that apply to the EIS. Thus, the investor, from one year before the investment to three years after it:

- must not be an employee (including being a paid director) of the social enterprise at any time in the period; and
- must not own more than 30% of the social enterprise's ordinary share capital, loan capital or voting rights. Investments of "associates" are included within this limit. "Associates" being business partners, trustees of any settlement of which the investor is a settlor or beneficiary, and relatives. "Relatives", for SITR purposes, are spouses/civil partners, parents and grandparents, children and grandchildren; but not brothers and sisters.

Importantly, there is no stipulation for SITR that the investor must be UK resident.

The investment itself can be either in newly issued shares or new qualifying debt investments, e.g. certain debentures.

If the investment is in shares, they must be ordinary shares, which includes not carrying any rights to a fixed return (whether a fixed amount or fixed by reference to the amount invested). The shares must also not carry any rights to the social enterprise's assets in the event of a winding up.

The social enterprise also has to meet a number of requirements. If the social enterprise ceases to meet one or more of these conditions, investors may have their tax relief withdrawn. The conditions to be met, at the time the investment is made, are:

- it must be a social enterprise (as defined above);
- it must be unquoted on any stock exchange (although it may become quoted later without the investors losing tax relief, but not if there were arrangements already in existence for it to become quoted when the shares were issued);
- it must have fewer than 500 full-time equivalent employees. If the social enterprise is the parent company of a group, that figure applies to the whole group. Where a social enterprise has part-time employees they should be included as a fraction that is just and reasonable;
- it must have no more than £15 million in gross assets immediately before the investment and £16 million immediately after the investment. If the company is the parent company of a group, that figure applies to the total of the gross assets of the company and its subsidiaries; and
- it, or a 90% subsidiary which is itself a social enterprise, must either be carrying on the "qualifying trade" for which the money was raised or preparing to carry on that trade, with the trade commencing within two years of the date of the investment.

In regard to the final point, a "qualifying trade" is one that is conducted on a commercial basis with a view to the realisation of profit. A trade does **not qualify** if it consists "wholly, or substantially" of "excluded activities". The following are some of the activities that are excluded:

- dealing in land, commodities or futures, shares, securities or other financial instruments;
- banking, insurance, moneylending, debt factoring, hire-purchase financing or other financial activities (with the exception of lending money to another social enterprise); and
- property development.

In addition, the social enterprise is restricted as to the amount of money it may raise under SITR. The restricted amount is given by a set formula that provides that the total amount of potential tax relief available must not exceed €200,000 (reduced by any other state aid received, such as government grants) for a three-year period from the day the investment was made.

9.5.5 Maintenance Payments

Income tax relief on maintenance payments is only available in very restrictive circumstances: on payments to support a spouse/civil partner or child after separation or divorce, provided at least one of the spouses/civil partners **was born before 6 April 1935**.

The main features of the relief are:

- The maintenance payment must be made to the divorced or separated spouse/civil partner for them or any children. It is not allowable if made direct to children.
- The maintenance payment must be legally enforceable. That is, they are not voluntary but are agreed in an official, legally binding agreement.
- Payments of up to £3,220 are allowable at 10%.

Income received as a maintenance payment is exempt from income tax, i.e. the recipient is not liable to income tax on it. If the recipient remarries, the maintenance payments become liable to income tax.

9.5.6 Married Couple's Allowance

Despite its name, the married couple's allowance (MCA) is technically a tax reducer as it reduces the income tax liability rather than directly affecting income. It is available to legally married couples/civil partners who live together for at least part of the tax year, so long as one of the spouses/civil partners was born before 6 April 1935. In other words, for 2016/17 one spouse must be aged 82 or over during the tax year.

For couples married before 5 December 2005, the MCA is generally claimed by the husband. However, the couple may elect that instead it be claimed by the spouse with the higher income. Application to do this must be made before the start of the first tax year in which the MCA is to have effect; and it will apply to all subsequent tax years and is irrevocable.

For couples who marry or register as civil partners from 5 December 2005, the MCA is automatically claimed by the spouse/civil partner with the higher income.

The MCA is £8,355 per couple in a given tax year and is deducted from the income tax liability of the claimant spouse. The relief is restricted to 10% of £8,355 (i.e. £835.50).

In the year of marriage/registration of civil partnership, the MCA is pro-rated for each complete tax month that the couple is not married/registered. The MCA is available in full in the tax year in which a couple divorce or separate, or in which one of them dies.

Restricted Married Couple's Allowance
The MCA is reduced if the claimant's net income exceeds £27,700. The MCA is reduced by £1 for every £2 of excess income over £27,700 but cannot, in any event, fall below a minimum amount of £3,220 (the limit for 2016/17). The income of the other spouse/civil partner is not taken into account.

The couple can **jointly** elect to set-off half or all of the £3,220 against the other spouse/partner's income. The election to set-off is subject to the following rules:

- the election must be made before the start of the tax year, except in the year of marriage/civil partner registration, when an election can be made during the tax year;
- if the election is revoked by the couple, the change will apply from the next tax year; and
- only the minimum amount of £3,220 can be transferred (half or all) by election.

If the claimant has no income to set-off against the MCA, or if the MCA exceeds their tax liability, then the unused ("surplus") MCA may be passed over to the other spouse/civil partner **without election**.

Example 9.14
Calculate the tax payable in 2016/17 by a husband and wife both aged 83 (both born in 1934) and married for many years if the husband's net income is £28,600 and the wife's net income is £18,560. Assume all income comes from non-savings sources.

Husband: Income Tax Computation 2016/17	£
Net income	28,600
Less: personal allowance	(11,000)
Taxable income	17,600
Income tax due:	
Basic rate band: £17,600 @ 20%	3,520.00
Less: MCA £7,905 @ 10% (Note 1)	(790.50)
Tax payable	2,729.50

Wife: Income Tax Computation 2016/17	£
Net income	18,560
Less: personal allowance	(11,000)
Taxable income	7,560
Income tax due:	
Basic rate band: £7,560 @ 20%	1,512
Tax payable	1,512

Notes
1. The husband's income is £900 over the income limit. MCA is reduced by £450 (£28,600 – £27,700)/2). This gives a revised MCA of £7,905 (£8,355 – £450).

9.6 Tax Credits

Tax credits are payments from the Government that are administered by HMRC. Currently there are two types of tax credit widely available:

- Child Tax Credit (CTC) – available to individuals who are responsible for at least one child or young person (see **Section 9.6.1**); and
- Working Tax Credit (WTC) – available to individuals who work, but are on a low income (see **Section 9.6.2**).

The Universal Tax Credit (UTC) is a new tax credit that is being gradually introduced across the UK, but which is not yet widely available (see **Section 9.6.3**).

Both CTC and WTC are not taxable.

Tax credits are awarded on an annual basis. They are initially based on the income of the claimant, or joint claimants, for the preceding tax year and then adjusted based on actual income in the tax year in which the credit is claimed. Broadly, "income" includes all taxable income, excluding the first £300 from pensions, savings, property or foreign assets.

Individuals must renew their tax credits once a year. Claims must be received by 31 July, but can be backdated depending on individual circumstances.

If actual income for 2016/17 falls by more than £2,500 (when compared with 2015/16), then the 2016/17 award is based on 2016/17 income minus £2,500.

Example 9.15

In 2015/16 Larry's income was £10,000 and in 2016/17 his income is £6,000.

The fall is more than £2,500; therefore Larry's 2016/17 final tax credit award will be calculated on his 2016/17 income plus £2,500, i.e. £8,500.

If annual income rises by more than £2,500, then the individual's award is based on current year's income minus £2,500.

Example 9.16

In 2015/16 Laura's income was £9,000 and in 2016/17 her income is £13,000.

The rise is more than £2,500; therefore Laura's 2016/17 final tax credit award will be calculated on her 2016/17 income minus £2,500, i.e. £10,500.

Table 9.1 shows the income thresholds and the withdrawal rates for tax credits.

TABLE 9.1: TAX CREDITS – INCOME THRESHOLDS AND WITHDRAWAL RATES

Income thresholds and withdrawal rates	2015/16	2016/17
Income threshold for those entitled	£6,420	£6,420
Withdrawal rate	41%	41%
Threshold for those entitled to CTC only	£16,105	£16,105
Income rise disregarded	£5,000	£2,500
Income fall disregarded	£2,500	£2,500

Where an individual's circumstances change during a tax year and different rates apply, the award is recalculated on a proportional, daily basis. Any changes in circumstance that result in a reduced tax credit entitlement must be notified to HMRC within one month. A £300 penalty can arise if there has been an overpayment of a tax credit.

Tax credits are paid directly into the claimant's bank, building society, post office or National Savings account.

9.6.1   Child Tax Credit

Child Tax Credit (CTC) is a means-tested allowance for parents and/or carers of children under 16 years of age, or for young people under 20 years of age who are in full-time, non-advanced education or approved training. As a means-tested allowance, it is dependent on the annual income (amongst other criteria) of the claimant.

CTC is paid directly to the main carer for all the children in a family. They can choose to receive payments weekly or every four weeks. The main carer does not have to be the child's parent to be eligible, but they must be the main person responsible for them. The CTC payment is made up of two elements:

1.   a family element, paid to any family with at least one child and worth up to £545 (2016/17 tax year); and
2.   a child element, paid for each child in the family and worth up to £2,780 (2016/17 tax year).

Additional amounts are provided for disabled children. A summary of the credits is given in **Table 9.2**.

TABLE 9.2: CHILD TAX CREDIT RATES

	2015/16	2016/17
Family element	£545	£545
Child element	£2,780	€2,780
Disabled child element	£3,140	£3,140
Severely disabled child element	£1,275	£1,275

9.6.2   Working Tax Credit

Working Tax Credit (WTC) is a payment to top up the earnings of low-paid individuals (whether employed or self-employed), including those who do not have children. It is based on household income and circumstances, so the claimant must provide the following information:

- income and the number of hours normally worked per week;
- if applicable, their partner's/civil partner's income and the number of hours they normally work per week;
- any benefits they are receiving;
- the number of children in the family and their ages; and
- the amount spent each week on childcare.

The WTC is comprised of a number of different elements that can be applied to specific circumstances, as shown in **Table 9.3**.

TABLE 9.3: WORKING TAX CREDIT RATES

	2015/16	2016/17
Basic element	£1,960	£1,960
Couple and lone parent element	£2,010	£2,010
30-hour element	£810	£810
Disabled worker element	£2,970	£2,970
Severely disabled element	£1,275	£1,275
Childcare element		
Maximum eligible cost for one child	£175 per week	£175 per week
Maximum eligible cost for two or more children	£300 per week	£300 per week
Percentage of eligible costs covered	70%	70%

If the claimant is part of a couple or civil partnership and both qualify for the WTC, they can decide who will get the WTC payments. HMRC pays the childcare element of WTC directly to the main carer for all the children in the family, along with CTC.

9.6.3 Universal Tax Credit

Universal tax credit (UTC) is a new benefit for people who are unemployed or on low incomes and is designed to replace a number of existing benefits with a simpler, single monthly payment. The UTC is exempt from income tax.

UTC will eventually replace all of the following:

- Child Tax Credit;
- Working Tax Credit;
- income-based Jobseeker's Allowance;
- income-related Employment and Support Allowance;
- Income Support; and
- housing benefit.

The amount of UTC will depend on a person's circumstances. It is made up of a standard allowance plus other "elements", e.g. for children, childcare, housing and caring. There is also an element for those with limited capability for work. If an individual qualifies, their monthly payment will cover everyone in their family who qualifies for support.

UTC was introduced on 29 April 2013 in selected areas of Greater Manchester and Cheshire and is being gradually rolled out to the rest of the UK from October 2013 and due to be completed by 2017. The UTC is not yet available in Northern Ireland, but is in operation in many areas of England. Until a taxpayer is advised that the UTC will start to apply to them, they should continue claiming their respective existing benefits under the current benefits system.

Questions

Review Questions

(See Suggested Solutions to Review Questions at the end of this textbook.)

In each of the following questions, assume the individuals were not born before 6 April 1938 unless it is specifically stated otherwise.

Question 9.1

Jane and John are married. John was born in August 1937 and has income of £20,000 (pension) in the 2016/17 tax year. Jane was born in March 1935 and has no income.

Requirement
Calculate John's tax liability for the 2016/17 tax year.

Question 9.2

Mr Smith was born in January 1935 and is married. He has total taxable income before personal allowances of £33,900.

Requirement
Compute Mr Smith's tax liability for 2016/17.

Question 9.3

Joe has total income from his employment of £50,000 in 2016/17. He has taken out a loan of £40,000 to invest in 10% of the share capital of a close company run by his neighbour. Interest on the loan was £1,000 in the year.

He made a gift aid donation of £780 to his church in the tax year.

Requirement
Compute Joe's tax liability for 2016/17.

Question 9.4

Rachel married John on 4 June 2016. She was born in March 1933. John was born in September 1936 and has no taxable income. Rachel's non-savings income was £30,000 in 2016/17. This arises from a sole trade. As part of the sole trade she paid £9,750 in copyright royalties. She received UK dividend income of £600.

Requirement
Compute Rachel's tax liability for 2016/17.

Question 9.5

Mr Frost is an employee of ABC Ltd and earned £30,000 in 2016/17. He suffered PAYE of £5,000.

He gave shares in BT Group plc, with a market value of £780, to Action Cancer, a registered charity, in the tax year.

He also gave £780 to his local Action Cancer shop's appeal. He has signed a gift aid declaration with Action Cancer.

Requirement

Compute Mr Frost's tax liability for 2016/17, and the amount of income tax reclaimable by Action Cancer.

Question 9.6

Compare and contrast the tax relief available on charitable donations made using gift aid and payroll giving donations.

Question 9.7

(a) Brian has no taxable income in 2016/17.
   What is his maximum pension contribution on which tax relief is available and why?
(b) Brian has employment income of £400,000 in 2016/17.
   What is his maximum pension contribution on which tax relief is available and why?
   Assume there is no unused annual allowance relating to the previous three tax years.
(c) Brian has employment income of £40,000 and property income of £10,000 in 2016/17.
   What is his maximum pension contribution on which tax relief is available and why?
(d) Brian has employment income of £50,000 and trading income of £60,000 in 2016/17.
   What is his maximum pension contribution on which tax relief is available and why?
   Assume there is no unused annual allowance relating to the previous three tax years.

Question 9.8

Sarah has trading income of £50,000 in 2016/17 and makes a gross pension contribution of £20,000 in the year. She also pays interest on a loan to buy into a qualifying partnership of £1,000.

Requirement

Compute Sarah's tax liability for 2016/17, and outline how the £20,000 will physically get into her pension fund.

Question 9.9

Molly has gross employment income of £50,000 in 2016/17 and made a £20,000 investment into an EIS company in the tax year. PAYE was deducted of £5,000.

Requirement

Compute Molly's tax refund for 2016/17.

Question 9.10

Neville has gross employment income of £25,000 and dividend income of £20,000. PAYE of £5,000 was suffered. He also made a £30,000 investment into a qualifying EIS company in the 2016/17 tax year.

Requirement
Compute Neville's tax refund for 2016/17.

Question 9.11

Irwin has gross employment income of £32,000, property income of £5,000 and dividend income of £9,000. PAYE of £7,000 was suffered. He also made a £60,000 investment in a qualifying EIS company in the 2016/17 tax year.

Requirement
Compute Irwin's tax refund for 2016/17.

Question 9.12

James has gross employment income of £325,000 and interest income of £5,000. He also receives a dividend of £9,000 from a US company, which gives James the choice of having the dividends paid in shares rather than cash; James chooses cash.

PAYE of £75,000 was suffered.

James made a charitable donation of £7,800 in the tax year. He also made a £600,000 investment into a qualifying EIS company in the 2016/17 tax year.

Requirement
Compute James's tax liability for 2016/17. What is his maximum pension contribution for the tax year, and his relevant earnings?

Question 9.13

Matthew and Jennifer were married on 5 July 2015. Matthew has trading income of £400,000 and gave a field to a UK charity in the period. The value of the field was £30,000. He received £2,000 of dividends from his £100,000 investment in a VCT that he had made on 10 April 2015.

He also received interest on UK gilts of £10,000 and UK stock dividends with a market value of £9,000.

Requirement
Compute Matthew's tax liability for 2016/17.

Question 9.14

Hamish is single and works 40 hours a week on a sheep farm as a labourer. He earned £9,000 in 2016/17 from this employment. He has no children.

Requirement

Calculate Hamish's WTC entitlement for 2016/17. How will he actually receive the credit?

Question 9.15

Sylvia and Ted are married and work full time in the local council. Sylvia earns £7,000 a year and Ted earns £20,000 a year. They have two small children for whom they pay childcare costs of £4,500 a year.

Requirement

What tax credits will the couple get for 2016/17?

The PAYE System

The Chartered Accountants Regulatory Board *Code of Ethics* applies to all aspects of a Chartered Accountant's professional life, including dealing with PAYE issues. As outlined at the beginning of this book, further information regarding the principles in the *Code of Ethics* is set out in **Appendix 2**.

10.1 Introduction

Pay As You Earn (PAYE) is the method used by HMRC to collect income tax and National Insurance contributions (NICs) on most **employment** income and pensions. Broadly speaking, it obliges an employer to deduct income tax and NICs from wages, salaries and other payments made to employees, such as bonuses, commission, vouchers exchangeable for cash, etc., **when the remuneration is actually paid**.

The PAYE system is a good example of the principle of deduction of **tax at source**, whereby the **payer** (the employer), and **not** the **recipient** (the employee) of the income is liable to account for the income tax and other deductions to HMRC. It is the employer that must account to HMRC for the tax/NICs deducted. Under PAYE, tax and other deductions are paid on a **cumulative basis**, i.e. each time the employee is paid. In this way much of the administrative cost involved in collecting income tax is, in effect, imposed on the employer. In recent years, the operation of PAYE has been significantly altered with the introduction of Real Time Information (RTI).

Although PAYE is most frequently used to collect income tax and NICs, it is also the mechanism used by HMRC to collect student loan repayments and CIS deductions (see **Chapter 12**).

In this chapter we will look in detail at how the PAYE system operates on a cumulative basis throughout the year, and the method by which HMRC allocates tax codes and how they are calculated. The operation of RTI is discussed, as well as the numerous payment methods available and the penalties that employers are exposed to if they do not operate correctly within the filing and payment deadlines. A number of National Insurance contribution categories exist and these are outlined, together with the recovery of statutory payments by employers in certain circumstances.

10.2 Calculating Income Tax through PAYE and Tax Codes

10.2.1 Calculating Income Tax through PAYE

PAYE is designed to collect tax from employees on a cumulative basis. To calculate income tax on a cumulative basis, specific steps need to be followed.

Step 1 Calculate gross pay to date.

Step 2 Deduct employee's allowances to date.

Step 3 Calculate income tax due to date.

Step 4 Deduct tax already paid.

Step 5 Finally, calculate tax due for the month/week.

Example 10.1

Pamela earned £3,500 in the months to 5 May 2016, 5 June 2016 and 5 July 2016, and paid PAYE of £700 each month. In the month to 5 August 2016, she earned £4,500. She is entitled to a personal allowance of £11,000 for 2016/17.

What PAYE will be deducted from Pamela's salary in the month to 5 August 2016?

		£
1.	Cumulative pay to date £3,500 × 3 + £4,500	15,000
2.	Personal allowances to date are £11,000 × 4/12	(3,667)
	Taxable pay	11,333
3.	Income tax due to date	
	£32,000 × 4/12 = £10,667 @ 20%	2,133
	£11,333 − £10,667 = £666 @ 40%	266
	Tax liability for year to date	2,399
4.	Less: tax paid to date £700 × 3	(2,100)
5.	Tax due in month to 5 August 2016	299

10.2.2 Tax Codes

Essentially a tax code is a shorthand 'instruction' from HMRC to an employer to explain how an employee's income should be taxed. All employees are assigned a tax code by HMRC.

When determining tax codes, the amount of the personal allowance is reduced by benefits in kind (BIKs) (see **Chapter 6.3.2**). If BIK exceeds the personal allowance, then a K code applies. This is a negative code, which is added to (rather than deducted from) pay. The K code is subject to a regulatory upper limit of up to 50% of gross pay.

Tax codes consist of numbers and/or letters − the number refers to the amount of tax-free income the employee is entitled to, i.e. their personal allowance entitlement, divided by 10; while the letter signifies the employee's particular circumstances and how it affects their personal allowance. The following letters comprise the main codes used:

■ Suffix letters, which follow one or more numbers:

L = standard personal allowance, i.e. 1100L, being £11,000 divided by 10;

T = temporary code is being used, e.g. if HMRC need to review the tax code;

M = marriage allowance, the recipient of transferred personal allowance;

N = marriage allowance, the transferor of transferred personal allowance.

■ Prefix letters, which precede one or more numbers:

D0 = all of the employee's pay should be taxed at the higher rate;

D1 = all of the employee's pay should be taxed at the additional rate;

K followed by one to four numbers = additional tax for benefits to be deducted (total allowances are less than total deductions). For example, an individual with the tax code K200 effectively has a negative tax code of £2,000. They are deemed to have taxable income of £2,000 that will increase their tax liability for the year. Such negative tax codes may arise as a result of a benefit in kind received and/or underpayments from previous years.

■ Letters only:

BR = all of the employee's pay should be taxed at the basic rate, i.e. no tax-free allowances.

NT = no tax is to be deducted.

An employee's tax code may have a 'W1' or 'M1' at the end. W1 (week 1) and M1 (month 1) are **emergency tax codes** and appear at the end of an employee's tax code. Where a W1 or M1 is present, the employee's tax should be calculated only on what they are paid in the current pay period, not the whole year.

Tax codes will change each tax year, generally due to changes to the personal allowance. For example, the personal allowance was £10,600 in the 2015/16 tax year and it has increased to £11,000 in the 2016/17 tax year. A change in an employee's circumstances will also affect their tax code.

HMRC will collect an underpayment of tax (on amounts up to £3,000) by reducing an individual's tax code for the next tax year. For example, if an individual had £1,000 of underpaid tax in 2015/16, then their tax code for 2016/17 would be 1000L (i.e. £11,000 personal allowance less £1,000 underpayment equates to £10,000, and divided by 10 = 1000)

An employer **must not alter** an employee's tax code unless HMRC notifies them to do so.

10.3 The Administration of PAYE: Real Time Information (RTI)

The PAYE system was transformed with the implementation of Real Time Information (RTI), which was introduced to improve its operation, as well as to support the introduction of the Universal Tax Credit (see **Section 9.6.3**). Essentially, RTI collects information on PAYE deductions each time an employer pays an employee. The information is provided by the employer and must be submitted electronically to HMRC on or before the day the employee is paid.

This marks a significant change from the previous (paper-based) system where employers didn't have to inform HMRC of an employee's PAYE deductions until six weeks from the end of the tax year. This meant that HMRC could not know whether people had paid the right tax until well into the next tax year.

10.3.1 Operation of RTI

The information submitted to RTI is generated by the employer's payroll software or payroll provider. There are a number of different submissions that can be made, the two main ones being:

1.   a Full Payment Submission; and
2.   an Employer Payment Summary.

A Full Payment Submission (FPS) is made each time an employer makes a payment to an employee, provided that the payment is greater than the "lower earnings limit". The lower earnings limit (LEL) is £112 per week (see **Section 10.5.1**). If there are no employees paid over the LEL, then there is no need to make a submission; however, if just one employee exceeds the LEL, then there is a requirement to supply the information for all employees, including those for whom no deductions have been made.

An FPS includes details of:

■   the amount of total pay to the employee(s) that is taxable, including any BIKs;
■   deductions, such as income tax and NICs; and
■   if applicable, starting and leaving dates of employees (see below).

An Employer Payment Summary (EPS) is submitted when no payments have been made during a pay period, or no payment has exceeded the LEL. An EPS is also used to notify HMRC of any reductions to payments already submitted. An EPS must be submitted within 14 days of the end of the pay period, i.e. by the 19th of the following month.

In some cases, where there is a reduction in the amount being paid to HMRC, employers may submit an EPS as well as an FPS. This may occur if they need to reduce the amount of PAYE or NICs they pay to HMRC to recover statutory payments (such as statutory sick pay, maternity pay, etc.), Construction Industry Scheme deductions (see **Chapter 12**) and NICs "employment allowance" (see **Section 10.5.1**).

There are other submissions an employer may also make under RTI. These include:

■   Employer Alignment Submission (EAS) – used to align employee records with HMRC records before the employer submits any other information. An EAS is only required for existing employers with a:
   ●   large PAYE scheme (over 250 employees); or
   ●   where their payroll is administered by two or more payroll systems, including those operated by different payroll providers.
■   National Insurance Verification Request (NIVR) – used to verify or obtain a National Insurance number for new employees.
■   Earlier Year Update (EYU) – used to correct, after 19 April, any of the year-to-date totals submitted in the final FPS for the previous tax year. This only applies to years after the employer started to send information in real time.

Starting and Leaving Employment

RTI has simplified the administrative burden of reporting and registering the details of employees who commence or leave employment. All the details pertaining to the individual, whether leaving or starting, are provided to HMRC by the employer's FPS.

On leaving an employment, the employer must provide the leaver with Parts 1A, 2 and 3 of their P45. The P45 details the income tax and NICs the individual has paid so far in the tax year. Using RTI, employers must still give the leaver their parts of the P45 but they no longer need to return Part 1 of the P45 to HMRC.

On commencing employment, the employer must obtain and record certain information that must be submitted on the FPS when the new employee is first paid. The information required is the employee's name, gender, address, date of birth and National Insurance number. If the employee has been previously employed and has a P45 from their last employment, Parts 2 and 3 of it should be given to the new employer. If the new employee does not have a P45, the employer must ask the new employee to declare their previous employment situation and confirm which of the following applies to their situation:

1. This is their first employment since the start of the last tax year (6 April) and they have not been receiving taxable Jobseeker's Allowance, Employment and Support Allowance, taxable Incapacity Benefit, the state pension or an occupational pension.
2. This is their only employment, but since the start of the last tax year (6 April) they have been employed elsewhere, or have received taxable Jobseeker's Allowance, Employment and Support Allowance or taxable Incapacity Benefit. In addition, they do not receive a state or occupational pension.
3. They have another employment, or receive a state or occupational pension.

The declaration effects the employee's designated tax code (see **Section 10.3**) and how much tax the employer must deduct. In the first instance the employer will be able to deduct income tax as normal, i.e. on a cumulative basis. This means the employee will get the benefit of the personal allowance from the beginning of the tax year.

In the second instance, the employer must operate an "emergency code", which deducts income tax on a non-cumulative basis (see **Section 10.2** for discussion on W1 and M1 additions to tax coding), so that the employee is given only a proportion of the personal allowance as a tax-free amount. For example, if an employee is paid monthly, then that month's pay is compared to one month's tax-free allowance, which is £11,000/12 = £916.60.

Finally, in the third instance, the employer must deduct tax at the basic rate (i.e. 20%) and without any personal allowances being given.

An employer is required to keep a written record of the new employee's answers and to include it on their FPS.

10.3.2 Aspects of PAYE Not Affected by RTI

The basics of the PAYE system, such as deductions from payments to employees and the frequency of payments to HMRC, were unchanged with the move to RTI. As noted above, employers still have to provide a P45 to an employee who is leaving, and they must also still provide each employee with a P60 (which indicates how much tax has been paid in the tax year) if applicable. Employees' expenses and benefits in kind (and the associated National Insurance contributions) are also still reported on forms P9D and P11D.

Other aspects of the PAYE system that are unaffected by RTI are:

- Tax code notices − employers can still choose how they receive tax coding notices for their employees.
- Reporting a change to HMRC, e.g. updating an employee's new name or address for HMRC records − a real-time submission does not update HMRC records. It is still the responsibility of the individual employee to notify HMRC of changes of details (such as name, address, etc.).
- The Construction Industry Scheme (CIS) payment and reporting process (see **Chapter 12**).

10.3.3 Payment of PAYE

As noted above, PAYE is used to collect income tax, NICs, student loan deductions and the CIS withheld from subcontractors. It is the employer's responsibility to ensure that payments are remitted to HMRC correctly and on time. Payment can be made either:

- electronically through a bank or post office − cleared payment for the full amount due must reach HMRC by the 22nd of the month (payment options include online/telephone banking, debit/credit card, CHAPS, BACS or direct debit); or
- by cheque (if not required to pay electronically) − payment must be processed by HMRC no later than the 19th of the month.

If an employer's average monthly total for PAYE is less than £1,500, they can choose to pay quarterly, i.e. tax quarters ending 5 July, 5 October, 5 January and 5 April. Cleared electronic payments are due by the 22nd of the month in which the quarter ends or, if paid by cheque, by the earlier date of the 19th of that month.

Large employers, which are those who have 250 or more employees, must make their monthly payments **electronically**.

10.4 Penalties under RTI

There are two main penalties under RTI:

1. in-year late filing penalties; and
2. in-year late payment penalties.

In-year penalties are penalties levied during the tax year rather than after the end of it.

10.4.1 Late Filing Penalties

An employer will incur an in-year late filing penalty for failing to file an FPS on or before payment to the employee (although HMRC have announced that penalties would not be imposed where the delay in filing is three days or less).

In addition, a late filing penalty may be issued where:

- the employer did not send the expected number of FPSs; or
- the employer did not submit an EPS when it should have.

The first instance where an employer fails to file an FPS on time will not incur a penalty; but the penalty will be applied if there is a repeat occurrence at any time in the future.

The amount of the late filing penalty depends on the number of employees within the PAYE scheme (see **Table 10.1**).

TABLE 10.1: PAYE LATE FILING PENALTIES

Number of employees	Amount of monthly penalty
1–9	£100
10–49	£200
50–249	£300
250 or more	£400

Ordinarily, HMRC will send employers a filing penalty notice quarterly (in July, October, January and April) where appropriate. These penalty notices show the amount of the filing penalty for each tax month identified in that quarter. For example, a penalty notice in July will show any filing penalties arising in the first quarter of the tax year – that is, month 1 (6 April–5 May), month 2 (6 May–5 June) and month 3 (6 June–5 July).

Penalties are due for payment 30 days following the date of the penalty notice. Penalties not paid on time will attract interest on a daily basis at a rate of 3% per annum.

Additional Penalties – Late Filing
Where a return is late for three months or more and the information that it would have contained has not been provided on a later return, a further penalty may be charged. This additional penalty is set at 5% of the tax/NICs that should have been shown on the late return. This will be used for the most serious and persistent failures.

Again, the penalty payment is due 30 days from the date of the penalty notice; and late payment attracts interest.

10.4.2 Late Payment Penalties

The penalty for late payment depends on the number of late payments in a tax year and the total amount that is paid late. The penalty is calculated as a percentage of the total amount that is late in the relevant tax month (ignoring the first late payment in the tax year) depending on the number of defaults (see **Table 10.2**).

TABLE 10.2: PAYE LATE PAYMENT PENALTIES

Number of defaults in a tax year	Penalty %	Amount to which penalty percentages apply
1–3	1%	The total amount that is late in the relevant tax month (ignoring the first late payment in the tax year, unless it is more than six months late).
4–6	2%	
7–9	3%	
10 or more	4%	

For example, if an employer paid months 2 to 6 late, the first late payment (month 2) is not counted as a default. This means that a penalty of 1% will be charged on the amount paid late for month 3. A penalty of 1% of the months 4 and 5 amounts, and 2% of the month 6 amount (because by month 6, there have been four defaults in the tax year) of PAYE paid late will be charged.

Late payment penalties are usually issued after each quarter. In which case, using the example above, the penalty for the defaults for months 4, 5 and 6 would generally be issued together on one notice from HMRC.

Late payment penalties are not issued automatically; instead they are reviewed and issued on a "risk assessed" basis (i.e. HMRC will review on a case by case basis).

Additional Penalties − Late Payment

If an employer has still not paid a monthly or quarterly amount in full after six months, an additional penalty of 5% of the amounts unpaid is incurred. A further penalty of 5% will be charged if they have not paid the amount after 12 months.

These penalties may be charged in addition to the penalties for monthly and quarterly payments described in the previous section and apply even where only one payment in the tax year is late.

If PAYE has been underpaid, i.e. the amount paid is less than the FPS or EPS declares for the corresponding period, and if the underpayment is not significant, then no penalty is applied. However, daily interest will continue to accrue on all unpaid amounts from the due and payable date to the date of payment.

10.5   National Insurance Contributions (NICs)

Individuals and employers pay National Insurance contributions (NICs). NICs are paid to provide for the State retirement pension, unemployment and sickness benefits; they are collected by HMRC.

NICs are based on an individual's "earnings". "Earnings", from an NIC perspective, comprises gross pay, excluding benefits that cannot be turned into cash by surrender (e.g. holidays). It includes readily convertible assets given to employees (e.g. quoted shares). No deduction is made for employee pension contributions. An employer's contribution to an approved pension scheme is not "earnings" for an employee; however, NICs are due on employer contributions to an unapproved pension scheme.

In general, income and NIC exemptions mirror each other, e.g. a company-provided mobile phone is not "earnings" for tax (see **Chapter 6.4.3**) or NICs.

In general, non-cash vouchers are subject to NICs. However, the following are exempt:

- Childcare vouchers up to £55 per week or £28 (higher rate taxpayer) and £25 (additional rate taxpayer).
- Vouchers for the use of sports and recreational facilities (where tax-exempt).
- Vouchers for meals on the employer's premises.
- Transport vouchers (where tax-exempt).
- Top-up vouchers for pay-as-you-go mobile phones where the provision of the phone itself is exempt from income tax.
- Vouchers for eye tests and glasses for employees using VDUs.
- Any other voucher that is exempt from income tax.

National Insurance is categorised into 'classes' depending on employment status − essentially whether the taxpayer is employed or self-employed and the level of earnings. The principal National Insurance classes are:

- Class 1 − an employee's earnings. This includes company directors, although they are subject to slightly different rules.
- Class 1A − an employee's expenses or benefits in kind.

- Class 2 — self-employed earnings above £5,965 per annum.
- Class 3 — voluntary contributions.
- Class 4 — self-employed earnings above £8,060 per annum.

Different rules regarding the calculation and the frequency and timing of payments apply to each class.

10.5.1 Class 1 and Class 1A NICs

Class 1 NICs apply to an employee's earnings, i.e. their gross pay, and are calculated for the employee's pay period, which can be weekly, monthly, quarterly or annually. This differs from income tax, which is always calculated on an annual basis. Company directors, however, are an exception and their NICs are calculated on an annual basis regardless of their pay period.

Individuals who have more than one employment are liable to Class 1 NICs in respect of each employment. Each employer will operate PAYE (including NICs) as they would for an employee with only one employer. If an employee with two employments pays too much in NICs over the two employments, a refund can be claimed after the end of the tax year from HMRC. To make a claim, the employee should write to HMRC attaching their two P60s.

There are a number of earnings thresholds and limits to be aware of when calculating Class 1 NICs. **Table 10.3** introduces these and provides the weekly, monthly and annual equivalents.

TABLE 10.3: THRESHOLDS AND LIMITS FOR CLASS 1 NICS

	Relevant for Class 1	**Weekly £**	**Monthly £**	**Annual £**
Lower earnings limit (LEL)	Primary contributions 2 employees	112	486	5,824
Primary earnings threshold (PT)	Primary contributions 2 employees	155	672	8,060
Secondary earnings threshold (ST)	Secondary contributions 2 employers	156	676	8,112
Upper earnings limit (UEL)	Primary and secondary contributions 2 employees and employers	827	3,583	43,000

Class 1 Primary NICs

Primary Class 1 NICs are those **paid by the employee**. That is, the employee's take home pay will be reduced by the amount of primary Class 1 NICs paid. The rates of primary Class 1 NICs are 0%, 2% and 12%. **Table 10.4** shows the weekly, monthly and annual limits and thresholds that impact on the percentage of primary Class 1 NICs paid.

TABLE 10.4: RATES OF CLASS 1 PRIMARY NICS

	Weekly £	Monthly £	Annual £	Employee Class 1 (Primary) %
Up to the lower earnings limit (LEL)	0–112	0–486	0–5,824	0
From the LEL to the primary earnings threshold (PT)	112–155	486–672	5,824–8,060	0
From the PT to the upper earnings limit (UEL)	155–827	672–3,583	8,060–43,000	12
Above UEL	Above 827	Above 3,583	Above 43,000	2

Employees over the national pension age, currently 66, are not required to pay primary Class 1 NICs.

Example 10.2
Matthew earns £52,000 gross employment income in the 2016/17 tax year and is paid weekly (£1,000 per week).

What are the Class 1 primary NICs due in respect of Matthew's pay?

Class 1 primary NICs are paid by Matthew on his earnings, calculated on the basis of the pay period (weekly in this case), as follows:

£155	× 0%	
(£827 – £155)	× 12% =	£80.64 per week
(£1,000 – £827)	× 2% =	£3.46
Total NICs		£84.10

Matthew's Class 1 primary NICs are therefore £84.10 per week. His employer will deduct this amount from his weekly salary and will pay it to HMRC.

Class 1 Secondary NICs
Secondary Class 1 NICs are **paid by the employer**. The rates of secondary Class 1 NICs are 0% and 13.8%. There is no upper limit for secondary NICs. **Table 10.5** shows the weekly, monthly and annual limits and threshold that impact on the percentage of secondary Class 1 NICs paid.

TABLE 10.5: RATES OF CLASS 1 SECONDARY NICS

	Weekly £	Monthly £	Annual £	Employer Class 1 (Secondary) %
Up to the secondary earnings threshold (ST)	0–156	0–676	0–8,112	0
From the ST to the upper earnings limit (UEL)	156–827	676–3,583	8,112–43,000	13.8
Above UEL	Above 827	Above 3,583	Above 43,000	13.8

Special rules apply to employers with employees under 21 years of age. In such cases the employer does not have to pay Class 1 secondary NICs on earnings up to the "upper secondary threshold" (UST) for those employees. The UST is equivalent to the UEL (£827 per week).

As mentioned above, no primary Class 1 NICs are payable once an employee reaches State pension age (currently 66); however, the employer's secondary Class 1 NICs remain payable.

Example 10.3

Matthew earns £52,000 gross employment income in the 2016/17 tax year and is paid weekly (£1,000 per week).

What are the Class 2 secondary NICs due in respect of Matthew's pay?

Class 1 secondary NICs are payable by Matthew's employer, calculated on the basis of the pay period, i.e. weekly, as follows:

$(£1,000 - £156) = £844 \times 13.8\% = £116.47$

Employment Allowance

In 2014, the Government introduced an "employment allowance", available to all businesses, to reduce their Class 1 secondary NIC liability. The allowance is intended to encourage business growth and to help small businesses in particular with the costs of employment. It can be claimed through the Employment Payment Summary (EPS) on RTI (see **Section 10.3.1**).

For 2016/17, the employment allowance is £3,000, and can only be offset against Class 1 NICs (not against Class 1A NICs). It is offset in full against the first monthly payment of the employer's Class 1 secondary NICs, provided this is equal to or greater than £3,000. Any unused allowance is carried forward until the next payment period. For example, if an employer's Class 1 secondary NICs are £1,200 each month, then £1,200 of the allowance would be offset to the first month's payment, and £1,800 would be offset to the next month.

If a business has multiple PAYE schemes, only one employment allowance can be claimed. The allowance can be claimed up to four years after the end of the tax year in which the allowance applies. For example, for the 2016/17 tax year, the claim must be made by 5 April 2021. If a business is up to date with their PAYE, HMRC will set any allowance award against their future or existing PAYE liabilities, unless specifically requested to refund the amount.

Class 1A NICs

Class 1A NICs apply to an employee's expenses and benefits in kind (see **Section 6.3.2**). They are collected from the employer only, on an annual basis, at a rate of 13.8%. Employee contributions are not charged on BIKs. Class 1A NICs are calculated on the amount of the BIK.

Example 10.4

Matthew's employer also pays his private medical insurance. The cost to his employer is £2,500 per annum.

What are the Class 1A NICs due in respect of Matthew's BIK?

Class 1A NICs will be calculated on an annual basis, as follows:

Total BIK   £2,500
Class 1A NIC = $£2,500 \times 13.8\% = £345$

Class 1A NICs are due for payment by 22 July (19 July if paying by post) following the tax year.

Summary: Class 1 Primary and Secondary NICs Rates and Thresholds

Table 10.6 summarises the thresholds and rates that apply to Class 1 primary and secondary NICs.

TABLE 10.6: RATES OF CLASS 1 PRIMARY AND SECONDARY NICs

	Weekly £	Monthly £	Annual £	Employee Class 1 (Primary) %	Employer Class 1 (Secondary) %
Up to lower earnings limit (LEL)	0–112	0–486	0–5,824	0	0
From LEL to primary earnings threshold (PT)	112–155	486–672	5,824–8,060	0	0
Up to secondary earnings threshold (ST)	0–156	0–676	0–8,112	0	0
From PT/ST to upper earnings limit (UEL)	155/156 –827	672/676 –3,583	8,060/8,112 –43,000	12	13.8
Above UEL	Above 827	Above 3,583	Above 43,000	2	13.8

Example 10.5

Melissa works for Sharp Tech Limited, and earns £42,000 gross employment income in the 2016/17 tax year. She is paid £3,500 monthly. She is also provided with a company car (list price of £18,000 and CO_2 emissions of 125g/km) and petrol for the car. The taxable value of the car BIK is £3,960 (i.e. £18,000 × 22%). The taxable value of the fuel BIK is £4,884 (£22,200 × 22%).

What are the Class 1 primary and secondary NICs and the Class 1A NICs due in respect of Melissa's pay and benefits?

Class 1 Primary NICs
Class 1 primary NICs are paid by Melissa on her earnings, calculated on the basis of the pay period (monthly in this case), as follows:

(£3,500 − £672) × 12% = £339.36 per month
Melissa's Class 1 primary NICs are therefore £339.36 per month. Her employer will deduct this amount from Melissa's monthly salary and will pay it to HMRC.

Class 1 Secondary NICs
Class 1 secondary NICs are payable by Melissa's employer, calculated on the basis of the pay period, i.e. monthly, as follows:

(£3,500 − £676) × 13.8% = £389.71 per month

Sharp Tech Limited will pay the monthly Class 1 secondary NICs of all employees, including Melissa, to HMRC by the 22nd of each month. Sharp Tech Limited can claim up to £3,000 relief per annum from its Class 1 secondary NIC liability.

Class 1A NICs
Class 1A NICs are paid by employers on the provision of most BIKs (unless the BIK is equivalent to cash, in which case Class 1 primary and secondary NICs are due, or the BIK is exempt from NICs). Employees do not pay Class 1A NICs.

Class 1A NICs will be calculated on an annual basis as follows:

Car BIK: £3,960
Fuel BIK: £4,884
Total BIK   £8,844

Class 1A NIC = £8,844 × 13.8% = £1,220.47

Sharp Tech Limited will pay this amount to HMRC by 22 July 2016.

Example 10.6
Taking Example 10.5, Melissa receives a bonus in July 2015 of £2,000. How does this affect her Class 1 primary and secondary NICs?

Class 1 Primary NIC
Class 1 primary NIC in respect of July 2015:

(£3,583 − £672) × 12% = £349.32
(£5,500 − £3,583) × 2% = £38.34

Melissa's Class 1 primary NIC liability in respect of July 2015 will be £387.66.

Class 1 Secondary NIC
Class 1 secondary NIC in respect of July 2015:

(£5,500 − £676) × 13.8% = £665.71

Melissa's Class 1 secondary NIC liability in respect of July 2015 will be £665.71.

Example 10.7
What difference would it make if Melissa was a director rather than an employee (assuming Melissa receives her bonus in July 2015)?

If Melissa was a director, Class 1 primary and secondary NICs would be calculated using the annual NIC thresholds for the 2016/17 tax year.

Class 1 Primary NIC

(£43,000 − £8,060) × 12% = £4,192.80
(£44,000 − £43,000) × 2% = £20

Total Class 1 primary NIC payable by Melissa is £4,212.80.

Class 1 Secondary NIC

(£44,000 − £8,112) × 13.8% = £4,952.54

A comparison of the Class 1 NICs payable by Melissa as an employee versus those payable as a director is set out below:

	Employee £	Director £
Class 1 primary: (£339.36 × 11) + £387.66	4,120.62	4,212.80
Class 1 secondary: (£389.71 × 11) + £665.71	4,952.52	4,952.54
Class 1A	1,220.47	1,220.47
Total	**10,293.61**	**10,385.81**

The difference in Class 1 primary NIC is due to the fact that more of the bonus payment is taxed at 2% when NICs are calculated monthly (£5,500 − £3,583 = £1,917) rather than on an annual basis (£44,000 − £43,000 = £1,000).

10.5.2 Class 2 and Class 4 NICs

Self-employed taxpayers pay Class 2 and Class 4 NICs. Class 2 NICs are payable at a flat rate. Class 4 NICs are paid at two different rates and the amount of Class 4 NICs due depends on the level of the taxpayer's trading profits. We will now look at each NIC class separately.

Class 2 NICs

Class 2 NICs are assessed on **self-employed** persons at £2.80 per week, if earnings exceed the small earnings exemption of £5,965. Therefore, if a taxpayer has trading profits of over £5,965 for 2016/17, then the amount of Class 2 NICs due will be 52 weeks at £2.80 per week. That is, £145.60.

Payments may be made voluntarily, if earnings are below this amount, so as to maintain a full contributions record for social security purposes. A Class 2 contribution record is very important as it goes towards State pension and social security benefits for the self-employed.

The amount of Class 2 NICs due is calculated based on the number of weeks of self-employment in the tax year and is, in most cases, determined when the taxpayer completes their self-assessment return and the Class 2 NICs are paid alongside their income tax (see **Chapter 11**) and Class 4 NICs (see below).

However, there are a number of specific cases where Class 2 NICs are not collected through self-assessment. This is the case where the taxpayer is:

- an examiner, moderator, invigilator or person who sets exam questions;
- running a business involving land or property;
- a minister of religion who doesn't receive a salary or stipend;
- living abroad and paying voluntary Class 2 contributions;
- a non-UK resident who is self-employed in the UK; or
- working abroad.

Where Class 2 NICs are not collected through self-assessment, HMRC will send a bill by the end of October each tax year instructing the amount of Class 2 NICs to be paid. Payment can then be made electronically or by post.

Class 4 NICs

Class 4 NICs are assessed on trading profits. The amount collected is 9% of profits from all trades in the tax year between the lower profits limit of £8,060 and the upper profits limit of £43,000. Class 4 NICs of 2% are collected on profits above the upper profits limits. Therefore, a taxpayer with trading profits of £50,000 will pay Class 4 NICs of £3,284.60. That is, £34,940 (£43,000 − £8,060) at 9% and £7,000 (£50,000 − £43,000) at 2%.

Class 4 NICs are paid by taxpayers at the same time as their associated income tax liability under self-assessment (see **Chapter 11**). Trading losses can be taken into consideration to reduce profit for Class 4 NICs, as well as for income tax. If income tax relief is claimed for a loss against non-trading income or against capital gains, the loss can still be set against future trading income for Class 4 NIC purposes.

Example 10.8: Class 2 and Class 4 NICs

Roberta runs her own business as a dance instructor. She earns trading profits of £80,000 in the 2016/17 tax year. Calculate her NICs in respect of the 2016/17 tax year.

Class 2 NIC
Weekly Class 2 NICs are due at a rate of £2.80 per week.
Roberta's Class 2 NIC liability will be £145.60 (£2.80 × 52 weeks).

Class 4 NIC
Class 4 NICs are calculated on the basis of trading profit as follows:

(£43,000 − £8,060) × 9% = £3,144.60
(£80,000 − £43,000) × 2% = £740.00

Roberta's total Class 4 NIC liability is £3,884.60.

10.5.3 Class 3 NICs

Class 3 NICs are **voluntary** contributions that can be paid by individuals who have a 'gap' in their NIC record, i.e. periods when they were not paying any NICs. Gaps can occur where:

- an employee's earnings were below the "lower earnings limit", i.e. £112 per week;
- the individual was unemployed and not claiming social security benefits;
- if self-employed, the individual's earnings were less than the £5,965 small earnings exception limit; or
- the individual was living abroad.

Gaps in an NIC record are important to consider as they may affect future eligibility to receive the full State pension. Class 3 contributions therefore allow an individual to maintain a full contribution record.

10.5.4 NICs Payable by a Taxpayer who is both Employed and Self-employed

If a taxpayer is both employed and self-employed, they are liable to Class 1 NICs as an employee, and to Class 2 and Class 4 NICs with regard to their self-employment income.

How much NICs need to be paid depends on the taxpayer's combined income from employment and self-employment. There is a maximum figure above which contributions will be refunded; however, the calculation of this figure is very complicated and has up to nine stages. The maximum figure is not a fixed amount and will vary according to the mix of employment/self-employment and the amounts earned. If a taxpayer pays the maximum amount of annual NIC by way of Class 1 and Class 2, then they may not need to pay the full amount of Class 4 NICs. However, the taxpayer will have to pay 2% Class 4 NICs on all profits above the level of £8,060. For the 2016/17 tax year and subsequent years, the Class 4 NIC liability will automatically be calculated as part of the self-assessment process.

10.6   Employer's Recovery of Statutory Payments

Employers who have made certain statutory payments – statutory maternity pay (SMP), statutory paternity pay (SPP) and statutory adoption pay (SAP) – to employees can reclaim some of the payments from HMRC. Since April 2014, statutory sick pay (SSP) is no longer recoverable. (See **Section 6.5** for details of the statutory payments.)

The amount an employer can reclaim depends on the **total gross** Class 1 secondary NICs paid in the appropriate tax year.

If an employer's annual liability for Class 1 secondary NICs is £45,000 or less, they can qualify for **Small Employers' Relief**. This allows them to claim:

- 100% of the SMP, SPP and SAP paid; and
- an additional 3% as compensation for the NICs that were paid on those statutory payments.

If the employer's annual liability for Class 1 secondary NICs is more than £45,000, they are entitled to 92% of the statutory payments made.

The employer will deduct the amount they can recover from money due to HMRC. Employers use their payroll software to see how much of the statutory payments can be claimed back. Details of the reclaimed amount will be included in the Employer Payment Summary (EPS).

Questions

Review Questions

(See Suggested Solutions to Review Questions at the end of this textbook.)

Question 10.1

Mary is 50 years old. She earns £30,000 from her employer in 2016/17 and also receives BIKs worth £400.

Requirement
What is Mary's tax code for 2016/17?

Question 10.2

Andrew was born in March 1935 and earns £20,000 in 2016/17. He has anticipated BIKs of £750. He has no other income. He is married to Mary.

Requirement
What is Andrew's tax code for 2016/17?

Question 10.3

Sean, a married man of 50, is employed by NEW Ltd. He is allowed unrestricted private use of a company van in the 2016/17 tax year and doesn't pay for any fuel. He earns £30,000 a year.
   Sean has an underpayment of PAYE from 2015/16 of £1,000.

Requirement
What is Sean's tax code for 2016/17? Explain what this means.

Question 10.4

Alison, aged 45, is married to Sean. She earns £60,000 a year and is provided with a company mobile phone for which the company picks up the bill (private calls were £750) and medical insurance for which the premium is £500.
   She has an overpayment of PAYE from 2015/16 of £150.

Requirement
What is Alison's tax code for 2016/17?

Question 10.5

Paul earned £2,500 in the month to 5 May 2016 and paid PAYE of £500. He is paid on a commission basis and earned £4,433 in the month to 5 June 2016. His tax code is 360L.

Requirement

What PAYE will be deducted from Paul's salary in the month to 5 June 2016?

Question 10.6

David has earned £17,000 in the tax year so far, and paid PAYE of £3,600. He earns £3,000 in the month to 5 October 2016. His tax code is K120.

Requirement

(a) What PAYE will be deducted from David's salary in the month to 5 October 2016?
(b) How would the answer be different if PAYE deducted had been £2,900 instead of £3,600?

Question 10.7

Brian is an employee with gross monthly earnings of £50,000 in September 2016.

Requirement

What NICs will Brian pay on this wage?

Question 10.8

Jonathan is 67 years old. He earned £4,000 in August 2016.

Requirement

What NICs will Jonathan pay on this wage?

Question 10.9

Sarah is 27 years old. She earned £12,000 in 2016/17, paid in equal instalments of £1,000 per month. Sarah was also self-employed in 2016/17, preparing accounts to 5 April. Her profits for the year ended 5 April 2016 were £22,000.

Requirement

What NICs will Sarah pay for 2016/17?

Question 10.10

Frank is a company director who earns an annual gross salary of £50,000 in 2016/17 and also receives the following benefits in kind:

1. Company car (over 2,000cc) with a list price of £20,000. CO_2 emissions are 300g/km. He had to pay £5,000 towards the cost of the car.
2. All fuel is paid for by the employer.
3. His employer pays his annual golf subscription of £800.

Requirement

What Class 1A NICs are payable for 2016/17?

11

Administration and Procedures

Learning Objectives

After studying this chapter you will understand:

- The operation of the self-assessment system and the taxpayer's responsibilities and obligations.
- How to register with HMRC as self-employed.
- How to register with HMRC for self-assessment.
- The procedures for submission of the annual self-assessment tax return as a paper copy or online.
- The due dates for payment of income tax and the various methods of payment, including the various payment plans available.
- The HMRC penalty system, including what is subject to a penalty, the accrual of interest charges and how penalties can be mitigated.
- The procedure for amending an error or mistake on a tax return, including the time limits for doing so.
- HMRC's powers in relation to enquiries and discovery assessments and the procedures for dealing with these, including the taxpayer's right of appeal.
- The provisions dealing with the dishonest conduct of tax agents.
- The General Anti-abuse Rule (GAAR).

The Chartered Accountants Regulatory Board *Code of Ethics* applies to all aspects of a Chartered Accountant's professional life, including dealing with various aspects of the tax system. As outlined at the beginning of this book, further information regarding the principles in the *Code of Ethics* is set out in **Appendix 2**.

11.1 Introduction

As we saw in **Chapter 3**, residency and domicile are key factors in determining if an individual is liable to income tax. If an individual is resident in the UK in a tax year, whether they are UK domiciled or not, they will be liable to pay income tax on all of their income for that year, including income from an overseas source.

Income tax is **payable by**:

- adults, on their own income and on their share of the income of a partnership;
- children, if they have sufficient income to pay tax; and

■ trustees (on the income of a trust or settlement) and personal representatives of the estate of a deceased person (not within the scope of the CA Proficiency 1 Competency Statement).

The following persons and organisations are generally **exempt** from income tax:

■ registered charities, except on some types of trading income and subject to various anti-avoidance provisions;
■ scientific research associations;
■ registered pension schemes;
■ representatives of foreign countries (e.g. ambassadors);
■ visiting members of foreign armed forces (on their service pay only); and
■ local authorities and local authority associations and trade unions (on certain types of income).

This chapter will look at the overall system for the administration of tax in the UK. The chapter will begin by looking at the self-assessment system for tax, whereby an annual tax return is filed. It is worth noting that not all taxpayers have to operate within the self-assessment system. For example, an individual who is only a PAYE worker (see **Chapter 10**) will not be obliged to operate within the self-assessment system, as all of their income tax and National Insurance contributions should be collected through the PAYE system.

For taxpayers within the self-assessment regime, the payment of tax to HMRC follows automatically from the self-assessment return and this chapter will look at the various dates, rules and regulations in this regard. In order for HMRC to encourage the correct operation of the self-assessment system in the UK, a penalty regime is in place. In addition, HMRC will also carry out enquiries and discovery assessments to ensure compliance with the various tax rules. Where a taxpayer is not happy with the decision of HMRC in respect of their taxes, an appeals procedure is available. This chapter will conclude by considering the recently introduced General Anti-abuse Rule (GAAR) in the UK, which was put in place to counteract tax avoidance.

11.2 Self-assessment

The term 'self-assessment' refers to the system under which the taxpayer is responsible for calculating their own tax liability, reporting it to HMRC on their tax return and also making payment of their income tax based on the information contained in their tax return. The self-assessment system places the responsibility on the taxpayer to calculate their income tax liability, allowing HMRC to devote more resources to checking the accuracy of the submissions and offering advice to taxpayers. Given the complexities of the tax system in the UK, many taxpayers will engage a tax agent, tax advisor or accountant to help with the calculation of their tax and the submission of their income tax return (see **Section 11.2.3**).

11.2.1 Registration for Self-assessment

Self-employed individuals, i.e. sole traders, must be registered as such with HMRC; registration means they will automatically be treated under self-assessment and will be liable for Class 2 self-employed NICs. All self-assessment registrations must be carried out online (even if the taxpayer intends to submit paper returns) by completing Form CWF1. The '**Government Gateway**' is an online central registration service for many of the different Government services, including self-assessment tax registrations and agent services (see **Section 11.2.3**).

When an individual commences self-employment, or anticipates starting to trade within the next 28 days, they must submit Form CWF1. HMRC also state that an individual should register no later than 5 October following the end of the tax year for which they need to send a tax return. Late registrations will not incur a penalty (see **Section 11.6.1**) where the required tax is paid by the self-assessment deadline (see below). HMRC advise that the registration process may take up to four weeks to complete.

When an individual registers for self-assessment, they will automatically receive a Unique Taxpayer Reference (UTR). This UTR will then be quoted on all tax returns they submit as a self-employed individual.

11.2.2 Tax Returns

A tax return is a taxpayer's declaration of their income in any particular tax year. All taxpayers that are registered for self-assessment are sent a tax return or, if registered for online filing (see below), a notice to file online. Generally these are sent by HMRC in April/May each year. In the 2015 Budget, the Government announced its intention to abolish tax returns by 2020 and introduce digital tax accounts. In December 2015, HMRC issued a roadmap entitled *Making tax digital* that sets out the policy and administrative changes for 2016–2020).

A tax return consists of a basic eight-page form, form **SA100**, plus a number of supplementary pages, each dealing with a different type of income, e.g. income from employment is SA102, self-employment is SA103 and property income is SA105. Taxpayers are sent only those supplementary pages that are thought to be relevant to their circumstances, but they can request further supplementary pages if needed. If a taxpayer is filing their tax return online, they can complete whichever supplementary pages they need.

Partnerships must file a separate return, form **SA800**, which includes a partnership statement declaring the firm's profit, losses, tax suffered, tax credits, the division between partners, etc. in the tax year. Each partner must then declare their share of partnership profits on their personal tax return.

The tax return includes details of all income, claims for allowances and tax reducers. A four-page **short tax return** (form SA200) may be issued to taxpayers with simpler tax affairs. For example, a short tax return can be used where a taxpayer was a paid employee or had taxable benefits, where a taxpayer was self-employed with an annual turnover of less than £83,000, or where a taxpayer had property income of less than £83,000 from rents or letting a room in their own home.

A taxpayer has the right to insist on completing a tax return where they feel the need to submit a self-assessment tax return.

In situations where a taxpayer is liable to income tax under self-assessment (for example, if they were in receipt of miscellaneous or property income, or they received interest income), but they have not been issued with a tax return, they must **notify** HMRC within six months of the end of the tax year in question, i.e. by 5 October. Failure to do so results in a penalty. Taxpayers can authorise someone else to complete their tax return, whether it be a family member, friend or a tax professional. However, the taxpayer is responsible for the information being submitted and they must sign the completed return.

Online Filing

Taxpayers (and their agents) are encouraged to file tax returns online using the self-assessment online service. The online service allows most individuals to file their tax returns this way; likewise, agents and tax practitioners can file clients' tax returns using the Self Assessment for Agents online service (see **Section 11.2.3** for more detail).

To file tax returns online, the taxpayer (or agent) must register to do so – this is a separate registration process from registering for self-assessment. The self-assessment online service is accessed through the Government Gateway portal. On registering, an 'Activation Code' is sent, within 10 working days, by post to the address held. The activation code is a 12-character security code that the taxpayer can then use to access online services.

Online filing of tax returns has a number of advantages over a paper return:

- the online return is checked and verified as it is completed;
- the income tax is calculated automatically;
- email notification provides immediate acknowledgement of receipt;
- greater security and data protection;
- significantly faster refunds on overpaid tax;
- later deadline for filing;
- ability to access statements and view liabilities and payments;
- email/SMS text message reminders of future due dates.

Tax Return Filing Deadlines

A **paper tax return** must be completed and submitted to HMRC by the "filing date", which is:

- 31 October following the end of the tax year; or
- if the tax return was issued after 31 October following the end of the tax year, three months after it was issued.

If the paper return is received before 31 October, HMRC will calculate the taxpayer's income tax liability and notify them before 31 January.

An **online return** must be submitted by 31 January following the end of the tax year. So, if a taxpayer misses the paper return deadline, they can file online without incurring a late filing penalty charge (providing they allow sufficient time to complete the registration process). If the first notice to file a return is issued to the taxpayer after 31 October, then the latest filing deadline is the end of three months following the notice.

For taxpayers who would like HMRC to collect any income tax they owe through their wages or pension, the tax return must be filed online by 30 December. For example, for the 2016/17 tax year, a taxpayer must file online by 30 December 2016 if they want HMRC to collect their income tax liability through the PAYE system.

Amending Tax Returns

The taxpayer can **amend** their tax return within 12 months after the filing date. This facility enables a taxpayer to deal with an error/omission discovered after the income tax return has been submitted. The taxpayer's income tax bill will be updated based on the amendments made and any extra tax due as a result of the amendment will need to be paid to HMRC immediately. If a refund arises as a result of the amendment, the refund should issue once HMRC have dealt with the amendment.

HMRC may amend a return for obvious errors or mistakes, e.g. simple arithmetical errors, or entries that the HMRC officer has reason to believe are incorrect in light of information available. HMRC have until nine months after the date the return is filed to amend in this manner.

Accounting Information

If declaring trading income and expenses, the tax return requires that the figures are presented in a "standard format", i.e. certain boxes on the tax return need to be completed. There is no requirement to submit accounts with the tax return.

Businesses with a turnover (or gross rents from property) of less than £83,000 (the threshold for VAT registration) need only include "three-line" accounts (i.e. income less expenses equals profit) on the tax return. The only boxes on the tax return that need to be completed in respect of such a business are: turnover; the total of allowable business expenses, rather than a breakdown of each expense; and the net profit or loss for the business. This is not as helpful as it might appear, as underlying records must still be kept when producing three-line accounts (see below).

Records

All taxpayers are expected to make, and keep, sufficient records for them to provide a complete and accurate return. HMRC's view is that it is reasonable to expect a person who does not understand a tax issue to take care to check the correct tax treatment, or to seek suitable advice from HMRC or a tax professional.

All individuals who carry on a business (e.g. a self-employed individual) are obliged to keep records of:

- all receipts and expenses;
- all goods purchased and sold; and
- all supporting documents relating to the transactions of the business, such as accounts, books, contracts, vouchers and receipts.

These records must be kept for five years after 31 January following the tax year.

Other taxpayers should keep evidence of income received for one year after 31 January following the tax year.

HMRC can inspect "in year" records, i.e. before a tax return is submitted to HMRC, if it believes it is reasonably required to check a tax position.

11.2.3 *Tax Agents, Tax Advisors and Accountants*

As previously noted, if a taxpayer authorises someone else to complete the tax return, it is still the taxpayer who is responsible for the information submitted. If a tax professional has been engaged to complete the tax return and it is a paper return, the taxpayer is required to sign and the date the return for submission.

If the tax agent is submitting the return online, they must be registered with the Self Assessment for Agents online service. When online filing, agents should still make a copy (either a softcopy or a photocopy) of the completed return for their client to sign (an electronic signature is valid) and approve.

HMRC encourages online filing and the online service for agents has a number of additional benefits. A registered agent can:

- view their clients' statements by name or UTR number;
- add other people within their organisation as 'users' and assign them the same access to services or register for new services; they can also create and delete other users from their organisation;
- create 'assistants', who have limited access to certain features but can send their organisation's forms to HMRC using appropriate software; and
- complete tasks, such as deleting users, changing the services that users are assigned to and making changes to their registration details.

11.3 Payment of Self-assessed Income Tax and National Insurance Contributions

Where a taxpayer pays their taxes under the self-assessment system, they may have to make up to three payments of income tax and NICs a year. In general, due dates of "payments on account" of **income tax and Class 4 NICs** are as follows:

- first payment on account by 31 January in the tax year;
- second payment on account by 31 July following the end of the tax year; and
- balancing, or final, payment by 31 January following the end of the tax year.

Self-assessed taxpayers are expected to know when they need to make their payments on account. If they are registered online with HMRC for filing their returns, then the HMRC's online system will remind taxpayers of their payment deadlines.

The first and second payments on account each equal **50% of the prior tax year's income tax and Class 4 NICs liability, i.e. less tax deducted at source**, such as PAYE. This is called the "relevant amount".

Payments on account are not required if:

- the relevant amount is less than £1,000; or
- if more than 80% of the income tax liability for the previous year was paid through PAYE.

At any time before 31 January following the tax year, a taxpayer can **claim to reduce** their payments on account. Such a claim can only be made if the tax payable for the current year is expected to be less than the payments on account, i.e. less than the tax payable for the previous tax year. An incorrect claim can lead to interest and penalties.

From 6 April 2015, Class 2 NICs are to be paid along with the balancing payment on 31 January following the end of the tax year. Class 2 NICs are not payable on account in the way that income tax and Class 4 NICs are.

Example 11.1

David has taxable trading profits of £73,724 for the tax year 2016/17. He also earned dividend income of £5,027. He paid £78 per month into a private pension scheme. David made payments on account in respect of income tax and Class 4 NICs for the tax year 2016/17 of £7,396.68 each in January and July 2017.

Calculate the tax payable by David on 31 January 2018 and the payment on account due on 31 July 2018.

David – Income Tax Computation 2016/17

	Non-savings £	Dividends £	Total £
Trading income	73,724		73,724
Dividends		5,027	5,027
Total income	73,724	5,027	78,751
Less: personal allowance	(11,000)	–	(11,000)
Less: dividend allowance		(5,000)	(5,000)
Taxable income	62,724	27	62,751

Income tax due:		
On non-savings income		£
Basic rate band:	£32,000 @ 20%	6,400.00
Extended basic rate band: Non-savings	£1,170 @ 20%	234.00
Higher rate band: Non-savings	£29,554 @ 40%	11,821.60
Higher rate band: Dividends	£27 @ 32.5%	8.78
	£62,751	18,464.38

continued overleaf

Tax liability			18,464.38
Class 4 NICs: £43,000 – £8,060 @ 9%			3,144.60
£73,724 – £43,000 @ 2%			614.48
			22,223.46
Payments on account:	Jan 2017	7,396.68	
	July 2017	7,396.68	(14,793.36)
Balance by 31 January 2018			7,430.07
Payments on account due for 31 January 2018 (£22,223.46/2)			11,111.73
Total income tax and Class 4 NICs due at 31 January 2018			18,541.80
Add: Class 2 NICs			145.60
Total payment due on 31 January 2018			18,687.40

Taxpayers have numerous methods by which they can pay their income tax. For example, HMRC can accept payment by online or telephone banking, CHAPS, by debit or credit card or by direct debit.

11.3.1   Underpayment of Income Tax and NICs

An underpayment of income tax or NICs will be subject to penalties and interest. See **Section 11.4** for more details in respect of the penalties for late payment of tax and also the interest charged on late paid tax.

11.3.2   Overpayment of Income Tax and NICs

Where an assessment to tax is excessive due to error or mistake in the return, the taxpayer can claim back the amount overpaid. The claim must be made by the taxpayer not more than four years after the end of the year of assessment.

A claim cannot be made where the tax liability was in accordance with the tax rules and practice prevailing at the time the return was made.

Interest on Overpayments of Tax/NICs
Interest, or repayment supplement, is paid by HMRC on an overpayment from the original date of payment. Tax deducted at source is assumed to have been paid on 31 January following the tax year. The interest rate of repayment supplements from 29 September 2009 is 0.5%.

11.3.3   Arrangements for Payment of Tax

Budget Payment Plan
A taxpayer can decide to make regular tax payments in advance under a budget payment plan. Such a plan allows a taxpayer to decide how much to pay each week or month and they can stop paying into the plan for up to 6 months. To set up a plan, a taxpayer must register online and must pay by direct debit. Where the total payments made by the taxpayer during the year do not cover their full tax bill, the difference should be paid by the normal payment deadline.

Time to Pay Arrangements
Where a taxpayer fails to pay an amount of tax, and before liability to a penalty arises, i.e. within the 30-day grace period, they can request a "time to pay arrangement". If HMRC agrees, then any penalty due will be suspended. The suspension will stop, however, if the taxpayer breaks the agreement and HMRC serves notice of the penalty. A time to pay arrangement is a negotiated agreement with HMRC to allow the taxpayer to settle their tax liabilities by regular instalments. The arrangement will take into full account the taxpayer's circumstances, such as illness, unemployment, unforeseen short-term business difficulties, etc.

Such an arrangement is normally subject to adequate provision being made to settle future liabilities on time. Interest will arise as normal by reference to the original due date and not the instalment date. Penalties, however, may be avoided where a time to pay arrangement is in force. Such arrangements must, after 3 August 2015, be paid by direct debit.

Managed Payment Plan

Managed payment plans are similar to time to pay arrangements except that payments are by instalments that are "balanced" equally before and after the normal due date. If the taxpayer pays all of the instalments in accordance with the plan, they are treated as having paid the total amount on the due date, meaning no interest or late payment penalties will be imposed. The introduction of managed payment plans has been deferred and no commencement date has yet been given.

11.4 Penalties for Late Filing and Late Payment

In an attempt to encourage taxpayers to pay their income tax and file their income tax returns on time, a penalty regime is in place that penalises taxpayers for non-payment of tax and non-submission of tax returns. Late payment and late filing penalties can be appealed (see **Section 11.7**).

See **Section 11.6** for further details of the unified penalty regime that applies to all taxes.

11.4.1 Late Filing Penalties

A fixed penalty system for the late filing of returns was introduced by Finance Act 2009. Under these provisions, the penalties for late filing of a tax return are:

1. Initial penalty of £100 for failure to submit the return on time.
2. After three months, HMRC can impose a daily penalty of up to £10 for a maximum of 90 days.
3. After six months, the penalty will be the greater of £300 or 5% of the tax due.
4. After 12 months, the penalty will again be the greater of £300 or 5% of the liability. If the taxpayer withholds requested information, the penalty can rise to 100% if the withholding is deliberate and concealed, and 70% if just deliberate. The 100%/70% thresholds may be reduced by voluntary disclosures under the new penalty regime for errors (see below).
5. Separate provisions have been included for the Construction Industry Scheme (CIS) (see **Chapter 12**).

A late filing penalty can be appealed if the taxpayer has a "reasonable excuse". A reasonable excuse is considered as "something unexpected" or outside the taxpayer's control that prevented them from filing on time. HMRC suggest the following would be considered a reasonable excuse:

- a partner or close relative died shortly before the filing date;
- a serious illness or an unexpected stay in hospital;
- a computer or software failure;
- a technical fault with the HMRC online service;
- destruction of records through fire, flood or theft; or
- an industrial dispute in the post office **after** the return was posted.

11.4.2 Late Payment Penalties

Similar to the late filing penalty, a fixed penalty system is in place if **full payment** of tax due is not received by HMRC by the required date. There is a 'grace period' of 30 days from the due date where no penalty is imposed; thereafter:

1. Any tax due that is outstanding more than 30 days after the due date, an initial penalty of 5% of the unpaid tax.
2. Any tax outstanding more than five months after the first penalty is charged (i.e. six months after the due date), a second penalty of 5% of the unpaid tax.
3. Any tax outstanding more than 11 months after the first penalty is charged (i.e. 12 months after the due date), a third penalty of 5% of the unpaid tax.

The above penalty regime will only apply where the tax liability is not discharged in full by 31 January following the tax year. For example, for the 2016/17 tax year, a penalty will only be incurred if payment has not been received by 31 January 2018. As noted previously, a taxpayer may have to make payments on account in respect of their tax liability, e.g. payments on account for the 2016/17 tax year will be due on 31 January 2017 and 31 July 2017. The late payment penalty regime outlined above does not apply to payments on account that are paid late.

Where an individual withholds information that would enable or assist HMRC to assess their liability to tax, HMRC can impose greater penalties after a period of 12 months commencing from the penalty date. The level of the penalty is determined by the individual's level of co-operation. See **Section 11.6.1** for further information on how co-operation can impact on the level of penalty imposed by HMRC.

Late payment penalties are due for payment within 30 days of their imposition. If the penalty is not paid in that time, interest at 3% per annum will accrue on it from the date the payment is due.

Interest on Late Payments
In addition to the fixed penalties above, late payments can incur interest charges on the amount of tax due. Interest, at 3% per annum is accrued from the due date to the day before payment is received.

For payments on account that are received late, interest would accrue for a maximum period from 31 January in the tax year to 31 July following the end of that tax year. Interest on late payment of a balancing payment would accrue from the later of:

■   31 January following the tax year; or
■   three months after the tax return was issued.

11.5 HMRC Enquiries and Discovery Assessments

HMRC has substantial powers to ensure compliance with the tax legislation. On an ongoing basis, HMRC carry out tax enquiries and compliance checks. If, during a tax enquiry, or outside the 12-month enquiry window, HMRC discover that tax has been underpaid by a taxpayer due to the omission of profits or the excessive claiming of a relief, then HMRC may issue an assessment (i.e. a discovery assessment) to recover the tax lost.

11.5.1 HMRC Compliance Checks and Enquiries

HMRC randomly selects tax returns for checking and enquiry as a matter of course. It also selects tax returns where there is an identified tax risk, e.g. a taxpayer who regularly files their return and pays tax late. Enquiries may be "full" enquiries (which will look at the tax return as a whole), or may be limited to "aspect" enquiries (which will look at a particular item in the return, e.g. interest income).

In the course of an enquiry, HMRC may require the taxpayer to produce documents, accounts or any other information required (see below for more detail on HMRC's powers of information and inspection).

Where a taxpayer has engaged a tax agent or tax advisor to look after their tax affairs, HMRC will usually correspond with the agent regarding the enquiry into the tax affairs of their client.

Notification of an Enquiry

HMRC do not need to have, or give, a reason for conducting an enquiry. In particular, they do not need to inform the taxpayer if they have been selected at random for enquiry. HMRC must, however, send written notice to the taxpayer that an enquiry is underway. This notification must be sent within 12 months of the date the return was filed or, if the return was filed late, within 12 months of the "quarter day", i.e. 31 January, 30 April, 31 July or 31 October.

If after these 12 months have elapsed it is discovered that a full disclosure has not been made, HMRC may conduct a **"discovery assessment"** (see below).

If the taxpayer **amended** the return after the due filing date, the enquiry 'window' extends to the quarter day following the first anniversary of the date the amendment was filed. Where the enquiry is not initiated within the period that would have applied had no amendment been filed, the enquiry is restricted to matters contained in the amendment.

Enquiries into partnership returns are subject to the same timeframe, including amended returns. A notice to enquire into a partnership return is deemed to incorporate a notice to enquire into each individual partner's return.

Enquiries may also be made into stand-alone claims (e.g. for certain reliefs such as investment in a venture capital trust), provided notice is given by the HMRC officer by the later of:

- the quarter day following the first anniversary of the making or amending of the claim;
- 31 January after the end of the tax year, if the claim relates to that tax year; or
- the first anniversary of the end of the period to which a claim relates if it relates to a period other than that tax year.

During an Enquiry

Once an enquiry is underway, the taxpayer is not allowed to make any amendments to the return being investigated. A prompted qualifying disclosure is one that is submitted after notification of the HMRC enquiry has been received but before the enquiry physically commences; once HMRC commences an investigation and finds errors or omissions, no prompted disclosure can be made (see **Section 11.6**).

At any time during the course of an enquiry the taxpayer may apply to the First-tier Tribunal to require HMRC to notify the taxpayer within a specified period that the enquiries are complete, unless HMRC can demonstrate that it has reasonable grounds for continuing the enquiry.

Disputes concerning a point of law can be resolved through litigation if both sides agree, without having to wait until the whole enquiry is complete.

In situations where a return indicates an overpayment of tax and that a repayment is due, and this return is then subject to enquiry, any repayment may be postponed until the enquiry is complete. HMRC has discretion to make a provisional repayment, but there is no facility to appeal if the repayment is withheld until the enquiry is complete.

Conclusion of an Enquiry

At the conclusion of an enquiry, HMRC must issue a closure notice to the taxpayer informing them that the enquiry is complete, stating their conclusions and amending the self-assessment, partnership statement or claim (e.g. the amount of a loss relief claim) accordingly.

The taxpayer has 30 days to either appeal the decision of the enquiry (see **Section 11.7** for further information on appeals), or to amend the self-assessment, partnership statement or claim to give effect to HMRC's conclusions.

Once an enquiry is concluded, the taxpayer has an opportunity to make any other amendments to their tax return that could have been made had the enquiry not been initiated (amendments cannot be made while enquiries are in progress and such amendments may not have been within the scope of the enquiry). If HMRC is not satisfied with the taxpayer's amendment, it has 30 days in which to amend the self-assessment, partnership statement or claim.

If a claim has been disallowed but it does not affect the self-assessment, HMRC must advise the taxpayer of the extent to which it has been disallowed.

Once an enquiry has been completed, HMRC cannot make further enquiries into that particular return; they may, in limited circumstances, undertake a discovery assessment if it believes that there has been a loss of tax.

Any underpaid tax arising as a result of the enquiry will need to be paid within 30 days (of the closure notice) plus interest and penalties (see **Section 11.6.1**). If a refund of tax is due, this will be paid by HMRC on foot of the amendments being submitted by the taxpayer.

11.5.2 Discovery Assessments

Where, during an enquiry or after the 12-month enquiry window has lapsed, HMRC 'discover' that a taxpayer has omitted income or gains that should have been taxed or where the assessment is insufficient or the claiming of a relief excessive, then HMRC may issue a discovery assessment to the taxpayer. Discovery assessments are generally undertaken to **recover tax** that is due.

Discovery assessments can **only** be initiated where:

- there has been "careless" or "deliberate" understatement by the taxpayer or their agent; or
- at the time that an enquiry was completed or could no longer be made, HMRC did not have information available to it to make them aware of the loss of tax.

Discovery assessments **cannot** be raised if:

- the return was made in accordance with prevailing practice at the time, e.g. where HMRC have changed their opinion on a certain matter, even if an error in the return resulted in tax lost; or
- full disclosure was made in the return, unless there was a loss of tax due to careless or deliberate conduct, e.g. where income was returned in the incorrect position on the tax return.

The normal **time limit** for these assessments is four years from the end of the tax year in question, but it is increased to six years if there has been careless understatement and 20 years if there has been deliberate understatement. A taxpayer can appeal against a discovery assessment within 30 days of issue.

For discovery assessments, HMRC is bound by rules regarding what can be treated as "available". Information is **available** if:

- it is contained in the taxpayer's return for the period (or for either of the two preceding/periods) or in any accompanying documents;

- it is contained in a claim (e.g. a loss relief claim) made in respect of that period or in any accompanying documents;
- it is contained in any documents produced in connection with an enquiry into a return (or claim) for the period or either of the two preceding periods; or
- it is information, the existence and relevance of which could reasonably be expected to be inferred by HMRC from any of the above, or which was notified in writing by or on behalf of the taxpayer to HMRC. The information supplied must be sufficiently detailed to draw HMRC's attention to contentious matters, such as the use of a valuation or estimate.

These rules do not prevent HMRC from raising assessments in cases of genuine discoveries, but prevent assessments from being raised due to HMRC's failure to make timely use of information or to a change of opinion on information made available.

11.5.3 Determinations by HMRC

Where a return is **not filed** by the filing date, HMRC may determine the amount of tax due. This determination is replaced by the actual self-assessment when it is submitted, if done so within 12 months of the date of determination. A HMRC determination must be made within three years of the due date for the return.

Such a determination must be made to the best of HMRC's information and belief, and is then treated as if it were a self-assessment. This **enables HMRC to seek payment of tax**, including payments on account for the following tax year, and to charge interest. Late submission and payment penalties will also apply (see **Section 11.6**).

11.5.4 HMRC Information Powers

In recent years, HMRC powers have been significantly extended. HMRC has one set of information and inspection powers – covering income tax, CGT, corporation tax, VAT and PAYE – to ensure that taxpayers comply with their obligations, pay the right amount of tax at the right time and claim the correct relief and allowances.

HMRC usually **informally** requests information and documents from taxpayers in connection with their tax affairs. If a taxpayer does not co-operate fully with an informal request, HMRC has statutory powers to request information and documents from taxpayers and/or relevant third parties. HMRC must send a written "**information notice**" requesting documents and other information, such as appointment diaries, board minutes, correspondence, contracts, etc.

HMRC can only issue an information notice if the information and documents requested are "reasonably required" for the purpose of checking the taxpayer's tax position. An information notice may be issued to a taxpayer either with or without the approval of the First-tier Tribunal (see **Section 11.7**).

Information Powers with regard to a Third Party

There are a number of rules and conditions regarding HMRC's powers to request information from third parties.

Notice to a third party can be issued either with the agreement of the taxpayer or with the approval of the Tribunal. However, where the Tribunal is satisfied that informing the taxpayer would prejudice the tax enquiry, it can approve the information request without the taxpayer having been informed.

An authorised HMRC officer must agree to the notice before it is referred to the Tribunal.

The taxpayer to whom the notice relates must receive a summary of the reasons for the third-party notice, unless the Tribunal believe it would prejudice the assessment or collection of tax. As with a notice to a taxpayer, the request must be "reasonably required" to establish the taxpayer's correct tax position.

Tax advisors and auditors cannot be asked to provide information connected with their functions when this work comes within **legal professional privilege**. For example, a tax advisor does not have to provide access to their working papers used in the preparation of the taxpayer's return where the papers fall within the definition of "relevant communications", i.e. information and documents relevant to the case. There are instances, however, when professional privilege does not apply. In a recent tax case, known as the *Prudential* case (*Prudential plc and another v. Special Commissioner of Income Tax and another* (2013)), it was held by the Court of Appeal that legal professional privilege did not apply to legal advice given by accountants. It was held that such privilege, outside the context of litigations, is applicable only in relation to advice from lawyers. Prudential appealed the decision to the Supreme Court. The Supreme Court, however, upheld the judgment and confirmed that legal advice given by non-lawyers does not enjoy the benefit of legal privilege.

HMRC has the power to request and inspect documents held in a person's possession to explicitly include documents held on a computer or recorded electronically in any way. Anyone obstructing HMRC in the exercise of its powers, or failing to comply within a reasonable time, may be charged a penalty of £300.

Legislation introduced in Finance Act 2013 extended HMRC's data-gathering powers in relation to third parties. HMRC can now issue information notices to card payment processors, requiring them to provide bulk data on businesses accepting credit and debit card payments. These powers are being used by HMRC in a targeted campaign (**Section 11.8**).

The data that will be provided, covering the monthly totals paid to merchants, is expected to be of significant value in identifying businesses that do not declare their full sales. The measure was also designed to enable compliance interventions (i.e. HMRC inspections and enquiries) to be better targeted at those who are underpaying tax, as part of HMRC's attempt to minimise tax leakage.

The type of information that can be requested includes information about credit, debit and charge card sales made by a retailer, and the retailer's name, address, VAT number (if available) and bank account details. It will not identify the details of the credit or debit card holder, just the total sales made by particular businesses in each month. These are then used by HMRC to crosscheck against VAT registrations and business income declared on tax returns.

11.5.5 HMRC Inspection Powers

An authorised HMRC officer has the power to enter the business premises of a taxpayer whose liability is being investigated (by way of enquiry or discovery assessment) to inspect the premises, business assets and business documents that are on the premises. The power does not extend to any part of the premises used solely as a dwelling.

If an information notice has been issued (see above), the documents specified in that notice can be inspected at the same time. As with the information powers, the inspection must be "reasonably required" for the purpose of checking the taxpayer's tax position.

HMRC will usually agree a time for the inspection with the taxpayer. However, an authorised HMRC officer can carry out the inspection at "any reasonable time" if either:

1. the taxpayer receives at least seven days' written notice, an "inspection notice"; or
2. the inspection is carried out by, or with the approval of, an authorised HMRC officer.

There is no right of appeal against an inspection notice.

HMRC are also statutorily entitled to enter the premises of an "involved third party" to inspect the premises, business assets and relevant documents. Again, the inspection must be "reasonably required" for the purpose of checking the tax position of any period or class of persons. For example, a payroll-giving scheme operator may be considered a "third-party provider".

HMRC are also entitled to enter premises for valuation purposes, if this is reasonably required to check the tax position.

11.6   Penalty Regime

A unified penalty regime applies to all taxes (i.e. income tax, corporation tax, capital gains tax, VAT, etc.). This penalty regime applies penalties in the event of a number of tax compliance failures. For example, a taxpayer will incur a penalty where they fail to notify HMRC that they are chargeable to tax, where they submit an incorrect return or where inaccurate information or documents is supplied.

11.6.1   Penalties for Non-compliance

The main aspects of the penalty regime are:

- If a taxpayer can demonstrate to HMRC that they have taken "reasonable care" to correctly calculate their tax, they will not be penalised if they make an error.
- If they do not take reasonable care, errors will attract penalties – and higher penalties if the error is deliberate.
- Disclosing errors to HMRC early will substantially reduce any penalty due.
- Penalties can be charged where information declared to HMRC, e.g. a tax return or supplementary accounts submitted in support of a tax return, contains an inaccuracy that results in:
  - an understatement of a liability to tax;
  - a false or inflated statement of a loss;
  - a false or inflated claim to repayment of tax; or
  - a false or inflated claim for allowances and reliefs.
- Penalties can also be charged where tax has been under-assessed due to a failure to make a return (i.e. notify HMRC of chargeability) or where an error has been discovered but the taxpayer has not taken reasonable steps to inform HMRC.
- The inaccuracy must be "**careless**", "**deliberate**", or "**deliberate and concealed**" for a penalty to be incurred. The amount of the penalty depends on the potential lost revenue as well as the taxpayer's behaviour (i.e. careless, deliberate or deliberate and concealed).
- Whether a taxpayer has taken "reasonable care" will be viewed in the light of their abilities and circumstances. For example, the same level of knowledge or expertise will not be expected from a self-employed and unrepresented individual as would be expected from a large multinational company; and a higher degree of care will be expected over large and complex matters than for simple straightforward ones.
- If the information provided to HMRC contains more than one error or inaccuracy, a penalty can be charged for each error.
- Taxpayers have the option to make prompted and unprompted disclosures to help reduce penalties.
- HMRC will publish the names of tax offenders in certain circumstances.

Potential Lost Revenue

Penalty charges are generally based on the additional tax (and subsequent Class 4 NICs) that are due as a result of correcting the error; this is known as the **potential lost revenue (PLR)**. Depending on the level of error, the following penalties can apply:

- careless behaviour – maximum penalty: 30%
- deliberate behaviour – maximum penalty: 70%
- deliberate and concealed behaviour – maximum penalty: 100%.

Example 11.2

Peter is a sole trader, and he files his tax return for 2016/17 on time. The return shows his trading income to be £50,000. In fact, his trading income was £55,000. This oversight was due to carelessness.

State the maximum penalty that could be charged by HMRC.

HMRC's potential lost revenue is:
£55,000 – £50,000 = £5,000 undeclared income
PLR = £5,000 × 40% (income tax) + 2% (Class 4 NICs)   £2,100
Peter's error is "careless", so the maximum penalty is: £2,100 × 30%   £630

Prompted and Unprompted Disclosures

The concept of prompted and unprompted disclosures was introduced by the unified penalty regime, with the aim of encouraging taxpayers to voluntarily declare any errors or under-assessment in their tax affairs. **Unprompted disclosures**, i.e. those where the taxpayer has no reason to believe that HMRC has discovered, or is about to discover, the inaccuracy or under-assessment, can substantially reduce the penalty charged. **Prompted disclosures**, i.e. those where an error has been admitted but it is in response to a HMRC investigation, such as a discovery assessment (see above), may also receive a reduced penalty charge, but it is not as generous as for an unprompted disclosure.

For errors and inaccuracies considered to be "careless", if they are rectified within 12 months of the disclosure, further reductions are available. **Table 11.1** shows the mitigation of penalty charges by prompted or unprompted disclosures.

TABLE 11.1: MITIGATION OF PENALTIES – PROMPTED AND UNPROMPTED DISCLOSURES

Behaviour	Maximum penalty	Minimum penalty with unprompted disclosure		Minimum penalty with prompted disclosure	
		Within 12 months	After 12 months	Within 12 months	After 12 months
Careless	30%	0%	10%	15%	20%
Deliberate	70%	20%		35%	
Deliberate and concealed	100%	30%		50%	

The reduced rates are the **minimum** penalty that can be imposed. Nevertheless, the reductions available, especially for unprompted disclosures, are significant. For instance, an unprompted disclosure of a "careless" error could have the penalty negated entirely if rectified within 12 months.

When considering the actual penalty to be imposed, HMRC will consider the "quality" of the disclosure. HMRC consider the following three elements as primary when deciding on a reduced penalty:

1. The fact that the taxpayer has informed HMRC of their error. HMRC will take into consideration whether the disclosure was unprompted or prompted;
2. the fact that the taxpayer has made a full disclosure and explained how the error arose; and
3. the taxpayer has given reasonable help to HMRC to calculate the unpaid tax, including providing access to records.

A taxpayer can appeal against:

- the fact that a penalty is being imposed;
- the amount of the penalty; and
- a decision by HMRC not to suspend a penalty and against conditions imposed by HMRC for suspension of penalties (see below).

For further information on the appeals procedures, see **Section 11.7**.

Suspended Penalties

Taxpayers who endeavour to improve their accounting systems (e.g. by keeping better records or using improved accounting systems so that payment and submission deadlines are not missed) to avoid errors or inaccuracies in reporting in the future, may escape a penalty charge. Conditions will be agreed and set and with HMRC and if they are met the penalty will be cancelled. If they are not met, the penalty becomes payable. The period of suspension can be up to two years.

Only a penalty arising from the "careless" category, i.e. failure to take reasonable care, can be considered for suspension.

11.6.2 Publication of Tax Offenders

All deliberate tax defaulters (i.e. both types of deliberate behaviour), whether individuals or companies, whose actions result in a tax loss to HMRC in excess of £25,000, will have their names and details (such as address, profession, tax, interest and penalties) published on the internet by HMRC.

Names will not be published of those who make a full unprompted disclosure or a full prompted disclosure within the required time. Details are published quarterly within one year of the penalty becoming final and are removed from publication one year later.

11.6.3 Serious Defaulters

Taxpayers who incur a penalty for deliberate evasion in respect of tax of £5,000 or more may be required by HMRC to submit returns for up to the following five years showing more detailed business accounts information and detailing the nature and value of any balancing adjustments within the accounts.

11.6.4 Failure to Keep and Preserve Records

The maximum penalty for failure to keep and preserve records for self-assessment returns in relation to any tax year is £3,000. Self-employment records must be kept for five years after the 31 January submission deadline of the relevant tax year.

11.7 Appeal Procedures

In **Chapter 1** we outlined the appeals system – the escalation of appeals from the First-tier Tribunal to the Upper Tribunal, and on to the Court of Appeal and finally to The Supreme Court. In this section we will look at the process in more detail, at the various rules and conditions that are in place.

11.7.1 Introduction

A taxpayer has the **right to appeal** against:

- any HMRC assessment to pay tax;
- a HMRC amendment to a self-assessment or a disallowance of a claim or election following an enquiry or discovery assessment;
- a demand for documents made by HMRC;
- the imposition of a penalty or surcharge;
- the reason for undertaking a discovery assessment, i.e. the taxpayer may feel that the reasons cited by HMRC do not exist;
- the decision of a discovery assessment; or
- "follower notices" (see below).

There is no right of appeal against:

- self-assessments. Where HMRC complete the tax liability calculation (i.e. a determination) because the taxpayer failed to submit a tax return on time, the submission of the actual self-assessment return by the taxpayer will automatically replace the determination. Therefore, there is no right to appeal a HMRC determination.
- an "inspection notice".

The **time limit** for appeal is 30 days from the issue of assessment, amendment, disallowance or demand.

11.7.2 Procedures to Appeal

For HMRC decisions regarding **direct taxes**, there are three options open to the taxpayer:

1. seek agreement with HMRC;
2. HMRC "internal review" – a taxpayer may request, or accept an offer from HMRC, to conduct an internal review, which would be carried out by a HMRC officer who is independent of the case; or
3. reject an offer or internal review and formally take an appeal to the Tribunal system.

A HMRC internal review is, perhaps, the more cost-effective resolution for the taxpayer and HMRC, as less professional fees should be incurred by both parties. Once an internal review has been agreed to, an appeal to a Tribunal cannot be made until it has ended.

Generally, where agreement cannot be reached between HMRC and the taxpayer, the taxpayer may be offered, or may request, an internal review. If an internal review is agreed to, HMRC has 45 days to undertake it. On the conclusion of the review, the taxpayer has 30 days to either accept the outcome of the review or to send a "notice of appeal" to the Tribunal (in most cases this will be the First-tier Tribunal). The Tribunal will then inform the other party (normally HMRC as it is usually the taxpayer who will wish to appeal) that the notice of appeal has been received. If, after the 30-day period, neither action has been taken, the decision of the internal review is considered as final and the taxpayer has no further recourse.

Disputes regarding **indirect taxes** must be sent directly to the relevant Tribunal; that is, there is no scope for agreement or internal review.

11.7.3 Appeal to Tribunals

Once the Tribunal has received a taxpayer's "notice to appeal" and has informed the other party involved, the case is reviewed by the Tribunal to determine its complexity. There are four categories:

1. *Paper cases* – are dealt with by the First-tier Tribunal and apply to straightforward matters, such as fixed filing penalties. They are usually dealt with in writing and without a hearing.
2. *Basic cases* – are heard by the First-tier Tribunal and are usually dealt with at the close of a hearing with minimal exchange of documents before the hearing.
3. *Standard cases* – are heard by the First-tier Tribunal; they tend to have more detailed case management and are subject to more formal procedures than basic cases.
4. *Complex cases* – require lengthy or complex evidence or a lengthy hearing; involve a complex or important principle or issue; and involve a large amount of money. Such cases will usually be sent directly to the Upper Tribunal.

A decision of the First-tier Tribunal may be appealed to the Upper Tribunal. Decisions of the Upper Tribunal are binding on the Tribunals and any affected public authorities. A decision of the Upper Tribunal may, however, be appealed to the Court of Appeal.

11.7.4 Appeal to the Courts

The First-tier Tribunal and the Upper Tribunal may confirm, reduce or increase a disputed assessment. A Tribunal's decision on a matter of fact is final; however, either HMRC or the taxpayer may express dissatisfaction with the decision on a **point of law** and take the appeal further, to the **Court of Appeal** and ultimately to the **Supreme Court**.

The costs of taking an appeal to the courts can be extremely high, and an unsuccessful taxpayer may be required to pay HMRC's costs in defending the appeal as well as their own costs.

11.7.5 Postponement of Tax Pending an Appeal

Postponement of Payments
In the case of disputed amendments to self-assessments and disputed discovery assessments, the taxpayer may apply to HMRC, within 30 days, to postpone payment of all or part of the tax that has been assessed, pending settlement of the appeal.

Applications to **postpone payment** are subject to HMRC agreement. If HMRC refuses an application to postpone payment, the taxpayer may take the application to the Tribunal, within 30 days of HMRC's refusal. A postponement application is heard by the Tribunal in the same way as an appeal; the Tribunal's decision is final.

Any non-postponed part of the tax due on a disputed assessment is payable on the due date in the usual way. If the appeal is subsequently determined in the taxpayer's favour, any overpaid tax is refunded.

Interest on Postponed Payments

The postponement of the payment of tax pending an appeal does not impact on the date upon which interest will accrue. If the conclusion of the appeal is that the tax is due, late payment interest will be charged from the same date (i.e. when the tax should have been paid) as if there had been no appeal.

11.7.6 "Follower Notices"

In cases where HMRC is of the view that the point in question has already been decided in another tax case, they can issue a "follower notice". These are designed to improve the speed at which tax avoidance cases are resolved. Many tax avoidance schemes will have been marketed and hence will have been used by a number of taxpayers. Therefore, if a particular scheme has been defeated in a tribunal or court, HMRC can issue a "follower notice" to a taxpayer who has used the avoidance scheme that has been shown in previous tax litigation to be ineffective. One of the features of follower notices is a penalty of up to 50% of the tax and/or NICs in dispute if the taxpayer does not amend their return or settle the dispute.

The taxpayer has a right of appeal against any penalty charged under these provisions.

11.8 HMRC Campaigns

HMRC frequently undertake campaigns targeted at specific sectors which, based on intelligence information, it believes are likely to include taxpayers who are not paying the right amount of tax. These campaigns offer an opportunity for a taxpayer to voluntarily put their tax affairs in order.

HMRC operate a campaign by:

- identifying a group to target;
- identifying information and intelligence that can be used to encourage and influence that group to come forward; and
- using that same information and intelligence to follow up with a programme of action, which can include criminal investigations, aimed at those who choose not to declare their full tax liability.

Each campaign focuses on different groups and has time limits for making notifications, disclosures and payment. Once the campaign opportunity expires, HMRC will clamp down on those who have failed to respond. HMRC is planning future campaigns.

As of July 2016 there are three 'live' campaigns:

- Second Incomes Campaign – "offers employees who have not declared additional untaxed income a chance to pay the tax they owe".
- Let Property Campaign – "targets the residential property letting market and offers a chance for landlords in this sector to get up-to-date or put right any errors they have made and then remain compliant".
- Credit Card Sales Campaign – "is aimed at individuals or businesses that accept credit or debit card payments. It offers them an opportunity to bring their tax affairs up-to-date".

11.9 Dishonest Conduct by Tax Agents

Chartered Accountants Ireland (CAI) requires its members and students to apply the highest professional standards to their professional work. CAI members and students should be guided by the *Code of Ethics* prepared by the Chartered Accountants Regulatory Board (see **Appendix 2**). The *Code of Ethics* includes five fundamental principles: integrity; objectivity; professional competence and due care; confidentiality; and professional behaviour. CAI members and students should apply these principles to particular situations they find themselves in in their professional life where their ethical standards may be compromised.

If we take, for example, the principle of integrity. CAI members and students should always remain honest in their professional and business relationships. They should not be associated with information that is materially incorrect or misleading.

The *Code of Ethics* includes the principle of professional behaviour. This principle requires that members and students comply with the relevant tax laws and regulations. In addition, it requires that members and students avoid any action that brings discredit to the profession. Where members and students are acting as tax agents for taxpayers, they are required to make sure that they apply the tax laws in an appropriate manner and that they do not become involved in the initiation or marketing of "abusive tax-avoidance schemes" (see **Section 11.10**), which HMRC may investigate and then counteract any tax savings the taxpayer achieved as a result of being involved in such schemes. Involvement in tax-avoidance schemes by a member or student brings both discredit to the profession and to the member or student themselves.

Where a tax agent does not adhere to the principles of the *Code of Ethics* and carries on dishonest activity, HMRC has introduced legislation from 1 April 2013 that allows HMRC to:

- investigate dishonest conduct by tax agents;
- charge civil penalties where there has been dishonest conduct and a person fails to supply information or documents HMRC has requested; and
- publish the details of tax agents who have acted dishonestly.

A tax agent includes any individual who, in the course of business, assists clients with their tax affairs. "Dishonest conduct" is when the tax agent does something dishonest with a view to bringing about a loss of tax revenue in the course of assisting clients with their tax affairs. It does not matter whether there is an actual loss of tax.

Dishonest conduct does not include negligence, nor is it poor quality work by a tax agent. When HMRC first contacts the agent, it will give a factsheet that explains the process and covers the agent's principal rights and obligations, along with their rights under the European Convention on Human Rights. When HMRC has evidence of dishonest conduct, a specialist officer will give the tax agent a "conduct notice" that sets out the evidence it has.

If the agent disagrees with the conduct notice, they can appeal by writing to the specialist officer dealing with the investigation within 30 days of the date of issue of the notice.

If the appeal is settled in HMRC's favour, or the agent does not appeal within the 30-day period, the specialist officer can then:

- ask for access to the agent's working papers;
- charge penalties if they do not get access to the working papers when requested;
- charge a penalty for dishonest conduct of between £5,000 and £50,000 (the minimum (£5,000), which will be charged where the agent discloses all the relevant details about their dishonesty to HMRC and did everything possible to help the investigation); and

- publish details about the agent if they are charged a penalty for dishonest conduct of more than £5,000.

When calculating the penalty amount, HMRC will consider:

- if the agent told it about their dishonest conduct;
- if they did tell, whether they did so before they had reason to believe HMRC was about to find out about their dishonesty;
- how much help they gave HMRC to establish the extent of their dishonesty; and
- how they complied with any file access notices.

HMRC will expect the agent to do everything they can to help with the investigation. If the agent gives any false information they could face a criminal prosecution.

11.10 General Anti-abuse Rule

The General Anti-abuse Rule (GAAR) is one part of the Government's approach to managing the risk of tax avoidance. It has been introduced to strengthen HMRC's anti-avoidance strategy and help HMRC tackle avoidance. It is targeted at users and promoters of "abusive" tax-avoidance schemes. The rule applies to income tax, NICs, corporation tax, CGT, inheritance tax, petroleum revenue tax, SDLT and the annual residential property tax.

The GAAR applies to "tax arrangements" that are considered "abusive". In broad terms, an abusive tax arrangement is one that attempts to obtain a tax advantage as its main purpose or one of its main purposes.

To ensure that the taxpayer is given the benefit of any reasonable doubt when determining whether an arrangement is abusive, a number of safeguards are built into the GAAR. These include:

- Requiring HMRC to establish that the arrangements are abusive; it is not up to the taxpayer to show that the arrangements are non-abusive.
- Applying a "double reasonableness" test. This requires HMRC to show that the arrangements "cannot reasonably be regarded as a reasonable course of action". This recognises that there are some arrangements that some people would regard as a reasonable course of action while others would not. The "double reasonableness" test sets a high threshold by asking whether it would be reasonable to hold the view that the arrangement was a reasonable course of action. The arrangement falls to be treated as abusive only if it would not be reasonable to hold such a view.
- Requiring HMRC to obtain the opinion of an independent advisory panel as to whether an arrangement constituted a reasonable course of action, before it can proceed to apply the GAAR.

If it is determined that an arrangement is abusive, then the GAAR provides that the tax advantage that the arrangement sets out to achieve will be counteracted. It should be noted that the GAAR applies in addition to other targeted anti-avoidance rules; it is there to be invoked when one of these specific anti-avoidance rules does not apply but where "abusive tax arrangements" are being used by a taxpayer.

There is a GAAR advisory panel whose role it is to make sure that GAAR is used where appropriate, that is, to challenge the most artificial, controversial and aggressive tax avoidance.

Questions

Review Questions

(See Suggested Solutions to Review Questions at the end of this textbook.)

Question 11.1

The senior partner of your firm has come to you with a letter from one of the firm's clients, John Murphy, who was previously an employee and has set up his own business on 1 July 2016. Mr Murphy will prepare accounts annually to 31 January. Mr Murphy is very worried about the self-assessment system.

Requirement
Write a brief letter to Mr Murphy describing the self-assessment system, including details on the self-assessment system for each of the following:

(a) income tax returns and penalties; and
(b) payment of tax liabilities.

Question 11.2

Explain briefly the details of a HMRC enquiry.
    If you have an issue with a HMRC enquiry that cannot be settled by agreement between yourself and HMRC, what options are open to you?

Question 11.3

Cian Connors is a single man, born in March 1970. His accounts for the year ended 31 October 2016 show a tax-adjusted profit of £48,000. £920 gross interest was received on gilts, i.e. UK Government stock (see **Chapter 7**).

Requirement
Compute the income tax and NICs due for 2016/17. What payments on account will be due, and when, for 2017/18?

Question 11.4

Mark Johnston is a single man, born in June 1968. He has employment income of £50,000 in 2016/17 and income from gilts of £5,500. PAYE deducted at source was £10,000.

Requirement
Will Mark have to make payments on account for 2017/18? Explain why.

Question 11.5

You are Tom, a newly qualified Chartered Accountant and you have recently joined the tax department of a medium-sized practice. The partner in the practice has asked you to help him draw up an aggressive tax planning scheme that will enable clients to reduce their tax liabilities to nil by undertaking a number of artificial transactions. Although you do not fully understand the steps in the tax scheme and the tax legislation involved, you are going to ring your 10 biggest clients to try to get them to buy into the scheme.

Requirement

Provide Tom with your comments in respect of the above situation. You should highlight the fundamental principles within the Chartered Accountants Regulatory Board's *Code of Ethics* that may be compromised, as well as the way HMRC might deal with the tax-planning scheme.

12

The Construction Industry Scheme

Learning Objectives

After studying this chapter you will understand:

- The mechanics of the Construction Industry Scheme (CIS) and how it operates, including:
  - determining whether work done falls within the CIS;
  - determining the status of an individual as a contractor or a subcontractor;
  - HMRC's registration and verification procedures; and
  - the appropriate deductions from payments made by a contractor to a subcontractor.
- The criteria for a subcontractor to qualify for gross payment status.
- HMRC's requirements regarding CIS returns and remittances.
- The penalties imposed for failure to adhere to the requirements of the scheme.

12.1   Introduction

The Construction Industry Scheme (CIS) was introduced with the main objective of reducing the level of tax evasion by subcontractors in the construction industry. The construction industry has such a large number of mobile, self-employed workers that the risk of tax evasion was significant. Therefore, the CIS is a special system designed around construction workers to help ensure tax compliance within the industry.

The first CIS was actually introduced in 1972, but the current scheme came into effect from 6 April 2007. The current CIS operates on a HMRC centralised database of contractor and subcontractor information. It places an onus on the contractor to operate the scheme correctly by deducting the correct amount of tax from payments to subcontractors (where necessary) and to file monthly returns recording specific subcontractor information.

HMRC's *Construction Industry Scheme: Guide for contractors and subcontractors* (CIS340) provides guidance on the operation of the current regime.

12.1.1   General Scheme

In simple terms, the Construction Industry Scheme (CIS) requires that where a "construction contract" is in place, that the "contractor" deduct tax from payments made to a "subcontractor", and that the amount deducted is then paid to HMRC. In essence it works on the same principle as tax deducted at source: it places the burden of tax collection on the contractor.

Deductions made by a contractor are either at the standard rate (20%) or the higher rate (30%) of the payment to the subcontractor, excluding the cost of materials.

In certain cases, where strict criteria are met, the CIS deductions can be waived, i.e. payments to a subcontractor can be "gross payments" (see **Section 12.2.4**).

The mechanics of the CIS are set out below, but before we look at the detail of how it works we must understand the very specific definitions contained in the legislation.

12.1.2 Definitions

"Contractor"

Under CIS legislation, "contractor" has a special, broader meaning that includes:

- any person carrying on a business that includes "construction operations" in the UK (these are referred to as "mainstream contractors");
- local authorities, NHS trusts, housing associations and a number of other specified public bodies that have spent, on average, at least £1,000,000 a year on construction operations over the last three years ending with their last accounting date; and
- persons not carrying on a construction business, but whose business has spent, on average, at least £1,000,000 a year on construction operations over the last three years ending with their last accounting date, e.g. retailers, banks, manufacturing entities, etc.

The last two categories in the list are referred to as "deemed contractors".

From this extended definition it is evident that private householders having work done on their own home would not be considered contractors and so are not included within the CIS.

"Deemed Contractor"

"Deemed contractors" are persons or bodies who do not operate as a construction business but who have spent at least £1,000,000 on "construction operations" over the last three years.

Deemed contractors can only cease to be deemed contractors, and so cease to operate the CIS scheme, when expenditure on construction operations is less than £1,000,000 in each of three successive years following a year in which the average £1,000,000 threshold was met.

"Subcontractor"

A "subcontractor" is a person, partnership (including a limited liability partnership (LLP)) or company that is employed to carry out, or provide labour for, "construction operations", or who is responsible for such operations being carried out by others.

"Payment"

Under the CIS, a "payment" is an amount paid out by the "contractor" to the "subcontractor" under a "construction contract". It includes cash, cheques or credit. An advance or a loan is credit and, as such, must be treated as a payment, and applies regardless of whether the payment was made directly to the subcontractor or not.

"Construction Contract"

A "construction contract" is a contract relating to "construction operations". The CIS scheme operates only in the UK (and its territorial waters), but it also includes non-UK businesses carrying on construction operations in the UK.

Some construction contracts may include a non-construction component, such as the delivery of materials. In such cases, the CIS applies to **all** operations under the whole contract, even if shown on separate invoices. However, if a contract exists solely for the delivery of materials, for example, it will fall completely outside the CIS.

"Construction Operations"

As a general rule, the CIS includes work done to a permanent building, a temporary structure and civil engineering work/installation. The legislation lists the following as "construction operations":

1. construction, alteration, repair, extension, demolition or dismantling of buildings or structures (whether permanent or not), including offshore installations;
2. construction, alteration, repair, extension or demolition of any works forming, or to form, part of the land, including (in particular) walls, road works, power lines, electronic communications apparatus, aircraft runways, docks and harbours, railways, inland waterways, pipelines, reservoirs, water mains, wells, sewers, industrial plant and installations for purposes of land drainage, coastal protection or defence;
3. installation in any building or structure of systems of heating, lighting, air conditioning, ventilation, power supply, drainage, sanitation, water supply or fire protection;
4. internal cleaning of buildings and structures, so far as carried out in the course of their construction, alteration, repair, extension or restoration;
5. painting or decorating the internal or external services of any building or structure;
6. preparatory operations, such as site clearance, earth moving, excavation, tunnelling and boring, laying foundations, erection of scaffolding, site restoration, landscaping and the provision of roadways and other access works.

The legislation specifically **excludes** the following list from the definition of construction operations:

1. drilling for, or extraction of, oil or natural gas;
2. extraction of minerals and tunnelling or boring, or construction of underground works for this purpose;
3. manufacture of building or engineering components or equipment, materials, plant or machinery, or delivery of any of these things to site;
4. manufacture of components for systems of heating, lighting, air conditioning, ventilation, power supply, drainage, sanitation, water supply or fire protection, or delivery of any of these things to site;
5. professional work of architects or surveyors, or of consultants in building, engineering, interior or exterior decoration or landscaping;
6. the making, installation and repair of artistic works, being sculptures, murals and other works that are wholly artistic in nature;
7. sign-writing or erecting, installing and repairing signboards and advertisements;
8. installation of seating, blinds and shutters; and
9. installation of security systems, including burglar alarms, closed-circuit television and public address systems.

12.1.3 Exceptions to the Scheme

HMRC recognises specific circumstances where the CIS need not apply. So, **deemed contractors** do not need to apply the scheme to expenditure that relates to property used for the purposes of its own business, or if the business is a company used within the same corporate group (greater than 50% shareholding relationship). This extends to offices, warehouses and nursing homes used for the business. This exclusion does not apply to property let out, held as an investment or up for sale/let.

HMRC can also authorise deemed contractors not to operate the scheme for construction operations that amount to less than £1,000 (excluding the cost of materials).

12.2   Mechanics of the CIS

The operation of the CIS is based on a centralised database of contractors and subcontractors. The information held in the database includes the contractor's/subcontractor's name, their unique tax reference (UTR) and their National Insurance number (NINO) if an individual or partnership, or the company tax reference and company registration number if a company.

The mechanics of the CIS relies upon:

1.   registration – contractors must register for the CIS; subcontractors' registration is optional;
2.   verification of a subcontractor's "payment status" by the CIS; and
3.   monthly returns and payments to HMRC by the contractor.

12.2.1   Registration for the CIS

Subcontractors
Subcontractors are not required to register for the CIS, but by doing so they qualify for the lower, standard rate of deductions (20%); unregistered subcontractors pay the higher rate of 30%. The rate that is applied is referred to as the subcontractor's "payment status".

Subcontractors can register using **Form CIS301**, or by telephoning HMRC with details of name, trading name, address, telephone number, UTR and NINO.

If a subcontractor fails to register with HMRC before a payment from the contractor is received, then the contractor is obliged to deduct the higher rate of 30% from the payment. HMRC may refuse payment under deduction of 20% if a subcontractor has a bad tax compliance record. In such cases a 30% deduction will apply.

If they meet certain conditions, subcontractors can also apply for "gross payment status", meaning that the contractor is permitted to pay the subcontractor in full with no deductions (see **Section 12.2.4**).

Registration or non-registration for the CIS does not affect a subcontractor's other tax obligations, that is they must still be registered for self-assessment income tax and Class 2 NICs (see **Chapter 10**).

Contractors
Contractors are **obliged** to register with HMRC before they 'take on' their first subcontractor, regardless of the "payment status" of that subcontractor. HMRC compile separate lists of contractors and subcontractors; therefore, if a business is a contractor **and** a subcontractor, two registrations are required. In regard to this, it is important to note that when a business is acting as a contractor, it must follow the compliance rules for contractors; likewise, when acting as a subcontractor it must follow the compliance rules for subcontractors.

Registration permits contractors to verify the payment status of a subcontractor. It also obliges the contractor to make monthly CIS returns and monthly CIS remittances.

Status of Relationship
The CIS operates only where the relationship is contractor–subcontractor; it does not operate where the relationship is employer–employee. The correct identification of the relationship is very important at the outset, and should be reviewed throughout the arrangement (see **Section 6.2**). Where there is a contract of employment, payments do not fall within the CIS – instead PAYE and NIC (Class 1) deductions should be operated (see **Chapter 10**).

HMRC emphasises that employment (i.e. employee) or self-employment (i.e. subcontractor) status is determined from the facts and from the terms of each engagement. If a worker who has been treated as self-employed is re-categorised by HMRC as an employee, the employer (i.e. previously the contractor) is exposed to PAYE, NICs, interest and penalty liabilities.

12.2.2 Verification by the CIS

Once a contractor is registered for the CIS, they can verify the "payment status" of the subcontractor, i.e. whether the standard rate of 20% or higher 30% rate should be deducted from payments, by phone or online.

The verification process consists of three simple steps:

1. The contractor provides their own name, unique tax reference (UTR), accounts office reference and employer reference.
2. The contractor provides the subcontractor's name, UTR and National Insurance number (NINO) for individuals and partnerships, or the company tax reference and company registration number for companies.
3. HMRC advises the contractor of the "verification number", which must be retained and included on the monthly return.

If the subcontractor has been included on the contractor's CIS monthly return for the current tax year or the previous two tax years, then verification of the subcontractor is **not** required and, in this instance, the contractor applies the same payment status as the last time the contractor paid the subcontractor, unless HMRC has notified the contractor of a change in payment status.

Example 12.1

Date contractor engages subcontractor A:	September 2016
Date contractor last paid subcontractor A:	Never
Date contractor proposes to pay subcontractor:	30 November 2016

Verification details: the contractor **must** verify this subcontractor before they can pay them under CIS on 30 November 2016. HMRC will tell the contractor whether a deduction should be made from this and all future payments to the subcontractor.

Example 12.2

Date contractor engages subcontractor B:	September 2016
Date contractor last paid subcontractor B:	February 2013
Details of last payment return:	Contractor made last payment return for the subcontractor in tax year 2012/13.

Verification details: as the period of the last payment return is not within the last two tax years before the tax year in which payment is now being made (2016/17), the contractor must verify this subcontractor with HMRC before they can pay them under CIS. HMRC will tell the contractor whether a deduction should be made from this and all future payments to the subcontractor.

12.2.3   CIS Returns and Payments

When a registered contractor has made a payment to a subcontractor, they are obliged to submit a CIS return, form CIS300, and remittance of the amount deducted from the payment to HMRC **within 14 days of the end of the tax month** (the payment deadline is extended to 17 days if payment is made electronically). For example, the return for 6 December 2016–5 January 2017 should be filed, along with any CIS payments, with HMRC by 19 January 2017 (payments can be made by 22 January 2017 if paying electronically). If a contractor has not made any payments to subcontractors in a tax month, they are not required to submit a return for that month, although they can submit a 'nil' return if they wish. In practice, it is advisable to submit a nil return to avoid HMRC assuming that a return has been missed or is late.

From 6 April 2016, online filing of all CIS returns is mandatory (except for those unable to access online resources by reason of age, disability, remote location or religious objection).

Where the average monthly payments of PAYE, NIC, CIS and student loan deductions are less than £1,500, i.e. "small" payers, the contractor can choose to pay quarterly instead – but monthly CIS returns are still required. The monthly CIS deductions remittance is included in **payslip P30BC** each month. It is important to note that the contractor is obliged to pay HMRC the required deductions, irrespective of whether or not the contractor has correctly deducted these sums from payments to the subcontractors.

Monthly CIS returns are pre-populated with details of subcontractors previously returned or verified within the last three months and are sent by HMRC to the contractor each month. The returns must be filed online or via some commercial CIS software.

The CIS return (CIS300) should include the following information on all "construction contracts" during that month:

- contractor's details – name, UTR, accounts office reference, NINO or company tax reference number (if known);
- Subcontractor's details, if not already included on pre-populated return;
- the verification number as provided by HMRC;
- details of **all payments** made to subcontractors, including to those with "gross payment status";
- cost of materials paid to the subcontractor in the month.

In addition, as part of the monthly return, the contractor must declare that:

- the employment status of each individual has been considered and payments have not been made under contracts of employment;
- each subcontractor has either been verified with HMRC or has been included in previous CIS returns in the current tax year, or the previous two tax years; and
- the information on the return is correct and complete to the best of the contractor's knowledge and belief.

Deductible Costs
CIS deductions are withheld from the gross payment to a subcontractor, excluding:

- VAT payable by the contractor;
- Construction Industry Training Board levy; and
- deductible costs.

Deductible costs are costs incurred by the subcontractor and include:

- materials (the VAT-exclusive cost of materials, i.e. the price before VAT);
- plant hire;
- fuel (except fuel for travelling to and from the work site);
- cost of manufacture or prefabrication of materials; and
- any irrecoverable VAT (see **Chapter 13**).

The contractor can ask the subcontractor for evidence of the direct cost of materials. If this information is not provided, then the contractor must make a fair estimate of the material costs involved.

Example 12.3

A subcontractor, registered for VAT, agrees to paint the interior of a building and to supply the materials. The painter pays £240 for the materials (including VAT of £40). The total cost to the contractor is £600 (excluding VAT). The subcontractor is not registered for the CIS.

Subcontractor invoice:

	£
Labour charge	400
Materials	200
Sub-total	600
VAT (@ 20%)	120
Amount due (invoice amount)	720

Calculation of CIS deduction:

	£	
Total payment (exc. VAT)	600	
Less: cost of materials (exc. VAT)	(200)	
Amount liable to CIS deduction	400	
Amount deducted @ 30%	(120)	
Net payment to subcontractor	600	[£720 – £120]

Entries on the contractor's monthly return:

	£
Total payment	600
Direct cost of materials used	200
Amount deducted	120

Contractor's Obligations to a Subcontractor

The contractor **must** issue a "**payment and deduction statement**" to subcontractors within 14 days of the end of the tax month that a payment has been made. A statement can be issued to a subcontractor each month; or for each payment if they are paid more often. This statement may be used by subcontractors to work out their income tax liability for the tax year or they may prepare their own payment analysis statements including the same information.

The contractor, if an employer in addition to having subcontractors, is still obliged to file a full payment submission under Real Time Information (RTI) and should include on the full payment submission (FPS) the total amount of CIS deductions due to be paid so that HMRC can reconcile the total payments made during the tax year.

CIS Deductions and Income Tax

From the subcontractor's perspective, the payment and deduction statement received from the contractor is evidence of tax withheld under CIS payments. As such it is an important document for the subcontractor as the sums withheld are included on the their income tax return for the tax year and credited against any income tax and Class 4 NIC liability due for that year.

Subcontractors who are companies may offset CIS deductions from the company's income against its PAYE liability or against CIS deductions withheld from other subcontractors in the same tax year. Subcontractors that are partnerships or self-employed cannot offset their CIS deductions in this manner.

12.2.4 Registration for "Gross Payment Status"

A subcontractor can apply to HMRC to be classed as "gross payment status" status, meaning that the contractor is permitted to pay the subcontractor in full without any CIS deductions. There are three criteria, all of which must be met, for the 12 months prior to application (the "qualifying period") in order to qualify for gross payment status:

- the business test;
- the turnover test; and
- the compliance test.

The Business Test

The business test requires that the subcontractor provide evidence that they carry out construction work in the UK or provide labour for construction work in the UK and that this business is substantially operated through a business bank account. HMRC will require evidence of business contact details and business activities, e.g. copies of invoices, bank statements, construction contracts, details of payments for construction work, the books and accounts of the business, etc.

The Turnover Test

HMRC will look at the subcontractor's net turnover from "construction operations" for the 12 months prior to application, ignoring the cost of materials and VAT. Depending on whether the subcontractor is an individual, a partnership or a company, turnover must be at least:

- Individual – £30,000 from labour on construction operations only.
- Partnership – £30,000 for each partner in a partnership, or at least £100,000 for the whole partnership.
- Company – £30,000 for each director of a company, or at least £100,000 for the whole company. If a company is controlled by five people or fewer, there must be an annual turnover of £30,000 for each of them.

The Compliance Test

Subcontractors (including all partners/directors/participators if a partnership or company) must have met all of their tax compliance obligations during the previous 12 months. This includes filing and paying all business taxes, PAYE, CIS and VAT on time, as well as filing and paying all personal taxes on time.

Withdrawal of Gross Payment Status

A subcontractor's gross payment status is reviewed annually by HMRC; this is referred to as an ongoing Tax Treatment Qualification Test (TTQT). HMRC may, on giving 90 days' notice, cancel a subcontractor's gross payment status if it appears that:

- an application for registration for gross payment, if made at this time, would be refused;
- an incorrect return or incorrect information under any provision of the CIS regulations has been made; or
- there has been a failure to comply with any provisions under the regulations. HMRC has set out a list of acceptable failures, such as minor breaches of due dates, e.g. three late submissions (up to 28 days late) of monthly CIS returns.

The conditions for acquiring and retaining gross payment status are, therefore, very stringent. The withdrawal of gross payment status is first notified to the subcontractor in question, who has a right of appeal (see **Section 11.7**). Contractors are then notified of the change of status of a subcontractor.

12.3   Penalties under the CIS

A penalty regime is in place to encourage contractors to file their CIS returns on time. The following penalties apply where a CIS return is submitted late:

How late the return is	Penalty
1 day late	£100
2 months late	£200
6 months late	£300 or 5% of the CIS deductions on the return, whichever is higher
12 months late	£300 or 5% of the CIS deductions on the return, whichever is higher

For returns submitted more than 12 months late, an additional penalty may be incurred of up to £3,000 or 100% of the CIS deductions on the return, whichever is the higher.

Questions

Review Questions

(See Suggested Solutions to Review Questions at the end of this textbook.)

Question 12.1

A subcontractor, who is not a taxable person for VAT, agrees to plaster part of the interior of a building and to supply the materials for a total cost of £4,600. The plasterer pays £900 for the materials, which includes VAT of £150. The plasterer provides an invoice to the contractor as follows:

	£
Labour charge	3,700
Materials	900
Amount due (invoice total)	4,600

The plasterer is registered and verified by HMRC for standard rate CIS deductions.

Requirement

Calculate the CIS deduction to be made by the contractor and the payment made to the subcontractor.

Question 12.2

A contractor contracts three new subcontractors, for the month ended 5 February 2017, to assist in the construction of an office block. The invoices received from the subcontractors for the period are as follows:

	Subcontractor A	Subcontractor B	Subcontractor C
	£	£	£
Labour	5,000	10,000	2,000
Materials	3,500	2,000	1,500
VAT	1,700	2,400	700
Total due	10,200	14,400	4,200

The contractor has verified the status of the subcontractors with HMRC, which has advised as follows:

Subcontractor A – Gross payment status
Subcontractor B – Standard rate deduction
Subcontractor C – No record on the system

The contractor and subcontractors are registered for VAT.

Requirement

Calculate the CIS deductions to be made by the contractor and declared in the CIS return for the period ended 5 February 2017. What are the payments made to each of the subcontractors?

Value-Added Tax (VAT): An Introduction

Learning Objectives

After studying this chapter you will understand:

- Who is a taxable person for VAT purposes.
- The registration and de-registration limits for VAT and how to calculate taxable turnover for the purposes of the registration limits.
- What goods and services are chargeable to VAT and the various rates that apply.
- The tax point for VAT and the specific rules in relation to what constitutes a supply of goods and/or services.
- The importance of the place of supply of goods and/or services for VAT purposes.
- How to register online as a taxable person for VAT, how to submit quarterly VAT returns online and pay VAT electronically.
- How to prepare a VAT return using either the invoice or cash receipts basis and calculate the amount of VAT due and the due date for payment.
- The rules in relation to the recovery of VAT.
- The various VAT schemes, including the flat rate scheme and the *de minimis* calculation for partially exempt supplies.
- Operation of the bad debt scheme and how relief for bad debts is obtained.
- Information to be shown on a VAT invoice or credit note to ensure they are valid for VAT purposes.
- The effect of offering and receiving discounts in relation to input VAT and output VAT.
- The rules in relation to VAT records and the appeals procedure.

The Chartered Accountants Regulatory Board *Code of Ethics* applies to all aspects of a Chartered Accountant's professional life, including dealing with VAT issues. As outlined at the beginning of this book, further information regarding the principles in the *Code of Ethics* is set out in **Appendix 2**.

This chapter introduces the general principles of value-added tax (VAT): who is chargeable to VAT and what goods and services are liable to VAT and at what rate. The requirements of VAT registration (and de-registration) are critical to understanding how the VAT system works so these are discussed in detail (**Section 13.3**) before looking at the various tax rates in operation in the UK and the types of supply under each category (**Section 13.4**). Consideration is then given to the amount on which VAT is chargeable (**Section 13.5**) and an outline of the basic concepts around the supply of goods and services (**Sections 13.6–13.8**). For businesses an important consideration in terms of VAT is the recovery of VAT that has been paid on purchases. **Section 13.9** covers this aspect in detail, including deductible and non-deductible VAT, VAT on partially exempt supplies and VAT relief on bad debts. **Section 13.10** deals with the administrative requirements, including the VAT return cycle, the VAT records to be maintained by a VAT-registered business and the penalties that a trader may be exposed to if they do not administer their VAT correctly. The chapter concludes with a discussion of some special VAT schemes that have been introduced to help certain types of business, depending on their size and sector.

This chapter deals mainly with UK-only VAT supplies. **Chapter 14** examines the more complex issues around trading with other countries, whether it is with businesses located within the EU (intra-EU "acquisitions" and "dispatches") or with countries outside the EU (i.e. "imports" and "exports").

13.1   Introduction

VAT is a tax on consumer spending. The basic principle of VAT is that it is charged at each stage in the supply of goods and services. This type of VAT, i.e. one that is charged on sales, is referred to as **output VAT**. If the customer is VAT-registered and uses the supplies for business purposes, a credit will be received for the VAT charged to them. This type of VAT is referred to as **input VAT**, i.e. VAT that is charged on purchases. As VAT-registered businesses can deduct their input VAT from their output VAT to establish if they have an overall VAT liability to pay to HMRC, the effect of VAT is not felt by VAT-registered businesses but is instead borne by the final customer.

The terms 'output VAT' and 'input VAT' will be referred to frequently throughout this chapter as they are central to understanding the operation of VAT. The subject of VAT also has its own specific terminology. Two key terms that are also referred to frequently are "taxable supplies" and "taxable person". "Taxable person", for VAT purposes, refers to an individual, partnership, company or other trading entity that is either registered for VAT or is required to be registered for VAT (see **Section 13.3**).

"Taxable supplies" are goods or services that are liable to VAT, whether at the standard rate, reduced rate or zero rate (see **Section 13.4**). Supplies that are exempt are **not** considered as taxable supplies. Examples of taxable supplies include:

- the sale of goods (including capital items);
- the sale of services;
- charges between associated businesses (such as management charges);
- the leasing or renting of goods or services;
- royalties from copyright;
- the sale of land and buildings; and
- recharging the salaries of staff, etc.

European Union Directives and Case Law
VAT is the only tax where the operational rules are decided by the EU. The UK and each other Member State are permitted to set the rates of VAT (within certain parameters) within their own territories, but the rules in relation to the operation of the system and the categorisation of goods and services for VAT-charging purposes are set by the EU.

The EU issues VAT directives to Member States and they, in turn, **must modify** their VAT legislation accordingly. In the event of any inconsistency, **EU law takes precedence**. Any judgment from the Court of Justice of the European Union (CJEU) takes precedence over UK case law on VAT, including determinations by Appeal Commissioners.

UK Legislation

VAT was introduced in the UK on 1 April 1973. Currently, the UK VAT legislation is consolidated in the Value Added Tax Act 1994 (VATA 1994). This Act provides the main framework for VAT. However, additional guidance and support can be found in statutory instruments and notices and leaflets published by HMRC.

The current standard VAT rate of 20% was increased from the previous rate of 17.5% on 4 January 2011, as a consequence of Finance (No. 2) Act 2010.

13.2   General Principles of VAT

Registered traders collect VAT on the **supply of goods and services** to their customers. Each trader in the chain of supply, from manufacturer through to retailer, will **charge VAT on their sales**, i.e. on their output on behalf of HMRC. The trader is entitled to **deduct** from this amount the **VAT paid on purchases**, i.e. on their inputs, before paying the net VAT over to HMRC. The effect of offsetting purchases against sales is to impose the tax on the **value added** at each stage of production – hence value-added tax. It is the final consumer, who is usually not registered for VAT, who absorbs VAT as part of the purchase price. This can be illustrated by way of a simple example.

Consider a wardrobe. The timber merchant sells the raw material to the manufacturer for £100 plus VAT at 20%, i.e. £120. The timber merchant keeps £100 and £20 is paid to HMRC.

The manufacturer uses the raw material to produce a wardrobe and sells the wardrobe to a retailer for £150 plus VAT at 20%, i.e. £180. The manufacturer keeps £150 and pays the VAT charged of £30, less the VAT of £20 (paid previously to HMRC) suffered on the purchase of the raw material. Therefore HMRC receives £10 at this stage.

The retailer sells the wardrobe to the final consumer for £200 plus VAT at 20%, i.e. £240. Similarly, the retailer pays the VAT charged (£40) less the VAT suffered on the purchase of the wardrobe from the manufacturer (£30) to HMRC. HMRC, therefore, receives £10 at this stage.

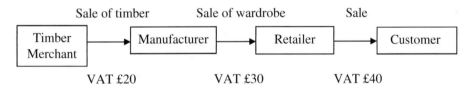

The final consumer is not registered for VAT and so cannot claim a deduction for VAT paid. The consumer has suffered VAT of £40. The total VAT received by HMRC through these transactions is also £40 (£20 + £10 + £10).

The combined effect of the transactions is that at each stage in the transaction a portion of the VAT due has been collected and paid over to HMRC, but the whole amount has been paid, in effect, by the **final consumer**.

13.3   VAT Registration and De-registration

Broadly, registration for VAT is compulsory if you make:

(a)   taxable supplies,

(b)   as a taxable person,

(c)   "in the course or furtherance of any business carried on".

Taxable supplies are standard rated (20%), reduced rate (5%) or zero-rated (0%) supplies, **not** exempt supplies. A **taxable person** is an individual, partnership, company or other trading entity that is either registered for VAT. A taxable person also includes someone who should have registered for VAT but has not yet notified HMRC.

The phrase "in the course or furtherance of any business carried on" is deliberately broad and vague as it is intended to be all-embracing. However, an individual can make a sale that is not part of their business. For instance, a furniture salesman could sell a piece of his own, private furniture and, unless it was on the shop floor, the sale would not be part of their "business".

Section 94 Value Added Tax Act 1994 (VATA 1994) states that the word "business" includes any trade, profession or vocation (see **Chapter 4**).

13.3.1 Registration Thresholds

For 2016/17, the VAT registration limit is £83,000 (previously £82,000). Registration for VAT is necessary if:

1. a trader's taxable supplies (excluding VAT), which include zero-rated sales, have exceeded the registration limit in the previous 12 calendar months (**the historical test**) – unless the trader can satisfy HMRC that their taxable supplies (excluding VAT) in the following 12 months will not exceed the de-registration limit (see **Section 13.3.5**);
2. there are reasonable grounds for thinking that the trader's taxable supplies (excluding VAT) in the next 30 days alone will exceed the limit, i.e. the trader will make a sale or sales within the next 30 days that will exceed £83,000 (**the future test**); or
3. a trader takes over another business and either 1. or 2. above applies.

Hence a trader should check the cumulative total turnover at the end of each calendar month to determine if registration is necessary. Note that in this context, the sale of a "capital asset" does not count towards the registration limit. However, the sale of a property on which you have "opted to tax" does count towards the registration limit (see **Section 14.6** for further details regarding VAT on property).

Three unusual, but important, categories should also be borne in mind, namely:

1. A business in another EU Member State that sells goods by mail order or over the internet to private customers (non-taxable persons, public bodies, charities, etc.) in the UK, and the value of its UK sales exceeds £70,000 per annum, must register for VAT in the UK as the place of supply is now the UK. This is called distance selling.
2. Where the value of acquisitions, i.e. goods purchased from an EU supplier, exceeds the registration threshold, the UK customer will be required to register for UK VAT.
3. Non-UK established businesses that sell either goods or services in the UK from a temporary presence are required to register for UK VAT within 30 days of making (or intending to make) taxable supplies in the UK, regardless of the value of taxable supplies they provide. For example, non-UK traders at farmers' markets or an Irish service supplier working across the border.

In all cases, the trader must notify HMRC:

- within 30 days of the end of the relevant month (where the threshold is exceeded as a result of past sales); or
- within 30 days (in the case of expected sales, i.e. where the trader believes that the taxable supplies in the next 30 days alone will exceed the registration threshold).

Notification to register is made on Form VAT1. See **Section 13.10** for more details on the administration and procedures around VAT. Once notification has been submitted the trader will be registered from either:

1. the **end of the month after that in which the annual limit was exceeded** (as a result of past sales); or
2. from the **beginning of the 30-day period** (for expected sales).

13.3.2 Voluntary Registration

A person can choose to register for VAT even if their taxable turnover falls below the registration limit. There can be many reasons for voluntary registration of VAT, for example:

- they may wish to recover input tax on purchases.
- it may depend on the status of his or her customers, i.e. if they are VAT-registered or not;
- the status of his or her outputs (i.e. are they exempt, zero-rated or standard rated?); or
- the business image that the trader wants to portray.

If the majority of a trader's customers are private individuals, the trader may prefer not to register if not compulsorily required to do so.

Registration for VAT can also be applied for when an individual intends to trade; evidence of the intention is required.

13.3.3 Specific Requirements by Business Type

The type of business in operation affects the VAT registration requirements.

Sole Trader
Sole traders can only have one VAT registration for **all** the "business" activities they own. If they have a number of businesses, VAT registration affects each business of the sole trader. It is the person(s) or the entity that is VAT-registered. Form VAT1 is used to register a business for VAT.

Partnerships
Each partnership must register separately for VAT if the partners are different. Hence, if a father and mother were one partnership, father and son another partnership and father and daughter another, the father would be required to make three separate VAT registrations.

When registering, partnerships must also complete Form VAT2 (in addition to Form VAT1). Form VAT2 requires the details of all partners.

Limited Liability Partnership
An ordinary partnership is not the same as a limited liability partnership (LLP). The partners in an LLP are not personally liable for debts the business cannot pay. Each partner's liability is limited to the amount of money they invest in the business. Each LLP must have its own separate registration. However, if the partners of the LLP have control over a limited company (or companies), then the LLP can be grouped with it.

Limited Company

A limited company must register for VAT on its own unless it is part of a VAT group. Companies under common control can be grouped together for VAT purposes, with one company acting as the representative member of the group (see below).

Other Organisations

Other kinds of organisations, such as clubs, societies and charities, are also potentially liable to register. It does not matter what you do, who you are or whether you make a profit, the overriding criteria is that you **must register for VAT if you make taxable supplies in the course or furtherance of your business where the taxable supplies exceed the registration limit in force**.

13.3.4 Group Registration

When a **group of persons under common control**, such as a number of interlinked companies, are registered for VAT, they may apply for group registration. This means that they are treated as a **single** taxable person. In these circumstances, one company acts as the "representative member" of the group. All inputs and outputs are treated as being those of the representative member. **Transactions between companies in the same VAT group are ignored (for VAT purposes)**.

All parties to the group are **jointly and severally liable** for all the VAT obligations of the other group members. The issuing of tax invoices in respect of inter-group transactions is not required.

Grouping does not increase the amount of input VAT recoverable, but it can prevent the creation of irrecoverable output VAT. One of the **advantages** of a group registration is that it offers a simpler means of accounting for VAT – because there is only one VAT return required for all the members within the group rather than separate, individual VAT returns.

The **disadvantages** of group registration include:

1. Every company within the group is responsible for the entire VAT debt of the group (e.g. a group company could become insolvent, which may disadvantage minority shareholders).
2. The liability for the VAT debt may take some time to materialise, but it can still have an effect on past or present group companies, e.g. even if the VAT debt relates to a member that is no longer in the group, the current group members will still be liable.
3. If a non-group company is due a repayment of VAT, it could move to monthly returns and receive the refund up to two months earlier than it would within a group registration.
4. Where the total VAT payable by a VAT group exceeds £2.3 million a year, the group must enter the Payments on Account Scheme. This will affect cash flow, as payments for a quarter will be due during the relevant VAT quarter (i.e. monthly payments of VAT are required, as opposed to quarterly payments). This £2.3 million threshold applies to all businesses and not just those in a VAT group.
5. If a company supplying exempt supplies is within the VAT group, this will restrict the VAT input recovery for the group (see partially exempt rules at **Section 13.9.3**).

Anti-avoidance legislation and the law on VAT grouping give HMRC extensive powers to refuse to allow a company to be grouped and/or to compulsorily de-group it.

13.3.5 De-registration

A person is eligible for **voluntary de-registration** if, in the upcoming 12 months, the taxable supplies (net of VAT and excluding capital assets) is not expected to exceed £81,000 (for 2016/17).

Also, traders may be **compulsorily de-registered**. De-registration is compulsory if, for example, the trader stops making taxable supplies, the business is sold, the business joins a VAT group, etc. Failure to notify a requirement to de-register within 30 days may lead to a penalty (see **Section 13.10**). There may also be a clawback of input VAT if de-registration is late.

Changes in legal status also cause de-registration, e.g. incorporation of a sole trader to a limited company, although the trader can request to keep his or her existing VAT registration number.

On de-registration, VAT is chargeable on all stocks and capital assets on which input VAT has been claimed and which are held at the date of de-registration. If VAT due is less than £1,000, it is disregarded. However, if it is £1,000 or more it must be paid to HMRC in line with the final VAT return.

13.4 VAT Rates

VAT rates depend on the type of goods or services in question. In the UK there are three rates:

	VAT rate*	VAT fraction**
Standard rate	20%	1/6
Reduced rate	5%	1/21
Zero rate	0%	0

* Used where the value of the supply/sale is quoted exclusive of VAT.
** Used where the value of the supply/sale is quoted inclusive of VAT.

In addition, goods or services can be categorised as exempt supplies, meaning they are not liable to VAT. **It is important not to confuse the two concepts of zero-rated and exempt supplies**, as a business that makes only exempt supplies is not eligible to register for VAT. Whereas, a business that makes only zero-rated supplies can register for VAT.

13.4.1 Standard Rate

The standard rate of UK VAT is currently 20% and has been since 4 January 2011. Standard-rated supplies are those that do not fall into the other categories, i.e. are not zero-rated, reduced rate or exempt.

The VAT portion for standard-rated supplies can be quickly calculated by:

Value of supply + VAT =	"gross consideration"
Rate of VAT 20%:	£100 + £20 = £120
VAT fraction	20/120 = 1/6
Quick calculation:	£120 × 1/6 = £20

13.4.2 Zero Rate

No VAT needs to be charged on zero-rated supplies. Therefore, VAT does not make these supplies more expensive to the end consumer. However, it is very important to recognise zero-rated supplies as they are "taxable supplies" and have 0% VAT added. A trader making zero-rated supplies can register for VAT and recover VAT incurred on making the zero-rated supplies, i.e. input VAT (see **Section 13.9**).

Table 13.1 lists some examples of zero-rated supplies.

TABLE 13.1: EXAMPLES OF ZERO-RATED SUPPLIES

Zero Rate (0%)	Notes/Exceptions
Food and drink for human consumption	Food and drink is, in general, zero-rated. "Luxury" items, however, such as alcoholic drinks, confectionery, crisps, savoury snacks, food for catering or hot takeaways (except for food that is "naturally cooling"), ice-cream, soft drinks and mineral water are all standard rated.
Baby and children's clothes and footwear	
Talking books and vision aids for blind people	Also, equipment for blind, partially sighted and disabled people.
Construction of buildings	Construction and sale of new residential buildings (NB: not commercial); construction and sale of new buildings for charitable purposes; building services for disabled people; protected buildings.
International services	Intra-EU supplies (where supplier and customer are VAT-registered).
Transport	Passenger transport that carries not less than 10 passengers.
Brochures, leaflets and pamphlets	Includes books, children's painting and picture books, maps, charts, magazines, newspapers, printed/copied music and publications generally (though online revisions are standard rated).

As is noted above, it is important to understand that a business that makes zero-rated supplies can still recover input VAT. Therefore, such a business will always be in a VAT recovery/refund position.

13.4.3 Reduced Rate

Table 13.2 lists some examples of reduced rate supplies.

TABLE 13.2: EXAMPLES OF REDUCED RATE SUPPLIES

Reduced Rate (5%)	Notes/Exceptions
Electricity, gas, heating oil and solid fuel	For domestic and residential use. (Where the supply is to a business the standard rate applies.)
Energy-saving material installed in residential premises	Air- and ground-source heat pumps, wood-fuelled boilers, central heating controls, insulation, solar panels, water and wind turbines, etc.
Smoking cessation products	Nicotine patches and gum.
Women's sanitary products	
Converting premises	Conversion into different living accommodation.
Renovating living accommodation	Renovation of an empty residential building.
Children's safety seats	Including booster seats.

The VAT portion for reduced-rate supplies can be quickly calculated by:

Value of supply + VAT =	"gross consideration"
Rate of VAT 5%:	£100 + £5 = £105
VAT fraction	5/105 = 1/21
Quick calculation:	£105 × 1/21 = £5

VAT is charged on the VAT-exclusive price. Prior to 1 April 2015, where a discount was offered for prompt payment, VAT was chargeable on the net amount even if the discount was not taken up. From 1 April 2015, however, suppliers must account for VAT on the amount they actually receive, i.e. VAT is due on the price that is actually paid.

13.4.4 Exempt Supplies

No VAT is chargeable on exempt supplies. A trader making only exempt supplies cannot register for VAT. Therefore, such a trader will not be able to recover VAT on the costs associated with making the exempt supplies, i.e. no input VAT is recoverable (see **Section 13.9**).

Table 13.3 lists some examples of exempt supplies.

TABLE 13.3: EXAMPLES OF EXEMPT SUPPLIES

Exempt	**Notes/Exceptions**
Physical education and sports activities	
Betting and lotteries and bingo	
Burial and cremation services	
Health and welfare	Medical services generally, e.g. services by doctors, dentists, opticians, pharmacists, etc.
Education, training or other services	Provided by an eligible body, like a school or college (currently under review with a view to extending).
Property	Grant or licence to occupy land or buildings.
Financial services and investments	Loans and credit facilities; insurance services.
Cultural services	Admission to museums, galleries, theatrical and musical performances.
Investment gold	

As noted above, it is important to understand the distinction between a trader making zero-rated supplies and one making exempt supplies. If a trader makes exempt supplies only, they are unable to recover any of the input VAT that is charged on those purchases that relate to the exempt sales.

Example 13.1

The fees charged by a university are exempt for VAT. However, the university will incur VAT on various costs that it needs to operate, for example, heat and light in the lecture theatres. The university will have to pay the reduced rate of VAT on its electricity and heating bills (either oil or gas).

A university making only exempt supplies will not be able to register for VAT and so it will not be able to recover the VAT it is charged on its heating and light costs.

13.4.5 Supplies Outside the Scope of UK VAT

Finally, as well as supplies that are exempt, there are other sales that are deemed to be outside the scope of UK VAT. There are three main kinds:

1. Sales/services for which the place of supply is treated as being outside the UK. The input tax incurred in the UK may or may not be recoverable and is dealt with later in relation to exports and imports (see **Chapter 14**).
2. Sundry transactions which, for a variety of reasons, are not subject to tax, e.g. a government subsidy, or transactions between companies within the same VAT group.
3. Transfer of a business where the conditions for transfer of going concern are met (see **Section 14.7**).

13.5   Amount on which VAT is Chargeable

The general rule for the supply of goods or services (and the acquisitions of goods from other EC countries, see **Section 14.1**) is that the amount on which VAT is chargeable is normally the **total sum** paid or payable for the supply of the goods or services, including all taxes, commissions, costs and charges, but **not including** the VAT chargeable in respect of the transaction.

Example 13.2
Clive is a Chartered Accountant and is registered for VAT. He bills his client £1,000 for his annual income tax return, £1,500 for the cost incurred in preparing his annual accounts and £500 for a meeting at his client's premises to discuss the controls in his business.

Clive's total fee will be £3,000 plus VAT of £600, i.e. a total fee of £3,600.

In some instances HMRC may determine that the **value** on which VAT is charged in relation to certain transactions **between connected persons** is the **open market value**. Where, for example, the actual amount charged is below market value because the supplier and the purchaser are connected.

13.5.1 Specific Rules

Imports
VAT on imports is charged on the cost, **plus** transport cost, **plus** any duty payable on the goods (its 'customs value'). (See **Chapter 14** for more detail.)

Goods or Services Supplied other than for Money
Where a customer agrees to pay the supplier in kind, the amount on which VAT is chargeable is the open market or arm's length value of the goods or services supplied.

Credit Card Transactions
In the case of credit card transactions, the amount chargeable to VAT is the total amount actually charged to the customer by the trader. Any amount withheld by the credit card companies from their settlement with the trader forms part of the taxable amount.

Packaging and Containers
When goods are supplied packaged for sale and **no separate charge** is made for the packaging in which the goods are contained, the rate of VAT chargeable is that **applying to the goods**. If containers

are charged for **separately** from the goods (e.g. where the goods and the container for transportation are billed for separately), the transaction is regarded as consisting of separate sales of goods and of packages and **each** such **separate sale** is chargeable at the appropriate rate.

Where containers are returnable and a separate charge in the nature of a deposit is included on an invoice (e.g. once the container is returned the deposit will be repaid), the containers are regarded as being the property of the supplier and the **deposit** is **not** subject to VAT. VAT **is** payable on the value of containers that are **not returned** to the supplier. This VAT may be accounted for at the time when the containers account is being balanced and a charge is being raised by the supplier against the customer for the value of containers not returned.

Mixed and Composite Supplies

Different goods and services are sometimes invoiced together at an inclusive price (a **mixed supply**). Some items may be chargeable at the standard rate and some at the zero rate, in which case the supplier must account for VAT separately by splitting the total amount payable in a fair proportion between the standard- and zero-rated elements; VAT is charged on each at the appropriate rate; there is no special way of making this apportionment (i.e. HMRC do not dictate any specific method)..

If a mixed supply cannot be split into different elements it is a **composite supply**, e.g. when one element of the supply is merely incidental to the main element. A composite supply must have a single VAT rate applied. For example, normal and necessary packaging (such as tins, bottles and jars) is treated as part of the goods that it contains, so that if the contents are zero-rated, then zero-rating also applies to the packaging (composite supply). If, however, the packaging is more than is normal and necessary, e.g. storage containers that could be sold separately from the contents, then it is a mixed supply and VAT is charged on the constituent elements at the appropriate rate.

13.6   Supply of Goods or Services

13.6.1   Supply of Goods

A taxable **supply of goods** means the **normal transfer of ownership** of goods from one person to another and includes the supply of zero-rated goods. This includes:

- the transfer of ownership of goods by agreement;
- the supply of any form of power, heat, refrigeration or ventilation or of water;
- the grant, assignment or surrender of a major interest (the freehold or a lease for over 21 years) in land;
- taking goods permanently out of the business for the non-business use of a taxable person or for other private purposes, including the supply of goods by an employer to an employee for his private use; and
- transfers under an agreement contemplating a transfer of ownership, such as a hire-purchase agreement.

Gifts of Goods

Gifts of goods are normally treated as sales at cost. VAT will therefore be due. However, business gifts are not supplies of goods if:

1. the total cost of gifts made to the same person does not exceed £50 in any 12-month period. If exceeded, output VAT is due on the full amount; or
2. the gift is a sample.

Self-supply of Goods

Where goods are **permanently** removed from the business for non-business purposes for no consideration, VAT must be accounted on their market value at that time.

If goods are loaned out **temporarily** to the proprietor personally, then a supply of services has been made for no consideration and not a supply of goods. VAT, in this instance, is due on the cost to the business of lending the goods out.

Example 13.3

One of the fixed assets of a business, a mini-digger, was loaned out for 40 days for private use to the proprietor.

The cost to the business of the mini-digger is the annual depreciation. If the annual depreciation is £2,000, then VAT is due at 40/365 × £2,000 = £220. Therefore the cost of the supply is £220, which attracts VAT at 20%.

VAT of £44 is due.

13.6.2 Supply of Services

For VAT purposes, a "service" is any commercial activity, **other than** a supply of goods (apart from a few specific examples), which is carried out in return for consideration. Consideration is any form of payment, in money or in kind, including anything which is itself a supply.

Typical services include:

■ caterers, mechanics, plumbers, accountants, solicitors, consultants, etc.;
■ hiring or leasing of goods;
■ supply of digitised goods delivered online – regarded as the supply of a service for VAT purposes, as is the physical supply of customised software;
■ restaurants – regarded as a supply of services not goods; and
■ contract work, i.e. the handing over by a contractor to a customer of movable goods made or assembled by him from goods entrusted to him by the customer.

Services also include **refraining** from doing something and the granting or surrendering of a right.

A supply of services also takes place if:

■ goods are lent to someone outside the business;
■ goods are hired to someone; and
■ services that were bought for business purposes are used for private purposes.

Certain services, including agents, banking agents and certain related agents, are **exempt** from VAT.

Self-supply of services are those services purchased for business use but put to private use instead. If that happens, then VAT must be accounted on the cost to the business of making the services available for private use. Such services could be computer software or building services.

13.7 Time of Supply of Goods or Services

VAT becomes due, or a liability for VAT arises, at the time when a **supply of goods or services takes place**. This is called the **tax point**. VAT must normally be accounted for in the VAT period in which the tax point occurs and at the rate of VAT in force at that time (unless the cash accounting scheme is being used, see **Section 13.11.3**).

13.7.1 Basic Tax Point

The basic tax point for a **supply of goods** is the date the goods are removed, i.e. dispatched to or collected by the customer. If the goods are not removed, it is the date they are made available for the customer's use.

The basic tax point for a **supply of services** is the date the services are performed or completed. The basic tax point is the default position that will apply if the 'actual tax point' is not used.

13.7.2 Actual Tax Point

In the case of both goods and services, where a VAT invoice is raised or payment is made before the basic tax point, there is an **earlier actual tax point** at the time the invoice is issued or payment is received, whichever occurs first.

In practice, there is usually a later tax point as the basic tax point is extended to the date the invoice is issued, if this is within 14 days (30 days at HMRC's discretion) after the basic tax point. However, this is subject to the overriding rule noted above regarding the actual tax points. If an invoice is not issued within the 14 days (30 days at HMRC's discretion) of the basic tax point, then the basic tax point rule applies. An actual tax point takes priority over a basic tax point.

Other specific rules apply for continuous supplies of services.

13.8 Place of Supply of Goods or Services

The place of supply rules are very important for VAT as goods and services are liable to VAT **in the place where they are supplied**, or are deemed to be supplied. For example, if a supply is in the UK, the UK rates of VAT apply. If instead the supply is in France, then no UK VAT would arise because it is outside the scope of UK VAT.

The complexities of the supply of goods and services internationally are dealt with in detail in **Chapter 14**. The general rules with regard to the place of supply of goods are outlined below.

13.8.1 Place of Supply of Goods

The place of supply of goods is deemed to be as follows:

1. If the supply requires the transportation of goods, the place where the transportation begins is deemed to be the place of supply.
2. In all other cases, the location of the goods at the time of supply determines the place of supply.

Generally, when goods leave the UK the place of supply will be treated as the UK. Conversely, where goods arrive from outside the UK, then the place of supply will typically be the supplier's country.

The supply of goods internationally can usually fall under one of four categories:

1. exports (where goods are sold to a customer outside the EU);
2. imports (where goods arrive in the UK from a non-EU supplier);
3. dispatches (where goods are sold to a customer in another EU country); or
4. acquisitions (where goods arrive in the UK from a supplier in another EU country).

13.8.2 Place of Supply of Services

The general rule for the place of supply of services is (subject to some exceptions) deemed to be:

1. (If the recipient is in business) in the country where the recipient of the service is located. These are known as business-to-business (B2B) supplies.
2. (If the recipient is not in business) in the country where the supplier is located. These are known as business-to-consumer (B2C) supplies.

There are some exceptions to the above general rule outlined above. For example, services relating to land are always treated as being supplied in the country where the land is located. See **Section 14.2.2** for further information on the exceptions to the general rule for the supply of services.

13.9 Recovery of VAT

13.9.1 Deductible VAT – Input VAT

In computing the amount of VAT payable in respect of a taxable period, a registered person may **deduct** the VAT paid by them on the purchase of goods and services, which are used for the purposes of the **taxable business**. To be entitled to the deduction, the trader must have a proper VAT invoice or relevant customs receipt as appropriate.

While a deduction of VAT is allowable only on purchases that are for the purposes of a taxable business, a situation may arise where a **portion** of a trader's purchases may be for the purposes of the taxable business and the remaining portion for the trader's **private use** (e.g. electricity, telephone charges, heating expenses, etc. where the business is carried on from his private residence). It may also arise that inputs may be used for **both taxable and non-taxable** activities. **In such cases, only the amount of VAT that is attributable to the taxable business is deductible**.

Similarly, where a trader engages in both taxable and exempt activities, it will be necessary to **apportion** the input VAT on a "just and reasonable" basis.

In general, VAT is deductible against a taxable person's liability in any of the following situations:

- VAT charged to a taxable person by other taxable persons on supplies of goods (including fixed assets) and services.
- VAT paid by the taxable person on goods imported.
- VAT payable on the self-supply of goods or services, provided that the self-supply is for business purposes (see **Section 13.6.1**).

There is no distinction between capital and revenue expenditure for VAT. This is in contrast to the position for income tax as outlined in **Chapter 4**.

13.9.2 Non-deductible VAT

No deduction is allowed in respect of VAT paid on expenditure on any of the following:

- VAT on expenses incurred on business **entertaining** where the cost of the entertaining is not a tax-deductible trading expense.
- VAT on **motor cars** not used wholly for business purposes. VAT is never reclaimable unless the car is acquired new for resale or is acquired for use in a taxi business, a self-drive car hire business or a driving school.

■ VAT on expenses incurred on domestic accommodation for directors/proprietors of a business.
■ VAT on non-business items passed through the business accounts.
■ VAT that does not relate to the making of supplies by the buyer in the course of a business (i.e. for VAT to be deductible, it must be incurred in respect of a cost that relates to the vatable supplies of the business).

Where input VAT is not recoverable, it forms part of the cost of the asset for income tax, CGT, corporation tax and capital allowance purposes. (Note, CGT and corporation tax are on the CA Proficiency 2 syllabus.)

Fuel

A VAT reclaim is permitted on business fuel only. If fuel is supplied for private purposes, all input VAT incurred on the fuel may be allowed to be claimed, but only if the trader accounts for output VAT using a set of scale charges **per VAT return** based on the CO_2 emissions of the car (CO_2 emissions are rounded down to the nearest 5%.). Scale charges are provided inclusive of VAT. See **Example 13.4** below for the inclusion of deemed output VAT in respect of the private fuel adjustment required in line with the VAT fuel scale charges.

Example 13.4

Adrian operates as a sole trader and is registered for VAT. All of his supplies are taxable. The following information is relevant to his VAT return for the quarter ended 31 March 2016:

1. Invoiced sales of £40,000 (excluding VAT). Sales were invoiced to customers in the UK and were standard rated.
2. Invoiced sales of £10,000 (excluding VAT). Sales were invoiced to VAT-registered customers in the EU and related to standard-rated goods.
3. Purchases of standard-rated stock in the amount of £12,000 (VAT exclusive), of which £600 was used by Adrian personally.
4. Payment of £200 (VAT inclusive) on a meal to entertain new clients.
5. Purchase of a new computer for the business at £1,800 (VAT inclusive).
6. Adrian uses his car for the business. Overall the car usage is 80% business and 20% personal. Adrian charges all of his petrol costs (£150 per month VAT inclusive) to the business. The car emits 150g/km of CO_2.
7. Adrian had an outstanding debtor of £1,500 (including VAT). The invoice was due for payment on 31 March 2015. Adrian received £750 in November 2015 as partial settlement and, in January 2016, he wrote off the remainder of the debt as irrecoverable.

Calculate the VAT payable to/repayable from HMRC in respect of the quarter ended 31 March 2016.

(Note: VAT scale charge for a car with CO_2 emissions of 150g/km is: £1,072 (12 months, inclusive of VAT); £267 (3 months, inclusive of VAT).)

	£
Output VAT	
Standard-rated sales (£40,000 × 20%)	8,000
EU sales (zero-rated in UK)	0.00
Petrol: fuel scale charge (£267 × 1/6) (Note 1)	44.50
Input VAT	
Stock ((£12,000 − £600) × 20%) (Note 2)	(2,280)
Meal (Note 3)	0.00
Computer equipment (£1,800 × 1/6) (Note 4)	(300)
Petrol (£150 × 1/6 × 3 months) (Note 5)	(75)
Bad debt relief (£750 × 1/6) (Note 6)	(125)
Total VAT payable to HMRC (£8,044.50 − £2,780)	5,264.50

continued overleaf

Notes:
1. This can be avoided if Adrian does not reclaim the input VAT on fuel.
2. Cannot reclaim VAT on items for personal use.
3. Cannot reclaim VAT on entertaining customers.
4. Input VAT reclaimed regardless of whether items are revenue or capital in nature.
5. A fuel scale charge is added to output VAT as a direct result of reclaiming the input VAT on petrol where there is private use.
6. Debt is over six months old and has been written off in the accounts.

13.9.3 Partially Exempt Supplies

Some businesses make both taxable and exempt supplies, e.g. a dentist, where normal dentistry work is exempt, while cosmetic procedures are standard rated. In such cases the business is partially exempt. The issue for businesses that are partially exempt is how much input VAT they can recover from HMRC. Where purchases can be directly attributed to taxable supplies, the input VAT on these is fully recoverable. Similarly, where purchases can be directly attributed to exempt supplies, VAT cannot be reclaimed.

Finally, there may be business purchases that cannot so easily be attributed as they relate to both taxable and exempt supplies, e.g. overheads such as electricity or telephone bills in a dentist practice that is used for both exempt and standard-rated supplies. This is "residual" input VAT and special rules apply to determine how it is allocated. Only the portion of this input tax that relates to taxable supplies can be recovered by a partially exempt, VAT-registered business.

There are two prescribed methods for calculating the amount of residual input tax that can be recovered:

1. HMRC's standard method; or
2. a special method, determined by the business itself, which is "fair and reasonable" and subject to HMRC approval before it can be used.

Standard Method
There are a number of different calculation bases under the standard method, such as the value-based and use-based calculations. The standard method is commonly used by smaller businesses as it is relatively simple to apply. The value-based calculation is outlined below:

The value-based standard method of apportionment of residual input VAT is:

$$\frac{\text{Total taxable supplies (excluding VAT)}}{\text{Total supplies (excluding VAT)}} \times 100 = \% \text{ of VAT recovery}$$

Self-supplies or supplies of capital goods used for the business are excluded from the calculation.

The percentage is usually rounded up to the nearest whole number (so, for example, 62.3% would be rounded up to 63%). This is then applied to the residual input tax to determine the amount that is recoverable.

De minimis *Input VAT*
Normally the input VAT on exempt supplies is not recoverable; however, HMRC relax this restriction for partially exempt businesses where the total input VAT on exempt supplies is below a certain limit – less than, or equal to, £625 per month on average **and** less than 50% of total input tax. Where a partially exempt business meets both of these stipulations, it is said to be *de minimis* and is allowed to reclaim the input VAT even though it relates to exempt supplies.

Note that the total exempt input VAT includes both the input VAT on purchases, which are directly attributable to exempt supplies, and the portion of the residual input VAT that relates to exempt supplies (as identified using the above methods).

There are two simplified *de minimis* tests that make it easier for smaller businesses to determine if they can fully recover input VAT on exempt supplies without having to perform the full calculations required under the normal *de minimis* test.

Test 1: total input VAT (compared to 'total input VAT on exempt supplies' under the *de minimis* test) incurred is no more than £625 per month on average and the value of exempt supplies is not more than 50% of the value of all supplies (compared to 50% of total input VAT under the *de minimis* test).

Test 2: total input VAT incurred less input tax directly attributable to taxable supplies is no more than £625 per month on average and the value of exempt supplies is not more than 50% of the value of all supplies.

These simplified tests should always be considered before the normal *de minimis* test.

Example 13.5
In the quarter to 30 June 2016, a sole trader incurred the following VAT-related costs:

	£
Taxable supplies (excluding VAT)	190,000
Exempt supplies	30,000
Input VAT relating entirely to taxable supplies	6,000
Input VAT relating entirely to exempt supplies	5,000
Input VAT relating to both taxable and exempt supplies	10,000

Taxable supplies include £10,000 (excluding VAT) for the sale of equipment during the three months to 30 June 2016.

What input VAT can the business recover?

The input VAT is equal to the input VAT on the purchases directly attributable to taxable supplies (£6,000) plus the portion of the input VAT relating to both taxable and exempt supplies (using the value-based standard method).

The portion is calculated as:

$$\frac{\text{Taxable supplies (excl. VAT)}}{\text{Total supplies (excl. VAT)}}$$

Capital goods are excluded from the calculation, so the £10,000 in relation to the sale of equipment must be excluded. The recovery % is therefore:

$$\frac{£180,000}{£210,000 \text{ (i.e. £190,000 + £30,000 – £10,000)}}$$

i.e. 85.7% (which is rounded up to 86%). This is applied to the residual input VAT of £10,000 to give the amount of input VAT that is recoverable (i.e. £8,600). The balance of residual input VAT is exempt, i.e. £1,400. The sole trade can therefore claim £14,600 (i.e. £6,000 + £8,600) of input VAT and the other £6,400 (£5,000 + £1,400) is not recoverable.

Simplified *de minimis* Test 1 is not met as the total input VAT for the quarter of £21,000 (i.e. £10,000 + £5,00 + £6,000) exceeds £625 per month (i.e. £1,875 for the quarter).

Simplified *de minimis* Test 2 is not met as total input VAT less input VAT directly attributable to taxable supplies is £15,000 (i.e. £21,000 – £6,000) and therefore greater than £625 per month on average.

The normal *de minimis* test is also failed as the total exempt tax (£6,400) is more than £1,875 (i.e. £625 per month).

Annual Adjustment

The residual input calculations are carried out for each quarter and, at the end of the trader's VAT year, an annual adjustment must be made. The same calculation applies, e.g. the value-based standard method, but this time it is the annual supplies and input tax that are used.

The *de minimis* calculation is also performed again using the annual limit: total exempt input tax is less than £7,500 (£625 × 12) and 50% of total annual input tax. The simplified *de minimis* tests can also be used for the annual adjustment review.

The trader compares the annual calculations to the sum of the quarterly ones and any difference is put through as an annual adjustment. The annual adjustment is accounted for on the first VAT return of the new VAT year (i.e. there are three VAT quarters in a VAT year. The adjustment will be in the first quarterly VAT return of a new VAT year).

Where a business passed the *de minimis* test in a given VAT year, it can provisionally treat itself as *de minimis* in each quarter of the following year. This means it can provisionally recover input tax relating to exempt supplies in each VAT period, saving the need for partial exemption calculations in every period. It would still be necessary to carry out an annual adjustment calculation at the end of the VAT year and, if the *de minimis* test is failed at this point, then input tax relating to exempt supplies that was previously recovered must be repaid to HMRC.

There is a cap of £1 million of input tax. So if a business expects input tax to exceed this in the next year, it cannot apply the simplified annual *de minimis* tests.

13.9.4 Pre-registration Input Tax

VAT incurred on goods purchased in the four years prior to VAT registration can be reclaimed in the first VAT return, provided they were still held at the date of registration.

VAT incurred on services purchased for the businesses in the six months prior to VAT registration can be reclaimed in the first VAT return.

13.9.5 Reclaiming Overpaid VAT

There is a four-year limit on the right to reclaim overpaid VAT. HMRC can refuse a repayment if it would unjustly enrich the claimant.

13.9.6 Bad Debts

Relief for VAT on bad debts is allowed where the debt is over six months old (measured from when payment is due) and has been written off in the trader's account. This means that VAT that has previously been paid to HMRC on an invoice basis (see **Section 13.2**) can be reclaimed through the VAT return, provided the above conditions are met. To reclaim the bad debt VAT amount, that amount is added to the input VAT being claimed for the current period.

Bad debt claims must be made within four years from the time the debt became eligible for relief.

A business that has claimed input tax on a supply, but which has not paid the supplier of the goods or services within six months of the date of the supply, must repay the input tax, irrespective of whether the supplier has made a claim for bad debt relief.

Bad debt relief does not apply to cash accounting recording (see **Section 13.11.3**) of VAT. Under the cash accounting scheme, cash is never received from a customer, hence no output tax needs to be accounted for – effectively bad debt relief is already given.

13.10 Administration of VAT

VAT is a self-assessed tax. The onus is therefore on a trader to recognise when they need to register for VAT and to report their VAT position to HMRC by making regular VAT returns. The records of the calculations and back-up documents used in the preparation of VAT returns must be retained in case HMRC need to verify the calculations.

13.10.1 Registering for VAT

A trader can register for VAT by using either a paper Form VAT1 or through the HMRC's VAT Online service.

The information required on the VAT registration form (both paper and online) includes:

- business turnover;
- business activity; and
- business bank details.

Once HMRC have processed the registration, the trader's VAT number will be received in writing (regardless of the method of registration).

13.10.2 VAT Returns and Payment of VAT

All VAT-registered businesses are required to submit their VAT returns and to pay any VAT amounts due to HMRC online. HMRC recognises limited exemptions whereby a business does not have to submit their VAT return online or pay their VAT electronically, namely:

- if the business is subject to an insolvency procedure; or
- HMRC is satisfied that the business is run entirely by practising members of a religious society whose beliefs prevent them from using computers.

From 1 July 2014, new categories of exemption from online filing were introduced after a September 2013 Tribunal decision upheld a number of joint appeals lodged against the requirement to file VAT online. The additional exemptions allow business owners to submit paper VAT returns where they satisfy HMRC that it is "not reasonably practicable" for them to use the online system. HMRC will also, in certain circumstances, approve telephone filing as an alternative method of electronic filing.

A VAT-registered person normally accounts for VAT on a quarterly basis. In the past, before improvements with electronic filing and payments facilities, HMRC was reluctant to allow all taxable persons to choose the same months on which to end their quarterly returns as it wished to have its workload spread evenly over the year. However, traders invariably wanted to have their accounting year-end to be coterminous with one of the VAT quarter-ends (for ease of bookkeeping, etc.). This has now been made possible and traders can, in essence, choose any dates to suit their particular entity.

VAT returns submitted online must be filed, and any VAT due paid, within one month and seven days of the end of the relevant quarter, e.g. a return for the quarter ended 31 March 2016 is due by 7 May 2016. Where a trader is constantly in a VAT refund situation, they may instead elect for monthly VAT returns so that their refund is processed quicker.

The VAT return (paper and online) has nine boxes for the following information to be inputted.

Box 1 VAT due in the period on sales and other outputs The output tax charged to customers.

Box 2 VAT due in the period on acquisition from other Member States of the EU Any tax owed on "acquisitions" (goods acquired from a supplier in another EU Member State). VAT is not collected when the goods enter the UK, but rather the taxpayer declares the "notional" VAT as acquisition VAT. In most cases no VAT is actually paid because the same amount is generally recoverable as part of the input tax in box 4.

Box 3 Total VAT due Total of boxes 1 and 2.

Box 4 VAT reclaimed in the period on purchases and other inputs (including acquisition from the EU) The input tax being reclaimed on the goods or services purchased. This includes tax on any capital expenditure, such as equipment and buildings, and is not restricted simply to the taxpayer's running costs. As stated above, also include the tax at box 2 (subject to certain conditions).

Box 5 Net VAT to be paid to HMRC or reclaimed The difference between the sum at boxes 3 and 4. If box 3 is greater, remit this amount to HMRC, while it will refund (in due course) the amount by which box 4 exceeds box 3.

Boxes 6 and 7 Total value of sales and all other outputs excluding VAT and **Total value of purchases and all other inputs excluding VAT** These boxes are for statistical information. Box 6 is the taxpayer's outputs, net of VAT. Box 7 deals with most of the running costs, but does not include wages or salaries, insurance and certain other items (i.e. value of purchases (net of VAT and before cash discounts) plus other inputs (excluding VAT) plus total in box 9).

Boxes 8 and 9 Total value of all supplies of goods and related costs (excluding VAT) to other EU Member States and **Total value of all acquisitions of goods and related costs (excluding VAT) from other EU Member States** These boxes record, where applicable, sales of goods to (box 8) and purchases from (box 9) other EU Member States. Note that these boxes are for goods and services related to **those "goods" only**.

Input and output VAT figures must be supported by the original or a photocopy of the invoices and records must be kept for at least six years.

As noted above, the VAT should be paid electronically and the payment deadline is the same as the filing deadline for the return.

Where the taxpayer pays by direct debit, it is stated that the direct debit will not be claimed by HMRC until three working days after the return is due – in essence, 10 days after the relevant month end. This provides the taxpayer with a cash-flow benefit.

In order to submit VAT returns online, the following action should be taken:

1. Register and enrol for the VAT online service. The VAT return will be submitted online using either commercial software or HMRC's free online service.
2. An accountant or tax advisor can file the VAT returns online where they have been authorised to do so.
3. Consideration should be given to whether any of the business processes for checking and signing-off the VAT return need to be adjusted.
4. Identify the preferred method of electronic payment (for example, direct debit, BACS, internet or telephone banking) and set up arrangements for this.

The online system can also be used to change business details, e.g. change of address, and to de-register. It is also possible to set up an e-mail reminder service to prompt a business when their next online VAT return is due.

13.10.3 VAT Records

Records to be Maintained

A VAT-registered trader must keep **full records** of all transactions that affect his liability to VAT. The records must be kept up to date and be sufficiently detailed to enable a trader to accurately calculate liability or repayment and also to enable HMRC to check the calculations, if necessary.

Purchases Records

The records of purchases should **distinguish** between purchases of goods for **resale** and goods or services **not for resale** in the ordinary course of business. The records should show the date of the purchase invoice and a consecutive number (in the order in which the invoices are filed), the name of the supplier, the cost **exclusive** of VAT and amount of VAT shown. Purchases at **each rate** of VAT must be recorded **separately**. The same information should be recorded in respect of imports, intra-EU acquisitions and services received.

Sales Records

The sales records must include the amount charged in respect of every sale to a registered person and a daily entry of the total amount charged in respect of sales to unregistered persons, **distinguishing in all cases** between transactions liable at each **different VAT rate** (including the zero rate) and **exempt** transactions. All such entries should be cross-referenced to relevant invoices, sales dockets, cash register tally rolls, delivery notes, etc. Traders who are authorised to account for VAT on the cash receipts basis are also obliged to retain all documents they use for the purposes of their business.

Businesses have requirements to retain evidence to support the zero-rating of goods dispatched to the EU, in particular proof that the goods have been sold to VAT-registered businesses and that they have actually been dispatched.

In **summary** the following records must be kept:

- Copies of VAT invoices, credit notes and debit notes issued.
- A summary of supplies made.
- VAT invoices, credit notes and debit notes received.
- A summary of supplies received.
- Records of goods received from and sent to other EU Member States.
- Documents relating to imports from and exports to countries outside the EU.
- A VAT account.
- Order and delivery notes, correspondence, appointment books, job books, purchases and sales books, cash books, account books, records of takings (such as till rolls), bank paying-in slips, bank statements and annual accounts.
- Records of zero-rated and exempt supplies, gifts or loans of goods, taxable self-supplies and any goods taken for non-business use.

Retention of Records

A taxable person **must retain** all books, records and documents relevant to the business, including invoices, credit and debit notes, receipts, accounts, cash register tally rolls, vouchers, ESLs and Intrastat returns, stamped copies of customs entries and other import documents and bank statements. These business records must be retained for **six years** from the date of the latest transaction to which they refer, unless written permission from HMRC has been obtained for their retention for a shorter period.

Information to be Included on VAT Invoices/Credit Notes

HMRC imposes strict requirements on the information given on invoices and credit notes. This information establishes the VAT **liability** of the supplier of goods or services and the **entitlement** of the customer to an **input deduction** for the VAT charged.

Traders who issue invoices and credit notes, and persons to whom these documents are issued, should ensure that the documents **accurately represent** the transactions to which they refer. For example, if an incorrect rate of VAT is used on an invoice, both the supplier and the customer are liable for VAT at the correct rate, unless the supplier has **overcharged** VAT and is therefore liable for the total amount of VAT invoiced.

Form of VAT Invoice/Credit Note

A taxable person who supplies taxable goods or services to **another taxable person** is obliged to issue a VAT invoice showing the following:

- name and address of the trader issuing the invoice;
- trader's VAT registration number;
- name and address of the customer;
- date of issue of the invoice;
- date of supply of the goods or services (tax point);
- full description of the goods or services;
- quantity or volume and unit price of the goods or services supplied;
- the amount charged, **exclusive** of VAT (expressed in any currency);
- the rate (including zero rate) and amount of VAT at each rate;
- the total invoice/credit note amount exclusive of VAT (in Sterling);
- the rate of any cash discount; and
- the total amount of VAT chargeable (expressed in Sterling).

For supplies to other EU Member States, the supplier's registration number must be prefixed by "GB" and, if the customer is VAT-registered, the customer's registration number (including the State code) must be shown. Reference should also be made to the fact that this is a reverse charge supply subject to charge in the country of receipt.

Self-billing arrangements are permitted where certain conditions are met, e.g. a formal agreement is in place. This is where the customer raises the invoice and sends it to the supplier, normally with payment. Invoices may be issued in a foreign currency; however, all values relating to VAT must be converted into Sterling.

A less detailed invoice may be issued by retailers where the invoice is for a total, including VAT, of up to £250.

A taxable person is not required to issue a VAT invoice to an unregistered person, but may do so if he or she wishes.

Following changes made by the EU Invoicing Directive (Council Directive 2010/45/EU), secondary legislation was introduced to simplify the VAT invoicing rules, with effect from 1 January 2013.

The changes removed a number of options that were previously available to individual Member States, which led to variances in the rules in relation to VAT invoicing in different EU Member States. The aim was to have a consistent set of rules that are uniformly applied across the EU, making things simpler and removing uncertainty for businesses.

In many cases the rules introduced reflected the current UK VAT invoice rules, so the changes required to existing UK VAT legislation were minimal. The changes to VAT invoice rules included the following:

- simplification of the rules for electronic invoicing;
- removal of the requirement to issue a VAT invoice for exempt supplies;
- use of a simplified VAT invoice for supplies up to £250 in value;

- reference on an invoice to explain the treatment of the supply; and
- time limit for issuing a VAT invoice for EU cross-border supplies.

Allowances, Discounts, etc.

When the amount of VAT payable as shown on an invoice is reduced because of an allowance or discount or similar adjustment, the trader who issued the VAT invoice must issue a credit note stating the amount of the reduction in the price and the appropriate VAT. This trader may then reduce his VAT liability by the amount credited in the accounting period in which the credit note is issued. Likewise, the customer or recipient of the credit note must increase his VAT liability by the same amount. All credit notes must contain a reference to the corresponding invoices.

Where a VAT-registered supplier and a VAT-registered customer **agree** in respect of a transaction **not to make any change** in the VAT shown on the original invoice, even though the price charged may subsequently be reduced, there is **no obligation** to issue a credit note in respect of the VAT. Such a practice saves trouble for both seller and purchaser. For example, if a discount taken by the purchaser is only on the goods, and the amount of VAT originally invoiced is allowed to stand, no adjustment for VAT is necessary and a VAT credit note is not required.

Alternatively, in the case of a prompt payment discount, if the supplier does not want to issue a credit note but wants to account to HMRC for the VAT on the amount he or she actually receives, the supplier must ensure that the invoice includes the terms of any prompt payment discount as well as a statement that the customer can only recover as input tax the VAT paid to the supplier.

13.10.4 Penalties

Late Registration Penalty

The total penalty depends on how late the registration is, how much VAT is due and whether the disclosure was prompted or unprompted. The biggest reduction to the penalty will be given if the taxpayer makes an "unprompted disclosure", i.e. where the taxpayer informs HMRC about the failure when they have no reason to believe that HMRC has discovered it or is about to discover it. Anything else is a "prompted disclosure". If an unprompted disclosure is made within 12 months of the date the VAT is due, the penalty may be reduced to nil.

The new penalty regime levies the penalty according to the behaviour of the individual (see **Table 13.4**).

TABLE 13.4: PENALTIES – LATE REGISTRATION FOR VAT

Behaviour	Maximum Penalty	Minimum penalty – unprompted disclosure	Minimum penalty – prompted disclosure
Careless	30%	>12 months 10% <12 months 0%	>12 months 20% <12 months 15%
Deliberate but not concealed	70%	20%	35%
Deliberate and concealed	100%	30%	50%

Penalties and Interest on Late Payments of VAT

HMRC record a 'default' for VAT if:

1. a VAT return is not received by the deadline; or
2. full payment for the VAT due on a VAT return is not paid by the deadline.

Surcharges

Where a trader has defaulted, they may enter a 12-month "surcharge period". If the trader defaults again during this time:

■ the surcharge period is extended for a further 12 months; and
■ the trader may have to pay an extra amount (a surcharge) in addition to the VAT owed.

The surcharge is a percentage of the VAT outstanding on the due date for the accounting period that is in default. The surcharge rate increases every time the trader defaults again in a surcharge period. No surcharge is payable on a first default.

Table 13.5 shows the surcharge rates in a 12-month surcharge period.

TABLE 13.5: VAT SURCHARGE RATES

Number of defaults within 12 months	Surcharge if annual turnover is less than £150,000	Surcharge if annual turnover is £150,000 or more
2	No surcharge	2% (no surcharge if it is less than £400)
3	2% (no surcharge if it is less than £400)	5% (no surcharge if it is less than £400)
4	5% (no surcharge if it is less than £400)	10% or £30 (whichever is the greater)
5	10% or £30 (whichever is the greater)	15% or £30 (whichever is the greater)
6 or more	15% or £30 (whichever is greater)	15% or £30 (whichever is the greater)

A trader will not be subject to a surcharge where a VAT return is submitted late and:

■ the VAT is paid in full by the due date;
■ no VAT is due;
■ or where a VAT repayment is due.

In addition to a surcharge, HMRC may also charge a penalty of up to:

■ 100% of any VAT under-stated or over-claimed if a return contains a careless or deliberate inaccuracy;
■ 30% of an assessment if HMRC issues an under-assessment and the taxpayer does not inform HMRC it is wrong within 30 days; or
■ £400 if a trader submits a paper VAT return, unless HMRC has advised that this is acceptable.

Example 13.6

Amanda's VAT return for the quarter ended 30 September 2016 was submitted late. The VAT due of £10,000 was paid on 20 November 2016.

Her return for the following quarter to 31 December 2016 was also submitted late – the VAT due of £15,000 was paid on 26 February 2017. Amanda's annual turnover is in excess of £150,000.

Outline the consequences arising from the late submission of the VAT returns.

1. Quarter ended 30 September 2016 – first default: surcharge liabilities notice issued. Surcharge period runs from the date of the notice to 30 September 2017.
2. (a) Quarter ended 31 December 2016 – second default (falls within surcharge period): surcharge period extended to 31 December 2017.
   (b) Surcharge penalty of £300 (i.e. 2% × £15,000) is due, but as this is below £400 an assessment will not be issued.

The position is slightly different for **small businesses**. A small business is one with a turnover below £150,000. When a small business is late submitting a VAT return or paying VAT, it will receive a letter from HMRC offering help. No penalty will be charged. A surcharge liability notice will be issued if there is a second default within 12 months of the letter offering help, again without penalty. However, on the issue of a third letter, a 2% penalty will apply, which increases to 15% on the issue of a sixth subsequent default.

HMRC may charge interest if the correct amount of VAT is not reported and paid. HMRC may also pay interest to a trader who has overpaid VAT. The rate of interest charged on late or unpaid VAT by HMRC is 3%. The repayment rate of interest HMRC will pay out to a trader who has overpaid is 0.5%.

Amend Errors

For accounting periods ending on or after 1 July 2008, errors can be corrected on the VAT return if the net value of errors found in the relevant period is **less** than the **greater** of £10,000 or 1% of turnover (excluding VAT) (subject to a maximum of £50,000). Errors above this limit must be disclosed separately in writing to HMRC.

HMRC can only raise an assessment to correct errors retrospectively for four years. The four-year cap works both ways. Although one cannot correct an overpayment made more than four years ago, in general one would not have to correct underpayments made more than four years ago either.

13.10.5 Appeals

A trader may appeal to the Tax Tribunal in the same way as explained earlier for income tax (see **Chapter 11**). VAT returns and payments must be filed and paid respectively before an appeal can be heard, subject to a relaxation in genuine cases of hardship.

13.11 Special VAT Schemes

HMRC operate special schemes in relation to specific business size, industries or sectors.

13.11.1 VAT Margin Schemes – Collectibles and Second-hand Goods

The principal feature of VAT margin schemes is that VAT is only payable on the margin, i.e. the difference between the purchase cost and the sales price. The schemes can be applied to the sale of second-hand movable goods, works of art, collector's items and antiques. For example, the correct VAT rate applicable is 16.67% on the difference between the purchase cost and the sales price.

A similar scheme operates in the second-hand motor vehicle sector, whereby VAT is only payable on the profit margin in respect of the purchase and resale of second-hand vehicles, including by way of trade-in. Qualifying cars remain outside the scheme and normal VAT rules apply.

13.11.2 Flat Rate Scheme

A trader can choose to avail of the flat rate scheme, in which VAT is charged at a flat percentage of turnover, with the percentage being aligned to the particular sector in which the trader operates. There are various conditions that apply before a business can join the scheme, the main one being that the expected taxable turnover in the next 12 months will not exceed £150,000 (net of VAT).

The purpose of the scheme is to ease administration for small businesses, and HMRC promote it on the basis that it is quicker, easier and less onerous for small businesses. However, the scheme is not simple and may not be beneficial for all small businesses. For example, the scheme is not suitable for traders who regularly receive VAT repayments, or for traders who make mainly zero-rated supplies.

The scheme works by enabling businesses to calculate VAT due by simply applying a flat-rate percentage to their **VAT-inclusive** turnover, including zero-rated and exempt supplies. Different sectors have different flat rates, fixed by HMRC. For example, the accounting services flat rate is 14.5%, whereas for hairdressing or other beauty treatment services the flat rate is 13%. However, under the scheme a trader cannot reclaim the VAT on purchases, except for certain capital assets over £2,000.

If the total value of the trade's tax-inclusive supplies (excluding sales of capital assets) is more than £230,000, the business must leave the scheme. However, if a business using the flat rate scheme exceeds the annual exit threshold as a result of a one-off transaction, but in the subsequent year expects its tax-inclusive annual flat-rate turnover to be less than £191,500, it may remain in the scheme with the agreement of HMRC.

A 1% reduction off the flat-rate percentage can be made by businesses in their first year of VAT registration. Note, invoices raised will show VAT at the normal rate and not at the flat rate.

Example 13.7

An accountant makes total supplies of £75,000, including VAT at 20%, in the VAT year. The flat-rate percentage is 14.5%. Assume the rate of VAT is 20% throughout the VAT year.

The VAT due to HMRC under the flat rate scheme will be 14.5% × £75,000 = £10,875. Under normal VAT accounting rules, the output tax would be £12,500 (£75,000 × 1/6).

Under the flat rate scheme no input VAT can be reclaimed.

13.11.3 Cash Accounting Scheme

VAT-registered traders normally become liable for VAT at the time of the **issue** of the invoice to their customers, **regardless** of whether they have received payment for the supplies made. For example, a trader must include in his or her VAT return for quarter ended 31 March 2015 all invoices issued during January, February and March 2015. This is known as the **invoice basis of accounting** for VAT.

Alternatively, small businesses can operate a cash receipts basis when accounting for VAT, whereby traders **do not** become liable for VAT until they have actually **received payment for goods or services supplied**. Likewise, they can only claim input VAT **when payment has been made for purchases** and not, as under the invoice basis, when the invoice for purchases is received.

The scheme can only be used by a trader whose annual taxable turnover (exclusive of VAT) does not exceed £1,350,000. If the value of taxable supplies exceeds £1,600,000 in the 12 months to the end of a VAT period, a trader must leave the scheme.

A trader who opts for the cash receipts basis of accounting is liable for VAT at the **rate in effect at the time the supply is made** rather than the rate in effect at the time payment is received.

Traders who opt for the cash receipts basis of accounting must **issue credit notes** for all discounts given to suppliers to ensure that a greater amount of VAT is not claimed by the purchaser than has been paid by the supplier.

The advantages of the cash receipts basis are that output VAT is not due until payment is received; in addition, there will be no VAT payable on bad debts (see **Section 13.9.6**). The disadvantages are that there will be no input VAT recovery until the trader pays the supplier. The business's accounting system may need to be modified to ensure that VAT (both input and output) is recorded only on payments or receipts.

13.11.4 Annual Accounting Scheme

Small businesses can choose to submit one return annually. In the meantime, they pay fixed sums to HMRC based on their previous year's VAT liability.

To be eligible to join the annual accounting scheme, the taxable turnover limit (excluding VAT) must not be expected to exceed £1,350,000 per annum over the following 12 months, and the taxpayer must leave the scheme if the taxable turnover is expected to exceed £1,600,000 per annum.

Under the annual accounting scheme, the taxpayer makes nine interim payments at monthly intervals or three quarterly interim payments based on the previous year's actual payments or, if newly registered, what is expected to be paid over the next 12 months. The first of these consecutive payments is made on the last working day of the fourth month of the scheme's accounting year. That is, 90% of the total payment is paid in nine equal instalments on the last day of months 4, 5, 6, 7, 8, 9, 10, 11 and 12 of the VAT year. The final payment is made when the annual return is submitted, which must be within two months of the end of the scheme's accounting year. Only one annual return is required.

A claim can be made to reduce the interim payments if the taxpayer believes that the annual VAT due in the current year will be less than in the previous year (obviously there can be many potential reasons for this).

Questions

Review Questions

(See Suggested Solutions to Review Questions at the end of this textbook.)

Question 13.1

Outline:

(a) the criteria for determining when a person making taxable supplies needs to register for VAT;
(b) how to register for VAT and the requirements regarding the payment of VAT due; and
(c) the records to be maintained and the information required to complete a VAT return form.

Question 13.2

Stephen has just started to trade as a seller of fine furniture. He has the following sales:

	£
May 2016	2,000
June 2016	6,500
July 2016	6,000
August 2016	8,000
September 2016	8,000
October 2016	15,000
November 2016	14,000
December 2016	23,000
January 2016	1,000
February 2017	70,000
March 2017	5,000

Requirement

(a) When is Stephen required to register for VAT, and when should he start to charge VAT?
(b) Would the answer to (a) be different if Stephen had thought he would make sales of £82,000 by September 2016 when he started trading?

Question 13.3

Outline the VAT rules for determining the tax point or time when a supply of goods or services is treated as taking place.

Question 13.4

What information must be included on a VAT invoice in order for it to be a valid VAT invoice on which input VAT can be reclaimed? (Assume the rules for simplified VAT invoices do not apply.)

Question 13.5

Michael, a friend of yours, has recently set up business in Bangor, Co. Down, selling computers. He has already registered for VAT.

Requirement
What penalties will arise if Michael does not consistently file his VAT returns on time?

Question 13.6

John Hardiman's business consists partly of the supply of VAT-exempt services and partly of services liable to VAT at 20%.

John's records for the VAT period September–November 2016 provide the following information:

1. Sales and cash receipts

Sales of services at 20% VAT (gross)	£24,000
Sales of services exempt from VAT	£2,000

2. Purchases

Purchases of goods and services at 20% VAT (gross)	£6,300
Purchases of goods and services at 5% VAT (gross)	£5,460

3. It has been agreed with HMRC that 10% of John's input VAT relate to his exempted activities. (Assume none of the costs is directly attributable to exempt or taxable supplies.)
4. Included in the purchases figures at 2 above are the following items:
   (a) An invoice for the servicing of his motor car amounting to £160 plus VAT at 20%. It has been agreed with HMRC that the private use of his car was 25% of his total mileage.
   (b) An invoice for the purchase of stationery amounting to £115 was included with purchases at 20% VAT. A closer examination of the invoice revealed that it had no supplier VAT number listed and no details of VAT rates or amounts.

Requirement

On the basis of the above information, calculate John's VAT liability/refund for the VAT period September–November 2016.

Question 13.7

Mr Byte supplies computers to business and retail outlets. You are given the following information in connection with his VAT return for the period July/August/September 2016. All figures are exclusive of VAT. He is not using the cash receipts basis of VAT accounting.

	£
Invoiced sales	100,000
Cash received	75,000
Purchase invoices received	42,000
Purchase invoices paid	50,000
Other expenses:	
Stationery	6,000
Wages	20,000
Electricity	10,000
Entertaining	1,000
Rent – landlord has not opted to tax building	2,400

Requirement

Compute Mr Byte's VAT liability for the period July/August/September 2016.

Question 13.8

Joe, who is a baker, supplies you with the following information from his books for the months of May, June and July 2016 (all figures are exclusive of VAT):

	May £	June and July £
Gross sales of bread	10,000	8,000
Cash discounts given	500	400
Purchase of ingredients	5,000	2,000
Stationery	1,000	1,000
Rent – building opted to tax	2,000	2,000
Bank interest	400	400

Requirement

Compute Joe's VAT liability for the period in question.

Question 13.9

What type of person/business would apply for voluntary registration for VAT? Discuss the reasons why they would choose to apply for voluntary registration.

Question 13.10

Discuss the place where goods and services are deemed to be supplied for VAT purposes.

Question 13.11

Andrew opened a coffee shop on 17 March 2016 and the transactions undertaken during the first VAT period, March–May 2016, were as follows:

Sales and Receipts

1. Net receipts in respect of sales of goods and services to sit-in customers amounted to £2,000.
2. Net receipts in respect of sales of cold food (not cakes) to take away amounted to £4,000.

Purchases and Payments

1. Purchases of food for re-sale: £588 inclusive of VAT at 20%
2. Purchase of stock for re-sale: £334 at zero-rated VAT
3. Purchase of tables and chairs: £440 plus VAT
4. Payment of rent to landlord: £373
5. Purchases of second-hand cash register on three months' credit. The invoice, dated 3 March 2015, was for £690 in total and included VAT at 20%.
6. Payment of £200 plus VAT at 20% to the tiler on 16 March 2015.
7. Payment of £750 on account to a solicitor for legal fees on foot of a bill received for £1,728 inclusive of VAT.
8. Purchase, for the business, of a commercial van for £10,350 inclusive of VAT. All invoices relating to the above transactions have been received unless otherwise stated. Assume that Andrew was registered for VAT prior to incurring any expenditure.

Requirement

Calculate the VAT liability/refund for the VAT period March–May 2015 (round amounts to the nearest £ for the purpose of the question). Andrew registered for VAT immediately when he commenced to trade.

VAT – Advanced Aspects

Learning Objectives

After studying this chapter you will be understand:

- The VAT treatment of the supply of goods and services within the European Union (EU).
- The VAT treatment of the supply of goods and services with non-EU countries.
- The procedures to reclaim VAT incurred in another EU country and for a non-EU business to recover EU VAT.
- An overview of VAT charges on property and the option to tax.
- An overview of the VAT treatment around a transfer of a going concern (TOGC).

Chapter 13 introduced the basic principles of VAT, concentrating mainly on UK domestic supplies. Businesses operating in today's world will most likely be engaged in doing business with customers and suppliers located in other European Union (EU) Member States, and indeed with customers and suppliers located outside the EU. This chapter concentrates on the more international aspects of VAT. It is highly recommended that you have read and understand the principles outlined in **Chapter 13** before reading this chapter.

This chapter begins by looking at the VAT rules that apply to the intra-EU supply of goods (**Section 14.1**) and services (**Section 14.2**). In particular, the VAT treatment in respect of EU 'acquisitions' and 'dispatches' is outlined. The importance of the general place of supply rule was discussed in **Chapter 13** and in this chapter we will consider it in the context of intra-EU transactions and also look at the main exceptions to the rule. The administration and reporting requirements of intra-EU transactions, including the 'reverse charge rule', are also covered in this section. **Section 14.3** deals specifically with intra-EU reclaims of VAT. In **Section 14.4** we move on to look at the VAT position associated with the import and export of goods to and from customers located outside the EU. The final sections of this chapter move away from cross-border and international trade to introduce the basic principles associated with VAT on property, a particularly complex area of tax legislation (**Section 14.6**), and the VAT issues connected with the categorisation of a transaction as a transfer of a going concern, which is often utilised in VAT on property transactions (**Section 14.7**).

14.1 Intra-EU Supplies of Goods

Following the introduction of the **Single Market** on 1 January 1993, the general principle was established that when supplying goods, a supplier does not need to account for VAT on a supply to a VAT-registered customer in another EU Member State. Usually, the customer will account for the

VAT on acquisition in their own Member State, although there are some exceptions to this general rule (see **Section 14.2.2**).

When considering the VAT position on intra-EU supply of goods, specific terms are used:

- intra-EU acquisition – when a customer makes a 'purchase' from another EU Member State. For example, a UK VAT-registered business buying goods from an Irish VAT-registered supplier; and
- intra-EU dispatch – when a 'sale' is made to another EU Member State. For example, a UK VAT-registered business selling goods to an Irish VAT-registered customer.

The EU comprises Austria, Belgium, Bulgaria, Croatia, the Czech Republic, Cyprus, Denmark, Estonia, Finland, France, Germany, Greece, Hungary, the Republic of Ireland, Italy, Latvia, Lithuania, Luxembourg, Malta, the Netherlands, Poland, Portugal, Romania, Slovakia, Slovenia, Spain, Sweden and the UK.

14.1.1 Acquisitions (Purchases) from other EU Member States

From a UK perspective, an 'acquisition' occurs when there is a supply of goods from another EU Member State into the UK.

Acquisitions of Goods by a UK VAT-registered Customer

The treatment for VAT on acquisitions from **VAT-registered suppliers** in other EU Member States depends on the **taxable status of the purchaser**, i.e. whether or not they are VAT-registered. For example, a German VAT-registered company may sell to VAT-registered businesses in the UK as well as to private individuals in the UK who are not registered for VAT. German VAT will not be applied to the sales to UK VAT-registered businesses, but it will be applied to sales to private individuals in the UK.

Of course, if the German company was not VAT-registered in Germany there would be no German or UK VAT implications, for either the business or the private customer in the UK.

When a UK VAT-registered trader purchases goods from a VAT-registered supplier in a Member State and these goods are dispatched to the UK, the UK trader must provide the supplier with their UK VAT number. Upon receipt and verification of this number and confirmation of the goods being dispatched to another EU Member State (i.e. the UK), the supplier, if satisfied it is an intra-EU acquisition, will zero-rate the supply of goods.

A VAT-registered UK purchaser must account for "acquisition VAT", in accordance with what is known as the '**reverse charge rule**'. The reverse charge rule refers to the method by which the purchaser must account for the VAT. So, a UK VAT-registered purchaser must:

1. declare a liability for the VAT as a sale (i.e. treat it as **output VAT**) in their VAT return using the appropriate UK VAT rate for the goods, which may be the zero, reduced or standard rate (see **Section 13.4**);
2. **simultaneously** claim the acquisition VAT as **input tax** (assuming the trader is entitled to full deductibility and is not partially exempt, see below); and
3. account for VAT on any subsequent supply of the goods in the normal manner (see **Section 13.2**).

As the transaction is entered as an output and an input on the VAT return, then, subject to the partial exemption provisions (see **Section 13.9**) the effect for the trader should be tax-neutral. Thus the trader is in the same position as he would have been if he had acquired the goods from a UK supplier.

For example, if a UK VAT-registered grocery business purchases goods from Ireland for use in its UK business, which only makes vatable supplies, the business will have full VAT recovery. If the purchased goods have a cost of £5,000 and are standard-rated, the business VAT position is summarised as follows:

Output VAT	Ireland acquisition (reverse charge)	£1,000
Input VAT	Ireland acquisition (reverse charge)	(£1,000)
VAT due to HMRC		Nil

If the grocery business had purchased the goods from a UK VAT-registered supplier, £6,000 (£5,000 + £1,000 VAT) would have been paid to the UK supplier for the goods and then the £1,000 VAT would have been claimed back in the VAT return. The overall net position for the grocery business is a VAT cost of nil.

Partially Exempt Supplies

Where the UK purchaser is registered for VAT in the UK but makes both vatable and exempt supplies, full VAT recovery will not be available. However, the UK purchaser will still be in a similar position as if they had bought the goods from a UK supplier.

For example, if a UK VAT-registered dentist purchases goods from Ireland for use in her UK business, which makes exempt (routine dentist work) and vatable (cosmetic procedures) supplies, the business will be partially exempt. If the VAT-recovery percentage (**Section 13.9.3**) is 25% and the purchased goods have a cost of £10,000 and are standard-rated, her VAT position is summarised as follows:

Output VAT	Ireland acquisition (reverse charge)	£2,000
Input VAT	Ireland acquisition (reverse charge)	
	% VAT recovery is 25%	(£500)
VAT due to HMRC		£1,500

If the dentist had purchased the goods from a UK VAT-registered supplier, she would have paid £12,000 (£10,000 + £2,000 VAT) for the goods and then reclaimed £500 in her VAT return. The overall net position for the dentist is still a VAT cost of £1,500.

Place of Supply and Time of Supply

The place of supply for acquisitions will generally be the UK if the goods are either removed to the UK or are acquired using a UK VAT number.

The time of supply for the acquisition of goods from another EU Member State is the earlier of:

- the 15th day of the month following the month of acquisition; or
- the date of issue of the invoice.

Acquisitions of Goods by a UK Customer who is not VAT-registered

If a UK trader who is not VAT-registered purchases goods from a VAT-registered supplier in another Member State, VAT is charged in accordance with the rates and rules in the other Member State. The VAT treatment in the UK depends on the value of the goods received.

Where a UK non-VAT-registered business customer purchases goods from an EU supplier, the UK customer pays the VAT charged by the supplier from the Member State and no additional UK VAT liability will arise. The place of supply is the country where the supplier is established.

However, where a UK non-VAT-registered business customer purchases goods from an EU supplier and the value of the acquisitions exceeds £83,000 in a year (i.e. the UK VAT-registration threshold), the UK customer must register for VAT in the UK. The reverse charge procedure, as outlined above, will apply to the acquisition.

14.1.2 Dispatches (Sales) to Other EU Countries

As noted previously, a 'dispatch' is the term used to refer to a supply of goods from the UK to another EU Member State. The VAT treatment of dispatches from the UK depends on whether the customer (i.e. the recipient) is VAT-registered or not in the other EU Member State.

Dispatches of Goods to VAT-registered Customers in another EU Member State
Where a UK VAT-registered supplier supplies goods to a VAT-registered customer within the EU, the transaction will be **zero-rated** in the UK, but will be liable to VAT in the Member State of the purchaser.

A VAT-registered trader in the UK may zero-rate the supply of goods to a business customer in another EU Member State, but only if:

■ the business customer is registered for VAT in the other EU Member State;
■ the customer's VAT registration number (including country prefix) is obtained and retained in the supplier's records;
■ this number, together with the supplier's VAT registration number, is quoted on the sales invoice; and
■ the goods are dispatched or transported to that other EU Member State (and evidence is retained to show this dispatch).

If any of the above four conditions are not satisfied, the UK supplier must charge UK VAT at the appropriate rate, i.e. the transaction is treated as if it had taken place between a UK supplier and a UK customer. If the conditions for zero-rating are subsequently established, the purchaser (i.e. the EU-VAT-registered customer) is entitled to recover the VAT paid from the UK VAT-registered supplier. The UK VAT-registered supplier can then make an adjustment in their VAT return for the period.

Dispatches of Goods to Non-VAT-registered Customers in another EU Member State
Generally, supplies made by a UK VAT-registered supplier to a non-VAT-registered person in another EU Member State are treated as taking place in the UK. Therefore, UK VAT must be charged accordingly.

Example 14.1
BM Tables Ltd, a UK resident and VAT-registered company, makes the following transactions:

(a) sale of top-of-the-range dining tables to Stylo Style SA, a VAT-registered company in Bordeaux, France;
(b) sale of dining tables to Lápis de Lucia, a non-VAT-registered business in Portugal.

What is the VAT treatment of each transaction?

(a) The customer is in the EU and is a VAT-registered business. BM Tables Ltd will zero-rate the supply where the EU customer has provided its VAT registration number. The customer must account for VAT (output VAT and input VAT) in France, using the rate in force there.
(b) The customer is in the EU but is not VAT-registered. BM Tables Ltd will have to charge VAT at the UK rate. The customer cannot reclaim any VAT as it is not VAT-registered.

14.1.3 Summary of VAT Treatment of Intra-EU Supply of Goods

The various permutations of the VAT treatment of the intra-EU supply of goods outlined in **Sections 14.1.1** and **14.1.2** are summarised in **Table 14.1**.

TABLE 14.1: VAT TREATMENT OF INTRA-EU SUPPLY OF GOODS

Country of establishment of supplier	Country in which customer is established	Status of customer	Place of supply	Person liable to charge and collect UK VAT
Dispatches (sales from the UK)				
UK	UK	Business (VAT-registered) or private (non-VAT-registered)	UK	UK supplier will charge UK VAT at the appropriate rate depending on the type of goods.
UK	Other EU Member State	Business (VAT-registered)	Other EU Member State	UK supplier will zero-rate the supply where the conditions are satisfied.
UK	Other EU Member State	Private (non-VAT-registered)	UK	UK supplier will charge UK VAT at the appropriate rate depending on the type of goods.
Acquisitions (purchases brought to the UK)				
Other EU Member State	UK	Business (VAT-registered)	UK	EU supplier will zero-rate the supply in their own country where the conditions for zero-rating apply. The UK customer must still account for acquisition VAT, which can be reclaimed in accordance with the UK purchaser's VAT position, i.e. if providing standard-rated, zero-rated or reduced rate supplies, then fully recoverable. If exempt supplies, no recovery; and if mixed, recovery will be based on partial exemption rules.
Other EU Member State	UK	Business (non-VAT-registered)	Other EU Member State	EU supplier will charge VAT at local rate in their country. Customer does not have to account for UK acquisition VAT. However, if the UK customer acquires goods worth £83,000 or more, they may have to register for VAT in the UK.

14.1.4 Distance Selling

Distance selling is the supply of goods by a business to a customer in another EU country, where the customer is not VAT-registered and the business is responsible for the delivery of the goods. The most common types of distance selling are mail order or internet sales to private individuals, unregistered businesses, charities or public bodies. The distance-selling rules only apply to goods and not to services.

EU Suppliers Selling to non-VAT-registered UK Persons
Usually, an EU supplier who sells goods to a non-VAT-registered UK person will charge VAT in accordance with the VAT rates in their own country (i.e. an EU Member State). If the value of such sales exceed £70,000 per annum, the EU supplier may become liable to register for VAT in the UK and account for VAT on these sales.

For example, if a French company, which operates a catalogue selling adult clothing, makes sales in excess of £70,000 a year to non-VAT-registered UK customers, the French company will have to register for VAT in the UK and charge UK VAT on its sales to UK customers.

UK VAT-registered Suppliers Selling to Non-VAT-registered Persons in the EU
UK suppliers selling to EU non-VAT-registered customers must be conscious of the distance-selling threshold in the various EU countries where their non-VAT-registered customers are located. Each EU Member State applies its own distance-selling threshold. For example, the Republic of Ireland's threshold is set at €35,000, whereas Germany's threshold is €100,000. Where a UK supplier breaches another Member State's distance-selling threshold, they must register for VAT in that Member State and charge VAT in accordance with the local rates in that Member State.

14.1.5 VIES (VAT Information Exchange System) and Intrastat

EC Sales List
When a UK VAT-registered trader makes **zero-rated supplies** of goods and certain services to a trader in another EU Member State, summary details of those **sales** must be returned to HMRC on a quarterly or monthly basis. This return, known as an EC Sales List (ESL), is to enable the authorities in each EU Member State to ensure that intra-EU transactions are properly recorded and accounted for. The return is made to the VAT authorities in the **Member State of the supplier** and should include:

■   the VAT number of the foreign Member State purchaser (this can be verified with HMRC); and
■   the total value (in Sterling) of sales to that purchaser in the quarterly period.

For online ESL submissions, the return must be submitted **within** 21 days, or within 14 days for paper ESLs, of the end of the period covered by the return.

Intrastat VAT Return
The Intrastat system is designed to ensure that all **statistical data** relating to purchases and sales of goods between Member States is available to each individual Member State and to the EU Commission. Certain thresholds of EU sales and EU purchases are required before an Intrastat return is required. The threshold for EU sales is currently £250,000, and for EU purchases it is £1,500,000 (increased from £1,200,000 from 1 January 2015). Services are excluded from Intrastat.

14.2 Intra-EU Supplies of Services

14.2.1 Introduction

A number of fundamental changes were introduced from 1 January 2010 on intra-EU supplies of services as a result of an EU-wide alignment of the VAT rules. Further changes were introduced on a phased basis, with the most recent changes coming into effect from 1 January 2015. These latest changes are specific to business-to-consumer (B2C) supplies of telecommunications, broadcasting and other electronic services.

Businesses involved in cross-border supplies of services are affected by the changes, either as a supplier or as a recipient. The measures introduced changes to the place of supply of service rules. As mentioned in **Section 13.8**, the place of supply rules determine the country where a supply of services is made, and where any VAT is payable. They also determine whether, if VAT is due on a supply, it should be accounted for by the supplier of a service or their business customer.

The new rules aim to ensure that, as far as possible, VAT is due in the country in which the service is consumed (e.g. where the customer is established), rather than where the supplier is established. The result for UK business customers is that they will be liable to account for UK VAT on most services provided by their overseas suppliers under the reverse charge provisions, rather than the supplier charging VAT.

14.2.2 Place of Supply of Services

Section 13.8 introduced the place of supply rules of goods and services. The general rule for the place of supply of services is (subject to a number of exceptions) deemed to be:

1. (If the recipient is in business) in the country where the recipient of the service is located. These are known as business-to-business (B2B) supplies.
2. (If the recipient is not in business) in the country where the supplier is located. These are known as business-to-consumer (B2C) supplies.

It is important to note that a customer does not need to be registered for VAT to be categorised as a business customer receiving a B2B supply of services. Most business customers will provide their EU VAT number as proof that they are in business; however, if a business customer is not VAT-registered (perhaps because they only make exempt supplies), other evidence may be obtained to confirm that the customer is in business. Such evidence may include a letter from the local tax authority or the local Chamber of Commerce. Therefore, the scope for B2B supplies of services is more extensive than it is for B2B supplies of goods (where VAT registration of the customer is required).

Example 14.2

A UK VAT-registered business provides services to the following:

(a) a Danish company, registered for VAT; and
(b) a private Italian customer.

Who is liable to pay UK VAT in each case?

(a) The customer is a business in the EU and the place of supply is Denmark. Therefore, there is no UK VAT (but reverse charge may apply to the Danish customer under its local VAT rules).
(b) The customer is in the EU but is not a business. The place of supply is the UK, the UK supplier will therefore charge output VAT at the standard UK rate.

However, there are exceptions to the general rule, some of which are outlined below.

Cultural, Artistic, Sporting, Scientific, Educational, Entertainment and Similar Services

Supplies of cultural, artistic, sporting, scientific, educational, entertainment and similar services, as well as valuation and work on goods (e.g. alterations and repairs) to non-business customers (B2C), are taxed where the service is performed. Business-to-business (B2B) supplies of such services are taxed where the customer is established (i.e. under the general rule).

Supplies of **admission** to cultural, artistic, sporting, scientific, educational and entertainment events are treated as supplied where the services are physically carried out, i.e. in the country where the event is being held.

Land-related Services

Land-related services, such as works of construction, engineering and architectural services, are supplied where the land is situated. Therefore if the land is situated in the UK, the supply of services will be deemed to be within the scope of UK VAT.

Hire of Means of Transport

The place of supply for the "hire of a means of transport" distinguishes between short-term hire (no more than 30 days, or 90 days for vessels) and long-term hire.

For short-term hire, the place of supply is where the vehicle is put at the disposal of the customer (for both B2B and B2C). For long-term hire to a non-business customer (B2C) and to a business customer (B2B), the place of supply is where the customer is established.

Restaurant and Catering Services

Restaurant and catering services are treated as supplied where they are physically performed. For restaurant and catering services carried out on board ships, aircraft or trains as part of transport in the EU, the place of supply is the place of departure.

Transport of Goods

The place of supply of the transport of goods made to non-business customers (B2C) is where the transportation begins. This rule does not apply to intra-EU transport of goods involving business customers (B2B), as these fall under the general place of supply rule.

Ancillary transport services (such as loading, unloading or handling services) are deemed to be supplied where they are physically carried out for non-business customers. For business customers these services fall under the general rule.

Passenger Transport Services

The place of supply of passenger transport services, for both B2B and B2C customers, is deemed as being the country where the transportation takes place and, in the case of more than one country, in proportion to the distances covered in each. For example, a passenger flight from London to Dublin will travel through UK and Irish airspace. The supply is treated as being partly performed in the UK and partly in Ireland. The distance travelled in each country's airspace will need to be quantified to establish how many miles/kilometres were travelled in the UK and how many in Ireland.

Broadcasting, Telecommunications and E-Services

The place of supply of services involving B2C supplies of broadcasting, telecommunications and e-services is determined by the location of the customer. This ensures that such services are taxed appropriately where they are consumed.

For businesses that provide such services, the administrative burden of registering and accounting for VAT in every Member State in which they have customers can be considerable. To simplify the process and ease the burden, the Mini One Stop Shop (MOSS) was introduced in January 2015. MOSS is an online service that gives businesses the option of registering in its 'home' country to account for the VAT due in respect of B2C supplies of digital services in all other Member States (at the appropriate rate of tax in each state). Only a single VAT return need be submitted to the home tax authority, e.g. HMRC.

Unless they opt to register for MOSS, businesses are required to register and account for VAT in every Member State in which they have customers.

The place of supply of services involving B2B supplies of broadcasting, telecommunications and e-services is determined under the general rule.

14.2.3 Time of Supply of Reverse Charge Services

Since 1 January 2010, the rules regarding the tax point for reverse charge services are governed primarily by when a service is complete, if this is earlier than when payment is made. A distinction is also made between single and continuous supplies. As noted previously, for single supplies, the tax point occurs when the service is completed or when it is paid for, if this is earlier. In the case of continuous supplies, the tax point is the end of each billing or payment period.

For example, if leasing charges are billed monthly or the customer is required to pay a monthly amount, the tax point is the end of the month to which the bill or payment relates. Again, if a payment is made before the end of the period to which it relates or before the end of the billing period, then that payment date, rather than the end of the period, is treated as the tax point.

For continuous supplies that are not subject to billing or payment periods, the tax point is 31 December each year, unless a payment has been made beforehand. In that case the payment created a tax point.

14.2.4 EC Sales Lists: Supplies of Services

Section 14.1.5 introduced the EC Sales List (ESL), which is required to be submitted in respect of intra-EU supplies of goods. From 1 January 2010, the persons required to complete ESLs were extended to include persons who make supplies of services to business customers in other EU Member States where the customer is required to account for VAT on a reverse charge basis.

This measure introduces a requirement for UK businesses that supply services where the place of supply is the customer's country, to complete ESLs for each calendar quarter. It will relate only to services on which the customer is required to account for a reverse charge in their country.

The main purpose of the extension of ESLs to services is to provide a system of control for intra-EU supplies of services whereby the customer is required to account for a reverse charge in their country, similar to that which already exists for goods.

14.2.5 Summary of the VAT Treatment of Intra-EU Supplies of Services

A summary of the permutations of the general rule on the intra-EU supply of services is shown in **Table 14.2**.

TABLE 14.2: VAT TREATMENT OF INTRA-EU SUPPLY OF SERVICES

Country of establishment of supplier	Country in which customer is established	Status of customer	Place of supply	Person liable to charge and collect UK VAT
UK	UK	Business or non-business/private	UK	Supplier
UK	Other EU Member State	Business	Other EU Member State	No UK VAT (reverse charge may be applied by the EU supplier under their local VAT rules)
UK	Other EU Member State	Non-business/private	UK	Supplier
Other EU Member State	UK	Business	UK	Customer (reverse charge to be applied by the UK customer)
Other EU Member State	UK	Non-business/private	Other EU Member State	No UK VAT (the EU supplier will account for any local VAT and charge the UK customer VAT)

14.3 Cross-border Reclaims of VAT

It may happen that a business that is registered for VAT in one Member State may incur VAT on goods and services purchased in another EU Member State. A UK VAT-registered business can reclaim certain VAT suffered in other EU countries.

Businesses established in the UK submit claims for EU VAT electronically, on a standardised form, to HMRC. Businesses are able to submit claims up to nine months from the end of the calendar year in which the VAT was incurred. The tax authorities in the Member State of refund have four months to make repayments, unless further information is requested, in which case the deadline extends up to a maximum of eight months. The Member State of refund pays interest in cases where the business meets all its obligations but deadlines are not met by the tax authorities. All EU Member States are required to afford a right of appeal against non-payment in accordance with the procedures of the Member State of refund.

Similarly, non-EU businesses that incur UK VAT while temporarily visiting the UK can now claim to recover UK VAT by filing Form VAT65A electronically. Claims must be submitted within 12 months following the year of claim.

14.4 Imports/Exports of Goods from/to Non-EU Countries

For VAT purposes, "imports" are goods arriving from non-EU countries; exports are goods that are sold and transported to a customer based outside the EU. In this context it should be noted that certain territories, e.g. the Canary Islands and the Channel Islands, are regarded as not being part of the EU for VAT purposes.

14.4.1 Imports from Non-EU Countries

Although the import of goods from non-EU countries is not a UK supply, VAT will be due on the import and it will be the customer's obligation to account for this import VAT. The fact that the place of supply is not the UK means that the overseas supplier will not have any UK VAT obligations. Imports are chargeable to VAT at whatever rate would have been applied if the goods had been bought in the UK. There is an exception for certain works of art and antiques imported from outside the EU, for which VAT is calculated at an effective rate of 5% on the full value.

An importer of goods from outside the EU must calculate VAT on the value of the goods imported and account for it at the point of entry into the UK. The importer can then deduct the VAT payable as input tax on their next VAT return if they are VAT-registered. HMRC issues monthly certificates to importers showing the VAT paid on imports.

If security can be provided, the **deferred payment system** can be used, whereby payment is automatically debited from the importer's bank account each month rather than being made for each import when the goods arrive in the UK. All incidental expenses (e.g. packing, transport and insurance costs) incurred up to the first destination of the goods in the UK should be included in the value of imported goods. Additionally, if a further destination in the UK or another Member State is known at the time the goods are imported, any cost incurred in transporting the goods to that further place should also be included in the value.

14.4.2 Exports to Non-EU Countries

All exports, irrespective of the type of goods, are zero-rated for VAT purposes. To be zero-rated, HMRC must be satisfied that the export has taken place and require evidence from the exporter to that effect. The evidence must take the form specified by HMRC and be submitted to it within three months of the date of supply.

Example 14.3

GJA Pens Ltd, a UK resident and VAT-registered company, makes the following transactions:

(a) sale of pen pots to Desktop Circus Inc., a VAT-registered company based in America; and
(b) purchase of pen cases from Canadian Cases Corp., a VAT-registered company based in Canada.

What is the VAT treatment of each transaction?

(a) The customer is outside the EU. The supply will be zero-rated (export), regardless of whether the customer is VAT-registered or not.
(b) The supplier, Canadian Cases Corp., is outside the EU. Although the place of supply is outside the UK, the UK customer (i.e. GJA Pens Ltd) must account for UK import VAT – but this should be reclaimable in full, unless GJA Pens Ltd is partially exempt.

If the supplier had been based in the EU, the supplier would have zero-rated the supply in their own country (when provided with the VAT number of GJA Pens Ltd). GJA Pens Ltd (the customer) would have accounted for UK output VAT on acquisition, which would then be fully reclaimable as input VAT (provided the business is not partially exempt).

14.4.3 Summary of VAT Treatment of Non-EU Supply of Goods

The VAT treatment of non-EU supply of goods is summarised in **Table 14.3**.

TABLE 14.3: VAT TREATMENT OF NON-EU SUPPLIES OF GOODS

Country of establishment of supplier	Country in which customer is established	Status of customer	Place of supply	Person liable to charge and collect UK VAT
UK (exporting goods)	Outside EU	Business or private	UK	UK supplier (zero-rated).
Outside EU (importing goods)	UK	Business	Outside EU	Although place of supply is outside UK, UK customer still accounts for UK import VAT (should be fully reclaimable if business is not exempt or partially exempt).
Outside EU (importing goods)	UK	Private	Outside EU	Although place of supply is outside UK, UK customer still accounts for UK import VAT (but it will not be reclaimable).

14.5 Non-EU Supplies of Service

VAT is an EU-wide tax. Therefore, non-EU (i.e. international) services refer to services received from suppliers located outside the EU or services provided by a UK business to customers located outside the EU.

Where a UK business has a customer (business or private) who is located outside the EU, the place of supply is deemed to be outside of the UK and the service is deemed to be outside the scope of UK VAT. Therefore, no VAT will apply to the sale.

Where a UK VAT-registered business receives services from a supplier who is located outside the EU, the place of supply of those services is deemed to be the UK. The UK VAT-registered business must apply the reverse charge to the service received.

Table 14.4 summarises the VAT treatment of non-EU supplies of service.

TABLE 14.4: VAT TREATMENT OF NON-EU SUPPLIES OF SERVICE

Country of establishment of supplier	Country in which customer is established	Status of customer	Place of supply	Person liable to charge and collect UK VAT
UK	Outside EU	Business or private	Outside EU	No UK VAT (outside scope of UK VAT).
Outside EU	UK	Business	UK	Customer (reverse charge to be applied by the UK customer).
Outside EU	UK	Private	UK	Supplier accounts for UK VAT.

14.6   VAT on Property

VAT on property is a complex and specialised area of tax law. Therefore, specialist VAT on property advice should be sought before a transaction is complete. The basic rules are as follows:

1.   Transactions on land may be zero-rated, standard-rated or exempt supplies.
2.   The construction of new dwellings or buildings to be used for residential or charitable purposes is zero-rated.
3.   The sale of the **freehold** of a "new" commercial building is standard-rated. The definition of "new" is less than three years old. The construction or renovation of commercial buildings is also standard-rated.
4.   Other sales and most leases of land and buildings are exempt.

Where an exempt supply is made (and in the absence of an 'option to tax', see below) any VAT suffered on costs relating to that supply are non-deductible. For example, an individual purchases a commercial unit for £500,000, on which VAT of £100,000 was charged with the intention of leasing it out to a tenant. If the landlord does not opt to tax the lease, they will not be able to recover the VAT charged on the purchase (£100,000).

14.6.1   Option to Tax

Owners of property may elect to treat sales and leases of land and **commercial** buildings as taxable instead of exempt. This is known as the 'option to tax'. The option to tax replaces an exempt supply with a standard-rated supply, which enables the owner to recover any input VAT paid. The owner must become registered for VAT (if not already so registered) in order to make the election.

An option to tax attaches to each interest in property separately, unless the taxpayer makes a real-estate election (e.g. where the intention is to buy a large portfolio of properties and opt to tax them all), which will apply automatically for each property acquired after making the election. The option to tax may be revoked on a particular property under certain conditions called the "cooling-off" provisions.

14.7   VAT and Transfer of a Going Concern (TOGC)

Normally the sale of the assets of a UK VAT-registered business will be subject to VAT. However, if a business is transferred as a going concern, the supply is not chargeable and it is considered outside the scope of VAT, i.e. it is not treated as a supply of goods or services and as such is not subject to VAT.

It is important to be aware that the TOGC rules are mandatory and not optional. Therefore it is important to establish from the outset whether the sale is, or is not, a TOGC.

For the TOGC provisions to apply, a number of conditions must be met:

1.   the assets must be sold as part of the transfer of a "business" as a "going concern".
2.   The assets are to be used by the purchaser with the intention of carrying on the same kind of "business" as the seller (but not necessarily identical).
3.   Where the seller is a taxable person, the purchaser must already be a taxable person or become one as the result of the transfer, i.e. be VAT-registered. In respect of land that would be standard-rated if it were supplied (which covers the supply of new commercial freehold buildings and the supplies of land on which there has been an option to tax (see **Section 14.6.1**)),

the purchaser must notify HMRC that they wish to elect to opt to tax the land no later than the date on which the supply of the land is treated as having been made, and must notify the seller that their option has not been dis-applied by the same date.

4. Where only part of the business is sold, it must be capable of operating separately.
5. There must not be a series of immediately consecutive transfers of "business".
6. There should be no significant break in the normal trading pattern before or immediately after the transfer. A short period of closure that does not significantly disrupt the existing trading pattern will usually be ignored.

The TOGC provisions are intended to simplify accounting for VAT when a business changes hands. They have the following main purposes:

- to relieve the buyer of a business from the burden of funding any VAT on the purchase, thereby helping businesses by improving their cash flow and avoiding the need to separately value assets that may be liable at different rates, or are exempt and which have been sold as a whole; and
- to protect Government revenue by removing a charge to tax and entitlement to input tax where the output tax may not be paid to HMRC.

Questions

Review Questions

(See Suggested Solutions to Review Questions at the end of this textbook.)

Question 14.1

Hermes Ltd distributes pet food to home and foreign markets. The following transactions were undertaken by the company during the VAT period March–May 2016:

Sales invoiced to customers within the UK	£250,000
Sales invoiced to customers in the US	£10,000

The above amounts are stated net of VAT. The VAT rate applicable to the company's sales is 20%. During the same period, purchase invoices were received in respect of the following:

	Gross Invoice Value	VAT Rate Applicable
	£	%
Stock purchased from suppliers in the UK	223,260	20
Stock purchased from suppliers in Ireland	50,000	20
Professional fees	5,880	20
Oil	1,050	20
Computer	8,934	20

The amounts stated include VAT where appropriate.

Requirement

Calculate the VAT due for the period March–May 2016.

Question 14.2

Elixir Ltd operates a UK-based business selling materials for the repair and maintenance of yachts and small boats. During the VAT period of three months ended 31 October 2015, it recorded the following transactions.

	VAT Rate	£
Sales of Services (exclusive of VAT)		
Sales in UK		950,000
Sales to Spain (to Spanish VAT-registered customers)		320,000
Sales to non-VAT-registered customers in Ireland		25,000
Sales to VAT-registered customers in Ireland		135,000
Sales to customers located in Singapore		46,000
Costs (inclusive of VAT where applicable)		
Purchase of materials from UK suppliers	20%	423,000
Purchase (acquisitions) of equipment from German supplier	20%	200,000
Purchase of machinery locally	20%	235,020
Rent of premises (Note 1)		11,748
Repairs and maintenance of office and equipment	20%	16,212
Audit and accountancy fees	20%	12,924
Electricity and gas	20%	2,520
Salaries and wages	n/a	167,000
Advertising costs	20%	35,250

Notes:
1. VAT at the rate of 20% is included in the amount of the rent paid on the company's premises.
2. All of the above purchases of goods and services (except for wages, salaries and acquisitions) are supplied by businesses that are registered for VAT in the UK. The acquisitions are purchased from a VAT-registered business in Germany.

Requirement

Calculate the VAT payable by, or repayable to, Elixir Ltd for the VAT period ended 31 October 2015.

Taxation Reference Material for Tax Year 2016/17

Income Tax Rates

	Rate %
Starting rate for non-dividend savings income up to £5,000	0
First £32,000	20 (Basic rate)
£32,001–£150,000	40 (Higher rate)
Over £150,000	45 (Additional rate)
Basic rate for dividends	7.5
Higher rate for dividends	32.5
Additional rate for dividends	38.1

Income Tax Allowances

	£
Personal allowance (1)	11,000
Income limit for personal allowance (1)	100,000
Income limit for married couples' allowance (2)	27,700
Marriage allowance (3)	1,100
Married couple's allowance (4):	
Maximum amount	8,355
Minimum amount	3,220
Blind person's allowance	2,290
Maintenance payments relief (5)	3,220
Dividend allowance (6)	5,000
Personal savings allowance (7):	
Basic rate taxpayers	1,000
Higher rate taxpayers	500

(1)   From 2016/17 onwards, all individuals are entitled to the same personal allowance, regardless of the individual's date of birth. This allowance is subject to the £100,000 income limit, which applies regardless of the individual's date of birth. The individual's personal allowance is reduced where their income is above this limit. The allowance is reduced by £1 for every £2 above the limit.

(2)   This allowance is subject to the £27,700 income limit. The individual's personal allowance is reduced where their income is above this limit. The allowance is reduced by £1 for every £2 above the limit, but is not reduced below £11,000 (unless the £100,000 income limit applies – see Note 1).

(3)   This transferable allowance is available to married couples and civil partners who are not in receipt of married couple's allowance. A spouse or civil partner who is not liable to income tax, or not liable at the higher or additional rate, can transfer this amount of their personal allowance to their spouse or civil partner. The recipient must not be liable to income tax at the higher or additional rate. The relief for this allowance is given at 20%.

(4)   This allowance is subject to the £27,700 income limit. The individual's married couple's allowance is reduced by £1 for every £2 above the limit. That reduction only applies after any reduction to their personal allowance (see Note 1). The individual's married couple's allowance is never reduced below the minimum amount. The relief for this allowance is given at 10%.

(5)   This is the maximum relief for maintenance payments where at least one of the parties was born before 6 April 1935.

(6)   From April 2016, the new dividend allowance means that individuals do not have to pay tax on the first £5,000 of dividend income they receive.

(7)   From April 2016, the new personal savings allowance means that basic rate taxpayers do not have to pay tax on the first £1,000 of savings income they receive and higher rate taxpayers will not have tax to pay on their first £500 of savings income.

Income Tax – Car Benefits Charges

Car Benefit Charge

CO_2 emissions (g/km)	% of list price		CO_2 emissions (g/km)	% of list price	
	Petrol	**Diesel**		**Petrol**	**Diesel**
Up to 50	7	10	155	28	31
51–75	11	14	160	29	32
76–94	15	18	165	30	33
95	16	19	170	31	34
100	17	20	175	32	35
105	18	21	180	33	36
110	19	22	185	34	37
115	20	23	190	35	37
120	21	24	195	36	37
125	22	25	200 or more	37	37
130	23	26			
135	24	27			
140	25	28			
145	26	29			
150	27	30			

Maximum percentage rate 37%.
*Subject to the diesel surcharge where appropriate.

Fuel Benefit Charge

The same percentage figure used to calculate the car benefit charge, as above, is used to calculate the fuel benefit charge. The relevant percentage figure is multiplied by £22,200 for 2016/17 (£22,100 in 2015/16).

Income Tax – Van Benefits Charges

Van benefit	£3,170
Fuel benefit	£598

The charges will not apply if a "restricted private use condition" is met throughout the year.

Capital Allowances

	2016/17 %	2015/16 %
Main pool	18	18
Motor cars on or after April 2009 – CO_2 emissions:		
< 75g/km	100	100
Between 76g/km and130g/km (Notes 1 and 2)	18	18
> 130g/km (Notes 1 and 2)	8	8
New and unused zero-emission goods vehicles	100	100
Special rate pool (Note 1)	8	8
Research and development	100	100
Energy-saving and water-efficient plant and machinery	100	100
Renovation of business premises (disadvantaged areas)	100	100

From 1 January 2016 there is a 100% annual investment allowance on the first £200,000 (£500,000 between 1 April 2014 and 31 December 2015) tranche per annum of capital expenditure incurred on or before 31 December 2015, per group of companies or related entities, on plant and machinery, including long-life assets and integral features, but excluding cars. The limits are subject to complex transitional rules.

Notes
1. These allowances are given on a writing down allowance reducing balance basis.
2. For cars purchased before 6 April 2013 the threshold was 160g/km.

Authorised Mileage Allowance Rates

Use of own vehicle:

Vehicle	Flat rate per mile with simplified expenses
Cars and goods vehicles – first 10,000 miles	45p
Cars and goods vehicles – after 10,000 miles	25p
Motorcycles (all miles)	24p
Bicycles (all miles)	20p

Use of company car (rates from 1 March 2016):

Engine size	Petrol	LPG
1400cc or less	10p	7p
1401cc to 2000cc	12p	8p
Over 2000cc	19p	13p

Engine size	Diesel
1600cc or less	8p
1601cc to 2000cc	10p
Over 2000cc	11p

National Insurance Contributions

Class I

Lower earnings limit:	Weekly	£112
	Monthly	£486
	Yearly	£5,824
Upper earnings limit:	Weekly	£827
	Monthly	£3,583
	Yearly	£43,000
Primary threshold (employee):	Weekly	£155
	Monthly	£672
	Yearly	£8,060
Secondary threshold (employer):	Weekly	£156
	Monthly	£676
	Yearly	£8,112
Upper secondary threshold (under 21) (employer):	Weekly	£827
	Monthly	£3,583
	Yearly	£43,000
Upper secondary threshold (apprentice under 25) (employer):	Weekly	£827
	Monthly	£3,583
	Yearly	£43,000

Employee's Contributions

- Not contracted-out rate:
  - on weekly earnings between £155 and £827   12%
  - on weekly earnings above £827   2%
- Contracted-out rate:
  - on weekly earnings between £155 and £827   10.6%
  - on weekly earnings above £827   2%
- Married woman's reduced rate:
  - on weekly earnings between £155 and £827   5.85%
  - on weekly earnings above £827   2%

Employer's Contributions

- Not contracted-out rate:
  - on weekly earnings over £156   13.8%
- Employer's allowance   £3,000

Other Classes

Classes 1A and 1B	13.8%

Class 2:
Self-employed per week	£2.80
Small profits threshold	£5,965

Class 3:
Voluntary per week	£14.10

Class 4:
Self-employment (rate on profits):
on annual profits between £8,060 and £43,000	9%
on annual profits above £43,000	2%

Beneficial Loans

Official rate of interest:
     3% (from 6 April 2015)
     3.25% (from 6 April 2014–5 April 2015)

Pension Scheme Limits

Annual allowance	£40,000*
Lifetime allowance	£1,000,000
Maximum contribution without earnings	£3,600
Lifetime allowance charge – if excess drawn as cash	55%
Lifetime allowance charge – if excess drawn as income	25%
Annual allowance charge on excess –	
linked to individual's marginal tax rate	20%/40%/45%

* From 6 April 2016, the annual allowance for those earning above £150,000 is reduced on a tapering basis. For every £2 of income above £150,000, an individual's annual allowance will reduce by £1 but is not reduced below £10,000.

Individual Savings Accounts (ISAs)

Overall annual investment limit: 2016/17   £15,240
                                             (split any way between cash and stocks/shares)

Tax Credits

	2016/17 £*
Working Tax Credit	
Basic element	1,960
Couple and lone parent element	2,010
30-hour element	810
Disabled worker element	2,970
Severely disabled element	1,275
Childcare element of Working Tax Credit	
Maximum eligible cost for one child	£175 per week
Maximum eligible cost for two or more children	£300 per week
Percentage of eligible costs covered	70%
Child Tax Credit	
Family element	545
Child element	2,780
Disabled child element	3,140
Severely disabled child element	1,275
Income Thresholds and Withdrawal Rates	
First income threshold	6,420
First withdrawal rate	41%
First threshold for those entitled to child tax credit only	16,105
Income rise disregard	2,500
Income fall disregard	2,500

* £ per year (unless stated).

Sufficient Ties Table – Statutory Residence Test

Days spent in the UK	Arrivers	Leavers
Fewer than 16 days	Always non-resident	Always non-resident
16–45 days	Always non-resident	Resident if at least 4 ties apply
46–90 days	Resident if 4 ties apply	Resident if at least 3 ties apply
91–120 days	Resident if at least 3 ties apply	Resident if at least 2 ties apply
121–182 days	Resident if at least 2 ties apply	Resident if at least 1 tie applies
183 days or more	Always resident	Always resident

Value-added Tax

Registration/Deregistration Limit	Annual Value of Taxable Supplies
Registration limit from 1 April 2014	£81,000
Registration limit from 1 April 2015	£82,000
Registration limit from 1 April 2016	£83,000
Deregistration limit from 1 April 2014	£79,000
Deregistration limit from 1 April 2015	£80,000
Deregistration limit from 1 April 2016	£81,000

Standard rate from 4 January 2011   20.0%
Reduced rate   5.0%
Zero rate   0.0%

Exempt Supplies
These include the following types of items: land and buildings, insurance, postal services, finance, education, health and welfare and professional subscriptions.

Zero-rated Supplies
These include the following types of items: food, water and sewage services, books, construction of buildings, transport, charities, children's clothing and international services.

Reduced Rate
These include the following types of items: supplies of domestic fuel or power, installation of energy-saving materials, women's sanitary products and children's car seats.

Standard-rated Supplies
Applies to all supplies of goods and services by taxable persons that are not exempt or specifically liable at 0% or 5%. Includes goods such as adult clothing and footwear, office equipment and stationery, drink and certain foods.

VAT Fuel Scale Charge from 1 May 2016

CO_2 Band (g/km)	VAT-inclusive 1-month period £	VAT-inclusive 3-month period £	VAT-inclusive 12-month period £
Up to 120	38	116	467
125	58	175	699
130	61	186	747
135	65	197	792
140	69	209	841
145	73	221	886
150	77	233	934
155	81	245	979
160	85	256	1,028

165	89	268	1,073
170	92	279	1,121
175	96	291	1,166
180	101	303	1,214
185	104	314	1,259
190	108	326	1,308
195	112	338	1,353
200	116	350	1,401
205	120	362	1,446
210	123	373	1,495
215	128	384	1,540
220	132	396	1,588
225 and above	135	408	1,633

VAT Fuel Scale Charge from 1 May 2015

CO_2 Band (g/km)	VAT-inclusive 1-month period £	VAT-inclusive 3-month period £	VAT-inclusive 12-month period £
120 or less	44	133	536
125	66	200	802
130	70	213	857
135	75	227	909
140	80	240	965
145	84	254	1,016
150	88	267	1,072
155	93	281	1,123
160	97	294	1,179
165	102	308	1,231
170	106	320	1,286
175	111	334	1,338
180	115	347	1,393
185	119	361	1,445
190	124	374	1,501
195	129	388	1,552
200	133	401	1,608
205	138	415	1,660
210	142	428	1,715
215	146	441	1,767
220	151	455	1,822
225 and above	155	468	1,874

Appendix 2

Chartered Accountants Regulatory Board *Code of Ethics*

Under the Chartered Accountants Regulatory Board's *Code of Ethics*, a Chartered Accountant shall comply with the following fundamental principles:

(a) **Integrity** – to be straightforward and honest in all professional and business relationships.

(b) **Objectivity** – to not allow bias, conflict of interest or undue influence of others to override professional or business judgements.

(c) **Professional Competence and Due Care** – to maintain professional knowledge and skill at the level required to ensure that a client or employer receives competent professional services based on current developments in practice, legislation and techniques, and act diligently and in accordance with applicable technical and professional standards.

(d) **Confidentiality** – to respect the confidentiality of information acquired as a result of professional and business relationships and, therefore, not disclose any such information to third parties without proper and specific authority, unless there is a legal or professional right or duty to disclose, nor use the information for the personal advantage of the Chartered Accountant or third parties.

(e) **Professional Behaviour** – to comply with relevant laws and regulations and avoid any action that discredits the profession.

As a Chartered Accountant, you will have to ensure that your dealings with the tax aspects of your professional life are in compliance with these fundamental principles. You will not be asked to define or list the principles, but you must be able to identify where these ethical issues arise and how you would deal with them.

Examples of situations that could arise where these principles are challenged are outlined below.

Example 1

You are working in the tax department of ABC & Co. and your manager is Jack Wilson. He comes over to your desk after his meeting with Peter Foley. He gives you all the papers that Peter has left with him. He asks you to draft Peter's tax return. You know who Peter is as you are now living in a house that your friend Ann leased from Peter. As you complete the return, you note that there is no information regarding rental income. What should you do?

Action

As a person with integrity, you should explain to your manager that your friend Ann has leased property from Peter and that he has forgotten to send details of his rental income and expenses. As Peter sent the information to Jack, it is appropriate for Jack to contact Peter for details regarding rental income and related expenses.

Example 2

You are working in the tax department of the Irish subsidiary of a US-owned multinational. You are preparing the corporation tax computation, including the R&D tax credit due. You have not received some information from your colleagues dealing with R&D and cannot finalise the claim for R&D tax credit until you receive this information. Your manager is under pressure and tells you to just file the claim on the basis that will maximise the claim. He says, "It is self-assessment, and the chance of this ever being audited is zero." What should you do?

Action

You should act in a professional and objective manner. This means that you cannot do as your manager wants. You should explain to him that you will contact the person in R&D again and finalise the claim as quickly as possible.

Example 3

Anna O'Shea, financial controller of Great Client Ltd, rings you regarding a VAT issue. You have great respect for Anna and are delighted that she is ringing you directly instead of your manager. She says that it is a very straightforward query. However, as you listen to her, you realise that you are pretty sure of the answer but would need to check a point before answering. What should you do?

Action

Where you do not know the answer, it is professionally competent to explain that you need to check a point before you give an answer. If you like, you can explain which aspect you need to check. Your client will appreciate you acting professionally rather than giving incorrect information or advice.

Example 4

The phone rings, and it is Darren O'Brien, your best friend, who works for Just-do-it Ltd. After discussing the match you both watched on the television last night, Darren explains why he is ringing you. He has heard that Success Ltd, a client of your tax department, has made R&D tax credit claims. Therefore, you must have details regarding its R&D. Darren's relationship with his boss is not great at present, and he knows that if he could get certain data about Success Ltd, his relationship with his boss would improve. He explains that he does not want any financial information, just some small details regarding R&D. What should you do?

Action

You should not give him the information. No matter how good a friend he is, it is unethical to give confidential information about your client to him.

Example 5

It is the Friday morning before a bank holiday weekend, and you are due to travel from Dublin to west Cork after work for the weekend. Your manager has been on annual leave for the last week. He left you work to do for the week, including researching a tax issue for a client. He had advised you that you were to have an answer to the issue by the time he returned, no matter how long it took. It actually took you a very short time and you have it all documented for him.

Your friend who is travelling with you asks if you could leave at 11am to beat the traffic and have a longer weekend. You have no annual leave left, so you cannot take leave. You know that if you leave, nobody will notice, but you have to complete a timesheet. Your friend reminds you that the research for the client could have taken a lot longer and that you could code the five hours to the client. What should you do?

Action

It would be unprofessional behaviour and would show a lack of integrity if you were to charge your client for those five hours.

Example 6

You act as tax agent for a friend of yours, John Smyth, who owns and runs his own sole-trade business. John's business has been doing well in recent times and he hints that, when the tax return is being prepared, it would be good if he could pay less tax or claim more business expenses and asks for your help as a long-time friend.

Action

It would be unethical to falsify business records or to underpay tax. You must explain to John that the tax return must accurately reflect the results of the business and highlight that if you were found to be providing false information, you could be prosecuted by HMRC under the legislation for 'dishonest conduct by tax agents' and charged a penalty of between £5,000 and £50,000.

Appendix 3

List C (as per Section 23 Capital Allowances Act 2001)

Note: the version of List C shown below has been modified for inclusion in this textbook.

Expenditure on any of the items on List C will be treated as expenditure on "plant" and will qualify for capital allowances. List C is a long list of specific items, most of which have been derived from case law.

List C
Expenditure unaffected by sections 21 and 22:

1. Machinery (including devices for providing motive power) not within any other item in this list.
2. Gas and sewerage systems provided mainly:
    (a) to meet the particular requirements of the qualifying activity, or
    (b) to serve particular plant or machinery used for the purposes of the qualifying activity.
3. [This item was withdrawn from List C as a result of Finance Act 2008.]
4. Manufacturing or processing equipment; storage equipment (including cold rooms); display equipment; and counters, checkouts and similar equipment.
5. Cookers, washing machines, dishwashers, refrigerators and similar equipment; washbasins, sinks, baths, showers, sanitary ware and similar equipment; and furniture and furnishings.
6. Hoists.
7. Sound insulation provided mainly to meet the particular requirements of the qualifying activity.
8. Computer, telecommunication and surveillance systems (including their wiring or other links).
9. Refrigeration or cooling equipment.
10. Fire alarm systems; sprinkler and other equipment for extinguishing or containing fires.
11. Burglar alarm systems.
12. Strong rooms in bank or building society premises; safes.
13. Partition walls, where moveable and intended to be moved in the course of the qualifying activity.
14. Decorative assets provided for the enjoyment of the public in hotel, restaurant or similar trades.
15. Advertising hoardings; signs, displays and similar assets.
16. Swimming pools (including diving boards, slides and structures on which such boards or slides are mounted).

17. Any glasshouse constructed so that the required environment (namely, air, heat, light, irrigation and temperature) for the growing of plants is provided automatically by means of devices forming an integral part of its structure.
18. Cold stores.
19. Caravans provided mainly for holiday lettings.
20. Buildings provided for testing aircraft engines run within the buildings.
21. Moveable buildings intended to be moved in the course of the qualifying activity.
22. The alteration of land for the purpose only of installing plant or machinery.
23. The provision of dry docks.
24. The provision of any jetty or similar structure provided mainly to carry plant or machinery.
25. The provision of pipelines or underground ducts or tunnels with a primary purpose of carrying utility conduits.
26. The provision of towers to support floodlights.
27. The provision of:
    (a) any reservoir incorporated into a water treatment works, or
    (b) any service reservoir of treated water for supply within any housing estate or other particular locality.
28. The provision of:
    (a) silos provided for temporary storage, or
    (b) storage tanks.
29. The provision of slurry pits or silage clamps.
30. The provision of fish tanks or fish ponds.
31. The provision of rails, sleepers and ballast for a railway or tramway.
32. The provision of structures and other assets for providing the setting for any ride at an amusement park or exhibition.
33. The provision of fixed zoo cages.

Suggested Solutions to Review Questions

Chapter 1

Question 1.1

(a) A paper income tax return is due on or before 31 October after the end of the tax year.
(b) An online return is due on or before 31 January after the end of the tax year.
(c) Payment of self-assessed income tax must reach HMRC by 31 January and 31 July after the end of the tax year. For example, for the 2016/17 tax year, income tax payments will be due as follows:
- first payment on account by 31 January 2017;
- second payment on account by 31 July 2017; and
- balancing, or final, payment by 31 January 2018.

Question 1.2

Under the Chartered Accountants Regulatory Board *Code of Ethics*, a Chartered Accountant shall follow the principle of confidentiality. This principle requires a Chartered Accountant to respect the confidentiality of information acquired as a result of professional and business relationships.

If Emma provides such confidential information about a client to Jack, she would be in breach of this principle. She should not provide the information to Jack.

Chapter 2

Question 2.1

Income tax computation for Pat for income tax year 2016/17

	Non-savings
	£
Income from employment	15,000
Total income	15,000
Less: personal allowance	(11,000)
Taxable income	4,000
Tax payable:	
£4,000 @ 20%	800
Less: tax deducted at source	(3,000)
Tax refund due for 2016/17	(2,200)

Income tax computation for Una for income tax year 2016/17

	Savings
	£
UK interest income	40,000
Total income	40,000
Less: personal allowance	(11,000)
Taxable income	29,000
Tax payable:	
£5,000 @ 0% (savings starting limit)	0
£1,000 @ 0% (personal savings allowance)	0
£23,000 @ 20%	4,600
Tax due for 2016/17	4,600

Question 2.2

Income tax computations for Paul for income tax year 2016/17

	Non-savings Income	Savings Income	Total
	£	£	£
Income from employment (Note 1)	29,000		29,000
UK property business	47,000		47,000
Interest income (Note 2)		300	300
Total income	76,000	300	76,300
Less: personal allowance	(11,000)		(11,000)
Taxable income	65,000	0	65,300
Tax payable:			
Non-savings income			
£32,000 @ 20%			6,400
£33,000 @ 40%			13,200
Savings income			
£300 @ 0% (personal savings allowance: £500 available)			0
Total tax liability			19,600
Less: tax deducted at source:			
PAYE			(5,000)
Tax due for 2016/17			14,600

Notes:
1. Grossed-up employment income is £24,000 net + £5,000 PAYE deducted at source.
2. Interest earned from a joint account is shared equally between the individuals. Paul's (and Jean's) share is thus £300 each.

Income tax computations for Jean for income tax year 2016/17

	Non-savings Income	Savings Income	Total
	£	£	£
Self-employment income	41,000		41,000
Bank interest		300	300
Total income	41,000	300	41,300
Less: personal allowance	(11,000)		(11,000)
Taxable income	30,000	300	30,300
Tax payable:			
Non-savings income			
£30,000 @ 20%			6,000
Savings income			
£300 @ 0% (personal savings allowance: £1,000 available)			0
Total tax liability			6,000
Tax due for 2016/17			6,000

Explanatory Notes
- The £50 Jean received from their neighbour for cutting his grass can be ignored as it is an exempt amount (less than £100).

Question 2.3

Income tax computations for M. Smyth for income tax year 2016/17

	Non-savings Income	Savings Income	Dividend Income	Total
	£	£	£	£
Income from employment	27,000			27,000
UK property business	10,000			10,000
Savings interest income		20,000		20,000
Dividend income			6,000	6,000
Total income	37,000	20,000	6,000	63,000
Less: personal allowance	(11,000)			(11,000)
Taxable income	26,000	20,000	6,000	52,000
Tax payable:				
Non-savings income				
£26,000 @ 20%				5,200

continued overleaf

Savings income	**£**
£500 @ 0% (personal savings allowance)	0
£5,500 @ 20%	1,100
£14,000 @ 40%	5,600
Dividend income	
£1,000 @ 0% (dividend allowance)	0
£5,000 @ 32.5%	1,625
Total tax liability	13,525
Less: tax deducted at source:	
PAYE	(4,000)
Tax due for 2016/17	9,525

Chapter 3

Question 3.1

2015/16

Hank is eligible for SYT for 2015/16 as:

■ he is UK resident for the current tax year (2015/16) (first automatic UK test – spends at least 183 days in the UK in 2015/16);
■ he is not UK resident for the previous tax year (2014/15);
■ he arrives part way through the tax year; and
■ he meets the Case 5 conditions, that is:
  ● he started full-time work in the UK during the tax year 2015/16 for a continuous period of at least 365 days; and
  ● he had no UK ties from 6 April 2015 to 18 May 2015.

Hank is therefore UK resident only from 19 May 2015.

2016/17

Hank spent more than 183 days in the UK in the 2016/17 tax year, therefore he is UK resident for the 2016/17 tax year under the first automatic UK test.

2017/18

Hank is resident in the UK having spent more than 183 days there in the tax year. However, as he is leaving to work full time overseas he may be able to qualify for SYT.

Note, if Hank had not been resident in the UK in 2017/18, then SYT would not be relevant, i.e. you only ever consider split year treatment when the person is UK resident in the tax year under review. (For example, if Hank had left on 15 April 2017 and had not returned, he would be non-UK resident in 2017/18 due to the first automatic overseas test (i.e. spends less than 16 days in the UK in the 2017/18 tax year). If this had been the case, his status would be non-resident for 2017/18 and split year treatment would not even be considered.)

Hank is eligible for SYT for 2017/18 as:

- he is UK resident in the current tax year (i.e. 2017/18);
- he was UK resident in the previous tax year (i.e. 2016/17);
- he is not UK resident in the following tax year as he meets the third automatic overseas test;
- he leaves part way through the current tax year; and
- he meets the Case 1 conditions, i.e. from 11 October 2017 to 5 April 2018 he:
  - works full time overseas, and
  - spends 16 days in the UK, which is less than the permitted 45 days (being 91 days pro-rated for the tax year of departure, i.e. $6/12$ months $\times 91 = 45$ days (round down) (the month of departure is treated as a whole month)).

Question 3.2

As none of the automatic tests apply to Sheila, we need to consider if there are sufficient UK ties that will result in her being treated as UK resident.

Sheila has not been UK resident in any of the three previous tax years prior to 2016/17 and has spent 98 days in the UK, therefore she must have at least three UK ties to be UK resident. Her ties are:

- the family tie (as her husband is UK resident); and
- the accommodation tie (as her brother is a "close relative" for these purposes and she stays with him for more than 16 days).

With only two ties, Sheila will not be considered UK resident.

Question 3.3

As none of the automatic tests apply to Sean, we need to consider the sufficient ties test.

Sean was resident in one of the three previous tax years and spent 52 days in the UK, in which case there must be at least three UK ties for him to be UK resident. Therefore, he will remain UK resident for 2016/17 as he meets the necessary three UK ties:

- family tie (wife and children are UK resident);
- accommodation tie (his time spent at the family home in Belfast); and
- 90-day tie (he spent more than 90 days in the UK in the previous tax year).

Question 3.4

As Mr Harris is neither resident nor domiciled, he is liable to UK tax only on income arising in the UK as follows.

Income tax computations for Mr Harris for income tax year 2016/17 as a US citizen

	£
UK property business (Note 1)	45,000
Total income	45,000
Less: personal allowance	0
Taxable income	45,000

continued overleaf

Tax payable:

£31,785 @ 20%	6,357
£13,215 @ 40%	5,286
Total tax liability	11,643
Less: tax deducted at source	(9,000)
Tax due for 2016/17	2,643

Note:

1. Always include the gross amount in the income tax computation: £36,000 + £9,000 = £45,000.

In general, non-resident individuals are not entitled to allowances, including the personal allowance. There are exceptions, for example, citizens of the EEA. Therefore a French citizen would be entitled to a personal allowance but a US citizen would not. The impact of this is shown in the calculation below.

Income tax computations for Mr Harris for income tax year 2016/17 as a French citizen

	£
UK property business	45,000
Total income	45,000
Less: personal allowance	(10,600)
Taxable income	34,400
Tax payable:	
£31,785 @ 20%	6,357
£2,615 @ 40%	1,046
Total tax liability	7,403
Less: tax deducted at source	(9,000)
Tax refund due for 2016/17	(1,597)

Question 3.5

Income tax computation for Laura for 2016/17

	£
Trading income	35,000
UK bank interest (Note 1)	500
Overseas bank interest (Note 2)	1,000
Total income	36,500
Personal allowance	(10,600)
Taxable income	25,900
Income tax:	
£25,900 @ 20%	5,180
Less:	
Double taxation relief (Note 3)	(150)
Income tax liability	5,030

continued overleaf

Less:

Tax deducted at source (Note 1)   (100)

Income tax payable   4,930

Notes:

1. UK bank interest is received net, with 20% tax deducted at source. The gross amount (i.e. ×
   100/80) must be included in the income tax computation, but relief is given for the tax
   deducted at source.
2. Always include the gross amount in the income tax computation.
3. Double taxation relief is given as credit/unilateral relief. It is the lower of the overseas tax
   and the UK tax on that source of income. In this case:
   * overseas tax = £1,000 × 15% = £150
   * UK tax on that source of income = £1,000 × 20% = £200

Therefore, double taxation relief is £150 (the lower of the two figures).

Chapter 4

Question 4.1

Year of Assessment	Basis
2014/15	**First year**: actual profits arising on time-apportioned basis from start of trading to the end of the tax year. Thus, 01/06/2014–05/04/2015: = 10/12 of £48,000 = £40,000
2015/16	**Second year**: there is a 12-month accounting date ending in the tax year and so the basis period is the 12 months to that accounting date. Therefore, taxable profits for the year are those arising in the 12 months ended 31/05/2015: = £48,000 There is an overlap period from 01/06/2014–05/04/2015, giving rise to overlap profits of £40,000 (10 months) – these profits have been taxed in both 2014/15 and 2015/16.
2016/17	**Third year**: there was an accounting date falling in the previous tax year. Therefore, the taxable profits for the 2016/17 tax year are £39,000 (as the basis period is the period of account ending in this tax year – i.e. the period to 31 May 2016).
2017/18	**Fourth year**: the trade did not cease in this year, so the period of account is the year ended 31 May 2017. Therefore, the taxable profits for the 2017/18 tax year are £37,200 (as the basis period is the period of account ending in this tax year – i.e. the one to 31 May 2017).

Question 4.2

Year of Assessment	Basis
2015/16	**First year**: actual profits arising on time-apportioned basis from start of trading to the end of the tax year. Thus 01/05/2015–31/10/2015 = £44,800. However, 31/10/2015 is not the end of the tax year, so we must time-apportion profits arising in the year ended 31/10/2016 to the period from 01/11/2015 to 05/04/2016: $= 5/12 \times £54,400 = £22,667$ Taxable profits for tax year 2015/16 = £44,800 + £22,667 $\qquad\qquad = £67,467$
2016/17	**Second year**: there is a 12-month accounting date ending in the tax year and so the basis period is 12 months to that accounting date. Therefore, taxable profits for year are those arising in the 12 months ended 31/10/2016, i.e. £54,400. There is an overlap period from 01/11/2015–05/04/2016, giving rise to overlap profits of £22,667.
2017/18	**Third year**: there was an accounting date falling in the previous tax year, and a 12-month accounting period ending in this tax year. Therefore, the taxable profits for this tax year are £53,600 (as the basis period is the period of account ending in this tax year, i.e. the one to 31 October 2017).
2018/19	**Fourth year:** the trade did not cease in this year, so the basis period is the year ended 31 October 2018 (as this is the 12-month accounting period ending in this tax year). Therefore, the taxable profits for the 2018/19 tax year are £46,400.

Question 4.3

(a)

Year of Assessment	Basis
2015/16	**First year**: actual profits arising on time-apportioned basis from start of trading to the end of the tax year, i.e. 01/05/2015–05/04/2016: $= 11/12 \times £48,000$ $= £44,000$
2016/17	**Second year**: there is a 12-month accounting date ending in the tax year and so the basis period is the 12 months to that accounting date. Therefore, taxable profits for year are those arising in the 12 months ended 30/04/2016, i.e. £48,000.

There is an overlap period from 01/05/2015–05/04/2016, giving rise to overlap profits of £44,000.

2017/18 **Third year**: there was an accounting date falling in the previous tax year.

Therefore, the taxable profits for this tax year are £60,000 (as the basis period is the period of account ending in this tax year – i.e. the year ended 30/04/2017).

2018/19 **Fourth year**: the trade did not cease in this year, so the basis period is the year ended 30/04/2018.

Therefore, the taxable profits for this tax year are £9,600.

(b) As Jim is a solicitor, this income arises from a profession.

Question 4.4

(a)

2015/16 No taxable profits arise. See letter below for explanation.

2016/17 The £10,000 profit on the job lot is a trading transaction – see below. It is therefore taxable in the 2016/17 year. This is also the year of commencement for her trade. Thus taxable profits are time-apportioned to 5 April 2016, i.e. for the period 01/09/2016–05/04/2017:

= 7/12 × £79,400 = £46,317

Total taxable profits in 2016/17:

= £46,317 + £10,000 = £56,317

2017/18 This is the second year and there is a 12-month accounting period ending in the tax year. This is the basis period and taxable profits are therefore £79,400.

There is an overlap period from 01/09/2016–05/04/2017, giving rise to overlap profits of £46,317. (Note: the initial profit made in June 2016 is not included in this calculation as it was not included in the accounts prepared for the year ended 31 August 2017.)

Income tax computations for D. Ross

	2016/17 £	2017/18 £
Trading income	56,317	79,400
Total income	56,317	79,400
Less: personal allowance	(11,000)	(11,000)
Taxable income	45,317	68,400
Tax payable:		
£32,000 @ 20%	6,400	6,400
£13,317 @ 40%	5,327	–
£36,400 @ 40%	–	14,560
Total tax due	11,727	20,960

continued overleaf

(b)

Ms Ross
2 Belfast Road
Belfast

1 May 2018
Re: Taxable income from eBay

Dear Donna,
I refer to our meeting last week.

Badges of Trade

In arriving at the above tax liabilities, it has been necessary to consider whether your eBay activities represent taxable income. This will generally only be the case if they arise from "an adventure in the nature of a trade".

The rules for deciding whether or not you were trading are governed by considerations called the "badges of trade" – of which there are six. These are outlined below, along with a brief narrative on how the fact pattern of your eBay activities fits into these badges.

The conclusion is that your eBay activity from 1 September 2016, together with the sale of the job lot of children's clothes in June 2016, is taxable as a trade. However, the initial sales of surplus items from your house are not taxable as trading income (they were probably sold for less than you purchased them) and, therefore, the £5,000 you received in 2015/16 does not represent taxable income.

Badges of Trade	Your Circumstances
Subject matter (if ownership does not give income or personal enjoyment, then sales indicate trading)	As your initial sales were of items bought originally for your enjoyment, this is not indicative of trading. However, later items were not bought for personal use.
Length of ownership (short indicates trading)	Initial sale items had been owned for quite a while until surplus to everyday needs. The 2016 job lot purchase and sale had a very quick turnaround, indicating trading.
Frequency (more over a long period indicates trading)	The initial transactions appear infrequent and opportunistic, not indicative of trading. However, the purchase and sale of the job lot, with subsequent focused trading, suggests trading.
Supplementary work indicates trading	As you didn't have a formal eBay shop until 2016, there is no indication of a concerted effort to obtain customers prior to this. Organised effort to obtain profit began with the job lot.
Circumstances, if opportunistic or unsolicited, refute trading	Until sale of job lot, sales had been opportunistic and, because the items sold were personal in nature, would counteract trading suggestion.
Profit motive	The evidence suggests the activity was merely to realise small amounts of cash until the sale of the job lot, at which case a clear profit motive was present.

In deciding if a trade is being carried on, all rules are evaluated and the whole picture is taken into account. The overriding evidence in your case suggests that no trading took place until the job lot was purchased for onward sale.

Overlap Profits
Due to the way the tax rules operate, profits of £46,317 apportioned to the period from 1 September 2016 to 5 April 2017 will be taxed twice. However, relief will be available for this amount either:

1. when you change your accounting date from 31 August to a date later in the tax year; or
2. when you cease your eBay trade.

I hope the above is helpful; however, please give me a call if you have any queries.

Yours sincerely

Question 4.5

2015/16
There is only one accounting period ending in this tax year and it is a 12-month period. The trade did not cease in the tax year. The basis period for this tax year is, therefore, the 12 months ended 31 May 2015.
    Taxable profits are therefore £72,000.

2016/17
The trade ceased in this tax year. The basis period thus runs from the end of the basis period in the previous tax year to the date of cessation, i.e. from 1 June 2015 to 31 December 2016. Taxable profits are therefore:

	£
£9,600 + £12,000	21,600
Less: overlap relief of £5,000	(5,000)
Taxable profits	16,600

Question 4.6

2015/16	There was an accounting date falling in the previous tax year. Thus the basis period for this year is the year ended 31 October 2015.
	Thus the taxable profits = £64,000
2016/17	The accounting date in the year is less than 12 months after the end of the previous basis period. The basis period is therefore the 12 months ending on the new accounting date.
	These 12 months are the 11 months ended on 30 September 2016, plus the month of October 2015.
	Therefore, the taxable profits = £24,000 + (£64,000 × 1/12) = £29,333

The profits for October 2015 have therefore been taxed twice. Thus, additional overlap profits of £5,333 arise, giving total overlap profits carried forward from 2016/17 of £20,333.

Question 4.7

Computation of taxable trading profit for Joseph Murphy y/e 31 December 2016

	£	£
Profit per accounts		9,874
Add:		
Drawings (Note 1)	8,500	
Interest on VAT (Note 2)	1,121	
Interest on PAYE (Note 2)	1,238	
Depreciation (Note 3)	13,793	
Subscriptions (political, football, old folks, sports) (Note 4)	525	
Repairs (£6,480 – £2,335) (Note 5)	4,145	
Bad debts – increase in general provision (Note 6)	2,875	
Legal fees (Note 7)	1,009	33,206
		43,080
Deduct:		
Dividend from URNO Co. (Note 8)	2,813	
National loan interest (Note 8)	2,250	
Deposit interest (Note 8)	170	
Profit on fixed assets (Note 9)	5,063	(10,296)
Trading profit		32,784

Notes:
1. Disallow Mr Murphy's salary of £7,500 and the £1,000 holiday trip – these are drawings.
2. Interest on late payment of tax specifically disallowed (except for corporation tax).
3. Depreciation is always added back – capital allowances are given instead.
4. Donations to political parties are never tax deductible.

In accordance with the tax legislation, in order for donations to be tax deductible as a trading deduction, it must be shown that the donations were provided for the purposes of the business's trade. In practice, these circumstances will be limited. An example could be where a donation is provided to a local football club in return for recognition in an article in the football club's monthly magazine.

It is possible, therefore, that the £50 to the football club, £150 to the old folks' home and £250 to the sports club could be claimed as a deduction under the above legislation. However, it has been assumed that this is not the case here. Full marks would be awarded for either approach, provided the student explained the basis of their answer. Subscriptions to traders' associations and for trade papers are wholly and exclusively business expenses and are therefore deductible.

Note: it is possible that even where donations have been disallowed as trading deductions, relief may still be available personally to the individual under the gift aid scheme (provided a gift aid declaration has been made).

5. The £3,000 on the new extension is capital expenditure and is therefore not tax deductible. The general provisions in the repairs account do not conform to IAS 37 and so are also not tax deductible. The only allowable repairs expense is the £2,335 for repairs expenditure during the period. The only amount to be added back is £3,000 (re. the new extension) + £1,145 (the increase in the repairs provision).
6. Only specific impairment provisions for bad debts are allowable for tax purposes.
7. Related to a capital item (freehold) and so disallowed.
8. Taxed as investment income and not trading income, so removed from computation of trading profit.
9. Capital and so disallowed – dealt with under capital allowances regime.

Question 4.8

Computation of taxable trading profit for Ann Reilly y/e 31 December 2016

	£
Net profit before taxation	49,560
Add: disallowed expenses:	
Motor vehicles (Note 1)	2,640
Depreciation – Equipment	2,500
– Motor vehicles	3,000
– Office equipment	900
Construction of garages (capital)	3,150
General bad debt provision	275
Drawings	10,000
Entertainment (Note 2) – Holiday	120
– Tickets	30
– Customer business meals	120
Taxable trading profits	72,295

Notes:	£	£
1. Total expenses for Andy Reilly's car		4,000
Disallow lease element 15% × £4,000	600	
Disallow personal element 60% (£4,000 – £600)	2,040	2,640

No disallowance for sales rep's cars as below 160g/km (the threshold when the lease was first entered into). Pre-5 April 2013 the limit was 160g/km.

2. Staff entertainment is allowable, although PAYE issues may arise if not within prescribed limits. Business entertaining is specifically disallowed.

Explanatory Note
■ Defalcations by Andy would clearly not be tax deductible. However, those by an employee are tax deductible.

Question 4.9

(a) Computation of adjusted trading profits for the 15 months ended 31 December 2016 and the 12 months ended 31 December 2017.

	15 months ended 31/12/2016		12 months ended 31/12/2017	
	£	£	£	£
Net loss per accounts		(4,350)		(7,400)
Add: disallowed expenses:				
Depreciation	3,000		2,400	
General provision for bad debts	2,500			
Entertaining	1,500		700	
Political donations	100			
Charitable donations	50			
Interest on late payment of VAT	250			
Drawings	15,000	22,400	12,000	15,100
		18,050		7,700
General provision bad debts				(500)
Adjusted profit		18,050		7,200

(b) Tony's taxable trading profit for 2016/17:

2016/17 is Tony's second tax year of trading. An accounting period for a period in excess of 12 months ends in the tax year – namely, the 15-month period ending 31 December 2016. Thus, Tony's basis period will be the 12 months ending on 31 December 2016. Taxable trading profits for 2016/17 are, therefore, the time-apportioned profits from the accounting period ending in the tax year, i.e. £18,050 × 12/15 = £14,440.

Question 4.10

Computation of taxable trading profits for John Smith for the 12 months ended 30 April 2016

	Notes	£	£
Profit per accounts			2,820
Add:			
Drawings (wages to self)		5,200	
Own NICs		200	
Depreciation		1,250	
Motor expenses	1	924	
Leasing charges	2	1,372	
Extension	3	1,500	

Provision for repairs	4	1,000	
Interest on late payment of tax	5	120	
Donation to church	6	970	
Life assurance	7	460	12,996
			15,816
Less: interest received			(390)
Adjusted trading profits			15,426

Notes: **Add back**

	£	£
1. Motor expenses	1,860	
Less: parking fine	(100)	100
	1,760	
Add: car insurance	300	
	2,060	
Less: private element 40%	(824)	824
	1,236	
		924
2. Lease charges on car	2,800	
Less: 15% disallowance	(420)	420
	2,380	
Less: private element 40%	(952)	952
	1,428	1,372
	(allowable)	(add back)

3. Extension to store is capital expenditure and, therefore, not tax deductible.

4. General provisions do not conform to IAS 37, so add back. Note, if painting the premises was required to make them suitable for trading, may also be disallowed. However, no further details are given in the question, so it is reasonable to assume that this cost is tax deductible, as normal painting costs are a repair and thus tax deductible.

5. Personal liability and so not allowed.

6. This charitable donation is not deductible against trading profits, but John should obtain tax relief for it personally if made under the gift aid scheme.

7. On the basis that these are for John personally, they are not tax deductible. If they were for an employee, then it is possible that they may be deductible.

Explanatory Note
▪ Sometimes the practice is to disallow key person insurance contributions on agreement with HMRC that the associated income, if received, would not be taxable. If a deduction is taken for the premiums, then the income paid out under the policy would be taxable.

Question 4.11

Computation of tax-adjusted profit for Polly Styrene for the year ended 31 December 2016

	£	£
Profit per accounts		2,500
Add back:		
Wages to self	8,000	
Light, heat and telephone (5/6 × 1,500) (Note 1)	1,250	
Repairs and renewals (Note 2)	3,400	
Legal and professional fees (Note 3)	300	
Bad debts (Note 4)	(600)	
Travel and entertainment (Note 5)	1,100	
Depreciation (Note 6)	5,000	
Sundries (Note 7)	1,549	19,999
Taxable trading profits 2016/17		22,499

Notes:
1. Non-business element disallowed.
2. Extension (capital) and general provision (not conforming to IAS 37) disallowed.
3. Surveyor's fees disallowed – related to capital purchase.
4. General provision decreases are not taxable.
5. Private use re. car expenses disallowed – £500 – as are customer entertaining costs of £600.
6. A trading deduction is available for interest payments on finance lease assets. However, they do not qualify for capital allowances; rather, under the provisions of SP3/91, a tax deduction is available for the accounting depreciation charge on finance lease assets (but not on operating lease assets). Thus the depreciation restriction is £20,000 – £15,000 = £5,000.
7. Political party subscription disallowed, parking fines disallowed (would be allowed if incurred by employees while performing their duties – not made clear here, so disallowed), charitable donation not allowed as trading expense, but Polly should obtain tax relief personally if it were made under gift aid.

Explanatory Note
■ Trade-related royalties are tax deductible on a gross basis, therefore no adjustment is required when computing taxable trading profits. The tax deducted at source should be paid to HMRC through self-assessment.

Question 4.12

Distribution of profits

	Total	Partner A	Partner B	Partner C
	£	£	£	£
Year ended 30/09/2012	20,000	10,000	10,000	Nil
Year ended 30/09/2013	25,000	10,000	10,000	5,000
Year ended 30/09/2014	30,000	12,000	12,000	6,000
Year ended 30/09/2015	30,000	Nil	15,000	15,000
Year ended 30/09/2016	35,000	Nil	17,500	17,500

Once the profits of a partnership have been allocated to each partner, then each partner is treated for tax purposes as a sole trader and the income is taxed using the basis period rules in exactly the same way. For instance, the year you become a partner, the commencement rules apply. The year you cease to be a partner, the cessation rules apply (unless you are the only partner left and are continuing the trade as a sole trader). Overlap profits are calculated and relieved by reference to each partner's individual circumstances, as if they were a sole trader.

Taxable profits for A, B and C are as follows:

Partner A	A's basis period for 2012/13 is the year ended 30/09/2012 and so taxable profits for that year are £10,000.
	A's basis period for 2013/14 is the year ended 30/09/2013 and so taxable profits for that year are £10,000.
	A ceases to be a partner in 2014/15. A's basis period is from 1 October 2014 (end of previous basis period) to the date A ceased to be a partner, i.e. 30 September 2014.
Partner B	
	A's taxable profits for 2014/15 are, therefore, £12,000 (less any available overlap relief). B has never left the partnership, so B's basis period for each of the 2012/13 to 2016/17 tax years is the normal accounting period. Therefore, B's taxable profits are:

2012/13 £10,000
2013/14 £10,000
2014/15 £12,000
2015/16 £15,000
2016/17 £17,500

Partner C	C commenced to trade on 1 October 2012. C's taxable profits are calculated as follows:

2012/13	**First year**: basis period is from date of commencement to end of the tax year. Therefore, taxable profits are actual profits arising on time-apportioned basis for the period, i.e. 01/10/2012–05/04/2013:

$$= 6/12 \times £5,000$$

$$= £2,500$$

2013/14	**Second year**: there is a 12-month accounting date ending in the tax year and so the basis period is 12 months to that accounting date. Therefore, taxable profits for the year are those arising in the 12 months ended 30/09/2013 = £5,000

There is an overlap period of 01/10/2012–05/04/2013, giving rise to overlap profits of £2,500.

2014/15	**Third year**: there was an accounting date falling in the previous tax year, and the accounting date in this year is 12 months from end of previous basis period.

Thus the taxable profits for this tax year = £6,000.

C's basis period for each of the 2015/16 and 2016/17 tax years is the normal accounting period. Thus C's taxable profits are:

2015/16	£15,000
2016/17	£17,500

Question 4.13

	£	£
Net profit y/e 30/04/2016		46,000
Disallowed expenses	26,000	
Partners' salaries	41,000	
Partners' interest	13,000	80,000
Assessable profit		126,000

	Total	Jack	John
	£	£	£
Salaries	41,000	20,000	21,000
Interest	13,000	6,000	7,000
Balance (50:50 share)	72,000	36,000	36,000
Total	126,000	62,000	64,000
Taxable trading profits for 2016/17		62,000	64,000

Chapter 5

Question 5.1

	AIA	Main Pool	Allowances Claimed
	£	£	£
TWDV b/fwd at 06/04/2016		20,000	
Additions (Note 1)		11,500	
Disposals		–	
		31,500	
Additions qualifying for AIA (Note 2)	12,100		
Allowances 100%	(12,100)		12,100
Remaining TWDV to main pool	–	–	
Allowances @18%		(5,670)	5,670
TWDV c/fwd at 05/04/2017		25,830	
Total capital allowances claim			17,770

Notes:

1. Cars with CO_2 emissions of 130g/km or less with no private use are treated as additions to the main pool, with WDA at 18%.
2. The maximum AIA for the year ended 06/04/17 is £200,000.

Explanatory Note

▨ Capital allowances are available on the filing cabinets as they were paid for before the year-end – even though they were not delivered until after the year-end. On the other hand, if they had been delivered before the year-end and not paid for until more than four months after the year-end, then the cost would only have qualified for capital allowances in the accounting period in which the bill was paid.

Question 5.2

	Special Rate Pool	AIA/FYA Pool	Main Pool	Allowances Claimed
	£	£	£	£
TWDV b/fwd at 1 September 2015			100,000	
Additions (Note 1)	40,000		10,000	
Disposals			—	
			110,000	
Allowances @ 8% (Note 2)	(3,200)			3,200
Additions qualifying for AIA		13,900		
AIA		(13,900)		13,900
Remaining TWDV to main pool		0	0	
Allowances @ 18%			(19,800)	19,800
TWDV c/fwd at 31 August 2016	36,800		90,200	
Total capital allowances claim				36,900

Notes:
1. AIAs or FYAs are not available on cars. Cars with CO_2 emissions more than 130g/km go to the special rate pool, with WDA at 8%.
2. The maximum AIA for the year ended 31/08/16 is £500,000 × 4/12 + £200,000 × 8/12 = £300,000

Question 5.3

	AIA/FYA	Main Pool 18%	Allowances Claimed
	£	£	£
TWDV b/fwd at 1 September 2015		120,000	
Additions qualifying for AIA	155,000		
Other additions (no AIA) – car		20,000	
Disposals		—	
		140,000	
AIA	(155,000)		155,000

continued overleaf

	AIA/FYA	Main Pool 18%	Allowances Claimed
	£	£	£
T/F to main pool/special rate pool	Nil	0	
		140,000	
WDA @ 18%		(25,200)	25,200
TWDV c/fwd at 31 August 2016		114,800	
Total capital allowances claim			180,200

Explanatory Notes

■ While the printing press (£110,000) is a special rate pool item, being a long-life asset > 25 years, it would normally qualify for WDA at 8%. However, it and the van (£15,000) and the miscellaneous plant and machinery (£30,000) all fall within the limits available on which AIA can be claimed.

■ The maximum AIA for the year ended 31/08/16 is £500,000 × 4/12 + £200,000 × 8/12 = £300,000.

■ Vans qualify for AIA and do not have to be kept in a separate pool, unlike expensive cars.

■ Cars do not qualify for AIA.

Question 5.4

	AIA/FYA	Main Pool 18%	Allowances Claimed
	£	£	£
TWDV b/fwd at 6 April 2016		20,000	
Additions		–	
Disposals (Note 1)		(15,000)	
		5,000	
Additions qualifying for AIA	10,000		
AIA (max. £200,000)	(10,000)		10,000
Excess to main pool (Note 2)	0	0	
Allowances @ 18%		(900)	900
TWDV c/fwd at 5 April 2017		4,100	
Total capital allowances claim			10,900

Notes:

1. Profit on disposal of the fixed assets will be disallowed in calculating the taxable trading profits for the period. However, the proceeds received on assets that have previously qualified for capital allowances must be included in the main pool. As the NBV was £10,000 and the profit £5,000, proceeds received are £15,000, and are deducted from the TWDV b/fwd before calculating the allowances due.

2. No excess as additions are less than the available AIA of £200,000.

Question 5.5

	Single Asset Pool – Car	Private Use Adjustment (25%)	Allowances Claimed
	£	£	£
2014/15			
TWDV b/fwd at 1 January 2014	–		
Additions	26,000		
Disposals	–		
Allowances @ 8%	(2,080)	520	1,560
TWDV c/fwd at 31 December 2014	23,920		
2015/16			
TWDV b/fwd at 1 January 2015	23,920		
Additions	–		
Disposals	–		
Allowances @ 8%	(1,914)	478	1,436
TWDV c/fwd at 31 December 2015	22,006		
2016/17			
TWDV b/fwd at 1 January 2016	22,006		
Additions	–		
Disposals	–		
Allowances @ 8%	(1,760)	440	1,320
TWDV c/fwd at 31 December 2016	20,246		

Question 5.6

	Single Asset Pool – Car	Private Use Adjustment (1/3rd)	Allowances Claimed
	£	£	£
2014/15			
TWDV b/fwd at 6 April 2014	–		
Additions 2014/15 (Note 1)	13,000		
Disposals	–		
Allowances @ 8%	(1,040)	347	693
TWDV c/fwd at 5 April 2015	11,960		

continued overleaf

	Single Asset Pool – Car	Private Use Adjustment (1/3rd)	Allowances Claimed
	£	£	£
2015/16			
TWDV b/fwd at 6 April 2015	11,960		
Additions	–		
Disposals	–		
Allowances @ 8%	(957)	319	638
TWDV c/fwd at 5 April 2016	11,003		
2016/17			
TWDV b/fwd at 6 April 2016			
Additions	–		
Disposals	–		
Allowances @ 8% (Note 2)	(880)	293	587
TWDV c/fwd at 5 April 2017	10,123		

Notes:

1. The CO_2 emissions of the car exceeded 130g/km and consequently an allowance of 8% is available. As a result of the private use, a single asset pool must be created.
2. The tax-deductible allowances in 2014/15 (and each of the years) are only two-thirds, as only two-thirds of the use of the car relates to business use. However, the TWDV carried forward is reduced by the full annual allowance each year.

Question 5.7

	AIA	Main Pool (18%)	Allowances Claimed
Period ended 30 September 2016	£	£	£
TWDV b/fwd at 1 January 2016		–	
Additions (Note 1)		11,000	
Disposals		–	
		11,000	
Additions qualifying for AIA (Note 3)	22,400		
AIA £200,000 × 9/12 = £150,000	(22,400)		22,400
Transfer to main pool	0	0	
Allowances @ 18% × 9/12 (Note 2)		(1,485)	1,485
TWDV c/fwd at 30 September 2016		9,515	
Total claim			23,885

Notes:

1. The car has CO_2 emissions of 130g/km or less and no private use is indicated, so it is added to the main pool. Cars do not qualify for AIA.
2. Accounting period is only nine months long. Therefore, the AIA and main pool allowances are restricted to nine months' worth.
3. Additions qualifying for AIA are less than the AIA available and so no excess to transfer to the main pool.

	AIA	Main Pool	Allowances Claimed
Year ended 30 September 2017	£	£	£
TWDV b/fwd at 1 October 2016		9,515	
Additions		–	
Disposals		–	
		9,515	
Additions qualifying for AIA	3,500		
AIA (max. £200,000) (Note 1)	(3,500)		3,500
Transfer to main pool	0	0	
Allowances @ 18%		(1,713)	1,713
TWDV c/fwd at 30 September 2017		7,802	
Total claim			5,213

Note:
1. Maximum AIA is £200,000.

Question 5.8

	Main Pool	Claim
	£	£
TWDV b/fwd	10,000	
Additions	–	
Disposals	(35,000)	
Balancing charge	(25,000)	(25,000)

No capital allowances are available in the period. Rather, taxable profits will be increased by the £25,000 balancing charge that arises when the assets are sold. This is taxable income.

The £35,000 proceeds are calculated as follows:

NBV of assets sold £10,000. Profit on sale £30,000. Thus proceeds are £40,000. However, the proceeds that go to the main pool on sale of an asset are **limited** to the cost of that asset – which was £35,000.

If plant was sold for £3,000 in the 2017/18 period, and no plant was purchased, the TWDV brought forward on the main pool would be £Nil, but proceeds of £3,000 would have been received. As such, a balancing charge of £3,000 would arise in 2017/18.

Question 5.9

	AIA	Main Pool (18%)	Special Rate Pool (8%)	Allowances Claimed
	£	£	£	£
Additions (Note 1)		11,000		
Disposals		–		
Additions qualifying for AIA	232,000			
AIA	(200,000)			200,000
	32,000			
Transfer to main pool	(32,000)	32,000		
Transfer to special rate pool	0		0	
	–	43,000		
Allowances @ 18%		(7,740)		7,740
Allowances @ 8%				
TWDV c/fwd at 31 March 2017		35,260	0	
Total capital allowances claim				207,740

Note:

1. Car has CO_2 emissions of 130g/km or less and no private use indicated, so an addition to main pool WDA @ 18% (cars do not qualify for AIA).

Explanatory Notes

■ Included are long-life asset (£200,000), van (£14,000), partition walls (£5,000), toilets (£4,000), desk (£1,000) and portable toilets (£8,000). Partition walls are qualifying plant and machinery if they serve a purpose of being moved to change the available space to reflect changing staff numbers or working patterns. Doors may be allowed if they serve a particular function, but none is specified here so they should be disallowed. The portacabin provided the setting for the business rather than serving a function for the business and so is not qualifying plant and machinery. When answering a question you should state your reasons for determining whether an asset is qualifying plant if there is any doubt.

■ The maximum AIA is £200,000.

Question 5.10

(a) Joe Bloggs's taxable trading income for 2015/16 is £11,223 – £6,592 = £4,631.

(b) Capital allowances claim for 2016/17 is £6,592.

Taxable trading profit for the year ended 31 March 2017

	£	£
Loss per accounts to 31 March 2017		(310)
Adjustments		
Add back:		
Wages to self	5,200	
Motor expenses 1/4 × £1,750	438	
Light and heat 1/4 × £1,200	300	
Christmas gifts	300	
Depreciation	900	
Charitable donation (Note 1)	105	
Cash register	380	
Shelving	2,920	
Display freezer	600	
Flat contents insurance	100	
Notional rent	2,000	
		13,243
		12,933
Deduct:		
Building society interest received	210	
Sale proceeds of equipment	1,500	
		(1,710)
Adjusted profits		11,223

Note:

1. Not a trading expense unless some form of trading benefit is obtained as a result of making it (not specified), but Joe will obtain tax relief through his personal tax computation if paid under gift aid.

Capital allowances computation 2016/17

	AIA	Main Pool	Single Asset Pool – Car	Private Use Adjustment (25%)	Claim
	£	£	£	£	£
TWDV b/fwd at 1 April 2016 (Note 1)		12,750	4,940		
Additions					
Disposals (Note 2)		(1,500)	–		
		11,250			

continued overleaf

Addition qualifying for AIA (Note 3)	3,900			
AIA	(3,900)	–		3,900
Transfer to pool	0	0		
Allowances @ 18%		(2,025)	(889)	222	2,692
TWDV c/fwd at 31 March 2017		9,225	4,051	
Total claim				6,592

Notes:

1. Capital allowances to date on car:

Purchased 2011/12	£14,000
WDA 2011/12 = £14,000 × 20%	£2,800 (as less than £3,000)
TWDV b/f 2012/13 = £14,000 – £2,800	£11,200
WDA 2012/13 = £11,200 × 20%	£2,240
TWDV b/f 2013/14 = £11,200 – £2,240	£8,960
WDA 2013/14 = £8,960 × 18%	£1,613
TWDV b/f 2014/15 = £8,960 – £1,613	£7,347
WDA 2014/15 = £7,347 × 18%	£1,322
TWDV b/f 2015/16 = £7,347 – £1,322	£6,025
WDA 2015/16 = £6,025 × 18%	£1,085
TWDV b/f 2016/17 = £6,025 – £1,085	£4,940

   Note that the main rate WDA in 2011/12 and 2012/13 was 20%.
2. Sale proceeds of old equipment; assume proceeds are less than cost.
3. Cash register (£380), shelving (£2,920), display freezer (£600) = £3,900.

Question 5.11

	£
Trading profits	–
Employment income	80,000
Total income	80,000
Less: current year loss relief against total income	(50,000)
Net income	30,000
Less: personal allowance	(11,000)
Taxable income	19,000

Linda's use of the losses is restricted by the cap on income tax relief, which is the greater of £50,000 and 25% of her adjusted total income (25% × £80,000). Her cap is therefore £50,000. Linda could also make a claim to carry back the excess £10,000 loss to the prior year (if she has enough taxable income in 2015/16).

Question 5.12

	£
Trading profits	–
Investment income	25,000
Employment income	50,000
Total income	75,000
Less: current year loss relief against total income	(30,000)
Net income	45,000
Less: personal allowance	(11,000)
Taxable income	34,000

When calculating the tax due, the loss can be set-off by the taxpayer in the most advantageous way possible, i.e. against income taxed at the highest rate. There is no restriction on the use of the losses by the cap on income tax relief (as the trading loss in the period is less than the permitted limit, which would be £50,000 here).

Question 5.13

	£
Profit	20,000
Less: capital allowances	(37,000)
	(17,000)
Add: balancing charge	10,000
Loss for 2016/17	(7,000)

This loss can be relieved in the same manner as other current year losses.

Question 5.14

(a) **John's net income for 2014/15, 2015/16 and 2016/17**

	2014/15 £	2015/16 £	2016/17 £
UK property business	20,000	30,000	25,000
Investment income	1,000	1,200	1,200
Trading income	30,000	0	45,000
	51,000	31,200	71,200
Loss relief	(51,000)	(31,200)	(45,000)
Taxable income	0	0	26,200

continued overleaf

(b) *Loss Memorandum*

	£
Loss arising 2015/16	187,000
Set against other income 2015/16 section 64 ITA 2007	(31,200)
	155,800
Carry back 2014/15 section 64 ITA 2007	(51,000)
	104,800
Carry forward 2016/17 section 83 ITA 2007	(45,000)
Loss to carry forward	59,800

The losses carried forward can only be set against income of the same trade, so taxable income arises in 2016/17 even though there are still unused trading losses from 2015/16. These unused losses shall be carried forward to set against future profits from the **same** trade.

Note: as the loss arose in 2015/16, it is affected by the cap on income tax relief. However, the cap does not apply to losses carried back or forward against income from the same source. The 2015/16 trade loss will be set against 2014/15 trade profit in the first instance. The cap will apply to "other income" in 2014/15. No restriction is required as "other income" totals £21,000, which falls below £50,000.

Question 5.15

	2014/15	2015/16	2016/17
	£	£	£
Trading income	Nil	7,000	30,000
Less: loss relief		(7,000)	(1,000)
Taxable income	Nil	Nil	29,000

Jim is obliged to take relief for the loss forward in the first year in which trading profits from the same trade are available. This occurs in 2015/16 and results in a waste of his personal allowances for that year. Jim would have preferred to defer relief for some of the loss until 2016/17 to avoid wasting his 2015/16 allowances. Unfortunately, this is not permitted.

Question 5.16

	2014/15	2015/16	2016/17
	£	£	£
UK property business	20,000	30,000	25,000
Investment income	1,000	1,200	1,200
Trading profits	80,000	–	45,000
	101,000	31,200	71,200
Less: loss relief	(37,000)	–	–
Taxable income	64,000	31,200	71,200

It is best to carry back the losses as this gives tax relief as soon as possible, and against income taxed at 40%. It also avoids wasting the personal allowance in 2015/16.

The loss arose in 2015/16 and is therefore affected by the cap on income tax relief. As the loss in 2015/16 is less than £50,000 (the minimum cap on relief), it is not restricted.

Chapter 6

Question 6.1

1. £70,000 –first £30,000 of **genuinely** ex-gratia termination payments is tax-free.
2. £2,000 – statutory sick pay is fully taxable in the hands of the recipient.
3. None – specific exemption applies.
4. None – specific exemption applies for payments on permanent disability leading to inability to work.
5. Full £2,400 is taxable.
6. Not taxable – specifically exempt.

Question 6.2

Income tax computation for Nuala Casey for tax year 2016/17

	Non-savings Income	
	£	£
Taxable element of termination payment (Note 1)	60,000	
Salary	33,750	
Total income	93,750	
Less: personal allowance	(11,000)	
Taxable income	82,750	
Tax payable:		
£32,000 @ 20%		6,400
£50,750 @ 40%		20,300
Total tax liability		26,700
PAYE		(7,300)
Tax due for 2016/17		19,400

Notes:
1. First £30,000 of termination payment exempt as non-contractual and entirely ex-gratia. No income tax liability arises when an EMI option is exercised.

Question 6.3

Income tax computation for Mr Houghton for tax year 2016/17

	£
Taxable element of termination payment (Note 1)	65,000
Salary	20,000
Share option income (Note 2)	5,000
Total income	90,000
Less: personal allowance	(11,000)
Taxable income	79,000

Tax payable:	
£32,000 @ 20%	6,400
£47,000 @ 40%	18,800
Total tax liability	25,200
Less: tax deducted at source (PAYE)	(7,000)
Tax liability for 2016/17	18,200

Notes:

1. Under general principles, the first £30,000 of a non-contractual, ex-gratia payment on termination would be tax-free. However, in this case the board of the company have created a general expectation amongst employees that they will receive a termination payment of this nature when they retire after a long period of service. This precedent has the effect of making the termination payment "deemed contractual" and so wholly taxable.
2. Gains on exercise of tax-advantaged/approved share options are generally tax-free. However, this is only the case if the options exercised have been held for at least three years. If the share option scheme rules allow "good leavers" to exercise their share options within three years of grant when they leave the company, then the gain on exercise will be subject to income tax. Thus the £30,000 gain arising on the options held for four years is tax-free, but the £5,000 gain arising on the options that are only 18 months old is taxable.

Question 6.4

Income tax computation for Dermot O'Donnell for tax year 2016/17

	£
Taxable element of redundancy package (Notes 1 and 2)	34,200
Salary (Super McBurgers)	37,000
Salary (Burger Palace) (Note 3)	18,200
Total income	89,400
Less: personal allowance	(11,000)

Taxable income	78,400

Tax payable:	
£32,000 @ 20%	6,400
£46,400 @ 40%	18,560
Total tax liability	24,960
Less: tax deducted at source	
PAYE (Burger Palace)	(2,900)
PAYE (Super McBurgers)	(9,500)
Tax liability for 2016/17	12,560

Notes:

1. Lump sums from approved pension schemes are tax-free. However, the gift of a car from an employer is treated as taxable income equivalent to the market value of the car at the date received. The total income from the termination payment that is taxable is, therefore, £64,200 (i.e. £1,200 + £22,500 + £40,500). However, it is then necessary to consider if the £30,000 ex-gratia payment rules may apply. It is not mentioned in the question whether the redundancy payments were contractual – but the fact that there is a £40,500 compensation payment implies that they were not. There is also no mention of it being a habitual payment for all leavers. Thus it is appropriate to claim the £30,000 exemption, although HMRC may challenge an exemption. HMRC approval should have been sought in advance of the package being agreed. The taxable income is £34,200 (i.e. £64,200 – £30,000).
2. The provision of a work mobile phone is a tax-free BIK – even if the company pays for all the personal calls that are made by the employee.
3. The £4,000 payment to join Burger Palace is taxable as an inducement payment. Therefore, his total salary from Burger Palace is £14,200 + £4,000 = £18,200.
4. Dividends on shares in the share incentive plan (SIP) are tax-free, provided the dividends are used to acquire additional shares in the company, which are then held in the SIP for a further three years. There is no limit on the amount of dividend that can be reinvested.

Question 6.5

Calculation of taxable benefits in kind – Sid Harvey

1. Round sum allowance of £100 a month – taxable income as there are no receipts to support the expenditure (assuming they are not covered by the exemption or a dispensation obtained by his employer pre 6 April 2016). If Sid were able to show receipts for genuine expenses, it would be possible to claim a deduction for these expenses in his tax return.
   Taxable BIK: £1,200
2. Company car – the starting point is the list price of the car when new. This will not always be the amount that was paid for the car by Sid's employer.
   The list price is £36,000/0.9 = £40,000 (before discount)
   The relevant % = ((145 – 95)/5) + 16% = 26%
   Basic charge is therefore £40,000 × 26% = £10,400
   However, a deduction is also available for employee contributions – £1,200 in this case.
   Taxable BIK: £9,200

3. Company car: fuel – no BIK arises as the full cost, including private use, is reimbursed to the company. (NB: HMRC has stated that it is almost impossible to confirm that all private fuel has been reimbursed, so very good records would need to be maintained to provide as evidence; otherwise HMRC may impose a fuel BIK.)

4. Household expenses – all treated as a BIK as these are private living costs.

   Taxable BIK: £890

   Apartment – normally it is the cost of providing the accommodation that is used to calculate the BIK that arises. However, as the company has owned the property for more than six years at the date it was first made available to Sid, the market value of the property when it was first made available to Sid is used instead of the cost of providing the accommodation when calculating the BIK.

Annual rateable value	£600
Additional taxable rent (£80,000 – £75,000) × 3%	£150

   Taxable BIK: £750

5. Staff canteen – available to all staff, therefore no BIK arises.

6. Preferential loan – a taxable benefit will arise on the waiver of an employee loan. It does not have to be a beneficial loan or amount to £10,000 to be a BIK here.

   Taxable BIK: £1,000
   Total BIK: £13,040

Income tax computation for Sid for tax year 2016/17

		£
Salary		40,000
BIK		13,040
Total income		53,040
Less: personal allowance		(11,000)
Taxable income		42,040
Tax payable:		
£32,000 @ 20%	£6,400	
£10,040 @ 40%	£4,016	
Total tax liability		10,416
Less: tax deducted at source (PAYE)		(13,900)
Tax refund due for 2016/17		(3,484)

Question 6.6

(a) Calculation of benefits in kind

1. Company car: the starting point is the list price of the car when new. This will not always be the amount that was paid for the car by the employer.
    The list price is £30,000
    The relevant % = 158g/km rounded down to the nearest five is 155g/km
    ((155 – 95)/5) + 16% = 28%.
    However, as the car is a diesel car, an additional 3% is added to the %.
    Basic charge is, therefore, £30,000 × 31% = £9,300.
2. The BIK on the fuel is £22,200 × 31% = £6,882; total benefit on car and fuel is £16,182.
3. BIK on golf club membership is £3,500.
4. Loan interest BIK:

	£
£125,000 × (3% – 2%) to give the taxable benefit	1,250
£4,000 × 3% to give taxable benefit on golf club loan	120
Total BIK on loans	1,370
Total BIK £21,052	

(b)

Income tax computation for Terry for tax year 2016/17

	Old	New
	£	£
Salary	75,000	70,000
BIK	0	21,052
Total income	75,000	91,052
Less: personal allowance	(11,000)	(11,000)
Taxable income	64,000	80,052
Tax payable:		
£32,000 @ 20%	6,400	6,400
Remainder @ 40%	12,800	19,221
Total tax liability	19,200	25,621
Net pay	55,800	44,379
Less costs: mortgage interest	(6,875)	(2,500)
Car	(10,500)	
Net cash in hand (new job leaves him better off)	38,425	41,879

Question 6.7

(a)

Income tax computation for Philip Stodge for tax year 2016/17

	£
Salary (Note 1)	49,600
BIK (Notes 2 and 3)	0
Total income	49,600
Less: deductions (Notes 4 and 5)	(5,360)
Less: personal allowance	(11,000)
Taxable income	33,240

Tax payable:	
£32,000 @ 20%	6,400
£1,240 @ 40%	496
Total tax liability	6,896
Less: tax deducted at source: PAYE	(7,900)
Tax repayment due for 2016/17	(1,004)

Notes:
1. Despite the fact that the sales commission is paid directly to his wife, it is taxable on Philip as it is earned by him. The employer's pension contributions are a tax-free benefit, so salary taxable is £43,600 + £6,000 = £49,600.
2. No taxable BIK arises from provision of a parking space at or near work for you by your employer, even if they have to pay for it.
3. Employers can pay up to £5 a night to employees to cover incidental costs arising when they are away from home without a taxable income arising.
4. If an employer does not reimburse an employee business mileage, the employee can claim a deduction of £0.45 per mile in their tax return for up to 10,000 business miles, and the remainder at £0.25 a mile. If the employer pays the employee less than these rates, the employee can claim the difference in their tax return. If the employee is paid more than these rates, the excess is taxable. Philip can, therefore, claim £0.45 × 10,000 = £4,500.
5. The cost of the suit is never allowed as a deduction from employment income. However, professional subscriptions and genuine expenses "wholly exclusively and necessarily incurred in the course of your work" can be claimed – thus phone, train and course are allowable.
    Deduction claimed = £4,500 + £400 + £180 + £150 + £130 = £5,360.

(b) You should advise your manager of the disposal by your client so that your manager can liaise with the client to establish whether there was some explanation for the omission. In line with the Chartered Accountants Regulatory Board *Code of Ethics*, a fundamental principle a Chartered Accountant should follow is professional competence and due care. The client should be advised of the need to return details of the disposal to HMRC and pay the tax due (if any). The likely penalties and interest that HMRC will charge if they discover the omission should be made clear to Philip.

Question 6.8

Income tax computation for Frank for tax year 2016/17

	£
Salary	50,000
Car BIK (Note 1)	42,550
Fuel BIK (Note 2)	8,214
Total income (Note 3)	100,764
Less: deductions (Note 4)	(800)
	99,964
Less: personal allowance	(11,000)
Taxable income	88,964

Tax payable:	
£32,000 @ 20%	6,400
£56,964 @ 40%	22,786
Total tax liability	29,186

Notes:

1. The list price is £120,000.

   However, a deduction is available for any capital contributions made by the employee. The available tax deduction is capped at £5,000.

   The cost of the car is therefore £115,000 (£120,000 less capital contribution £5,000 restricted).

   The relevant % = ((300 − 95)/5) +16% = 57%.

   However, this is also capped at 37%.

   The car benefit is therefore £115,000 × 37% = £42,550.

2. Fuel benefit = £22,200 × 37% = £8,214.

3. No BIK arises on the grant of the share options despite the fact that they have increased in value at the year-end from their value at the date they were granted. This is because the BIK arises on actual gains made on exercise – paper gains between exercise and grant are not taxable income.

4. Professional subscriptions are generally allowable as a deduction against employment income, provided the organisation to which they are made appears on the approved HMRC list (available on HMRC's website).

Chapter 7

Question 7.1

Income tax computation for Maeve for tax year 2016/17

	Non-savings income £	Savings income £	Dividend income £	Total £
NSB interest		6,300		6,300
Credit union		1,200		1,200
Pension	7,800			7,800
Dividend income			21,244	21,244
Total income	7,800	7,500	21,244	36,544
Less: personal allowance	(7,800)	(3,200)		(11,000)
Taxable income	0	4,300	21,244	25,544

Tax payable:

Non-savings income:

£0 × 20%	0

Savings income:

£1,000 × 0% (personal savings allowance)	0
£3,300 × 20%	660

Dividend income:

£5,000 × 0% (dividend allowance)	0
£16,244 × 7.5%	1,218
Total	1,878

Remember: NISA interest is tax-free.

Question 7.2

Income tax computations for David Lee for tax year 2016/17

	Non-savings Income £	Savings Income £	Total £
Bank interest		625	625
Salary	42,000		42,000

Government loan interest		1,130	1,130
Building society interest		175	175
Total income	42,000	1,930	43,930
Less: personal allowance	(11,000)		(11,000)
Taxable income	31,000	1,930	32,930

	£
Tax payable:	
Non-savings income:	
£31,000 × 20%	6,200
Savings income:	
£500 × 0% (personal savings allowance)	0
£500 × 20%	100
£930 × 40%	372
Total	6,672
Less: tax deducted at source:	
PAYE (Note 1)	(4,900)
Tax due for 2016/17	1,772

Note:

1. NICs are not deductible expenses for income tax purposes.

Explanatory Notes

▦ Lottery winnings, interest from National Savings certificates and premium bond payouts are specifically exempt from tax under section 692 ITTOIA 2005.

NB: National Savings certificates are different from National Savings accounts, interest on which is taxable and is received gross.

▦ A gift from a neighbour for a one-off job will not be subject to income tax. If David had done the shopping every week for a set amount, that income would then be taxable.

Chapter 8

Question 8.1

	Properties			
	A	**B**	**C**	**D**
	£	£	£	£
Rent receivable (Note 1)	6,000	8,000	4,250	52
Premium on lease	–	6,000	–	–
	6,000	14,000	4,250	52

continued overleaf

Less: allowable expenses (Note 2)

Bank interest	(5,500)	(7,200)	–	–
Storm damage	–	(1,400)	–	–
Advertising	–	–	(130)	–
Roof repairs	–	–	–	(1,600)
Blocked drains and painting	–	–	(790)	–
Net rent (Note 3)	500	5,400	3,330	(1,548)

Summary	£
Property A	500
Property B	5,400
Property C	3,330
Property D	0
UK property business	9,230

Notes:

1. Property A
   Although the rent for February was not received until after the end of the tax year, it is still taken into account in 2016/17 as property income is assessed on an **accruals basis**. If the £500 rent due on 28 February 2017 was subsequently never received, a bad debt charge could be included in the property business accounts for the 2017/18 tax year, and loss relief would then be available.

   Property B
   Let from 01/08/2016, i.e. eight months @ £1,000 p.m. = £8,000
   Assessable portion of premium:
   $$£10,000 - (£10,000 \times (21 - 1)/50) = £6,000$$

Property C	£	
£6,000 × 1/12	500	(one month to 30/04/2016)
£9,000 × 5/12	3,750	(five months to 31/03/2017)
	4,250	

2. Allowable Expenses

   Property B
   Expenses incurred to get the property into a fit state for letting prior to a first letting are not allowable (i.e. dry rot and windows). There is an argument for these repair costs being either deductible or non-deductible and the available marks would be given for student rationale in assessing the information. Repairs would not be deductible if they were required for the house to be fit for letting; however, if the house was in a fit state and available for letting and the repairs were undertaken when the house was vacant, then a tax deduction should be available for the repairs (*Odeon Associated Theatres Ltd v. Jones* (see **Section 4.3.5**)).

As a property business is already in place, the bank interest cost of £7,200 p.a. is fully deductible.

Property C
Although the property was vacant when the expenditure was incurred, this was only a temporary cessation and the expenditure is allowed in full.
3. Relief for losses on Property D
In general, losses on one UK property may be offset against the net rental profits arising on other UK properties. However, the loss arising on property D is ignored for tax purposes as it arises on a non-commercial rent charged to a connected party (favoured lease).

Question 8.2

UK property business income assessable 2016/17

	Prop. 1	Prop. 2	Prop. 3	Prop. 4	Prop. 5	Total
	£	£	£	£	£	£
Gross rents (Note 1)	16,000	8,000	9,600	6,750	120	
Expenses (Note 2)	(4,300)	(1,200)	(1,600)	–	(10)	
Interest	–	–	(1,400)	–	–	
Net rents (Note 3)	11,700	6,800	6,600	6,750	110	31,960

Notes:
1. The taxable rent for the year is calculated on an accruals basis whether or not rent is actually received in the year (Property 4 = 9/12 × £9,000).
2. The expenses for Property 3 are increased by £800 as it is assumed that the income from December 2015 would have been taxed in the 2015/16 tax year on the accruals basis, but now the debt has been proved bad, a tax deduction for this amount will be available in the 2016/17 tax year.
3. The profits on Property 5 are taxable, even though it is rented to a connected party. However, if a loss was incurred as a result of higher expenses (say, £150 of expenses would lead to a £30 loss), the loss would not be allowed as it is a favoured letting (compare with the solution to **Question 8.1**. See Note 3 to the solution specifically).

Chapter 9

Question 9.1

Income tax computation for John for income tax year 2016/17:

	£
Total income	20,000
Less: personal allowance	(11,000)
Taxable income	9,000
Tax payable:	
£9,000 @ 20%	1,800
Less: tax reducers:	
MCA – full @ 10%	(836)
Tax due for 2016/17	964

Question 9.2

Mr Smith is entitled to a personal allowance of £11,000 and the MCA of £8,355 as he was born before 6 April 1935. However, as his total income exceeds £27,700, this is reduced by £1 for every £2 his income exceeds £27,700.

£33,900 – £27,700 = £6,200

£6,200/2   = £3,100

Thus the MCA is £8,355 – £3,100 = £5,255. This gives a tax reducer (at 10%) of £525.50.

Income tax computation for Mr Smith for income tax year 2016/17:

	£
Total income	33,900
Less: personal allowance	(11,000)
Taxable income	22,900
Tax payable:	
£22,900 @ 20%	4,580
Less: tax reducers:	
MCA	(526)
Tax due for 2016/17	4,054

Question 9.3

Income tax computation for Joe for income tax year 2016/17:

	£
Employment income	50,000
Less: relief for deductions (Note 2)	(1,000)
Net income	49,000
Less: personal allowance	(11,000)
Taxable income	38,000
Tax payable:	
£32,000 @ 20%	6,400
£975 @ 20% (Note 1)	195
£5,025 @ 40%	2,010
Total tax liability	8,605

Notes:
1. The gift aid payment operates to increase the basic rate band by £780/0.80 = £975. Note, the charity can reclaim the £195 direct from HMRC and relief from higher rate tax is given to Joe.
2. Qualifying loan interest is restricted under the cap on income tax relief. However, this is well below the £50,000 minimum cap and therefore no restriction is required.

Question 9.4

Income tax computation for Rachel for income tax year 2016/17:

	Non-savings Income	Dividend Income	Total
	£	£	£
Non-savings income (Note 1)	20,250		20,250
Dividend income		600	600
Total income	20,250	600	20,850
Less: personal allowance	(11,000)	—	(11,000)
Taxable income	9,250	600	9,850

Tax payable:
£9,850 @ 20% — 1,970
£600 @ 0% (covered by dividend allowance) — 0
Total tax liability — 1,970
Less: tax reducers
MCA (£8,355 × 11/12 = £7,659 @ 10% = £766) (Note 2) — (766)
Tax due for 2016/17 — 1,204

Notes:
1. Copyright royalties paid in connection with the trade are deductible from trading income, i.e. £30,000 – £9,750 = £20,250 (trade income).
2. Rachel and John married on 4 June 2016. The MCA is reduced for each complete month they were not married, i.e. 6 April–5 May = one month.

Question 9.5

Income tax computation for Mr Frost for 2016/17:

	£
Non-savings income	30,000
Less: deductions	(780)
Net income	29,220
Less: personal allowance	(11,000)
Taxable income	18,220
Tax payable:	
£18,220 @ 20%	3,644
Less: tax deducted at source: PAYE	(5,000)
Tax repayment due for 2016/17	(1,356)

The tax reclaimable by Action Cancer is £195. This arises only on the cash gift of £780. Action Cancer cannot reclaim any gift aid on the gift of quoted shares as this is treated as a deduction from income, and the taxpayer gets relief as a deduction from total income.

Note that as the taxpayer does not have any income at the higher rate or additional rate band, there is no need to increase the basic rate or higher rate band by the amount of the gross cash gift to Action Cancer. If net income had been in the higher rate band, then the basic rate band would have increased from £32,000 to £32,975 and, if an additional rate taxpayer, then in addition to the basic rate band being extended to £32,975, the higher rate band would also have increased from £150,000 to £150,975.

The gift of shares would not increase the basic rate or higher rate band.

Question 9.6

Donations made under gift aid are made net of basic rate tax at 20% – as they are made by the taxpayer out of after-tax income. The charity receiving the gift reclaims the basic rate tax that has been paid on the gift.

If the taxpayer has not paid sufficient income tax to cover the income tax reclaimed by the charity, the taxpayer must pay it over to HMRC on their tax return.

If the taxpayer is a higher rate taxpayer, the basic rate band is increased by the gross gift, i.e. gift/0.80, so that the higher rate tax relief is obtained on the gift; if they are an additional rate taxpayer, the higher rate band is also increased by the gross gift.

Donations made under the payroll giving scheme are deducted by the employer from gross earnings of the employee before tax is applied. The employer will pay the amount withheld from the employee's salary to the relevant charity. Tax relief is therefore given at the taxpayer's marginal rate at the time of the donation.

Question 9.7

(a) £3,600 – anyone can make a gross pension contribution of up to £3,600 a year. They pay an amount net of basic rate tax (so a net contribution of £2,880 would be required to make a gross contribution of £3,600) and the government pays the balance into the pension fund – even if the individual has no taxable income.
(b) £40,000 – the upper limit on pension contributions in 2016/17.
(c) £40,000 – property income (unless from furnished holiday home lettings) is not counted as relevant earnings for pension purposes.
(d) £40,000 – the upper limit on pension contributions in 2016/17. Both trading and employment income are treated as relevant earnings for pension purposes.

Question 9.8

Income tax computation for Sarah for income tax year 2016/17:

	£
Trading income	50,000
Less: deductions	(1,000)
Net income	49,000
Less: personal allowance	(11,000)
Taxable income	38,000
Tax payable:	
£32,000 @ 20%	6,400
£6,000 @ 20% (Note 1)	1,200
Total tax liability	7,600

Note:

1. Increased basic rate band due to pension contribution. The maximum potential increase in the basic rate band is £20,000; however, there is not enough income to utilise this, so some higher rate relief on the pension is lost.

   The £20,000 would be paid into the pension pot as follows:

   Sarah would pay £16,000 to the pension company. The pension company would then reclaim £4,000 from HMRC. Total would be £20,000. This is because the payment is made net of basic rate tax and HMRC then pays the basic rate tax over to the pension fund.

Question 9.9

Income tax computation for Molly for income tax year 2016/17:

	£
Non-savings income	50,000
Less: personal allowance	(11,000)
Taxable income	39,000
Tax payable:	
£32,000 @ 20%	6,400
£7,000 @ 40%	2,800
	9,200
Less: tax reducers:	
EIS investment (Note 1)	(6,000)
Income tax liability	3,200
Less: tax deducted at source: PAYE	(5,000)
Tax refund for 2016/17	(1,800)

Note:
1. Relief at 30% of EIS investment, £20,000 $\times$ 30% = £6,000.

Question 9.10

Income tax computation for Neville for income tax year 2016/17

	Non-savings Income	Dividend Income	Total
	£	£	£
Employment income	25,000		25,000
Dividend income		20,000	20,000
Total income	25,000	20,000	45,000
Less: personal allowance	(11,000)		(11,000)
Taxable income	14,000	20,000	34,000
Tax payable:			
Non-savings income			
£14,000 @ 20%			2,800
Dividend income			
£5,000 @ 0% (dividend allowance)			0
£13,000 @ 7.5%			975
£2,000 @ 32.5%			650
(£32,000 – £14,000 = £18,000 but only £15,000 dividends taxable)			
Total tax liability			4,425
Less: tax reducers:			
EIS investment @ 30%			(4,425)
Total tax liability			0

continued overleaf

Less: tax deducted at source:

PAYE	(5,000)
Tax repayment due for 2016/17	(5,000)

Explanatory Note

■ EIS investment relief is a maximum of £30,000 × 30% = £9,000. However, EIS relief cannot give rise to a refund in 2016/17; but it may be possible to carry back to the 2015/16 tax year. The EIS relief is restricted to the total tax liability of £4,425.

Question 9.11

Income tax computations for Irwin for income tax year 2016/17

	Non-savings Income	Dividend Income	Total
	£	£	£
Employment income	32,000		32,000
UK property business	5,000		5,000
Dividends		9,000	9,000
Total income	37,000	9,000	46,000
Less: personal allowance	(11,000)		(11,000)
Taxable income	26,000	9,000	35,000
Tax payable:			
Non-savings income:			
£26,000 @ 20%			5,200
Dividend income:			
£5,000 @ 0% (dividend allowance)			0
£1,000 @ 7.5%			75
£3,000 @ 32.5%			975
Total tax liability			6,250
Less: tax reducers:			
EIS investment @ 30% (Note 1)			(6,250)
Total tax liability			0
Less: tax deducted at source:			
PAYE			(7,000)
Tax repayment due for 2016/17			(7,000)

Note:

1. £60,000 at 30% is £18,000. However, as it is a tax reducer, it cannot give rise to a tax repayment – so EIS relief is restricted to the tax liability for the year; however a carry back to 2016/17 should be considered.

Question 9.12

Income tax computation for James for income tax year 2016/17

	Non-savings Income	Savings Income	Dividend Income	Total
	£	£	£	£
Employment income	325,000			325,000
Investment income		5,000		5,000
Dividends (Note 1)			9,000	9,000
Total income	325,000	5,000	9,000	339,000
Less: personal allowance (Note 2)				
Taxable income	325,000	5,000	4,000	334,000

Tax payable:

Non-savings income

£32,000 @ 20%		6,400
£9,750 @ 20% (being extension to basic rate band) (Note 3)		1,950
£159,750 – £32,000 – £9,750 = £118,000 @ 40% (being extension to higher rate band)		47,200
(£325,000 – £159,750) = £165,250 @ 45%		74,363

Savings income

No personal savings allowance as additional rate taxpayer

£5,000 @ 45%	2,250

Dividend income

£4,000 @ 38.1%	1,524
Total tax liability	133,687
Less: tax reducers:	
EIS investment @ 30% (restricted) (Note 4)	(133,687)
Total tax liability	0
Less: tax deducted at source:	
PAYE	(75,000)
Tax repayment due for 2016/17	(75,000)

Notes:
1. Cash dividends from foreign companies are subject to UK income tax.
2. Personal allowance is not available as James's total income exceeded £122,000. For every £2 of income over £100,000, the personal allowance is reduced by £1.
3. This is the charitable donation of £7,800 grossed up by 100/80. It extends the basic rate band of £32,000 and also the higher rate band of £150,000.
4. The relief is the investment of £600,000 at 30% = £180,000. This is restricted to the tax liability of £133,687. Income tax relief is restricted to the tax liability; however a carry back to 2015/16 should be considered.

Explanatory Note

■ James's maximum pension contribution for the period will be restricted to the upper limit of £40,000 as his relevant earnings exceed this amount. The relevant earnings are just those from his employment – £325,000. The other income does not qualify.

Question 9.13

Income tax computation for Matthew for income tax year 2016/17

	Non-savings Income	Savings Income	Dividend Income	Total
	£	£	£	£
Trading income	400,000			400,000
Investment income		10,000		10,000
Dividends (Note 1)	———	———	9,000	9,000
Total income	400,000	10,000	9,000	419,000
Less: deductions (Note 2)	(30,000)			(30,000)
Total income	370,000	10,000	9,000	389,000
Less: personal allowance (Note 3)	–	–	–	–
Taxable income	370,000	10,000	9,000	389,000
Tax payable:				
£32,000 @ 20%				6,400
£118,000 @ 40%				47,200
£230,000 @ 45%				103,500
£5,000 dividends @ 0% (dividend allowance)				0
£4,000 dividends @ 38.1%				1,524
				158,624
Less: tax reducers:				
VCT investment @ 30% (Note 4)				(30,000)
Total tax for 2016/17				128,624

Notes:

1. UK stock dividends are taxed on their market value in the same way as UK cash dividends (see **Section 7.1.1**). No tax is due on dividends from first £200,000 invested in a VCT in a tax year.
2. The deduction is the land given to the UK charity at market value (this does not gross-up the basic rate band).
3. Personal allowance is not available as Matthew's total income exceeded £122,000. For every £2 of income over £100,000, the personal allowance is reduced by £1.
4. VCT investment of £100,000 at 30% = £30,000.

Question 9.14

	£
Basic credit	1,960
Additional for working at least 30 hours a week	<u>810</u>
Maximum credit	2,770
Less: reduction due to income (£9,000 − £6,420) × 0.41	<u>(1,057)</u>
Available credit	<u>1,713</u>

This credit is not taxable income.

The tax credit will be paid direct from HMRC into Hamish's bank, building society, post office or National Savings account (if it accepts direct payments), either weekly or every four weeks.

Question 9.15

	£
Basic credit	1,960
Being a couple entitlement	2,010
Additional for working at least 30 hours a week	810
Extra for having a family	545
Childcare element (70% of up to £300 a week)	3,150
Child element (£2,780 × 2)	<u>5,560</u>
Maximum credit	14,035
Less: reduction due to income (£27,000 − £6,420) × 0.41	<u>(8,438)</u>
Available tax credits for 2016/17	5,597

Chapter 10

Question 10.1

	£
Personal allowance for 2016/17	11,000
Less: BIK	<u>(400)</u>
Net allowances	10,600
Tax code: 1060L	

The tax code is arrived at by taking the net allowances and removing the last digit. The L suffix merely indicates that Mary is a normal taxpayer and therefore not entitled to any special allowances.

Question 10.2

	£
Personal allowance for 2016/17	11,000
Less: BIK	(750)
Add: impact of MCA	4,180
Net allowances	14,430
Tax code: 1443L	

The starting point for the tax code is always the personal allowance entitlement for the year.

He is also married and thus entitled to the MCA as he was born before 1938. Thus, we need to factor in the benefit of this known tax reducer into the tax code. The full MCA is £8,355. At 10%, this gives an allowance of £836. To give effective tax relief on this at 20% (as Andrew is a basic rate taxpayer) we need to increase the allowances available to him by £836/0.2 = £4,180. No marriage allowance is available as he was born before 6 April 1935.

Question 10.3

	£
Personal allowance for 2016/17	11,000
Less: BIK	(3,768)
Impact of underpayment	(5,000)
Net allowances	2,232
Tax code: 223L	

Value of benefit of van is £3,170 flat rate. Van fuel benefit is £598.

In general, small over- or under-payments of PAYE from previous tax year will be collected through the PAYE system, via adjustment of the notice of coding.

Thus we need to adjust the notice of coding to take into account the fact that additional tax of £1,000 needs to be collected. As Sean is a basic rate taxpayer, this is done by dividing £1,000 by 0.20 and deducting the answer (£5,000) from his allowances remaining after deducting the impact of a BIK.

Question 10.4

	£
Personal allowance for 2016/17	11,000
Less: BIK	(500)
Impact of overpayment	375
Net allowances	10,875
Tax code: 1088L	

The mobile phone is not a taxable benefit but the medical insurance is. The benefit is the amount of the gross premium.

As Alison is a higher rate taxpayer, we divide the £150 (her 2015/16 overpayment for which she is due credit) by 0.40 to determine the adjustment to her tax code.

The £375 is added to her personal allowance, less benefit deduction, to give the net allowances.

Question 10.5

	£
Cumulative pay to date (Note 1)	6,933
Less: 2/12ths of annual tax-free amount (Note 2)	(600)
Taxable pay	6,333
Tax payable (Note 3):	
£5,333.30 @ 20%	1,067
£999.70 @ 40%	400
Tax liability for year to date	1,467
Less: tax paid to date	(500)
PAYE due in month to 5 June 2016	967

Notes:
1. £2,500 for April (i.e. month to 5 May), plus £4,433 for May (i.e. month to 5 June).
2. Tax code of 360L indicates annual tax-free amount of £3,600. As we are in the second tax month of the year, he is due 2/12ths of this amount at the time of this payment: £3,600 × 2/12 = £600.
3. To determine the rates at which tax is payable, we take 2/12ths of the annual basic rate, i.e. £32,000 × 2/12 = £5,333.30. Paul's taxable pay exceeds this amount by £999.70. Therefore £5,333.30 is taxed at the basic rate and £999.70 is taxed at the higher rate.

Question 10.6

(a) PAYE deductions for David for month to 5 October 2016

	£
Cumulative pay to date (Note 1)	20,000
Plus: 6/12ths of annual tax-addition amount (Note 2)	600
Taxable pay	20,600
Tax payable (Note 3):	
£16,000 @ 20%	3,200
£4,600 @ 40%	1,840
Tax liability year to date	5,040
Tax paid to date	(3,600)
PAYE due in month to 5 October 2016	1,440

continued overleaf

Notes:
1. £17,000 for year to date plus £3,000 for this month.
2. September, i.e. month to 5 October, is the sixth month in the tax year and so 6/12ths of David's annual tax addition amount (as is the case where there is a K code) of £1,200 should be credited by this month.
3. To determine the rates at which tax is payable, we take 6/12ths of the annual basic rate, i.e. £32,000 × 6/12 = £16,000. David's taxable pay exceeds this amount by £4,600. Therefore, £16,000 is taxed at the basic rate and £4,600 is taxed at the higher rate.

(b) Change to PAYE deducted to date of £2,900

	£
Cumulative pay to date	20,000
Plus: 6/12ths of annual tax-addition amount	600
Taxable pay	20,600
Tax payable:	
£16,000 @ 20%	3,200
£4,600 @ 40%	1,840
Tax liability year to date	5,040
Tax paid to date	(2,900)
	2,140
PAYE due in month to 5 October 2016 (Note 1)	1,500

Note:
1. When a K code is in operation, tax deducted in each payment period is limited to 50% of the gross pay in that period. As £2,140 exceeds 50% of the gross salary of £3,000, actual PAYE deducted is £1,500.

Question 10.7

NIC works on an earnings period basis. As the earnings period in this case is one month, the NICs are calculated as follows:

- 12% Class 1 primary NICs payable on earnings between £672 and £3,583
  = (£3,583 – £672) × 12%
  = £349.32
- 2% Class 1 primary NICs payable on earnings in excess of £3,583
  = (£50,000 – £3,583) × 2%
  = £928.34

Total Class 1 NICs payable = £1,277.66

Question 10.8

No Class 1 primary NICs will be due by Jonathan as he is over 66 years of age. No NICs are payable by employees who are over State pension age. However, Class 1 secondary NICs will be still be payable in respect of these earnings.

Question 10.9

Sarah's earnings from employment were paid in 12 equal instalments, therefore we can calculate the Class 1 NICs on an annual basis, as follows:

- 12% Class 1 primary NICs payable on earnings over £8,060 (Sarah's earnings fall well below the annual upper earnings level of £43,000)
  = (£12,000 – £8,060) × 12%
  = £472.80

Sarah is also self-employed and so is required to pay Class 2 and Class 4 NICs on these earnings, as follows:

- Class 2 NICs are payable (Sarah's earnings exceed the small earnings exemption of £5,965 in the tax year) at £2.80 per week:
  = £2.80 × 52
  = £145.60
- 9% Class 4 NICs on earnings over £8,060 (Sarah's earnings fall well below the upper earnings limit of £43,000):
  = (£22,000 – £8,060) × 9%
  = £1,254.60

Total NICs payable by Sarah for 2016/17:

Class 1	£472.80
Class 2	£145.60
Class 4	£1,254.60
Total NICs	£1,873.00

As Sarah did not pay Class 1 or Class 4 NICs above the upper thresholds, she will not have overpaid NICs and so will not be in a position to apply for a refund or deferment.

Question 10.10

Income tax computation for Frank for tax year 2016/17

	£
Car BIK (Note 1)	5,550
Fuel BIK (Note 2)	8,214
Golf subscription BIK	800
Total BIKs	14,564
Class 1A NICs	
£14,564 × 13.8%	2,010

Notes:
1. The list price is £20,000.
   The relevant % = ((300 – 95)/5) +16% = 57%.
   However, this is also capped at 37%. The car benefit is therefore £15,000 × 37% = £5,550.
2. Fuel benefit = £22,200 × 37% = £8,214.

Chapter 11

Question 11.1

Mr Murphy
3 High Street
Banbridge

19 August 2016

Re: Self-assessment

Dear Mr Murphy,

I refer to your letter requesting information regarding the HMRC system of self-assessment. I have outlined below the main features of HMRC's self-assessment system.

Notice of liability

It is the taxpayer's responsibility to submit a tax return if he has uncollected tax or National Insurance contributions (NICs) for a tax year. For example, uncollected tax and NICs may arise where an individual's tax/NICs are not paid in full under PAYE or otherwise deducted at source. This would be the case where a taxpayer has income from other sources such as property. This is the case whether or not they have been issued with a tax return by HMRC – it is the taxpayer's obligation to notify HMRC if they are in receipt of income that is liable to tax.

In your case, you must register as self-employed with HMRC before 5 October 2017. Failure to notify HMRC by this date may result in a penalty being imposed.

Any penalty amount would depend on whether or not the failure is "careless" or "deliberate". The penalties range from 30% to 100% of the "potential lost revenue", i.e. the tax due for the year that by reason of failure remains unpaid on 31 January following that year.

Penalties imposed may be mitigated by making a prompted or unprompted disclosure. No penalty would be due if the taxpayer has a reasonable excuse that is acceptable to HMRC.

The first year for which you will be required to complete a self-assessment tax return (SA100) will be the tax year ended 5 April 2017. If you want to file a paper return, it must be filed by 31 October 2017 or, if HMRC issued the return after that date, three months after the date it was issued.

You can also file your return online, the deadline for which is 31 January 2017, or three months after the date HMRC notified you that you must complete a tax return. You may wish to appoint a tax agent to look after your tax affairs with HMRC.

Record-keeping

A taxpayer must keep sufficient records to enable them to complete their tax return. These records must be retained once the tax return has been filed in case HMRC requests to see them during an enquiry into the return.

Your new business must keep a copy of all receipts of income, all expenses and all supporting documents relating to business transactions, i.e. contracts, purchases, VAT returns, bank statements, how you calculate your closing stock, etc. These records must be kept for five years after 31 January following the end of the tax year to which they relate.

HMRC can charge you a penalty of up to £3,000 if you fail to keep proper records.

Late filing penalties

If you do not submit your tax return by the required date, as outlined above, you may be liable to a late filing penalty. The penalties for late filing are as follows:

- Initial penalty of £100 for failure to submit the return on time.
- A daily penalty of £10 per day for a maximum of 90 days can be imposed if the return is more than three months late.
- If six months late, the penalty will be the greater of £300 or 5% of the tax due.
- If 12 months late, the penalty will be the greater of £300 or 5% of the tax due.

Tax payments and interest

All taxpayers within the self-assessment system are required to pay their income tax liability by 31 January after the end of the tax year. Payments on account are paid before the income tax return is submitted and before the tax liability for the year is finalised. Payments on account are usually based on the previous tax year's liability. The balancing amount of tax is the difference between the tax due for the tax year per the final tax return and the payments on account already made in respect of the tax year.

However, payments on account on 31 January in the tax year and 31 July after the end of the tax year are required, if, in the previous tax year:

(i) less than 80% of the income tax liability was collected by deduction at source; and
(ii) the amount not collected was more than £1,000.

Each payment on account will be 50% of the amount not collected at source in the previous tax year. In your case, no payments on account will be required for 2016/17 as you only commenced your sole trade in that period. However, they are likely to be required for 2017/18.

The balancing amount of tax for any tax year is then due on 31 January after the end of the tax year. Any amount of tax that has not been paid 30 days after the end of the due date is subject to a late payment penalty of 5% of the unpaid tax. Interest is also charged on late payments. If any amount of tax is unpaid after 31 July, a further penalty of 5% of the amount of unpaid tax is due and a further 5% penalty if any tax is unpaid by the following 31 January.

If your payments on account exceed your tax liability for the year, HMRC will refund the overpaid amount. HMRC may also pay interest on the refund that you are due. It is possible to elect to reduce your payments on account – however this should only be done if you are reasonably sure that the tax due for the year will be lower than the tax liability for the previous tax year, as interest will be payable on any amounts underpaid. HMRC may also impose penalties if it considers payments on account have been reduced without good reason.

If you require any further information, please do not hesitate to contact me.

Yours sincerely,

Question 11.2

HMRC can issue an enquiry into any income tax return that is made. No reasons need to be given as to why the return has been selected for enquiry – it may be due to a risk assessment, or merely chosen at random from all the returns that have been filed.

1. HMRC must give written notice to the taxpayer when opening an enquiry; this must be sent: within 12 months of the date the tax return was filed; or
2. if the tax return was filed late, by the next 31 January, 30 April, 31 July or 31 October following the anniversary of the date the return was actually filed or amended.

If the return is amended by the taxpayer, then an enquiry into the amendment can be raised by HMRC by the next 31 January, 30 April, 31 July or 31 October following the anniversary of the date the amended return was filed.

If an enquiry is not raised within these time limits, then the return is treated as final except for exceptional circumstances. If the returns filed give rise to a deliberate understatement, HMRC can seek to amend them under the discovery assessment provisions up to 20 years later.

Once an enquiry is completed, HMRC will issue a final assessment to the taxpayer. If the taxpayer feels this is incorrect, they may request, within 30 days, that HMRC conduct an "internal review". If after the internal review the taxpayer still disagrees with the decision, they can send a "notice of appeal" to the Tribunal within 30 days. However, once a return is final, it cannot be the subject of a further enquiry (except in the case of "careless" or "deliberate" underestimates).

If the taxpayer appeals to the Tribunal, the appeal may be heard by the First-tier Tribunal or the Upper Tribunal, depending on the complexity of the case. If either the taxpayer or HMRC consider that the Tribunals have erred on a point of law, then they can proceed with the case to the Court of Appeal, and finally to the Supreme Court. However, this is very expensive.

Question 11.3

Income tax computation for Cian Connors for tax year 2016/17

	Non-savings Income £	Savings Income £	Total £
Non-savings income	48,000		48,000
Investment income		920	920
Total income	48,000	920	48,920
Less: personal allowance	(11,000)		(11,000)
Taxable income	37,000	920	37,920
Tax payable:			
£32,000 @ 20%			6,400
£5,000 @ 40%			2,000
£500 @ 0% (personal savings allowance)			0
£420 @ 40%			168
Total tax liability			8,568
NIC Class 4:			
(£43,000 – £8,060) @ 9%			3,144.60
(£48,000 – £43,000) @ 2%			100.00
Total self-assessment liability for 2016/17			11,812.60

Payments on account for 2017/18 of £5,906.30 each will be due for payment on 31 January 2018 and 31 July 2018.

Question 11.4

Income tax computation for Mark Johnston for tax year 2016/17

	Non-savings Income £	Savings Income £	Total £
Non-savings income	50,000		50,000
Investment income	_____	5,500	5,500
Total income	50,000	5,500	55,500
Less: personal allowance	(11,000)	_____	(11,000)
Taxable income	39,000	5,500	44,500
Tax payable:			
£32,000 @ 20%			6,400
£7,000 @ 40%			2,800
£500 @ 0% (personal savings allowance)			0
£5,000 @ 40%			2,000
Total tax liability			11,200
Tax deducted at source			(10,000)
Tax due			1,200

Tax due is more than £1,000. Thus, if less than 80% of tax due was collected at source, payments on account will be due for 2017/18.

Eighty per cent of £11,200 is £8,960. No payments on account are due for tax year 2017/18, as tax deducted at source was £10,000.

Question 11.5

Tom should be aware that a General Anti-abuse Rule (GAAR) has been introduced in the UK. The GAAR is targeted at users (i.e. Tom's clients) and promoters (i.e. Tom and the partner in the practice) of "abusive" tax-avoidance schemes. The GAAR applies to income tax, which is what the scheme is trying to aggressively reduce to nil through a serious of complicated and contrived transactions. The scheme proposed could be described as an abusive tax arrangement, one that has the intention of obtaining a tax advantage as its main purpose.

Importantly, if Tom sells the scheme to his clients and HMRC subsequently determine that the arrangement is abusive, then the GAAR provides that the tax advantage that the arrangement sets out to achieve will be counteracted.

If Tom markets or sells this tax planning scheme to a number of his clients, then he will potentially be in breach of a number of the Chartered Accountants Regulatory Board's *Code of Ethics*. Namely: integrity; professional competence and due care and professional behaviour.

Tom will be in breach of the principle of integrity as the scheme will be seen as misleading if his clients pay him to put the scheme in place and it turns out to be deemed a tax-avoidance scheme, which HMRC will then counteract to remove the tax advantage.

Tom will be in breach of the professional competence principle as he is going to market and sell the scheme, despite not fully understanding how the scheme operates.

Finally, Tom will be in breach of the principle of professional behaviour as he is marketing and selling a scheme that may be viewed as not complying with the relevant tax laws and regulations. As a Chartered Accountant, Tom's involvement in the scheme could also have a damaging impact on the profession as the scheme does not apply the tax laws in an appropriate manner and it is likely that the scheme could be deemed an abusive tax-avoidance scheme by HMRC.

Chapter 12

Question 12.1

Calculation of CIS deduction and payment to subcontractor:

	£
Total payment	4,600
Less: cost of materials (inclusive of VAT) (Note 1)	(900)
Amount liable to CIS deduction	3,700
Amount deducted @ 20% (standard rate)	740
Net payment to subcontractor (£4,600 – £740)	3,860

Note:
1. The cost of materials is the VAT-inclusive amount because the subcontractor is not VAT-registered. If the subcontractor was VAT-registered, then they would not suffer the VAT cost as this would be deemed input VAT (see **Chapter 13**), i.e. the amount deducted would be £750 £900 – £150) rather than £900.

Question 12.2

Calculation of CIS deduction and payment to subcontractors:

	Contractor A	Contractor B	Contractor C
	£	£	£
Total payment (exclusive of VAT)	8,500	12,000	3,500
Less: materials (exclusive of VAT)	(3,500)	(2,000)	(1,500)
Amount liable to CIS deduction	5,000	10,000	2,000
Amount deducted	Nil	2,000	600
Payments to the subcontractors	10,200	12,400	3,600

Total monthly payment by the contractor for the period ended 5 February 2017 is £2,600. This amount should be paid online to HMRC by 22 February 2017.

Chapter 13

Question 13.1

(a) Obligation to register
If you are operating a business that is making taxable supplies, i.e. selling goods that are within the charge to VAT, then you must register with HRMC if at any time the total value of taxable supplies made in the previous 12 months exceeds the registration threshold – currently £83,000. This is the historical test.

There is also a second test: if you believe that in the next 30 days alone (i.e. without regard to a previous period) your taxable supplies will exceed the registration threshold (£83,000), you must notify HMRC. This is the future test.

2

The two tests interact, such that the test that gives the earliest date is the one that applies.

Under the historical test, you must notify HMRC within 30 days of the end of the month in which you exceeded the limit; with the future test you must notify HMRC within 30 days of the date you anticipate exceeding the limit. If you are required to register under the historical test, you will then be registered for VAT from the first day of the second month after the month in which you exceed the £83,000 limit. Under the future test, you must start charging VAT immediately from the start of the month the threshold will be exceeded.

(b) How to register and make payment

If a new trader is required to register for VAT (or if they voluntarily wish to do so) they must submit Form VAT1 to HMRC, either in paper format or online using HMRC's VAT Online service.

VAT due to HMRC must be paid electronically seven days after the end of the month following the VAT quarter-end. Very severe penalties can be imposed for repeated failure to file returns on time and failures to file online. For example, for the VAT quarter ended 31 December 2016, the return will need to be filed and payment made by 7 February 2017.

(c) Records and information

A taxable person must keep full and true records of all business transactions that affect, or may affect, their liability to VAT. The records must be kept up to date and must be sufficiently detailed to enable the trader to accurately calculate the VAT liability or repayment and, if necessary, for HMRC to check.

Under VAT legislation, there are specifically noted records that must be kept (for at least six years):

- business and accounting records;
- VAT account documentation;
- copies of all VAT invoices issued;
- copies of all VAT invoices received;
- all certificates prepared that relate to the acquisition or disposal of goods or services to or from other EU Member States;
- copy documentation in relation to imports or exports to or from non-EU Member States; and
- copies of all credit notes issued and received.

A basic VAT return will contain details of:

(i) output VAT on taxable supplies made;
(ii) VAT due on items acquired from other EU Member States;
(iii) recoverable input VAT;
(iv) total value of all sales;
(v) total value of all purchases; and
(vi) total value of all sales to and purchases from other EU Member States.

Question 13.2

(a) January 2017 is the first period in which sales within the previous 12-month period exceed £83,000. Thus, Stephen will have to register with HMRC by 28 February 2017 and start to charge VAT on 1 March 2017.
(b) No – the second test would only apply if he had thought he would make sales of more than £83,000 within 30 days of starting to trade.

Question 13.3

Initially, we must determine the basic tax point. For goods, this is the time that they leave the vendor and go to the buyer. For services it is when the service has been completed, e.g. when an accountant finishes preparing an income tax return and any associated work.

The basic tax point can be adjusted in a number of circumstances. For example, if a payment is received or if an invoice is issued before the basic tax point is reached, the tax point moves forward to either the date the payment is received or the date the invoice is issued. Also, if an invoice is instead issued within 14 days (30 days at HMRC's discretion) of the work being completed (i.e. after the basic tax point), then the actual tax point will move to the date the invoice is issued.

This is important as it may move the sale on to a different VAT return and so to a later, or earlier, VAT payment date.

Question 13.4

A valid VAT invoice must contain the following information:
1. An identifying invoice number.
2. The date of the supply.
3. The date of issue of the document.
4. The name, address and VAT registration number of the supplier.
5. The name and address of the person to whom the goods and/or services are being supplied.
6. Description sufficient to identify the goods and/or services supplied.
7. For each item so described, the quantity of the goods or extent of the services, the rate of VAT charged and the amount payable (excluding VAT).
8. The gross amount payable, excluding VAT.
9. The rate of any cash discount offered.
10. The total amount of VAT chargeable in Sterling.
11. The unit price if the goods are sold in units.

Question 13.5

Michael will need to be careful to file his VAT returns on time because if he does not the penalties that can arise can be very punitive.

The first time he files a late return, HMRC will issue a warning notice to him. This will advise him that if another default (i.e. a late filing) occurs in the next 12 months, he will be liable to a penalty. If Michael subsequently defaults in this 12-month period, he will be liable to a penalty of 2% of the unpaid tax due on the late return. Thus, if the tax is nil or a repayment is due, no penalty will be due.

However, a further consequence of the second late return is that the 12-month "on notice period" is extended to 12 months from the end of the VAT quarter in which the second VAT default occurred. This extension will continue to occur on subsequent defaults until Michael reaches the end of the extended period without another later return. However, the amount due as a penalty continues to rise as further defaults occur in the extended period, as follows:

Third default – 5% of unpaid VAT
Fourth default – 10% of unpaid VAT
Rest of defaults – 15% of unpaid VAT

Thus the penalties can be very large. Penalties can also arise for failure to file online.

The position is slightly different for small businesses – one with a turnover below £150,000. When a small business is late submitting a VAT return or paying VAT, it will receive a letter from HMRC offering help. No penalty will be charged. A surcharge liability notice will be issued if there is a second default within 12 months of the letter, again offering help without penalty. However, on the issue of a third letter, a 2% penalty will apply, which increases to 15% on the issue of a sixth, subsequent default.

Question 13.6

	£	£
VAT charged		4,000
Total input credits 20% (Note 2)	1,050	
5% (Note 4)	260	
Less: private use	(8)	
Less: no valid invoice (Note 6)	(19)	
Total creditable VAT	1,283	
Less: 10% re. exempt supplies (Note 5)	(128)	
Claimable input VAT		(1,155)
VAT due		2,845

Notes:
1. Gross purchases charged at 20% = £6,300.
2. VAT charged on these purchases = £6,300 × 1/6 = £1,050 (1/6 is the VAT fraction for standard rated supplies/services at a 20% VAT rate).
3. Gross purchases charged at 5% = £5,460.
4. VAT charged on these purchases = £5,460 × 1/21 = £260 (1/21 is the VAT fraction for reduced rate supplies/services).
5. Partial exemption rules apply to all purchases as none are directly attributable to taxable/exempt supplies.
6. Purchase of stationery (gross) is £115. VAT charged was 20%. Therefore VAT is £115 × 1/6 = £19.
7. Private use on the invoice for servicing of car £160 × 20% = £32 × 25% (private use) = £8.

Question 13.7

VAT liability of Mr Byte for the period July/August/September 2016:

	£	£
VAT charged (Note 1)		20,000
Total input credits		
Purchases (Note 2)	8,400	
Stationery	1,200	
Electricity	2,000	
Claimable input VAT	11,600	(11,600)
VAT due		8,400

continued overleaf

Notes:
1. As Mr Byte is not using the cash receipts basis, the sales in the period will be the relevant amount for calculating the output VAT that he has to charge.
2. Based on the tax point being the date of invoice, the £42,000 purchases figure is the relevant one when determining the recoverable input VAT on purchases.

Explanatory Notes
■ No input VAT is reclaimable on client entertaining costs.
■ No VAT is charged on wages, so none is recoverable.
■ As the landlord has not opted to tax the building, no VAT will have been charged on the rent, so none is recoverable.

Question 13.8

	£	£
VAT charged (Notes 1 and 4)		0
Total input credits		
Purchases (Note 2)	0	
Stationery (Note 3)	400	
Rent (Note 3)	800	
Claimable input VAT	1,200	(1,200)
VAT due		(1,200)

Notes:
1. Since Joe supplies goods at the zero rate of VAT, he will be in a permanent VAT-repayment position.
2. Joe's purchases of ingredients will also be zero-rated, so he will not be entitled to recover any input VAT on these ingredients.
3. Joe will be able to recover input VAT suffered on the stationery and on the rent (as the building is opted to tax, the landlord will be required to charge VAT at 20% on the rent charged).
4. Cash discounts are irrelevant here as the sales are zero-rated.

Explanatory Notes
■ No VAT is suffered on interest received, so none is recoverable.

Question 13.9

Persons who are not required to register for VAT (due to their turnover not exceeding the registration threshold) may consider voluntary registration. In general, a person might choose to voluntarily register their business for VAT if:

1. They are a small supplier with total sales under the registration threshold, and do not want their customers to realise how small their business is – a VAT registration can give the impression of a larger and more reputable business to customers.

2. They are a start-up business whose sales have not yet exceeded the registration threshold – again, this would help to give the impression to customers that they are a more established business, which may enable them to gain a wider range of customers.
3. They purchase a lot of goods or services from VAT-registered persons, but make zero-rated supplies, or supplies to other registered persons. This will enable them to claim input credits on purchases.
4. They have not actually commenced supplying taxable goods or services, but will soon become a taxable person. This will enable them to obtain credit for VAT on purchases made before trading commences.
5. They are in a net VAT-repayable position even though they are making standard-rated supplies below the registration threshold (generally would apply only if they were making losses in early years).
6. Their customers are all or mostly all VAT-registered.

Question 13.10

The place of supply of goods is deemed to be:

1. in a case where it is a condition of supply that the goods are transported, it is the place where such transportation starts; and
2. in all other cases, it is where they are located at the time of supply, i.e. when ownership is transferred.

The basic rule for supplies of services to non-business customers is that the place of supply is where the supplier is established. For business-to-business supplies of services, the place of supply is where the customer belongs. There are exceptions to this general rule. For example, land-related services are deemed to be supplied where the land is situated.

Question 13.11

	£	£
VAT charged (Note 1)		400
Total input credits		
Food for resale (Note 2)	98	
Tables and chairs (Note 3)	88	
Cash register (Note 4)	115	
Tiler (Note 7)	40	
Solicitor	288	
Van	1,725	
Claimable input VAT	2,354	(2,354)
VAT due		(1,954)

Notes:
1. VAT is not due on most foodstuffs (essentials) taken away cold to eat off the premises, so no output VAT would be charged on the £4,000 receipts in respect of sales of cold food.
2. £588 × 1/6 = £98.
3. Businesses can recover VAT on capital items in the same way as they can on revenue items, unless they fall within the capital goods scheme (the capital goods scheme only applies to land

and buildings costing more that £250,000, or computers costing more than £50,000, so it does not apply here).
4. The tax point is used to determine when input VAT can be recovered. Thus, even though he has not paid for some items to date, he can recover the input VAT. If he delays paying for over six months, then bad debt relief will apply and he will have to charge himself the VAT he recovered, and claim it back in the VAT period in which he actually pays it.
5. Stock is zero-rated, therefore no VAT to reclaim.
6. In respect of the rent paid, it is assumed that the invoice received included no VAT as there is no option to tax on the premises.
7. A standard-rated VAT invoice was received from the tiler for the amount paid.

Chapter 14

Question 14.1

Calculation of Hermes Ltd VAT liability for March–May 2016:

	Net of VAT	VAT Payable
	£	£
VAT on Sales		
Supplies in UK	250,000	50,000
Supplies to US (Note 1)	10,000	0
Purchases from Ireland (Note 2)		10,000
VAT on sales		60,000

	Net of VAT	VAT Recoverable
VAT on Purchases		£
Purchase of stock from UK suppliers (£223,260 × 1/6)	186,050	37,210
Purchase of stock from Ireland (Note 2)	50,000	10,000
Professional fees (£5,880 × 100/120)	4,900	980
Oil (£1,050 × 100/120)	875	175
Computer (£8,934 × 100/120)	7,445	1,489
		49,854
VAT on sales	60,000	
VAT on purchases	(49,854)	
VAT payable	10,146	

Notes:
1. An export, therefore the supply is zero-rated irrespective of the type of goods sold.
2. Where goods are purchased for business purposes from another EU country, the supplier will not charge VAT, provided they are given the VAT number of the EU purchaser. The purchaser must account for VAT on the reverse charge basis in their VAT return (assume 100% VAT recovery and partial exemption rules do not apply).

Question 14.2

	Net of VAT £	Output VAT £
VAT on Sales (output VAT):		
Sales in UK (£950,000 × 20%)	950,000	190,000
Sales to Spain (to Spanish registered customers)	320,000	0
Sales to non-VAT-registered customers in Ireland		
(£25,000 × 20%)	25,000	5,000
Sales to VAT-registered customers in Ireland	135,000	0
Sales to customers located in Singapore	46,000	0
VAT on sales		195,000
VAT on EU acquisitions (£200,000 × 20%)	200,000	40,000
Total VAT on sales		235,000

	VAT Inclusive £	VAT Content £	Total VAT Content £
VAT on costs (input VAT):			
Purchase of materials from UK suppliers			
(£423,000 × 1/6)	423,000	70,500	
Purchase of machinery locally			
(£235,020 × 1/6)	235,020	39,170	
Rent of premises (£11,748 × 1/6)	11,748	1,958	
Repairs and maintenance of office and equipment			
(£16,212 × 1/6)	16,212	2,702	
Audit and accountancy fees			
(£12,924 × 20%)	12,924	2,154	
Electricity and gas (£2,520 × 1/6)	2,520	420	
Salaries and wages	167,000	0	
Advertising costs (£35,250 × 1/6)	35,250	5,875	
			122,779
EU acquisitions	200,000	40,000	40,000
VAT on costs			162,779
VAT payable (£235,000 – £162,779)			72,221

Index

subscriptions 58; *see also* professional
   subscriptions
subsistence allowances 132
sufficient hours, definition 22
sufficient ties test (residence) 23–6
supply of goods
   gifts of goods 257
   intra-EU 277–82
   non-EU 286–8
   overview 257
   place of supply 259, 279
   self-supply of goods 258
   time of supply 258–9, 279
supply of services
   intra-EU 283–6
   non-EU 288
   overview 258
   place of supply 260, 283–5
   self-supply of services 258
   time of supply 258–9, 285
Supreme Court 7, 231
suspended penalties 229

targeted anti-avoidance rules (TAARs) 8
tax-adjusted profits *see* computation of taxable
   income
tax agents and advisors
   dishonest conduct by 233–4
   fees allowable as deduction against trading
      income 62
   income tax returns completed by 218
   information requests and professional
      privilege 226
tax avoidance 8, 232, 234
tax codes 198–9
tax credits
   Child Tax Credit 191
   income thresholds 190
   overview 189–90
   Universal Tax Credit 192
   Working Tax Credit 191–2
tax evasion 8, 229
tax-exempt special savings accounts
   (TESSAs) 154
tax rates and bands
   income tax
      dividend income 12–13, 152–3

   non-savings income 12, 13
   overview 11, 13
   savings income 12, 13, 151–2
National Insurance contributions 205, 206,
   208, 210
VAT
   reduced rate 254–5
   standard rate 253
   zero rate 253–4
tax reducers
   definition 11
   Enterprise Investment Scheme 185
   maintenance payments 188
   married couple's allowance 188–9
   overview 183
   Seed Enterprise Investment Scheme 186
   social investment tax relief 186–8
   venture capital trust scheme 184
tax relief, definition 11; *see also* allowances
   and reliefs
taxable income, definition 11; *see also*
   computation of taxable income
taxable persons (VAT) 248
taxable supplies (VAT) 248
telecommunications services, place of
   supply 285
terminal loss relief 108–9
termination payments
   exempt payments 137–8
   income tax treatment of 136–8
   payment in lieu of notice 137
   redundancy payments 62, 137
   unfair dismissal payments 138
time to pay arrangements 220–21
trade
   badges of 45–6
   definition 44
trade debt impairments 59
trade unions, exemption from income
   tax 215
trademark registration and renewal 62
trading income
   badges of trade 45–6
   basis of assessment
      cessation years 52–3
      changes in accounting date 50–52
      commencement years 47–50

THANKS FOR JOINING US

We hope that you are finding your course of study with Chartered Accountants Ireland a rewarding experience. We know you've got the will to succeed and are willing to put in the extra effort. You may well know like-minded people in your network who are interested in a career in finance or accountancy and are currently assessing their study options. As a current student, your endorsement matters greatly in helping them decide on a career in Chartered Accountancy.

How can you help?

- If you have an opportunity to explain to a friend or colleague why you chose Chartered Accountancy as your professional qualification, please do so.

- Anyone interested in the profession can visit **www.charteredaccountants.ie/prospective-students** where they'll find lots of information and advice on starting out.

- Like us on **Facebook**, follow us on **Twitter**.

- Email us at **studentqueries@charteredaccountants.ie**

We can all help in promoting Chartered Accountancy to the next generation and in doing so, strengthen our qualification and community. We really appreciate your support.